PYRAMIDS AND NIGHTCLUBS

D1191030

PYRAMIDS & NIGHTCLUBS

A Travel Ethnography of Arab and Western Imaginations
of Egypt, from King Tut and a Colony of Atlantis to Rumors
of Sex Orgies, Urban Legends about a Marauding Prince,
and Blonde Belly Dancers

▲ ▲ ▲ ▲ ▲ ▲ ▲ ▲ ▲ ▲ ▲ ▲ ▲ ▲ ▲ ▲ ▲ ▲ ▲

L. L. WYNN

UNIVERSITY OF TEXAS PRESS, AUSTIN

COPYRIGHT © 2007 BY THE UNIVERSITY OF TEXAS PRESS
Printed in the United States of America
First edition, 2007

Requests for permission to reproduce material from this work
should be sent to:
    Permissions
    University of Texas Press
    P.O. Box 7819
    Austin, TX 78713-7819
    www.utexas.edu/utpress/about/bpermission.html

♾ The paper used in this book meets the minimum requirements
of ANSI/NISO z39.48-1992 (R1997) (Permanence of Paper).

Library of Congress Cataloging-in-Publication Data
Wynn, L. L., 1971–
Pyramids and nightclubs : a travel ethnography of Arab and Western imaginations
of Egypt, from King Tut and a colony of Atlantis to rumors of sex orgies, urban
legends about a marauding prince, and blonde belly dancers / L. L. Wynn. —
1st ed.
       p.   cm.
Includes bibliographical references and index.
ISBN 978-0-292-71701-5 (cloth : alk. paper)
ISBN 978-0-292-71702-2 (pbk. : alk. paper)
1. Urban anthropology—Egypt—Cairo.   2. Culture and tourism—Egypt—Cairo.
3. Cairo (Egypt)—Public opinion.   4. Cairo (Egypt)—History.   5. Cairo (Egypt)—
Social life and customs.   I. Title.
GN648w96   2007
306.4'819096216—dc22
2007022652

FOR DAVID INGLIS

CONTENTS

A NOTE ABOUT TRANSLITERATION AND NAMES

Arabic words in this book which are italicized have been transliterated without using diacritical marks, except for ʻ for the letter ʻayn and ʼ for hamza. Otherwise my transliteration system follows that of the *International Journal of Middle East Studies* (IJMES).

I have not used a uniform transliteration system for proper nouns, including people's names, because most of the Egyptians I quote and cite have preferred English spellings for their names. In some cases my spelling of names is idiosyncratic, as in my spelling of Prince Tork bin Abd al-Aziz, which can be found rendered as Tork, Turk, or Turki in English-language news accounts. I generally use the common English names for cities and towns, so, for example, *al-ʼuqsor* is here rendered Luxor and *al-ghardaqa* is Hurghada.

Many names have been changed to protect people's privacy, with the exception of those people to whose published works I refer, and who intriguingly blur the line between anthropological informants and academic references. When only a first name is given, this is generally a pseudonym. Ashour, the last name of the family I describe in Chapter 5, is also a pseudonym. Names in fieldnotes excerpts have also been changed to be consistent with the pseudonyms I give them in the text.

ACKNOWLEDGMENTS

Field research in Cairo was funded by an American Research Center in Egypt (ARCE) research grant. I am thankful to Madame Amira Khattab and the rest of the staff at ARCE for all their help, and especially for securing me a research visa. Even before I started my fieldwork, I had a year of language study at the Center for Arabic Study Abroad (CASA) at the American University in Cairo, and a year of pre-dissertation research funded by a Foreign Language and Area Studies (FLAS) scholarship. I am grateful to Jeffrey Herbst at the Woodrow Wilson School for nominating me for the latter, which gave me the extra time I needed to conduct a large research project with many different subprojects.

My greatest intellectual debts are to my professors and fellow graduate students in the Department of Anthropology at Princeton University (though of course none of them is responsible for this final project). I had a committee of advisors whose approaches were wonderfully complementary. Listening to Abdellah Hammoudi speak is like listening to a poem, and Abdellah has a neat trick of taking any subject and turning it over, and over, and over again, shaving off blunt corners and rough edges, until he can reveal a dozen new facets to the matter. Abdellah also gave me much theoretical advice before entering the field that helped me to consider the ethics of representation and to orient my methodological approach to researching Arab tourism.

Jim Boon has been a constant inspiration. I often daydream about what it would take to be like Jim Boon—I calculate that I would have to spend hours every day reading the classics of anthropology, literature, and philosophy, not to mention watching every Hitchcock film ever made—and I usually conclude my daydreams feeling a little low because I know that *nobody* will ever be like Jim Boon. But if I can never be as knowledgeable and well read as he is, at least

I can aspire to the approach he takes when examining any work, whether it is a movie or a classic of anthropology, and the lesson I always try to take from Jim is to avoid dogmatism and simplistic explanations. I'm sure that, in spite of all my best efforts, there are still enough gross generalizations in this book to make Jim wince repeatedly as he reads it.

Larry Rosen signed on to be an advisor somewhat later in my graduate education, while I was in the field, and I am constantly amazed by the whole-hearted support, encouragement, and practical advice he gives me. I used to labor under the belief that the hallmark of academia was to take an apparently simple issue and complicate it, but Larry has taught me that it can be even better to take a complicated issue and render it simple and comprehensible. Larry has provided constant encouragement and direction during the revisions of this book, and the final form that this book takes owes much to him.

Julie Taylor suggested that I take belly dancing classes to gain insight into the work of those whom I wished to study, and it was great advice. Vincanne Adams was an early advisor, and her approach to studying tourism was influential in my own research project. Khaled Fahmy kindly took the time to teach me much about Egyptian history. Robert Vitalis from the University of Pennsylvania generously agreed at the last minute to be an outside reader at my defense and offered both support and gentle criticism. James Trussell was my mentor during a three-year postdoc at Princeton University's Office of Population Research, and I cannot sufficiently express thanks for all that he has done for me, especially for his support for the many disparate projects I've worked on at OPR, including revisions of this book.

The other professors in Princeton University's anthropology department with whom I have studied have influenced me in innumerable ways, and I am grateful to Walter Armbrust, Isabel Clark-Decès, Hildred Geertz, Rena Lederman, Gananath Obeyesekere, and Kay Warren for what they have taught me. It's been sad to return from fieldwork to a department without Kay, Obey, and Hilly. But it has been a pleasure to be able to learn from new additions to the department: João Biehl, John Borneman, Carol Greenhouse, and Carolyn Rouse, who have offered much useful advice and insight.

Many brilliant teachers and students helped me learn Arabic, in Cairo, Middlebury, and Princeton, including Dr. Esam Rifaat, Abbas al-Tonsi, Nabila al-Asyuti, Sinan Antoon, Ahmed Karout, Chris Stone, Margaret Larkin, Lara Deeb, and Hadi Deeb.

As I was writing the dissertation that eventually became the basis for this book, I was lucky enough to have a couple of groups of fellow graduate students read chapters and discuss them with me. Many thanks to Ken Croes, Alex Edmonds, Heiko Henkel, Alison Lake, Kavita Misra, Rachel Newcomb,

Nathalie Peutz, Sarah Pinto, and Susanna Trnka for their comments and advice. While turning the dissertation into a book manuscript, I benefited from the critical readings of the Anthro Cyber Writing Group, which included Alex Edmonds, Rachel Newcomb, Alison Lake, Kristi Latta, Sarah Pinto, Kirsten Scheid, Tom Strong, Susanna Trnka, and Haley Duschinski. Before going into the field, my research project was shaped through conversations with my cohort; John MacDougal, Alison Lake, Ken Croes, Alex Edmonds, and Kristi Latta were intellectual companions and also great friends. I owe a great intellectual debt to both Omnia El-Shakry and Marwa El-Shakry, who influenced my thinking about Egypt in so many ways. Paul Amar shared his theories and passed on his Mounira apartment and clawfoot bathtub. I am grateful to Carol Zanca for her friendship, and to Melanie Adams for her help and encouragement while working on the book manuscript. Thanks also to the many people who offered bibliographical suggestions, including Laleh Khalili, Wendy Willems, Celia Applegate, Maksym Kyrczaniw, Eric G. E. Zuelow, Forrest Pass, Eric Kaufman, Paul Arpaia, Sylvia Maier, Matthew Hayday, and Krzysztof Jaskulowski.

I benefited from the opportunity to present a chapter of this book at New York University's Kevorkian Center for Near Eastern Studies and am thankful for the insightful readings that scholars there offered me. I am deeply grateful for the close readings and critiques of an earlier manuscript version by Mitch Rose, Donald Cole, Laleh Khalili, and Rania Salem, and for the editorial insights of Wendy Moore, Lynne Chapman, and Jim Burr at the University of Texas Press. A special thanks to Wendy for her enthusiasm for this book project.

A shout out to Maria McMath, Courtney Williams, Nancy Khalek, Angel Foster, Caroline Moreau, Bonnie Ghosh-Dastidar, Darren Rand, Barry Rand, Babur Habib, Philipp Sadowski, Raquel Salvatella, Sylvain Champonnois, Keith and Amy Morton, Brian and Kathy Inglis, Robert Inglis, Nicole and Ron Brouwer, Lorraine Hebert, Laurence Feist, and Jessica Toepfer, for their encouragement and friendship. All the usual disclaimers apply: none of these people is responsible for whatever errors or skewed interpretations this book may contain, but they may freely claim responsibility for any moments of insight.

In the field, many people selflessly helped me out in my research. Wow: I can't even convey how great they all were to me. Dr. Ali Omar Abdallah, Dean of the College of Tourism at Helwan University, was my Egyptian research supervisor. He kindly introduced me to many people and provided critical orientation to my research on tourism in Egypt. At the pyramids, Zahi Hawass was both a primary informant and a mentor, and I learned much about Egypt, both modern and ancient, from him. He was extremely generous with his time. I will always be grateful for the help and friendship of Mahmoud Afifi,

Mansour Boryak, Tariq el-Awady, Nashwa Gaber, Shaaban Abdelgawwad, May Samir, Ahmed Ebaid, Abeer Awad, Nermine Abdelmo'men, Sahar Mabrouk, Al-Husein Abdelbaseer, Sally Ahmed Zakaria, Mohamed Ismail, Ahmed Allam, Esam Bebars, Ayman Wahbi, Marco Naguib, Ramadan al-Badri, Noha Abdel Hafiz, Fareed Hassanein, and Adel Abdelhaty, all of whom worked at the Giza Pyramids. I also learned much from conversations with archaeologists Ed Brovarsky, Angela Milward Jones, Michael Jones, and Mark Lehner. Robert Schoch and John Anthony West generously shared their theories with me.

In Cairo, there were many dancers, teachers, performers, and choreographers who explained the intricacies of the world of Oriental dance. My greatest debt is to Diana (Anne-Corrine Mahiou), who was my dance teacher and also a dear friend. Just about everyone interesting whom I met in Cairo, I met through her. I am also grateful for multiple enlightening, in-depth conversations about dance that I had with Liza, Yasmina, Semasem, Caroline, Dunya (Bushra), Asmahan, Lucy, Ashraf Amin, Wael Ibrahim, Adel Shokry, and Ashraf Sobhi. I am indebted to Francesca Sullivan for introducing me to, and lending me her extensive collection of, the trade publications of the international community of Oriental dancers.

In the Khan el-Khalili, Abdelaziz and Osama Mohamed Amin welcomed me into their shop and let me make it my home base for doing research on tourism. Layla Gamal was a dear friend who kept me thinking straight. Samah, Emad, Nadia, and Salah were patient as they explained things to a slow-witted anthropologist who didn't always understand their jokes and wordplay.

Gamal Amer introduced me to Fustat and pointed out where architecture for tourists was, literally, just a façade. Tour guides Hiba and Randa both gave me insights into the art of presenting oneself for others. Inas and Fatima were both kind and funny as they taught me about how a hotel is run. In Nazlet el-Semman, Mahmoud el-Khattab and Ali el-Shaer showed me around and supplied introductions. Dr. Ibrahim Dessouki Abaza from the Wafd Party and Dr. Rifaat Saeed from the Tagammu' Party gave me interviews. Dr. Abaza sadly passed away before this book was published.

There are a large number of other informants who would not appreciate being named, and to them I offer warm thanks and a commitment to preserving their anonymity. Naturally, none of these people is responsible for the final work that my research produced.

Then there were so many friends who were not specifically informants but who taught me much about Egypt in general. They are the reason I loved the country and why I had so much fun living in Cairo, no matter how hard research sometimes was. First and foremost I thank Nada Abaza, Mohamed Sarawat Selim, and Mohamed Nasr for being my best friends, for taking care of me when I was sick, for constantly driving me around Cairo, for picking me up from and dropping me off at airports, and for helping me do my research. Nada and Hamada and Nasr always looked after me like a sister. (Actually, Nada still calls me her "baby," even though she is several years younger than I.) Mohamed Anwar was my close friend and also my doctor; I doubt I could even count the number of medicines he prescribed for me as I got sick over and over again. He also kindly arranged to have Mahmoud Abbas Elbadawi take a number of excellent photographs to illustrate this book.

I thank the Abaza family and the Selim family for inviting me into their homes. Dr. Sarawat Selim took care of me in his hospital when I was sick, and Hisham Farouq pulled out wisdom teeth while entertaining me with his wry perspectives on life in Egypt. Oumnia Abaza and Zainab Abaza often had me in stitches with their dry humor. Abdelhalim Gaafar, Amal, Injy, Camelia, and Loubna were a surrogate family to me. Amal Osman took me into her home and shared her life with me. Ramy Lakah, Minister Abdelmenaem Emara, and Ambassador Hamdi Saleh kindly furthered my research. Anwar Esmat and Lucy Iskander were dear friends. I owe a special debt to Dr. Hassan Moustafa.

Thanks to all my friends who came to visit me while I was in Egypt: Chris Rawlins and Tad Mike, Louise Wynn, Margot Lovinger, Mike Call and my uncle John Aldous, and Zahra. They helped me to see a familiar field site with new eyes. They also lent me some of the pictures that illustrate this book, for which I am doubly grateful.

I thank my then-husband Mohamed Ashour for his support. Although we constantly had differences about my research, I learned much from discussing it with him.

My family—Jeff, Louise, Jared, Valerie, Cory, and DonRaphael—was my pillar through hard times. I cannot sufficiently express my thanks to my parents for their love and support.

I was lucky enough to meet my husband, David Inglis, when I returned to Princeton after fieldwork. I hope to soon introduce David and our children, Saiph and Rigel, to Egypt. (Maybe one day David will even read this book.) If I were ever going to leave any graffiti on the monuments in Egypt, as countless travelers before me have done, it is David's name that I would scrawl. Instead, I would like to dedicate this book to him.

▲ ▲ ▲ ▲ ▲ ▲ ▲ ▲ ▲ ▲ ▲ ▲ ▲ ▲ ▲ ▲ ▲ ▲ ▲ ▲

FROM THE PYRAMIDS TO THE NIGHTCLUBS
OF PYRAMIDS ROAD

Imagine two Egypts. The first is a mystical, antique land. A vast shimmering desert is bisected by a narrow strip of lush green running from south to north. Along the fringes of the fertile Nile Valley lie the ruins of ancient civilizations, more than five millennia old, whose pyramids and temples and tombs have been preserved through the centuries by the sand and the dry desert climate. Secret passages have been found in the pyramids, low crawling passageways that open out onto hidden inner chambers with empty sarcophagi. Ancient avenues are guarded by sphinxes and obelisks, sunbeams frozen in stone. Towering granite statues of long-dead kings and queens preside over vast, echoing halls of temples in the south. You can walk through these ruins, dwarfed by huge columns carved with lotus flowers, your heels echoing on the stone floor, and imagine that they were the palaces of a long-extinct race of magician-giants. These ancients had sophisticated astronomical knowledge and built their monuments to align with the sun and the stars on solstices and equinoxes.

The land of Egypt today is peopled by the descendents of these pharaohs. The ruins are best toured in the winter, but if you have to come in the summer, you go to bed early and rise with the sun so you can visit the monuments in the morning, before the blinding sun reflected off the glassy desert sand makes your eyes ache from squinting and you wilt in the intense afternoon heat. The evening is reserved for trips to the Khan el-Khalili, the maze-like bazaar where you can buy gold and silver pendants with your name worked in hieroglyphs, or you can haggle with shopkeepers over souvenirs made by local artisans such as mother-of-pearl inlaid boxes, alabaster vases, or delicate hand-blown glass bottles containing fragrant oils that the shopkeepers will tell you are the same scents that perfumed the bodies of Nefertiti and Cleopatra.

Figure 0.1. Western tourists riding camels on the Giza Plateau. Photograph by W. H. Chow.

The other Egypt is vividly alive, and its pharaonic ruins are mere background for more modern dramas. The pyramids, on the outskirts of Cairo, are the set for romantic trysts in numerous Egyptian films where lovers steal kisses on the tumble of lower blocks. In this Egypt, Cairo is the center of the Arab world, and it's like Hollywood and New York all rolled into one big, dusty, overcrowded city of more than fifteen million. In the more elegant neighborhoods of Mohandiseen and Zamalek, people keep their eyes peeled for a glimpse of a famous movie star or singer. Omar Sharif has retired to an apartment in Mohandiseen, and many fondly remember how forty years ago he was so smitten by actress Faten Hamama that he converted to Islam to marry her, only to be divorced by her a few years later because of his gambling addiction. When the beloved classical singer Umm Kalthoum died in 1975, millions thronged the streets to walk in a funeral procession more than a mile long, and the entire Arab world mourned "the Lady." This Egypt is a political powerhouse, with an outspoken foreign minister (now head of the Arab League) who mediates regional conflicts, and a popular singer who achieved instant stardom all over the Arab world with his hit single, "I Hate Israel." This Egypt brings to mind visions of glamorous belly dancers who whirl in sequined costumes that glitter like the surface of the Nile at night as it reflects the colored lights of the city. The beautiful dancer Dina performs wearing a four-carat diamond on her dainty foot; it is rumored that a wealthy admirer gave it to her and she had it set in a toe ring to show her disdain for him.

In this Egypt, the only time to visit is the summer, when throngs from all over the Arab world come to Cairo for vacation. The days are hot and dull, so you sleep through them, waking up in the late afternoon and going down to the garden cafés of the hotels for a breakfast of stewed fava beans, and you sit and watch young women promenading along the length of tables while you leisurely smoke an apple-scented *shisha* (water pipe). This Egypt comes alive after sunset, when the uniform brown of the dusty city dissolves into a cool night of velvet indigo, speckled with pinpricks of light from streetlamps and towering office buildings and neon shop signs. You stay up all night, going to restaurants and theaters and discotheques. You go to see the latest Alaa Wali Eddin summer blockbuster hit, and when you go back home you will gloat about seeing it long before it came out on videotape. You might go with your family to see a belly dancer perform on a boat that cruises down the Nile, or you might take in a "Russian show" where five or six Eastern Bloc beauties wearing thong leotards over fishnet stockings and feather headdresses execute a perfectly synchronized dance routine to a medley of Western and Arab tunes. You don't visit the pyramids, but you see them from a distance when you make a pilgrimage to Pyramids Road, the long street leading from Cairo to the pyramids which is famously lined with nightclubs and cabarets that are open from late evening until six or seven o'clock in the morning. There, patrons show their appreciation for a favorite dancer by literally showering her with money, handing a wad of ten-pound bills to the stage manager, who fans the notes and lets them spill over the dancer's body as she shimmies, scattering onto the stage where they are quickly retrieved by a waiter while the dancer steps over to her admirer's table to thank him with a smile and a nod. You leave the nightclub as the sun is starting to rise, and you stumble back into your hotel just as the Western tourists are filing onto tour buses destined for the Giza pyramids or Saqqara or the Egyptian Museum.

For most Westerners, Egypt evokes mummies and pyramids. Westerners have been touring Egypt since the ancient Greeks, following a well-traveled tourist route up the Nile River. The Nile has been the central axis of civilization in Egypt, from ancient to modern times, and, except for the development of beach resorts in the Sinai and on the Red Sea and Mediterranean coasts, the Nile cruise remains the basic tourist route even today.

So entwined is the West's image of Egypt with its ancient monuments that it seems self-evident to Europeans and Americans that the pyramids are Egypt's

Figure 0.2. Arab League Street in Mohandiseen, a popular summer hangout for Arab tourists. Photograph by Mahmoud Abbas Elbadawi.

number one tourist attraction. But the pyramids are low on the list of destinations for Gulf Arabs visiting Egypt. Arabs engage with a more contemporary imagining of Egyptian culture, one that is grounded in the regional circulation of singers, dancers, and movie stars. Tourists from Saudi Arabia, Kuwait, and the United Arab Emirates are famous for spending their time not at the pyramids but rather in the nightclubs of Pyramids Road. The difference between Arab and Western tourism is literally night and day: the pyramid tours start early in the morning to beat the midday heat, while nightclub evenings don't come to an end until the early-morning light.

Arabs and Westerners don't see the same Egypt. What they see is influenced by their own culture, language, religion, history, and politics. These different imaginations of Egypt have in turn shaped Egypt's own view of itself, creating overlapping layers of identity: Egypt as the land of the pharaohs, pyramids, and mummies, but also Egypt as the center of Arab cinema, Arab music, and belly dancing. Centuries of transnational exchanges have produced layers of imaginations of Egypt.

Ultimately these different views of Egypt reveal as much about Westerners and Gulf Arabs as they reveal about Egypt. The Western fascination with pharaonic Egypt cannot be understood without seeing how Egyptology was intertwined with the history of European imperialism. And the Egyptian stereotype of Gulf Arabs as spending long nights salivating over belly dancers is symptomatic of a Middle Eastern migrant labor economy marked by cultural differences and resentment over the uneven distribution of oil wealth. This book explores parallel Western and Arab experiences with Egypt as a way of reflecting back their differences and similarities.

HERODOTUS AS THEIR TRAVEL GUIDE

For millennia it was tradition for Western travelers—from Greeks to Romans to nineteenth-century Europeans—to read Herodotus as a kind of travel guide to Egypt. The "Father of History" traveled to Egypt around 460–455 BCE, and his travels generated a peculiar mix of history, observed fact, hearsay, and myth. He described the most ancient of the Seven Wonders of the World, the Great Pyramid of Giza, and claimed that the pharaoh's daughter funded its construction by prostituting herself:

> Now the priests told me that Cheops enjoined all the Egyptians to work for him. . . . Cheops, they continued, descended so low, that for want of money he placed his own daughter in a chamber, and charged her to get a certain sum of money. . . . She not only obtained the sum appointed by her father, but on her own account was minded to leave a memorial behind her, and asked each of her visitors to give her one stone for the work. Of these stones, they said, the Pyramid was built which stands in the middle of the three before the Great Pyramid.[1]

Herodotus's combined fascination with the pharaohs' monumental buildings and his erotic fantasies of the exotic were echoed more than two millennia later by Gustave Flaubert, whose letters gave an account of his travels up the Nile, where descriptions of climbing pyramids are interspersed with graphic accounts of his visits to dancing girls and prostitutes. Having read in Herodotus that the Pyramid of Menkaure (Mykineros, as the Greeks called it) was built by order of a Greek courtesan named Rhodopis, in his notes, Flaubert insisted on calling it the Pyramid of Rhodopis.[2] The European Orientalist imagination of the mythically decadent sexuality of the East that Rana Kabbani, Edward Said, and others have written about has a very long pedigree indeed.[3]

From Herodotus to Flaubert to modern-day tourists, travelers have followed a well-traveled route that starts in Alexandria, proceeds on to the monuments of Giza and Memphis (Saqqara), and then up the Nile to Karnak, Thebes, and Aswan. The West's ancient fascination with pharaonic monuments received

Figure 0.3. A Victorian engraving shows the Sphinx buried to its shoulders in sand, before its re-excavation by Europeans.

new impetus in the modern period with Napoleon's invasion of the country in 1798. The French imperial spirit was self-consciously represented as a scientific expedition, concerned, among other things, with investigating ancient monuments. As historian Robert Tignor has observed, this gave it the noble pedigree of Enlightenment progress (Tignor 1993:1–15). A legacy of empire, the tourism industry in Egypt today directs Western tourists to see an ancient Egypt littered with the excavated monuments of a pharaonic past.

The touristic appeal of ancient Egypt seems obvious to a Westerner. But Gulf Arab tourists in Egypt rarely spend much time visiting pharaonic sites, nor do they constitute any substantial percentage of the tourists taking Nile cruises to Luxor. Instead, Gulf tourists bypass the pyramids and engage with a more contemporary imagining of Egyptian culture.

Within a Middle Eastern context, Egypt is more a contemporary cultural and media giant than it is the "antique land" of Shelley,[4] broadcasting its movies, television serials, and popular music to the entire Arab world (Armbrust 1996,

Abu-Lughod 2004). For Arabs, Egypt evokes images not just of pyramids but also of famous politicians, such as Gamal Abd el-Nasser of Arab nationalism fame, Nobel Prize–winning author Naguib Mahfouz, revered singers such as Umm Kalthoum, pop culture heartthrobs like Amrou Diyab, comedians such as Adel Imam and Alaa Waly Eddin, dramatic actresses and actors such as Nadia el-Guindi and Ahmed Zaki, and famous belly dancers Fifi Abdou, Lucy, and Dina.[5] Arabs are all aware of the Egyptian pyramids, but in the Arab world

Figure 0.4. Western tourists mounted on camels in the 1930s. Photographer unknown; collection of L. L. Wynn.

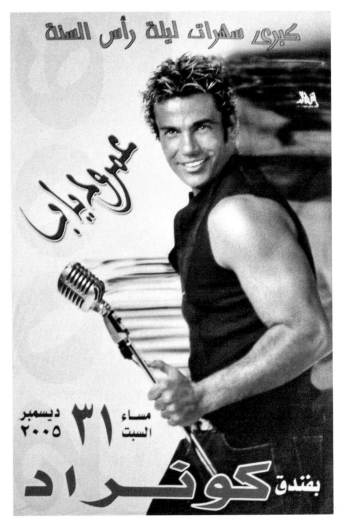

Figure 0.5. A poster advertising an Amrou Diyab concert at one of Egypt's newest luxury hotels. Photograph by Mahmoud Abbas Elbadawi.

the more immediate picture that Egypt brings to mind is an exotic accent that everyone has heard in songs, movies, and television serials since childhood.

Even though I am American and was myself raised on images of pyramids and mummies, I first became interested in the topic of tourism in Egypt while living in Saudi Arabia and hearing accounts of my Saudi friends' vacations in Cairo. A monarchy ruled by the al-Saud family, Saudi Arabia is the site of Islam's two holiest cities. Its vast oil wealth also makes it a magnet for migrant workers from all over the world. I went to Saudi Arabia when I was twenty years old. My father, a geophysicist, had gone to work there, so I decided to leave school and go live for a while in Saudi Arabia with my family. It was just after the Gulf War had brought images of the Arabian peninsula to Americans, and my friends in New York thought that it sounded like a miserable place to live, but I didn't care. It sounded terribly exotic to me, and I was excited to go.

Saudi Arabia is indeed exotic for an American. Men (and it is almost exclusively men) sign contracts to work there, and if they are sufficiently high ranking in their company, they get to bring their families. Western expatriates live in compounds behind high walls. In recent years, with increasing violent opposition to Western occupation of Middle Eastern countries, the walls have a security function, but when I lived there in the early 1990s, the walls seemed to be primarily designed to separate cultures. Within them, women could dress as they pleased and not offend with their immodesty or worry about intrusive stares.

When I lived there, it was difficult for expatriate women to find work in Saudi Arabia. Many just worked on their tennis games, or swam a lot in the compound pool. Families would often make the decision to go there when they had young children and the mother had decided to take some time off from her career to raise them. Expatriate men work with Saudi counterparts, so they have a measure of intercultural exchange with their colleagues. My father's company would sometimes host traditional Saudi meals of roast lamb and rice (*kabsa*) for its Saudi and expatriate employees. The Saudis would teach the foreign men the art of tearing off a piece of meat and rolling a ball of rice with the right hand without using silverware. The expatriates were informed that the eyeballs of the lamb were a delicacy, and the brave ones would give it a try. I often heard expatriate men talking about the different lamb roasts (popularly referred to as "goat grabs") they had been to and comparing notes on who had eaten the eyeballs.

Life in Saudi Arabia is marked by strict gender segregation, so while expatriate men work and even socialize with their Saudi coworkers, they almost never meet a Saudi woman. Expatriate men are warned that it is rude to even politely inquire after the health of a Saudi colleague's wife. Saudi boys and girls go to separate schools from age six, and Saudi men and women do not work together except in rare cases (and then it is usually kept a secret to avoid getting the *mutawwaʿīn*, enforcers of religion and tradition, involved).[6] Saudi men also politely avoid interacting with their expatriate colleagues' wives and daughters. As a result, even expatriate women rarely have the opportunity to know Saudi women, since they can't even hope to be introduced to the wives of their husbands' coworkers. Saudi women are a mystery for most foreigners working in the Kingdom, as is expressed by two phrases I heard Americans use to refer to Saudi women: "UBOS," or "Unidentified Black Objects," and "walking black trash bags," a derogatory reference to the silky black 'abāya (cloak) and tarha (headscarf used to cover their heads and veil their faces) that they would see Saudi women wearing in the supermarkets and shops. Few Westerners speak Arabic, which further entrenches the cultural barriers that keep Saudi and expatriate women from interacting.[7]

One day not long after arriving in Saudi Arabia, I got a call from an American woman whose husband worked with my father. She knew a Saudi woman who had lived for years in Colorado, and this Saudi woman was looking for a photography and English teacher for the girls' school where she was headmistress. I applied for both jobs, and for a year I taught English classes to the fourth, fifth, and sixth grades, and three photography classes for the seventh through twelfth grades.

Over the course of that year, I got to know other teachers at the school and I became close to several of my photography students, who, after all, were only a few years younger than I. I also got to know Susan, a Saudi woman who was the school's official photographer. She photographed school events and many of the engagement parties of the students, and I worked for her, too, photographing weddings and engagement parties when she was already booked for another event on a given night. After a year of teaching, I returned to college, but I spent two more summers in Saudi Arabia before I started graduate school. I would meet up with my Saudi friends then and work during the summers for Susan.

I was close to the family of Meriam, a former student of mine, and many summer evenings, once the heat of the day had cooled, her father and mother would take us out. They would take us to a mall and buy ice cream for Meriam's younger brothers while we went to different shops, and her father, a laughing, crinkly-eyed man, advised me on the best Arabic music to buy. Rashed al-Majed was a good Saudi singer, he told me, but the best music as far as he was concerned was that of Egyptians Mohammed Abdelwahab and Abdelhalim Hafez. Once Meriam's father drove us to a place on the Corniche where we could park the car and walk, with a sea breeze to keep us cool. Meriam and I were wearing 'abāyas and tarhas. Her father, wearing a white thōb (the long white garment worn by Saudi men) and the red and white checked ghutra on his head, walked ahead, holding the hand of Meriam's youngest brother, who was wearing trousers and a T-shirt. We passed a group of young men all wearing white thōbs who were having a picnic in the grass between the road and the sidewalk. As we passed by, they let out a cheer and started chanting something. Meriam took the edge of her headscarf and shyly drew it across her face, but she was smiling as she told me that they were reciting a verse in our honor. Her father genially ignored the flirting going on behind him. Thus did we entertain ourselves in the summer.

The last summer I was in Jeddah, I met Omar, who introduced me to several of his friends who were both male and female, including an unmarried couple who were dating—secretly, of course. All this Saudi male-female mixing was a little risqué, but it was not entirely new to me: I knew that a few of my high-school-aged former students had boyfriends they had met through friends, or in shopping malls in Jeddah, or at the beaches at ʿObhur, a lagoon resort area north of Jeddah where all the land was privately owned so the *mutawwaʿīn* (the so-called "religious police") could not patrol and enforce strict sex segregation as they did elsewhere.

Another place that young Saudi men and women met and dated was on summer vacation in Cairo. Saudi friends often planned their vacations to coincide and would meet up while abroad. The place people mostly went to at that time was Egypt: Cairo, Alexandria, and sometimes the beaches of Hurghada. Meriam had spent part of the summer with her fiancé in Egypt, and she had met other Saudi men and women there with whom she would keep in touch back in Jeddah. One of Meriam's friends had met her boyfriend—later her fiancé—while on vacation in Cairo.

I was fascinated, and I asked my Saudi friends what they did in Egypt, how they dressed (did they wear cloaks and veils?), how they met people of the opposite sex, and how it was that they got away from their parents to hang out with a mixed group of friends. I still have a picture Omar gave me that had been taken the last time he was on vacation in Cairo with his Saudi friends: the picture shows Omar and his best friend Abdullah in a hotel room in Egypt. Omar, just back from the pool, is wearing shorts and a T-shirt, orange or yellow, and he has longish, wavy hair that he now complained made him look like a hick from Jizan (a district in the southwest of Saudi Arabia). He is leaning back against the hotel room's dresser, his legs casually crossed at the ankle, and smiling broadly. Abdullah, a serious, almost haughty expression on his face, is standing next to him. He has a mullet and a thin moustache, and he is already dressed to go out that evening, wearing a Versace silk shirt with a colorful, intricate print of red and yellow and green. I was struck by how different this vacation photo was from the vacation photos of Westerners I knew who had visited Egypt. Those generally featured pyramids, sphinxes, and pharaonic temples. None of Omar's Cairo vacation pictures showed any of these monuments in the background; instead they usually featured hotels or pools.

Omar told me surprising stories about vacation in Egypt. He had lost his virginity in Egypt, he told me, to a Saudi girl. She was young, not even twenty, and he claimed that she had seduced him. After they had sex, he saw there was blood and he was suddenly terrified that it meant she was a virgin. But she just laughed and told him that it must be her period starting. When I acted shocked, he brushed it off: it was perhaps surprising, he conceded, that such a young Saudi girl wasn't a virgin, but not unheard of; he told me that he had later had sex with other Saudi women he dated, in Egypt and in Saudi Arabia.

I don't know how unusual his story was. I heard more surprising stories than that while I was in Saudi Arabia, but they came from liberal middle- and upper-class elites. (At the other extreme was my friend Nejwa, a strictly conservative Saudi woman who would not even show so much as her eyes to a strange man, wearing sunglasses to cover the space between her head covering and the veil she drew across the bridge of her nose.) Still, such stories unsettled my assumptions about strict Saudi conservatism and alerted me to ways that the younger generation, especially unmarried men and women, challenged the prevailing state-enforced cultural norms of sex segregation. Not only did they date to amuse themselves, they also managed to avoid arranged marriages this way and select their own partners (Wynn 1997).[8]

When I came to graduate school to study anthropology, I doubted that I would ever get a research visa to do fieldwork in Saudi Arabia. But it occurred to me that I could still do an ethnography of Saudi Arabia—only the fieldwork site would be Egypt. I would explore the Saudi summer vacation as a window onto generational changes in Saudi culture and investigate the extent to which Saudi tourists upheld or deviated from Saudi cultural norms while they were on vacation in a more liberal Arab country.

But when I tried to find Western academic literature on Arab tourism in Egypt, I drew a blank. There was very little on the topic. At first I thought this was just because there was relatively little social science writing about Saudi Arabia in general. While there are plenty of Egypt "specialists," there are not nearly as many social scientists who write about Saudi Arabia, and even fewer of them have done research in the country;[9] even for Western speakers of Arabic, Saudi dialects are little known.

But as I pored through the tourism literature, I realized that the near-absence of any discussion of Gulf tourism in Egypt was not just attributable to the scant English-language scholarship on the Gulf states. It also had something to do with the implicit assumptions of the literature, which generally portrayed tourism as a Western phenomenon. To understand why, it helps to quickly review social science writing about tourism.

"PHONY FOLK"

In the 1960s, social scientists first started to write and theorize about tourism as a unique category of travel. One of the earliest was John Forster, who argued that the tourist industry created "a 'phony folk' with a 'phony folk culture'" (Forster 1964:217–227). Forster was interested in the cultural problems or paradoxes that emerge as a result of the "commercialization of courtesies," whereby a "moral nexus" (e.g., courtesies such as giving directions) becomes converted into a "cash nexus" (when someone takes money for that courtesy, which otherwise would be given willingly), or when ceremonies are turned into spectacles of tourist consumption, or when people dressed in traditional costume insist on a fee to be photographed by tourists.

With his use of the term *moral* in connection with a social exchange, Forster proposed that there were certain arenas within a culture that were overtly held separate from the realm of economic exchange and where commodification of such an exchange was morally reprehensible. For Forster, it was the way tourism turned common social interactions into commodities to be bought and sold that threatened to destroy cultural authenticity.

Over the next two decades, Forster's argument about the cultural inauthenticity engendered by tourism was echoed by many theorists. These sociologists and anthropologists bemoaned the way tourism was transforming cultures (e.g., V. Smith 1989, Greenwood 1989). For these commentators, it was the commodification of cultural forms (and not merely courtesies) that rendered traditional culture inauthentic and therefore meaningless. This perspective, a common theme in the tourism literature, seemed to derive from a fundamental pessimism about capitalism and modernization. In this view, culture is seen as the last refuge of meaning, and through tourism, even culture is being assaulted by the onslaught of capitalism and its tendency to commodify and consume everything in sight (MacCannell 1976, Graburn 1989, K. Adams 1997).

In these writings, modernity was portrayed as an alienating state, and the meaninglessness of work in industrial society led people to seek meaning and authenticity in culture. This quest took the form of tourism, since viewing one's historical past (as in historical tourism sites such as those which attempt to re-create colonial times or a Viking village) or another contemporary, less industrialized way of life serves up the cultural authenticity of other people as a substitute for the loss of one's own. In this perspective, the tourist and the touristed are locked in a dialectic: authenticity lost and sought, authenticity voyeuristically consumed and thereby eroded. Unsurprisingly, this literature portrayed tourism as a devourer of culture that was destroying the very thing it consumed.

Dean MacCannell, a sociologist, proposed that there was a direct relationship between the alienation of modernity and mass tourism. Grounding his argument in anthropologist Edward Sapir's formula for "genuine" and "spurious" culture, MacCannell argued that the work experience under capitalism was inherently devoid of cultural meaning and satisfaction. For Sapir (1985), whenever there was insufficient integration between economic and other cultural spheres (religion, art, kinship, ritual) in a society, that culture was "spurious" and life in such a culture was spiritually unfulfilling. Similarly, for MacCannell it was the splitting off of cultural meaning from the economic part of life that produced the alienation of modern humans. This alienation, in turn, propelled the modern quest for authenticity through other people's lives and cultures. Modern men and women traveled to see other cultures, as if to prove to themselves that cultural authenticity still existed and to find a brief respite from their own culturally and spiritually barren lives.

The assumption that tourism is a kind of travel that is a paradigmatic practice of modernity has pervaded much of the literature since MacCannell's influential argument in *The Tourist: A New Theory of the Leisure Class* (1976). MacCannell saw in tourism not just a harmless fetishization of other peoples, cultures, and places, but a deliberate desire to categorize, demarcate, and exclude. In this view, the difference between tourist and touristed is not just their positioning in a global economy but a concomitant worldview.[10]

The link drawn by these theorists between tourism and modernity is a critical one, because it led to a set of assumptions about tourists that colored anthropological research on tourism: with tourists as paradigmatic moderns, and modernity generally regarded as a Western phenomenon, the tourism literature has been heavily biased toward describing tourism as an almost exclusively Western category.[11] There is often an implicit assumption that not only is authentic culture only to be found in the lifestyles of non-Western peoples, the only authentic *tourist* is the Westerner. For example, John Urry assumes that non-Westerners have better things to do than to waste their time and money on tourism, and he lumps non-Western travelers together under a friendly view of the eager, industrious, practical immigrant, claiming that "[m]any recent immigrants at least would consider that travel should have a more serious purpose than this: to look for work, to join the rest of one's family, or to visit relatives" (Urry 1990:142–143).

These theorists' assumption that the tourist is a Westerner is partly reasoned on the idea that it is only Western society that possesses the economic base to generate mass tourism, but it also derives from the association of tourism with modernity and a distinct attitude toward travel as leisure. However, in Egypt, Arabs from the Middle East and North Africa constitute approximately one-third of the foreign visitors each year, with Gulf tourists comprising roughly half of that group.[12] Further, Gulf tourists stay longer and spend more money than their Western counterparts, making Arab tourism a significant component of the tourist economy.[13] Arab tourists are not only prominent in Egypt, they also flock to Beirut, Morocco, and other European and American cities in the summer months. Recognizing the category of Arab tourists is important not only because it challenges an outdated image of the tourist, but also because it unsettles assumptions about the relationship between modernity and Western culture.

AUTHENTICITY: ELUSIVE OR ILLUSIVE?

For tourism theorists such as Kathleen Adams, Valene Smith, and Dean Mac-Cannell, cultural authenticity was eroded not only by the commodification of culture, but also in the way tourism demarcates appropriate matter for tourist spectating. The tourist wants to see authentic cultural rituals, so those rituals must be performed for the tourist. But once these rituals are performed for the tourist, they cease to be authentic. The tourist's quest for authenticity leads to a search for the backstage—every ritual performance geared to a tourist audience generates a search for the social reality behind the performance. But the backstage is elusive, always slipping away from the tourist's grasp. The backstage can never really be found, because once the tourist sets eyes on it, it is no longer the genuine backstage. Tourism produces performances that mimic a backstage scene. Yet the voyeuristic gaze of the tourist contaminates the relationship between tourist and "native," preventing the tourist from ever really getting backstage, since once the ceremony or cultural process is performed for tourists, it is no longer an authentic cultural ritual.

Many theorists writing about tourism have drawn on sociologist Erving Goffman's idea of frontstage and backstage to describe the touristic encounter. But whereas early tourism writers have seen the performative aspects of the tourism industry as resulting in inauthentic cultural forms, Goffman himself did not equate performance with inauthenticity. For Goffman, *all* social interaction in everyday life, whether touristic or otherwise, is to some extent staged. Performance is not an aberration resulting from mass tourism and integration of small communities into a market economy; performance is what social life everywhere is all about. Moreover, Goffman suggests that this quest for the backstage is not something unique to the touristic encounter, but a quality of "everyday life," and he too describes multiple layers of performance and revelation which characterize the "information game—a potentially infinite cycle of concealment, discovery, false revelation, and rediscovery" (Goffman 1959:8). Finally, Goffman argues that acting is not "just" a front, nor does it engender inauthentic identities. On the contrary, Goffman argues that, "[i]n a sense, and in so far as this mask represents the conception we have formed of ourselves—the role we are striving to live up to—this mask is our truer self, the self we would like to be" (ibid.:19). The social persona is constituted in and through performance, and social events are marked by both ritual and creativity, which are the basic stuff of human encounters, and meaningful precisely in their ritualistic, performative, and creative dimensions.

(Yet MacCannell is right to point out that there is a particular kind of tourism that revolves around a quest for authenticity that is perpetually—indeed, definitionally—elusive. This modern yearning for an experience that embodies authenticity, tradition, and culture produces a paradoxical situation in which authenticity can never be achieved, because once it is marked off as such, it is no longer authentic. There is a dialectical process of production and erosion of authenticity that frames the prototypical tourist experience. This is a persuasive argument, since whether or not authenticity is a valid category for academic analysis, it is doubtless true that authenticity is one of the most powerful semiotic operators within a certain kind of cultural tourism [Culler 1981].)

Anthropology and the social sciences have come around to a different perspective on tourism than that which characterized the early theorizing. Many of the theorists have become skeptical of their earlier concern that tourism eroded cultural authenticity.[14] Cultural performance, this new perspective argues, is created through a dialogue and a dialectic. And just as Goffman showed how we can understand how individuals' self-identities are constructed through performance, so too does anthropology need to examine how cultural and national identities are constructed through performance, tourism, travel, and encounters with cultural and national others.

But as Judith Butler (1993, 1989) has demonstrated in her feminist application of the concept of "performativity," the relationship between performance and identity is also a process imbricated with power (see also Mitchell 2002). This point is critical to my examination of Western and Arab tourists in Egypt. Both groups are in a position of power vis-à-vis most Egyptians: Western tourists have economic power vis-à-vis the majority of the Egyptians working in the tourism economy, and Western interest in pharaonic antiquities has its roots in centuries—even millennia, if we include the ancient Greeks and Romans— of imperialism in Egypt. Gulf Arabs, too, are in a position of power, through the oil wealth that enables them to both employ Egyptians in their home countries and make Egypt their summer playground. Egyptian critiques accuse Arab tourists of using that wealth to spread moral corruption, from the sexual exploitation of Egyptian women to their patronage of lowbrow, ribald theatrical productions that are put on in the summer for a mostly Gulf Arab audience.

An unequal power differential between tourist and touristed compels people to submit to external definitions of cultural authenticity to fulfill tourist expectations and fantasies.[15] But though "collaborative" projects of defining Egyptian culture may be shaped by the fantasies of Western and Arab tourists, we have to be cautious against seeing such efforts as inauthentic or meaningless for the touristed. In Nepal, for example, anthropologist Vincanne Adams has shown how Sherpa identity is constituted through mimesis with a Western image of Sherpas as hardy, hospitable, spiritually enlightened mountain climbers. Since cultural representations "are the crux of ongoing development aid and tourism, both of which are desired by Sherpas and Westerners," such self-definition is an important political project for Sherpas (V. Adams 1996:22). However, it is not merely a political project in which Sherpas cynically engage for economic gain. This image is also a source of meaning and pride for most Sherpas, who actively seek to fulfill this cultural identity.

A similar point could be made for Egypt, where Western and Arab tourism in Egypt have both contributed to the development of an Egyptian national identity. This book examines how the history of Western travel, colonialism, and tourism are intertwined and how they have contributed to the contemporary national self-image of Egypt as an ancient, pharaonic state. Three centuries ago, Egyptians showed minimal interest in the pyramids, even while Europe was going through a phase of "Egyptomania." Today, Egyptians regard the pyramids as part of their national heritage and many feel pride in the pharaonic past. The West's historical fascination with ancient Egypt has certainly contributed to the elaboration of Egyptian identity as an ancient and pharaonic land, but the colonial origins of Egyptology do not render the image of Egypt's pharaonic past any less meaningful or authentic for those Egyptians who identify with the mystical grandeur of the pharaonic age and see the monuments as an essential component of their national heritage.

But the pharaonic past is only one component of Egyptian national identity; for most Egyptians, Egypt is as much the home of Umm Kalthoum as it is the land of pyramids. The point is not to find one or two sources of Egyptian identity, or to figure out which is the most authentic identity, but rather to see how multiple, sometimes conflicting identities are created and defined through points of transnational contact with outsiders.

ETHNOGRAPHIES OF TRAVEL AND TOURISM

By the mid-1990s, when I entered graduate school, a number of theorists were calling for ethnography to expand beyond the traditional localized village study and instead examine the movement of peoples and things, rejecting bounded, spatiotemporally fixed ideas of culture and of dwelling.[16] Anna Tsing's *In the Realm of the Diamond Queen* (1993) exemplified this approach, abandoning the fixed locale of the village to follow her Meratus informants, whose communities, she argued, could be understood only when their constant mobility was taken into account. Another approach I was smitten with was the creative ethnography of Amitav Ghosh, who described a village in Egypt's Nile Delta as having "all the busy restlessness of airline passengers in a transit lounge" (Ghosh 1992, cited in Clifford 1997:1).

To me, the idea of doing an ethnography of travel seemed rather cutting edge at the time, even postmodern. Anthropologists have always been travelers, and they have often written about travel, but usually by portraying themselves as travelers in juxtaposition to fixed native cultures found in a set place, a stable village, a localized community. Writing about Arab and Western tourists in Egypt, I thought, was a really new project. (This hopeless question must be the stuff of late-night contemplation for many an anthropology graduate student trying to formulate a fieldwork project and a career trajectory: what can I study and write about that will be really *new*?)

But one of my professors, James Boon, had a better historical grasp of anthropological writing, and he gently pointed out to me that my generation of anthropologists was not the first to write about hybrid identities and peoples on the move, nor even was his. As far back as 1955, Claude Lévi-Strauss's *Tristes Tropiques* was one of the first great ethnographies of travel that portrayed the ethnographic subject as equally displaced and hybrid as the anthropologist. Lévi-Strauss describes how, when he first arrived in São Paulo and started looking for a people to study, "the nearest anthropological curiosity was a primitive village about fifteen kilometers away, whose ragged inhabitants had fair hair and blue eyes which betrayed their recent Germanic origin" (Lévi-Strauss 1981 [1955]:139).

In *Tristes Tropiques*, Lévi-Strauss tracked histories of immigrants, colonists, missionaries, and Indians who were always on the move. The natives he encountered deep in the Amazon jungle were wise to anthropological customs even before he could introduce those customs to them:

> Young anthropologists are taught that natives are afraid of having their image caught in a photograph, and that it is proper to overcome this fear and compensate them for the risk they think they are taking by making them a present in money or in kind. The Caduveo had perfected the system: not only did they insist on being paid before allowing themselves to be photographed; they forced me to photograph them so that I should have to pay. (Ibid.:176)

Writing about travel was still an appealing trend, whether or not Lévi-Strauss had scooped us half a century ago. Just before I left for the field, I devoured

James Clifford's 1997 book *Routes,* which argued persuasively that contemporary anthropology's subjects were transnational and transcultural, revealed through travel and through contact with others.[17] By the time I returned to Princeton after years in the field, I realized, somewhat belatedly, that the tradition of anthropologists writing about travel was not only well established, it had become de rigueur, and anyone who didn't take into account travel and transnational points of contact between peoples was setting herself up for a "culture garden" critique.[18]

But even as anthropologists have turned to examine *travel* and movement as critical elements of the cultural and social milieux that they describe, anthropological and social science writing about *tourism* has remained more ambivalent. While *travel* and *traveler* seem to be neutral terms, tourism has been a much more lowbrow subject for anthropological inquiry, and the anthropological literature has often portrayed tourists laughingly, as butts for scorn, objects of parody, and foils for contrasting to deep anthropological knowledge about exotic cultures that the tourists inelegantly consume and disrupt.[19] Ironically, such disciplinary hierarchies of knowledge and authority mimic the practices of tourism itself, which, as Graburn notes, is "rife with snobbery" (Graburn 1989:35).

While tourism can be read both as a discourse on modernity and as a practice of modernity, at the same time it subverts the confident, secure categories of modernity—jumbling anthropologist, tourist, and native, modern and traditional, high and low. This kind of subversion of categories is particularly evident in recent essays on anthropology and tourism that describe the anthropologist as "tourist"—or vice versa—to unseat or at least unsettle the authoritative category of traveler which we call anthropologist (Crick 1985, V. Adams 1996, Boon 1992, Bruner 2004). Crick wrote an early and definitive essay pushing this comparison. He begins his essay by asking "What is the difference between being an anthropologist, being a tourist, and being an anthropologist studying tourism?" (1985:74). He suggests that there is an intimate historical connection between anthropologists and travelers/tourists, and the former have sought to distance themselves from the latter precisely because of the frightening similarities between both. This, he suggests, may explain the reluctance of anthropologists to undertake research on tourism.

> It is my suggestion that one of the reasons tourism has not become a matter for greater attention in anthropology is precisely because tourists are relatives of a kind; they act like a cracked mirror in which we can see something of the social system which produces anthropologists as well as tourists. More than that, tourists remind us of some of the contexts,

motives, experiential ambiguities and rhetoric involved in being an anthropologist. (Ibid.:78)

Crick itemizes some of the areas where we might look for similarities between tourists and anthropologists. Both are temporary and marginal residents in another culture, often existing in an "environmental bubble" which
the anthropological myth of "immersion" belies. Both involve stereotyping and
the use of rhetorical conventions in writing about other cultures; "the rigid
distinction between monographs and tales is not sustainable" (ibid.:79). Both
use the other to create the self; "instrumentalism and distance" characterize
both the world of the tourist and the scientific method. And both are parasitic
on cultural brokers, be they tour guides or informants. Crick asks whether we
need to maintain the distinction between anthropology and tourism, and gives
important reasons why it is useful to break it down. He suggests that anthropologists must consider the comparison if only because the tourist role is one
that anthropologists can strategically adopt at any time (as when the politically
sensitive query of the anthropologist quickly transforms into the mere tactless
curiosity of the tourist to defuse a tense situation).

Yet while Crick uses the concept of tourism, where authenticity is always
in doubt, as a way of challenging the authenticity and authority of the anthropologist as cultural interpreter and spokesperson, James Boon (1992) uses the
comparison "to explore the ludic possibilities of inauthentic cross-cultural encounters taking on fuller authority." He suggests that, by accepting tourist encounters as valid objects of ethnographic study, anthropologists might manage
to give up some of our conventional ideas about what constitutes an authentic informant, a proper fieldwork encounter, and genuine fieldnotes material,
recognizing the richness of ethnographic insights gleaned through encounters
with hybrid identities and disconcerting "cosmopolitan moments."[20] In this
study, that means a wide range of hybrids/informants, including: an Australian belly dancer who challenged in Egyptian court a new law that prohibited
non-Egyptians from working as belly dancers in Egypt; a villager from Nazlet
el-Semman, next to the pyramids, who had lived for decades in the West as a
satellite engineer and now had returned to open a tourist "bazaar" on a spot of
land coveted by Egyptologists who wanted to dig there for pharaonic remains;
an American geologist who contested the Egyptological dating of the Giza
monuments and who was in Cairo for both research and a lecture tour with a
New Age author on ancient Egypt; and a young Saudi woman who spent her
summers in Egypt where her father lived while her mother shuttled back and
forth between her job in Jeddah and her family in Cairo. And it means seeing
all these characters not as exceptionally cosmopolitan people and juxtaposing

them against some more stable, culturally authentic characters, but rather seeing their peregrinations and hybrid identities as authentic aspects of human societies and cultures at the turn of the millennium.

So studying tourism raises two key theoretical issues for anthropology. One is the location of identity—and perhaps "culture"—itself. The comparison of Arab and Western experiences in Egypt reveals how national identities are created partly through encounters with cultural others. This research links up the cross-cultural projects of tourism, archaeology, and cultural performance as components in the production of multiple, contested, and often competing imaginations of nation and people.[21] Describing a nation as "imagined" does not mean that nations and people are imagined ex nihilo; there is always something prior to the encounter. However, this prior something is given form and force as "imagination" is incarnated in institutions: from archaeological sites, museums, and monuments to hotels, media, and cultural productions.

The second theoretical issue raised by tourism studies is that of cultural "authenticity" and the location of anthropology itself: what should anthropologists study, and what should they encapsulate in their description of a "culture" or people? A number of recent theoretical works have highlighted how travel and cross-cultural encounters have contributed to the production of subjectivities in the nation-building project.[22] When one group encounters another, they each define both self and other, drawing boundaries and making sense of difference. As Chris Prentice observes, "the very constitution of 'self' and 'other' is inseparable from their mutual contamination by each other" (1994:50). The tourist economy in Egypt illuminates the creative projects of cultural production that occur in such boundary-zones and "borderlands."[23] This book builds on cross-disciplinary work that examines how public identities are constructed through processes at once mimetic and oppositional in encounters with others.[24] In short, the tourist economy in Egypt illustrates how, through encounters with Others, the Self is defined.

But while both colonialism and postcolonial identities may be described using metaphors of travel and itineraries, or what Ha (1997:159) calls "the trope of nomadic space," the concepts of travel and cross-cultural contact are insufficient for explaining the processes by which one group comes to define itself for another. We have to also examine: what brought these groups into contact? What incentive or forms of violence compel one to define itself for the other? What expectations or fantasies on the part of one group does the other group seek to fulfill or defy, mimetically reproduce or defiantly deconstruct?

In studying tourism, it is useful to combine a trope of consumption with the tropes of travel and cross-cultural contact for understanding the processes of identity construction that ensue. Though Western tourism in Egypt has its roots in colonial encounters which were coercive, sometimes violently so, tourism today has a different basis of power: the economic power wielded by an international class of consumers operating in a poor country where tourism revenue is consistently one of the top earners of international currency. That does not mean talking about consumption in the sense that some earlier tourism theorists proposed, where economic exchange with tourists somehow sullied authentic indigenous culture, but seeing instead how the consuming tourists provide incentives for those working in tourism, in service industries, in cultural production (from belly dancers to "whirling dervishes" who perform for Western tourists near the Khan el-Khalili to theatrical productions in the summer Arab tourism season)—and even in archaeology—to engage with a certain imagination of Egypt.[25] At the same time we need to be cautious when using terms such as *incentive*, which connotes a voluntary exchange, that we not neglect two things. The first is the link(s) between contemporary tourist consumption of Egypt and imperialisms past and present. The second is the fact that for a poor country like Egypt, financial "incentives" have high stakes for people whose livelihoods depend on tourist dollars, euros, and riyals, and the structures of the ostensibly liberal international market actively exclude certain groups and classes from benefiting from the tourist economy, in coercive and sometimes violent ways (Mitchell 1995, 2002; Tsing 2005).

Near the start of this chapter, I described the roundabout way that I got interested in my research topic, after living with my family in Saudi Arabia (during which time I was also a tourist in Yemen and Jordan). The almost painful description of the expatriate community in Jeddah of which I was a part, with our enthusiasm for "goat grabs" and ethnic Saudi dolls and sneering descriptions of Saudi women, is no mere whimsical detour into an embarrassing moment from my past before I "became an anthropologist" and supposedly acquired a more sophisticated perspective on cultural difference. It is a deliberate effort to ground my own narrative here in a particular history of transnational imaginations. It is also a reminder that anthropology of the Middle East goes hand in hand with other forms of knowledge-acquisition, political and economic exchanges in the region, and even Western military occupation. Expatriates and tourists are relatives of anthropologists; they act like a "cracked mirror" in which we can see something of the social system which produces anthropologists as well as tourists (Crick 1985:78). Just as the discipline grapples with the ways that anthropologists of the colonial era worked from particular positionings that were a mixture of cooperation with, dependence on, and opposition to colonial authority,[26] so must contemporary anthropologists of the Middle East take into account the ways that our entry into the Arab world is conditioned, enabled, and hindered by the reach of American and European military incursions into and cultural hegemony in the region (Asad 1991). My early introduction to the Arab world as the dependent of an American scientist in Saudi Arabia is a part of that.

If arrival scenes are an iconic staple of ethnographic writing that typically portray the first contact that the ethnographer has with her planned fieldwork-situation (Pratt 1986), contemporary anthropologists often have a few arrival scenes, even before the official start of fieldwork, since the acquisition of anthropological knowledge is frequently predated by other modern (and post-modern) forms of cultural encounter, such as those anthropologists who first visit their fieldwork site as a tourist, or as the employee of an international development agency or other nongovernmental organization, or as an English teacher, or as a belly dancer, or . . . (the list of possible "first encounters" could go on and on). And for "native" (Limon 1991) and "halfie" (Abu-Lughod 1991) anthropologists, fieldwork is a return, rather than a first, second, or later encounter.[27] In line with this contemporary state of ethnographic inquiry, therefore, the arrival scene I describe at the beginning of Chapter 2, "Buried Treasure," is one of a series of arrivals that date back to the moment that I decided to accompany my parents to Saudi Arabia. That fact and other aspects of the circumstances of my research in Egypt deserve more explication, and so, prior to launching into ethnographic description, the next chapter, Chapter 1, picks up this thread again with a discussion of the "Ethics and Methodology of a Transnational Anthropology." It discusses the terms of my stay and research in Egypt and some of the ethical issues of doing ethnographic research among small, highly visible and well educated groups of informants, whose careers and personal lives might be affected by the publication of this ethnography. It also addresses some of the methodological problems that inhere in doing a transnational, multi-site ethnography in an urban environment.

Methodological issues are also addressed in Chapter 2, where I relate some of the problems I encountered trying to find informants who would take the time to talk to an anthropologist who seemed strikingly ignorant about some of her subject matter, and in Chapter 4, where I discuss the difficulty of study-ing tourists, especially for an American anthropologist who wants to know what Gulf Arab tourists are up to in Egypt.

Chapter 2, "Buried Treasure," reviews the history of Egyptology, starting in the days when it was less archaeology than a mad, free-for-all European trea-sure hunt. There are colorful stories to tell, such as the Indiana Jones–style race between a German and a French archaeologist to acquire the spectacular Zodiac of Dendera. Medieval Muslims were interested in the pharaonic past, seeing it as evidence of an ancient race of giant-magicians. But for centuries

Egyptology has been dominated by Westerners, and even today Egyptian Egyptologists are still forced to publish in English, French, and German, while few Western Egyptologists even speak—much less write—Arabic. The explanation lies not in Arab disinterest in pharaonic Egypt, but rather in the history of Western colonialism in Egypt and colonial control over local institutions regulating Egypt's antiquities.

Pharaonism, the identification with ancient Egypt, is one key strain of modern Egyptian nationalism. Egyptologist Zahi Hawass's discovery of the tombs of the pyramid builders in the 1990s was hailed in the Egyptian press for proving that the pyramids were built by Egyptian laborers and not Israelite slaves, a point of pride vis-à-vis Israeli claims that it was *their* ancestors who built the pyramids. But for other Egyptians, "pharaoh" does not evoke a proud cultural past but rather idolatrous despotism. Sadat's assassins proudly shouted, "Pharaoh is dead!" and some Muslim tourists refuse to crawl through the narrow inner passages of the pyramids, lest they appear to bow to pharaoh. This chapter and the next examine these conflicting attitudes toward national pride in Egypt's pharaonic past.

Chapter 3, "Atlantis and Red Mercury," tackles the politics of archaeology from a different angle, examining New Age rewritings of pharaonic history. Both Arabs and Westerners have mystical imaginations about ancient Egypt, and this chapter reviews a wide range of myths and legends about ancient Egypt, from Plato's Atlantis to the psychic Edgar Cayce, who believed he was the reincarnation of an ancient Egyptian high priest and predicted that a chamber with the secrets of a lost civilization would be discovered under the paw of the Sphinx. This chapter shows why New Age theories offend patriotic Egyptians, which in turn explains some of the conspiracy theories that New Agers develop about the mire of bureaucracy that swamps those who wish to excavate Egypt's past. But it also shows that Egyptologists and New Age theorists have a lot in common, no matter how hard the former try to dissociate themselves from the latter: from the shared colonial history that influences both popular and academic narratives of ancient Egypt, to their shared audience of Western tourists who consume their theories.

Both Chapters 2 and 3 show that the aspects of Egypt and Egyptian identity that Westerners take for granted, as though they were natural things, are in fact historically constituted. Westerners visit the pyramids not because they are intrinsically monumental, but because they have been constructed as monumental through processes of European colonialism, the discipline of Egyptology, and the way both construct civilizational history. Both of these chapters also explore how the science of archaeology is tied to social, cultural, and political projects like nationalism.

Chapter 4, "Sex Orgies, a Marauding Prince, and Other Rumors about Gulf Tourism," turns to encounters between Egyptians and Gulf Arabs and their representations. Among Egyptians, the stereotype about Gulf Arabs is that they come to Egypt to do things that are forbidden in their own country: visit prostitutes and have sex parties, drink alcohol and gamble. Hence they are popularly associated with the morally suspect nightclubs of Pyramids Road. Stories circulate about Gulf sex orgies in hotels, and a favorite topic of conversation in 1999 was the exploits of a Saudi prince living in Cairo with a large entourage of servants and bodyguards who were famous for roughing up anyone who got in their way. These urban legends about sex, power, wealth, and exploitation turned this prince into the mythical prototype for the stereotypical wealthy Gulf Arab who thinks that he can buy everything. These negative images of Gulf Arabs can be understood only in the context of Arab identity politics, labor migration, and the regional political economy. I explore these stereotypes of Arab tourism within the context of anthropological investigations of urban myths, rumor, and gossip.

In Chapter 5, "Transnational Dating," Gulf tourism is seen from a very different perspective, that of two young Saudi women. The popular Egyptian stereotype about Gulf tourists holds that they come to Egypt to indulge in scandalous activities and exploit poor Egyptians. But a look at Saudi youth vacationing in Cairo shows that, for these Arab tourists, summer vacation in Egypt is as much about meeting other Saudis as it is about taking advantage of Egyptian freedoms. Saudi girls love coming to Egypt so that they can date young men in an atmosphere which is more liberal than back in Saudi Arabia, yet still basically defined by Saudi social and cultural parameters. As a fundamentally Saudi cultural phenomenon that takes place *outside* the borders of Saudi Arabia, the Saudi summer vacation in Egypt is an extraordinary example of transnational culture.

Chapters 4 and 5 portray encounters between Egyptians and Gulf Arabs to compare the imaginations that each group constructs of the other. Moments of cultural contact become opportunities for defining self and other: Egyptians nurture stereotypes whereby Gulf Arabs embody the transgression of social proprieties, while Saudis see Egyptians as obsequious economic mercenaries. Both groups portray the other as sexual predators. Linguistic and cultural differences between the groups get mapped out on a regional economy marked by labor migration and extreme differences of wealth.

In both these chapters, identity—of self and other—appears as central. Yet the discussion of identity is not an end in itself but a strategy for examining "culture," the traditional domain of anthropological research. I am interested in describing the moments of cross-cultural contact that suddenly shake people into an awareness of their own, otherwise unremarked cultural traditions by way of their contrast with those of others, and then exploring what people make of those differences. For example, in relating stories about how Egyptians describe the way that Gulf Arabs eat, dress, and behave in public, or the ways that Gulf Arabs criticize Egyptian terms of polite address when speaking to one another, I show how being confronted with these small markers of cultural difference throws into relief each group's own cultural norms. Then, I show how these differences provoke discussions about what such markers of cultural difference mean — both sides take these differences as evidence of civilization and political histories, among other things. In short, I examine how culture gets tied to civilizational narratives — or how "culture" is tied to "Culture."

The concluding chapter, "Palimpsest, Excavation, Graffiti, Simulacra," examines the phenomenon of foreign (non-Egyptian, non-Arab) belly dancers in Egypt. Belly dancing has become popular outside the Arab world, and American, European, and Japanese women who have become professional belly dancers dance all over Europe and the Middle East, but their ultimate goal is to make it in Cairo — for belly dancers, if you can make it there, you can make it anywhere. This phenomenon uniquely brings together elements of both the Western and the Eastern imaginations of Egypt. Foreign belly dancers perform for tourist audiences, both Arab and Western, in Cairo's hotels, nightclubs, and Nile cruises. But many of these dancers first came to Cairo as tourists themselves, and that trip marked their first exposure to Oriental dance. Examining the roots of Oriental dance in Egypt reveals that this "traditional" cultural phenomenon was shaped by a history of cross-cultural encounters between Egypt and the West as well as Egypt and the Arab world, encounters which have substantially modified the art form as it is performed today.

Though the research topic centers on Cairo, this book tracks characters through locations across the globe, from Saudi youth who come to Egypt in the summer to play out elaborate dating and courtship rituals, to archaeologists and New Age groups producing conflicting histories of the Giza pyramids for television, to European belly dancers trying to make a name for themselves in Cairo. These chapters map out but a few points on the paths of the various transnational networks crisscrossing through Cairo; for all of them, tourism is a common denominator. But there is more than just the theoretical category of tourism and an anthropologist bringing these apparently disparate subjects together. This book is a study of different imaginations of Egypt as a people, culture, and history. It links up political history, regional and international economies, and cultural production with an ongoing process of national identity construction. It is a tentative mapping of transnational networks and cross-cultural encounters between different peoples, nationalities, languages, classes, religions, and ideologies that all intersect in the country—and imagination—of Egypt.

The history of anthropology is a history of travels and cross-cultural encounters. Tourism is a variation on the kinds of travel and cross-cultural transactions—imperialism, colonialism, religious and intellectual pilgrimages, the Grand Tour, archaeology, anthropology, and more—which have for centuries been critical elements in the building of nations and subjectivities. It is only by taking into account these processes that constitute a history of transnational encounters that we can begin to understand how the idea of Egypt as a place, a culture, a history, a people, a country, and a nation is actively constructed and enacted.

▲ ▲ ▲ ▲ ▲ ▲ ▲ ▲ ▲ ▲ ▲ ▲ ▲ ▲ ▲ ▲ ▲ ▲ ▲

CHAPTER 1

ETHICS AND METHODOLOGY OF A

TRANSNATIONAL ANTHROPOLOGY

THE METHODOLOGY OF TOURISM RESEARCH

There are certain methodological problems inherent in doing research on tourism (Graburn 2002). One is structural: tourists are only present for a short period of time. Western tourists might stay in Cairo for a week or two at the most; Arab tourists tend to stay longer, a month or more. Even so, a month is not the ideal length of time for really getting to know them, talking to them, and letting them speak freely—the ideals of qualitative ethnographic research. Another is the fact that tourists are taken out of their own cultural context, which makes it harder to fit their travel experience into the rest of their life. For example, theorists speculate that tourism is driven by the alienation of modernity or the quest for another more authentic way of life. But when you are talking to tourists on vacation in Egypt, you can ask questions about their lives back home, but you will never have a direct knowledge of whether they are alienated moderns, postmoderns, or something else entirely.[1]

This problem—the difficulty of situating tourist experiences within their daily lives—was mitigated somewhat in the case of some of my Arab informants, those I knew from Saudi Arabia. Having lived in Jeddah for two years, I had many contacts among the students and teachers at the school where I had worked, people whom I used to see every day and knew well. For these, I could make connections between their lives back in Jeddah and their vacations in Cairo. But for other Arab and Western informants, there was simply no way to engage in in-depth participant observation over an extended period of time, which is the hallmark of anthropological research.

However, it *was* possible to take the time to get to know Egyptians working in the tourism industry, as well as various expatriates (such as the foreign belly

Figure 1.1. The author typing fieldnotes in her Mohandiseen flat in Cairo. Photograph by Nada Abaza.

dancers) in Cairo who work in the tourism industry. As a result, I determined that the main focus of my research would have to be tourism from the perspective of the touristed. The exception was my study of Saudi tourists in Egypt, where my Cairo research was supplemented by previous knowledge of their social world.

I spent a total of three and a half years in Egypt, from the beginning of June 1998 to the end of November 2001, with a one-month follow-up visit. The first year was devoted to language study at the American University in Cairo, in the Center for Arabic Study Abroad (CASA) program. This entailed the intensive study of Modern Standard and Egyptian Colloquial Arabic. Another year of "pre-dissertation research," to narrow the parameters of my project, was funded by a Foreign Language and Area Studies grant which I was awarded by Princeton's Woodrow Wilson School. The remainder of the time was spent conducting fieldwork, with funding from the American Research Center in Egypt (ARCE) and the Mellon Foundation.

I had a research visa obtained through ARCE. The terms of research permission allowed archival research and formal interviews with government representatives, tourism officials, and any other contacts I could make, but it forbade quantitative research such as randomly sampled interviews and surveys. An Egyptian research supervisor was assigned to me, both to facilitate and to keep an eye on my research. Dr. Ali Omar Abdellah, the Dean of the College of Tourism and Hotels, Helwan University, was extremely helpful. He suggested interesting paths for my research to take, facilitated interviews and contacts, gave me wise advice about how to deal with people, and spoke candidly about sensitive aspects of my research topic which I raised with him.

The organization that sponsored my research, ARCE, informed me that the terms of my research permission, which prevented me from conducting quantitative surveys, were standard for anthropologists at that time. Although there are limits to what kind of information one can get from formal interviews, I had initially hoped to gain some valuable data that way that I couldn't have gained through qualitative research with smaller numbers of informants. For example, I could have gotten some figures for how many Arab tourists travel with their extended families, how big the groups were that they came in, and whether they met friends from back home during their vacation, or whether they kept an anonymous profile in Egypt. That would have answered some key questions I had about how Arabs spent their vacations in Egypt. There is a widespread belief in Egypt that Arabs come to Egypt to engage in scandalous activities that aren't available in their own countries—partying, drinking, and procuring the services of prostitutes—protected by the anonymity of Cairo's crowding. On the other hand, most Saudis I knew portrayed their Egyptian vacation as wholesome family fun, with a few of the things that were forbidden to them at home, such as going to see a movie in the cinema, going dancing at a disco, or taking in a belly dancing show during dinner—but nothing so scandalous as the Egyptian stereotype held. Of course, questionnaires wouldn't provide accurate data on how many Arab tourists came to Egypt for sex tourism. But with questionnaires, I *could* find out how many came to Egypt with their family, and how many came alone, or with friends of the same sex, which would provide some clues to the kinds of activities they *might* engage in. What's more, by asking if they met other friends from their own country while in Egypt, I could have tested a hypothesis of mine, which was that, for Gulf Arabs, an Egyptian vacation was not about escaping to the freedom of Cairo from the oppressive social strictures that prevailed back home. Instead, I suspected that it was a kind of extension of that social world, rather than an escape from it—a place to come hang out with friends and extended family, and make new contacts among other vacationers from back home.

But without research permission to do surveys, I concluded that I would have to find other ways of talking to Gulf tourists, rely on introductions, and use contacts I already knew from Jeddah, and snowball from there.

Though the results do not provide representative data, I interviewed dozens of Arab tourists this way. And, in the environment in which I was doing my research, there were good reasons for using this methodology. I found evidence of scams targeting wealthy Arab tourists, in which con artists would approach people to ask them a few apparently innocent questions under the pretext of a market survey. This may have made Arab tourists reluctant to talk to an unknown researcher. On the other hand, people tended to be very open with me when I came recommended by someone they knew, often speaking candidly about topics that I had thought would be taboo. I gathered fascinating information this way that I could not have gotten through random sampling.[2]

FIELDWORK ETHICS

Official research permission is often difficult to obtain in Egypt, especially for anthropological research. Some social scientists do research without permission because it is so easy to stay in the country for long periods of time on tourist visas. Others submit research proposals to the authorities describing a research agenda substantially different from their intended research project when they suspect that research permission will be difficult to obtain.

There are different schools of thought about the ethics of doing research without permission, or lying about one's research subject in an application because it is a sensitive or taboo subject. Some foreign researchers argue that they are not in the field of public relations and should not be expected to research only topics that the Egyptian government likes. They argue that they have a responsibility not to the Egyptian political elite, but to the masses. So, to give an example, while the regime may disapprove of research that exposes poverty, institutional corruption, and the like, the Egyptian people may benefit from it if the embarrassment that such studies create results in policy changes.

Others, however, argue that foreign researchers who want to delve into scandals should focus on their own societies and leave Egyptian scandals to Egyptian researchers. The latter are more tied to their communities with a greater sense of social responsibility than outsiders, who, like mercenaries, come to Egypt to get their data and leave with their booty, publishing with an eye to their own career objectives without a sense of accountability to the community where they did their research.

I am explicit about the terms of my research permission because it is relevant to debates I encountered in the foreign research community about how to do research in Egypt. At the time I was doing research, it was said to be difficult for anthropologists to get official research permission. On the other hand, it was very easy for Americans and Europeans to live in Egypt for extended (almost unlimited) periods of time on tourist visas. So there was a lot of debate among young researchers that I met about how to do their research. Many people conducted research while living on tourist visas. Others wrote research proposals for projects they didn't actually intend to research, so that they could get research visas approved and get the big grants that were issued only to researchers with permission. In our small community of academic fledglings, rumor had it that this had been done in the recent past by a researcher who had proposed one line of research and then gone on to write a history of prostitution in Egypt, which had deeply offended the government and provoked them to refuse to give research visas for some time. I don't know if this was true, but the merits of such a research tactic were widely debated by my peers at the time. Some held that it was a reasonable way to do research on sensitive topics that the government would never approve but that were relevant to the research community and to other Egyptians not in control of state power. Others argued that this was not only unethical, it also endangered the future research of others.

Some of my peers have their own good reasons for doing underground research without a permit, but I decided that it was not a strategy that I could ethically use. I certainly would have liked to research a number of topics that the Egyptian government would not have approved of, such as the network of real estate brokers who allegedly supply Gulf Arab male tourists with not only furnished apartments but also prostitutes during their stay in Egypt (e.g., el-Gawhary 1995). But I didn't have permission to do this sort of research, so I only discuss rumors about prostitution, which are inescapable when talking to Egyptians about Gulf tourism, and I largely focus on the existence of much less scandalous forms of Gulf tourism. Similarly, I do not discuss the link between tourism and terrorism, i.e., the historical and ongoing tactics of Islamist opponents of the current regime who have attacked tourists as a way of harming the lucrative tourist industry and thus the state.

Some interlocutors have in the past taken me to task for omitting a discussion of terrorism and actual prostitution (rather than just rumors of it) in this analysis of transnational connections. It is not an oversight but rather a deliberate attempt to avoid dwelling on topics that would offend my Egyptian hosts (see also Tsing 2005:xii). The code of ethics of the American Anthropology Association (AAA), to which I adhere, reminds anthropologists to "recognize their debt to the societies in which they work," and also states that anthropologists "are not only responsible for the factual content of their statements but also must consider carefully the social and political implications of the information they disseminate" (AAA 1986).

There are all kinds of researchers with varying ties back to the communities where they did their research, and with different ideas about loyalty to informants, the Egyptian people, and the state. I designed a project that I hoped would be interesting to academics and social scientists, as well as relevant to Egyptian policy makers. I sought to avoid topics that were sensitive or that might be inappropriate for a foreigner to address, such as rare tourist-targeting terrorist attacks, or sex tourism. However, I found it impossible to avoid certain topics, because in the course of my research, they came up again and again, even without my specifically inquiring about them. The obvious example is prostitution. When one talks to Egyptians about Arab tourism, the vast majority either allude to or directly mention prostitution. The same applied when I talked to people about belly dancing. While I did not conduct research specifically on the subject of prostitution, I still address the issue in its discursive dimensions in Chapter 4.

Regardless of whether I was conducting a formal interview with a tape recorder or speaking off the record, I informed every person from the first time we spoke that I was an anthropologist researching transnationalism in Egypt and comparing Western and Arab tourism. When, in 2001, I gave a public talk at the American Research Center in Egypt presenting some of the preliminary results of my research, it was attended by several informants, including Egyptologists, a French and an Australian belly dancer who were informants, and an Arab tourist I had recently interviewed and invited to attend the talk. That public lecture sketched out the three main foci of the current book manuscript: Egyptology and the New Age fascination with the Giza monuments; Arab tourism and its representation in the Egyptian media; and foreign belly dancers in Cairo.

I mention this lecture because it is important to know that my informants were aware of the broader focus of my research, that is, that I was comparing Egyptology with "New Age" imaginations of ancient Egypt, and juxtaposing these with Arab tourism and foreign belly dancers. This is important to know because belly dancers occupy a morally liminal position in Egyptian society, and I worried that some informants might not take kindly to being examined alongside dancers. One of my key informants, Dr. Zahi Hawass, was so magnanimous that not only did he tolerate my plan to write about dancers, Egyptologists, New Agers, and Arab tourists in the same book, he introduced me to his ideological opponents in interpreting ancient Egyptian history, and he provided me with a warm introduction to the famous Egyptian belly dancer Lucy, who graciously granted me an interview on Dr. Hawass's recommendation.

After I completed my research, I asked Dr. Hawass to be the outside reader at my dissertation defense, and he graciously agreed. I was excited about the chance to make a primary informant also a formal evaluator of the final product. This is something that has not often been done in the history of anthropology, but is increasing, thanks to anthropology's growing interest in science.[3] It is to my enduring regret and embarrassment that I was not able to come up with the funds to pay for Dr. Hawass's travel to attend this dissertation defense, and I could not allow him to pay for the trip himself, although he generously expressed a willingness to do so. (I reiterate that this does not mean that Dr. Hawass supports or even agrees with any of the conclusions I reach in this book.)

My volunteer work at the pyramids, which I discuss in Chapter 2, was another part of my attempt to be an ethical researcher, and give something back to the informants who generously shared their time and insights with me. Again, this is in accordance with the AAA's code of anthropological ethics, which notes anthropologists' "obligation to reciprocate with people studied in appropriate ways."

PSEUDONYMS AND PROTECTION OF HUMAN SUBJECTS

I have tried, I hope successfully, to protect my sources. That sometimes raises difficult methodological issues: often when you want to hide someone's identity, it is insufficient simply to change the name of that source when she or he is giving you details about her or his life. Other people would be able to recognize the person being described without a name. On the other hand, if you change enough details to protect the person's identity, you risk creating a fictional character; if you merely leave out details, then you either run the risk of them being identified by the few descriptive characteristics you *do* mention, or you don't provide enough information to contextualize them. This is one of the ethical dilemmas of representation in contemporary anthropology, when we have to assume that our informants and those in their social circles will read what we write about them. I believe that the ethical imperative of protecting

Figure 1.2. Lucy, one of Egypt's most celebrated belly dancers, actresses, and singers, who performs in the Pyramids Road nightclub owned by her husband, Parisiana. Here Lucy has invited a young Arab tourist in the audience of her late-night show to dance on stage while she sings. Photograph by L. L. Wynn.

one's informants takes precedence over the obligation to describe them accurately using identifying details.

Throughout my ethnography, I have scrupulously changed not only names but also any identifying details when I talk about informants (again, required by the AAA's ethics code). The obvious exceptions to this are when I talk about Egyptologists such as Dr. Hawass, a few "New Age" authors, and the geologist Robert Schoch. Such are the quirks of doing anthropology of science: my informants are interlocutors with their own academic credentials and extensive publications (see, for example, Traweek 1988). Whenever Dr. Hawass, Dr. Schoch, or Anthony West is quoted by name, I am citing either on-the-record interviews or one of their published works. There was a great deal of interaction with named informants that I had to assume was off the record, even when they did not specifically warn me of this. When I refer to such, they are not identified by name.

There was one group of informants with whom I interacted extensively and intimately to the extent that I gained information about their private lives (and they of mine), the publication of which would have been deeply scandalous: this was the foreign belly dancer community. Although they all knew I was researching dancers, we became friends, and friendship entails its own sorts of revelations about private lives that are a far cry from what might normally be revealed to a researcher. In such cases I had to assume that such revelations did not occur in the context of informed consent, because at the time that they told me such things, they were not thinking of me as a researcher but as a friend. When it came time to write up my dissertation, I struggled with how to write about these matters while still giving my informants anonymity. In the end I came to the conclusion that it could not be done in the format of a standard ethnography. Because the foreign dance community was small, and its affairs were known by many in the group, and because many in the dance community—not just dancers, but also agents, stage managers, the wealthy patrons of dancers, and so on—all knew which dancers I associated with, I could not change identifying details enough to hide the identities of my informants without effectively creating fictional characters.

The result is that, despite the fact that more than one-third of my fieldnotes deal with the dance community, in this ethnography I deal very little with dancers, save for a brief discussion of certain generic career trajectories for foreign belly dancers that I use to make some theoretical points in the concluding chapter. In the future I hope to find other strategies for writing about this community and the very interesting dilemmas that dancers grapple with, living on the moral margins of a foreign society and negotiating their sexual identities in a cross-cultural context.

METHODS AND INFORMANTS

The most important component of my research was qualitative, participant observation with groups of people whom I spent a significant amount of time with, came to know well, and by and large considered my friends. These mostly consisted of foreign dancers, dance teachers, and choreographers; Egyptian workers and salespeople in a shop in the *sagha* area bordering the Khan el-Khalili; Egyptian hotel workers in a three-star hotel that catered to Arab tourists; Egyptian archaeologists and antiquities inspectors on the Giza Plateau; Egyptian tour guides; families from Nazlet el-Semman, the village adjacent to the Sphinx and Giza pyramids; and several extended Saudi families that spent each summer vacationing in Egypt. I also interviewed Arab tourists from Saudi Arabia, Yemen, Oman, the United Arab Emirates, Morocco, Lebanon, Syria, and Palestine, and Western tourists whom I encountered at the pyramids, in the Khan el-Khalili, and at other tourist sites. My sample of tourists was limited to those who spoke English, Spanish, or Arabic, the languages I speak.

In addition to the core groups of informants that I describe above, I also conducted numerous formal and informal interviews with tour guides and travel agents, *khurateyya* (tourist "hustlers"), officers in the Tourism Police, teachers at the Tourism College, a former director of the Cairo museum, museum curators, archaeologists and Egyptologists (Egyptian, European, and American), alternative theorists of the history of pharaonic Egypt (this includes those theorists usually categorized as "New Agers"), Egyptian and foreign belly dancers, dance agents and managers, nightclub managers, dance teachers and choreographers, hotel management and labor, taxi drivers, tourism developers, artists and artisans who produce tourist art and souvenirs (from silver workers to papyrus painters), shop owners and salespeople in tourist "bazaars" in the Khan el-Khalili, stable owners and other residents of the village of Nazlet el-Semman, Egyptian journalists, representatives of the various government bureaucracies that supervise tourism development and control, and representatives of two opposition political parties.

I usually recorded and transcribed formal interviews. However, I respected people's wishes whenever they asked not to be recorded or not to have their names associated with what they told me.

By the end of the 2½ years of research (and 3½ years in Egypt), I had many interviews, but I used no random sampling and my data is not representative, and I do not analyze it as such. I try to analyze the observations that informants made in several different contexts: the context of the people who said them, their situations in Egypt, and (for tourists) their situations back home in their own social worlds. Then I try to put that in a broader cultural, historical, economic, and political perspective. In some cases, it would not have been possible to do quantitative research, anyway, because there were not enough people involved in any given profession or subculture (such as foreign belly dancers) to allow random sampling.

Quantitative surveys of some of my research populations, which I was not able to conduct, could have resolved some important questions that are left unanswered. However, even if I had been permitted this methodology by the terms of my research visa, identifying truly representative groups to interview would in any case be extremely difficult for the kind of urban, multi-site ethnography that mine is. For each group that I write about, I talked to approximately thirty to forty people from that group. With multiple interviews and encounters described in thousands of pages of fieldnotes, this was a great deal of data to draw on. Yet, because the numbers were still relatively small and not randomly sampled, I was cautious about what kinds of conclusions I reached from such data. With a sample this size, it makes little sense to report statistical results, because of the large margin of error associated with such a sample size. My strategy instead is in the anthropological tradition of "thick description" (Geertz 1973): I take a particular social fact, such as the way an Egyptian friend made certain assumptions about the exploits of Arab tourists, and I then contextualize and explain that fact, what lies behind those assumptions, how they are interpreted by others, how they might change over time, who might share and who might challenge these assumptions, and so on. I do not infer from this conversation that this Egyptian friend's assumption represents the assumptions of a certain percentage of Egyptian society; I only try to describe what it means and why it is.

Written sources supplemented interviews and participant observation: I consulted websites (especially those which deal with conspiracy theories about the Giza Plateau), academic journals (especially archaeological and geological), and trade publications (particularly those for belly dancers). I also relied on two archives for contemporary (circa 1980s–2000) Egyptian media coverage of the topics investigated in this book: these were the files of news clippings maintained by CEDEJ (Centre d'Etudes et de Documentation Economique, Juridique et Sociale) and those of the office of the Giza Plateau Antiquities Inspectorate. Media representations form a substantial component of my analysis in Chapter 4, which examines Egyptian media accounts of the Arab-Egyptian "summer marriages" phenomenon and the exploits of Prince Tork bin Abd al-Aziz al-Saud and his entourage. Here my analysis is less concerned with the factual escapades of the Saudi Prince Tork's bodyguards, for example, than it is with the way Prince Tork and his bodyguards were treated in the press, the way the newly appointed public prosecutor used the media to make himself into a popular folk hero by proclaiming that he would prosecute Tork's bodyguards, and the way that Egyptians discussed and debated the topic among themselves. Prince Tork's actual scandals had very little personal impact on most Egyptians, but he was taken personally and turned into a popular symbol of the hated Arab tourist who abuses poor Egyptian workers, then thinks he can buy or bully his way out of any difficulty. (This methodological issue is discussed in greater detail in Chapter 4.)

My research involved dealing with disparate groups who sometimes have hostile attitudes toward one another, or, at the very least, negative stereotypes about each other: Egyptians and Arab tourists; Egyptians and Western tourists; Egyptologists and New Agers; and archaeologists and villagers from Nazlet el-Semman. In some cases I seek to explain the basis for these stereotypes, or disprove their validity. In other cases, they are not provable, or their status as fact is irrelevant: rumors and stereotypes are analyzed as social facts. I should not be misunderstood as condoning those beliefs, rumors, and stereotypes, just because I examine them. I merely try to explain why they are circulated and believed.

I describe several groups that are intellectual opponents. I have done my best to respectfully and non-judgmentally represent each group's point of view. The place where staying value-neutral was the most difficult was in comparing Egyptologists and alternative theorists of the archaeological record in Egypt, which is covered in Chapter 3.[4] There were two reasons for this. First of all, I am not entirely value-neutral myself. I do have my own beliefs about dating the Giza monuments, right or wrong. Second, it is difficult for an anthropologist to get some distance from archaeologists, because there has always been a close historical link between anthropology and archaeology. Even when most of contemporary cultural anthropology has very little to do with physical anthropology and archaeology, the organizational link is still there (anthropology and archaeology traditionally being part of a single department at many universities), and because of that, many cultural anthropologists are trained in the basics of physical anthropology or archaeology (although I'm not one of those, coming from a university that focuses on cultural anthropology). So studying archaeologists put me a little closer to the people I was studying than is the case with anthropologists who do studies of, say, mathematicians or physicists.

Nevertheless, the anthropology of science does not attempt to evaluate the merits of a particular science. Rather, it is concerned with the culture of the science, the social world of the scientists, the way that group reproduces itself and its knowledge, the boundaries that define one field and exclude others from it, and the way these boundaries determine whose theories are acceptable—even before they are evaluated on the basis of their scientific merits or lack thereof. In looking, therefore, at the theories held by different groups about the origin of the Giza monuments, I do not present a conclusion about which is right and which is wrong. First of all, it would not be fair to my informants. While some of my principal informants were orthodox Egyptologists working on sites near the Giza pyramids, I also interviewed their intellectual opponents who were kind enough to give me their time and openly share their theories with me. I would be betraying the trust of one set of informants if I were to spend my efforts trying to prove that they are wrong.

But it's not just a question of not taking sides—in truth, I'm not remotely qualified to decide the merits of any one side. I am not an Egyptologist or an archaeologist, I do not read hieroglyphs, I have only the most basic knowledge of ancient Egyptian dynastic history and the Hermetic texts, and the only geology I know is what little I have picked up from my father, a geophysicist—all of which, we will see, are among the knowledge bases used by different people in advancing their theories about dating the Giza pyramids and the Sphinx.

The fact that I tried to stay value-neutral does not mean, however, that I was able to attain some sort of Archimedean position and obtain data untainted by my own situation in the field. On the contrary: I was doing research that compared Western and Arab tourism in Egypt, and everyone I talked to perceived me as an American and a Westerner, which undoubtedly figured in the way people dealt with me. Egyptians—if I may be permitted to indulge in a generalization—are tactful people. They do not like to insult someone to his or her face. I was reminded of this every time I asked a stranger his or her opinion on the difference between Western and Arab tourism in Egypt, and that person gave a glowing description of Western tourists and then gleefully badmouthed (Gulf) Arab tourists. I always wondered, How would they have answered the question differently if I were an Arab asking it?

Let me offer two examples of encounters with taxi drivers that illustrate this point. I had determined that I would interview taxi drivers on the subject of tourism, since they are an important component of the tourism industry in Egypt. Every time I got into a taxi, I would strike up a conversation with the driver about the differences between Arab and Western tourists whom they'd had as passengers. While some would express polite reservations about American foreign policy, for the most part, they would report positive encounters with Westerners. Then, as often as not, they would compare Arab tourists in a negative light to these Westerners, as the following encounter, taken from my fieldnotes, describes:

I asked him about his experience with different tourists who were passengers in his cab. He said that Europeans were *munazzamīn*, ordered, and they keep their word. They have morals and principles (*ikhlāq wa mabādi'*), which was something that, contrary to what many people thought, had nothing whatsoever to do with religion. You could trust them and count on them. In contrast, he opined, Arabs were disordered, unreliable, spoiled. They were a recently developed civilization who just a few decades ago had been Bedouins scratching around in the dust, he said, so what could you expect? [Fieldnotes, 28 July 1999]

Not only did people almost certainly avoid saying bad things about Western tourists to avoid insuJting me, others may have done so strategically (particularly in the case of taxi drivers, who hoped to get a good tip). This point was driven home to me when I was interviewing a man named Mohamed who vacationed in Egypt many summers. He told me a joke that he and a Saudi friend liked to play on sycophantic taxi drivers. They would get in the taxi and the driver would ask them, conversationally, where they were from, to which they would reply that they were from Kuwait. The taxi driver would warmly say to them, "*ahsan nās*"—a polite expression meaning "the best of people," a common Egyptian phrase said to anybody when he or she says where he or she is from. Mohamed would say, "Oh, so you like Kuwaitis?" The taxi driver, eager for a tip, would carry on about what good people they were. "What about Saudis?" Mohamed would then ask. The taxi driver would say, "Oh, no, they're assholes! I can't stand them! Arrogant bastards. Not friendly and warm like Kuwaitis." Mohamed would then say, "Excuse me, sir, but we are Saudi," and then he and his friend would enjoy watching the man squirm as he tried to backtrack from the insults he'd just doled out.

Mohamed told me this story to illustrate how toadying Egyptian taxi drivers were (see Chapter 5 for a critical examination of Saudi views on Egyptian tourism workers). But it conveys a more universal message, which is that, in a social encounter, few people, Egyptian or otherwise, will say negative things about you (or the social group you are perceived as belonging to).

I had to keep this in mind constantly during the course of my research. (That said, I did encounter people who told me how much they disliked Americans, or how much they liked Gulf Arabs.) Assuming bias, I was careful not to reach conclusions based on some sort of simplistic tabulation of the number of taxi drivers who said they liked Western tourists versus the number who liked Arab tourists, and then use those data to calculate who won the popularity contest. Instead, whenever someone said that she or he liked or disliked Arabs or Westerners, I always asked why. It was the reasons that they offered that were telling, as they spoke volumes about the political, social, and economic interactions that characterized different groups of people.

Most of my informants are eager to see what I produce with the information they have given me. I hope that I do not embarrass, disappoint, or betray them. I look forward to their feedback and I regard this work as part of a continuing dialogue.

▲ ▲

CHAPTER 2

BURIED TREASURE

The first time I visited the Giza pyramids was in December 1999. I had been living in Egypt for a year and a half, but I kept putting off the obligatory pilgrimage. Egyptians and foreigners alike were always shocked when they heard I hadn't been there. What American living in Cairo didn't go to see the pyramids? Of course, I'd *seen* the pyramids—you can see them from most tall buildings in Cairo. They're located in Giza, which is technically a separate governorate from Cairo, but by the end of the twentieth century, the two cities had merged into one vast urban sprawl, and the pyramids were about a thirty-minute drive (depending on traffic) from downtown Cairo. But I hadn't seen them up close.

I finally visited the pyramids and the Sphinx when a couple of American friends came to Egypt for the turn of the millennium. The Great Pyramid is the oldest of the Seven Wonders of the World, and the only one remaining. The Giza site is the single biggest tourist draw in a country which does not lack tourist draws—some claim that, owing to the preservative qualities of its desert climate, Egypt contains half of the world's antiquities (Horn 1992). And yet I wasn't prepared for the vastness and grandeur of the pyramids and the Sphinx. It is almost enough to make you forget that there are several thousand other tourists swarming around it with you. Almost.

The second time I visited the pyramids was a month later, when I had my first interview with Dr. Zahi Hawass. Dr. Hawass is famous to any American who has watched one of the National Geographic or Fox Television specials on ancient Egypt. I didn't have a TV in graduate school, so I didn't know his face, but in my second year of graduate school, my advisor, James Boon, had given me a *New Yorker* article about the restoration of the Sphinx that talked

Figure 2.1. One of the pyramids of the Giza Plateau with the haze of Cairo in the background. Photograph by W. H. Chow.

about Dr. Hawass (Stille 1997), and I'd dreamed of meeting him ever since. The reality of the meeting dashed some of my naive fantasies about how to do anthropological fieldwork, but it also introduced me to a number of the issues that would concern my ethnographic inquiries into this Mecca of Western tourism in Egypt.

From my fieldnotes:

Just came back from my interview with Dr. Zahi Hawass. My appointment was for 11:00 and I was running late, so I took a taxi there. All along the road leading up to the pyramids, next to the Mena House Hotel, people from shops and tourist kiosks were shouting at the taxi and running alongside, trying to stop it, telling the taxi driver in Arabic that he should take me to such-and-such a store, or such-and-such a stable (where of course he would get a commission). They actually came hurtling towards the car head-first as if about to collide with it, and then would suddenly veer to a parallel course and run along with the car, hanging on to the door on the driver's side, so they could pretend to be having an intimate conversation with [the] driver, while trotting along at a fantastic pace so as not to lose him. The taxi driver just kept yelling out, "She's not a tourist!" because I had told him I had an appointment with the Director of the Pyramids in his office.[1]

When we had neared a place where there were guards, someone dressed all in black stopped the taxi by standing right in front of the car, sticking his hand out in front of him. "Ticket?" he said in Arabic, making a hand gesture. The taxi driver said that I had an appointment, I didn't need a ticket. The man came over and said that we couldn't proceed any further by car and I would have to get out there. I said I was there to see Dr. Zahi Hawass and the man said I would have to get out of the car and walk up to his offices, pointing vaguely up the hill, and he said he would take me there.

While I was debating this with the taxi driver, who seemed as bewildered as I was, a tourist policeman came over from the guard station and grabbed the man who had stopped us by the collar and started physically hauling him off and hitting him on the head. Not hitting him hard, just sort of whacking him on top of the head like an older brother does to his younger siblings. Then he let go of the man, who straightened his clothes and trotted off in the direction of the horse stables below the pyramids.

Turns out that he was a tourist hustler trying to force me out of the car to get some sort of guide fee for taking me around. It should have occurred to me that he had no uniform, but he spoke very authoritatively about cars not being allowed past that point. Once he had vanished, the taxi driver, as confused as I was, apologized and said he didn't know what was going on and what was the system there. We drove ahead to a police officer to whom I complained about con artists; the policeman smiled vaguely and benevolently, said, "*Ma'leish*"—translates either to "never mind" or "sorry about that"—and answered our questions about where to drive—cars were indeed allowed—to get to Dr. Hawass's office. [Fieldnotes, 25 January 2000]

That odd encounter turned out to be typical for tourists visiting the pyramids without being attached to a tour group. Once I finally made it to the offices of the archaeologists who work on the Giza Plateau, I was privileged to overhear a conversation that struck me as a titillating primer on the intersection of cultural politics and archaeology in Egypt. And my first introduction to Dr. Hawass himself made me rethink my own research methodology. To continue from the same day's fieldnotes:

I had the appointment for 11 A.M. I went in to the reception area and told a woman sitting at a desk that I had arrived for my appointment with Dr. Hawass. There were a number of other people also there to see Dr. Hawass, but they seemed to not have appointments. And it was abundantly clear that Dr. Hawass thought I was right at the bottom of the totem pole because he saw everybody else before me, even though they didn't have appointments. So

I sat in the outer office about 45 minutes before I was called in. This proved to be useful because I observed some interesting interactions between foreign and Egyptian archaeologists in the foyer of his office while I was waiting.

There was a European woman and an Egyptian man, both speaking Italian somewhat haltingly with each other. Then they switched over to English.

SHE: . . . the European woman can do four things at once: she can talk, listen, think, answer . . .

HE: You are not superwoman.

SHE: I tell you all European women can do this.

HE: What is Europe? Europe is nothing.

SHE: Europe is 2000 years of development and you copy it—Egyptians copy it, Americans copy it—look at what you are wearing! (sweater, pants)—this is European!

HE (with a smirk and an incredulous glance at one of his Egyptian colleagues): It's Egyptian!

SHE: I am talking about the form, not the fabrication. *Pantalon,* shirt, this is European, 2000 years of development.

HE: It is Egyptian.

SHE: 2000 years of development. You are just wearing *galabiyya* [robe] and *shibshib* [sandals] before this.

HE: You developed our design.

SHE: No, you copy and that's it.

HE: We invented it and you developed it. Europe is nothing, a piece of shit.

SHE: You are nothing, you only copy.

They were both joking and smiling. There was an edge to the conversation, but it was also clear that they were long partners in bickering.

Another man asked the first man:

2ND MAN: You are going to America when?

SHE: He is a terrorist, he can't go there. I am going to call the U.S. Embassy and tell them he's a terrorist and to not allow him to go there, and they'll send him right back. Just look at his face, you can see he's a terrorist.

HE (replying to the woman): Don't worry, my dear, I will come back for you. I won't leave you for America.

She made a face at him. The two men started looking at pages from some magazine, an article with glossy color pictures about one of their excavation projects.

HE: This is my tomb here (pointing out a picture to her).

SHE: You are buried there? (laughing, teasing)

HE: No, I was director of excavations in this tomb. (He starts describing the project and what they were doing there.)

SHE (still teasing, grabs the pages and shows them to someone else in the office): Look, pictures of his family.

He grabbed the pages back, folded them over, offended, and refused to give them back to her, even as she begged for them penitently . . .

Just then I was called in to Dr. Hawass's office. I went in and sat down. There were still some other people in there talking to him, a couple of French journalists and a Polish archaeologist. Dr. Hawass introduced us all, ordered a minion to bring some hibiscus tea, then continued his conversation with them. While he was talking to them, I looked around. Bookshelves covered two walls and were filled with archaeology books in Arabic, English, French, Italian and German. His desk was stacked high with papers and envelopes, and had about ten different pyramid-shaped paperweights made of everything from plastic to granite. On the wall was a pyramidal arrangement of framed photographs. In the center was Dr. Hawass receiving an award from President Mubarak. The surrounding photos showed Dr. Hawass with the Egyptian Minister of Culture, with Omar Sharif, with Princess Diana, Hilary Rodham and Chelsea Clinton, Barbara Bush, Brooke Shields, and a group of TWA stewardesses. Dr. Hawass was simultaneously talking to his guests, writing something on a yellow legal pad, and fielding phone calls. Someone commented on his ability to multitask. "Oh, this is nothing," he said. "I can do 5 or 6 things at once. I'm writing my next book on Bahariya, the Valley of the Golden Mummies." He gestured to the yellow legal pad he was writing on. "It's going to be translated into five languages. Harry Abrams Press."

Finally the other guests left, and he turned to me. I asked him questions about the millennium and secret chambers underground and site management, and he answered in between incoming phone calls. Whenever he was talking on the phone, he would pass me an article or book of his to look through. For every question I asked him, he referred me to some article. "I can make a copy for you, or you could look it up in the library." Implication seemed to be that I was ill-prepared for this interview, as obviously I was, since he'd written something on nearly every single thing I wanted to ask him about, and I'd read nothing that he'd written.

He dismissed me after a short interview. I suppose that everybody wants a piece of him, and he doesn't have much time for a minor anthropology grad student to pester him. I trudged home after ascertaining that there were no more interesting debates going on in the outer office about whether pants and shirts were of Egyptian or European provenance.

I walked down the hill from the pyramids and waited for the bus to come. A fierce sand storm was blowing up and I had to put on my sunglasses and huddle in the enclosed booth of the bus stop. On the wall was some graffiti in Arabic:

> O my beloved Egypt,
> Happy twenty-first century
> I wish flourishing and progress
> To Egypt, the beloved, the precious

It was signed "Alaa Saqr." I remembered what one Saudi tourist I interviewed had said: that there was no one in the Arab world with more national pride than Egyptians.

After I came home that first day, I contemplated my next step. I was discouraged. I wanted to research Egyptology from a social perspective and I had a goal of getting to know the archaeologists around the pyramids. It was true that the answer to many of the questions I wanted to ask Zahi Hawass could be found in his published writings. However, I also knew that there were questions I didn't even know to ask at that point, and things to be learned by extended contact with informants over time that couldn't be learned in a formal interview or in published articles. But it was clear that Dr. Hawass had no time for me.

I realized that I'd been subconsciously working on a model of fieldwork based on the outdated premise that my informants would have plenty of time to sit around and chat and share their lives with me. But I was trying to secure an informant who clearly did *not* have time to sit around and chat. Hawass was busy, his time was valuable, and he had plenty of his own friends to sit and chat with in his spare time. I had to find another way to get access to the offices of the archaeologists.

Eventually, after reading a number of his articles and securing another meeting with him, I worked out a deal in which I would volunteer around his office. The work I did consisted of typing up and proofreading some of the articles that he publishes in English. This arrangement had several advantages. First, I was helping Dr. Hawass out. That made me feel like less of a parasite; I wasn't just mooching off him for my dissertation research. Second, it gave me a reason to be physically present in the offices of the Giza Plateau archaeologists on a regular basis, so I could observe the everyday life of the antiquities inspectors at the pyramids. And when Dr. Hawass had a spare moment, he would often talk to me about his work, or when he was giving a television interview next to one of the excavations, I could tag along. Third, as I typed up his articles, I learned more about his research and the issues he thought were important, and I learned a little about Egyptology, a subject about which I was appallingly ignorant.

Finally, being at the pyramids three days a week for about a year, I got to know Dr. Hawass's staff, the archaeologists who work with him in his offices.

While I was typing on the computer in a back room, Sahar would be typing responses to Dr. Hawass's e-mails, Tariq would be organizing slides of the latest excavation work, Nashwa and May would be answering phones, Ayman would be going through a large reference book to beef up his knowledge of some Middle Dynasty tomb, Sally would be poring through the daily newspapers and clipping all the articles on archaeology-related subjects for the office's files, Nermine would be alphabetizing the archaeology books in Dr. Hawass's office, al-Husseini and Ramadan would be working on their grad school applications to do their Ph.D.s in Egyptology in the United States and the Czech Republic, and Mohamed and Shaaban would be detailed to take visitors around the pyramids. Mahmoud Afifi, Chief Inspector of the Giza Plateau, and Ahmed Haggar, the Director of the Pyramids, had offices next door and would pop in to say hello, and sometimes, at the end of a day directing the excavations of the pyramid builders' tombs, Mansour Boriak would come into the office to take a break and chat. After hours trudging around in the hot sun, he should have been exhausted, but he had apparently boundless energy, and he would do one of his famous impressions of people to make me laugh. When we weren't busy working on something for Dr. Hawass, Sally and Nashwa would help me look through their archives for articles relevant to my own research project.

Dr. Hawass's team of Egyptian Egyptologists has been responsible for some of the most important archaeological finds in recent history. In 1990, Hawass's team started excavating the tombs of the builders of the pyramids, which had long been sought in the sands of Giza, unsuccessfully, by a number of Egyptologists (Hawass and Lehner 1997). This work is changing how archaeologists see ancient Egyptian state-building and the relationship between ruler and subject. For example, the pyramid shape was long thought to be a sacred form that only kings could use. But miniature pyramids and proto-pyramids have been found as grave markers above the tombs of the artisans, engineers, and craftsmen who worked on the pharaohs' pyramids, indicating that it was a folk tradition not reserved exclusively for royalty (Hawass 1996). More important, the tombs are inscribed with names and epitaphs, providing information about the identities of the builders, indicating that they were Egyptian workers who were organized into teams and remunerated for their labors, thus laying to rest popular theories about the pyramids being built with ancient Israelite slave labor.

The other big find that Hawass's team was working on during the period of my fieldwork was in Bahariya Oasis, Giza Governorate. There, a vast underground necropolis was found dating to the Greek-Roman period in Egypt, when Bahariya was a major wine producer and trading post for desert caravans. It has been dubbed "The Valley of the Golden Mummies" by Hawass, because dozens of mummies with gold masks have been found in family tombs. Mummies of all different class levels have been found, shedding new light on both the class structure and burial practices of a previously obscure period of Egyptian history (Hawass 2000a).

Hawass's is an all-Egyptian team that receives funding only from the Egyptian government. Today there are many Egyptian archaeologists working on everything from Old Kingdom to Greek-Roman sites. But until recently there were only a handful of well-known Egyptian Egyptologists.[2] Only in the latter half of the twentieth century have there been significant numbers of Egyptian Egyptologists, and the field is still dominated by non-Egyptians. The majority of the texts are in French, German, and English. Egyptologists, including some Westerners, bemoan the dearth of texts that are translated into Arabic and vice versa, but there is no structural impetus to propel change.

It was no accident that Egyptians did not participate in the field of Egyptology until recently. For years, they were deliberately excluded from it by Europeans who did not want to lose their monopoly over the country's Antiquities Service. When I first asked to interview Mark Lehner about his research in Egypt, he insisted that I first read Donald M. Reid's article, "Indigenous Egyptology: The Decolonization of a Profession" (1985), before he would talk to me. Lehner assigns the article to all his archaeology students at the University of Chicago to instill in them an awareness of the politically charged history of their field. Egyptology has, from its very inception, been intimately connected with European imperialism, and it experienced its own period of gradual decolonization.

IMPERIALISM, COLONIALISM, AND EGYPTOLOGY

The contemporary politics of Egyptology cannot be understood without knowing something of the history of the field and its relationship to European colonial powers, starting with Napoleon's invasion of Egypt in 1798. So let us first turn to a review of this history as recounted by some of the discipline's historians.[3]

When Napoleon invaded Egypt, he brought with him chemists, biologists, mineralogists, botanists, linguists, artists, draftsmen, mathematicians, and engineers. The French styled the invasion a scientific expedition, and the scientific team studied and reproduced drawings of the ancient tombs and monuments (along with other aspects of Egypt), eventually compiling their research into the enormous twenty-volume *Description de l'Egypte*. Bonaparte was a member of the Institut de France, a prestigious French scholarly organization, and less than two months after arriving in Egypt, he inaugurated the Institut

Figure 2.2. A tourist photograph from the 1930s. On the back is penciled "Scene of Napoleon's victory; Sakkara in the distance, Giza." (The tourist imagination projects meaning onto an apparently featureless landscape.) Photographer unknown; collection of L. L. Wynn.

d'Egypte along the same lines, with its goals to study the country and to enlighten Egypt (Brier 1999:48).

From the beginning, there was an intimate association between archaeological investigations in Egypt and colonialism—not to mention war. Many of the drawings and accounts compiled in *Description* were the direct products of battles that cleared the way for the French artists and scientists to work uninterrupted. The team followed the French army, and they were dispatched to various sites almost immediately after battles had concluded. It was 1 July 1798 when French soldiers landed near Alexandria. The next morning, from the base of Pompey's Pillar, they attacked, and they took the city by midday. The following day, the artists and scientists were taken ashore, and the day after that, they were already at work, sketching Pompey's Pillar and taking its measurements, while the army was still fighting. When French artist Denon ran out of pencils later in the expedition, he melted down lead bullets to draw with (France 1991:17).

Before long, Alexandria and Cairo were both subdued, and Napoleon went to work forming the Institute of Egypt from the members of the Commission of Arts and Science, installing the Institute in mansions of the conquered elite. The French made meticulous drawings of mosques and the citadel, the pyramids, the Sphinx, and numerous other monuments. They compared what they were seeing to the records of Herodotus, Strabo, Pliny the Elder, and other ancient writers who had visited Egypt. In 1799, they mounted an expedition to Upper Egypt, passing through Assiut, Qena, and Aswan, visiting and sketching the temples of Dendera, Philae, Esneh, Edfu, Kom Ombo and Luxor on the way. The artists traveled with the soldiers, and sometimes they were given only a few minutes to sketch a temple before they had to move on.

The Commission members not only sketched and documented monuments, they also documented the natural history, mineral resources, local customs, and farming techniques of the people. They hunted and stuffed birds and animals; drew plants; collected seeds, insects, and minerals; and made annotations about irrigation practices. Most important for our purposes, they collected a large number of portable artifacts. A French engineer by the name of Lieutenant Pierre François Xavier Bouchard found the famous Rosetta Stone. The stone consisted of the remnants of an ancient political decree repeated in three languages: hieroglyphs, Demotic (a cursive form of hieroglyphs), and Greek. It would later be the key to deciphering hieroglyphs and would profoundly transform modern understanding of ancient Egypt.[4]

The French occupation of Egypt ended three years later, when they were defeated by the British. The Commission had continued to work through months of political turmoil. During the last days of battle, Commission members had attempted to leave Egypt, but were forced back to Alexandria by British forces. General Menou surrendered to England on 30 August 1801, and the British allowed the French to take home all of the antiquities and natural history specimens they had collected, but the British kept the original Rosetta Stone, recognizing its tremendous importance. The French went home with just a wax impression. Egypt reverted back to Ottoman rule, but now with a strong European presence. It was the beginning of a long reign of European imperialism in Egypt.

Napoleon's expedition had kicked off a fad of Egypt mania in Europe which affected art, architecture, fashion, jewelry, and literature.[5] His invasion also launched a period of intensive European treasure hunting in Egypt. The main players in the rush for antiquities, especially in the beginning, were England and France. England's consul in Egypt was Henry Salt, and France had Bernardino Drovetti. Between them, these two managed to carve up all of Egypt into "spheres of influence," as Fagan describes it, for their own personal tomb raiding. They obtained *firmāns*, or decrees, giving them access to diverse and remote areas, which translated into almost exclusive rights over treasures of

Figure 2.3. The Rosetta Stone. Photograph by Vladimir Korostyshevskiy.

antiquities all over the country, to the dismay of other lesser consuls, missionaries, and adventurers who were also hunting for treasures and had to negotiate terms when invading the turf of the British and French consuls.

There was an intimate relationship between politics and treasure hunting
in those days. Several historians have argued that Muhammad Ali Pasha, then
ruler of Egypt, didn't give a fig about the monuments himself, but he recognized that they appealed to the foreigners with whom he wanted to preserve
good relations, so he allocated various treasures and digging rights as gifts. In
the early days of the European presence in Egypt, the fiercely competitive Salt
and Drovetti managed to get their hands on the vast bulk of the antiquities,
thanks to their positions as representatives of the two most important foreign

governments—governments which had already proved their ability to militarily conquer and occupy Egypt. They often obtained their *firmāns* from the Pasha himself.

Excavating teams would sometimes raise the flag of their country over their
tents or their ships to claim for themselves diplomatic immunity—even when
they were not diplomats or working for one of the consuls—to prevent competing Europeans, or lesser provincial governors, from raiding their excavations
and taking away the artifacts they had found.[6] This continued even after 1835,
when the first ordinance was passed preventing the exportation of antiquities
and the destruction of monuments. Even the pieces that made it to Egypt's first
museum were all eventually given away by the Ottoman rulers of Egypt as gifts
to important European visitors of state.

Tomb robbing has a long pedigree in Egypt. The Abbott and Amherst Papyri record a court case against a gang of tomb robbers operating more than
2,700 years ago in Thebes. (When questioned why he stole from the Pharaoh's
tomb, the robber replied that, if the Pharaoh was a god as everyone said, why
didn't He stop him?)[7] But while ancient Egyptian tomb robbers were primarily
interested in the valuables that they could take from the tombs, Europeans
were also interested in chunks of the tombs themselves. Vast quantities of
monuments, both large and small, were removed from the country. The big
players took large pieces from tombs, such as sarcophagi and sections of wall
inscriptions; others scavenged for smaller portables, and even traded in the
occupants of the tombs themselves. Indeed, for at least two centuries before
the French conquest, there had been a lively European trade in mummies,
which were ground up and the powder sold as a staple medicine in apothecar-
ies. (This was apparently a result of a confusion between the black resin used
in preparation of mummies and *momia,* a Persian word meaning pitch or black
bitumen, which may have therapeutic properties. The powder of mummified
corpses was applied to cuts and fractures, and taken internally for a wide range
of ailments. One hates to imagine the effect of the powder on Europe's sick,
especially since a shortage of real mummies led many traders in the substance
to imitate mummies by wrapping and then leaving the corpses of the recent
dead out in the sun to dry.)[8]

But soon the craze for all things Egyptian drove a trade that went well beyond powdered corpses. As early as 1819, de Montule, a European traveler,
remarked that Gurna villagers on the West Bank in Luxor were making a living
for themselves digging for monuments, mummies, statues, and other artifacts
in response to European demand (Greener 1966:107). In 1833 the European
"lust to own the exotic," as Fagan aptly puts it, prompted one monk to remark
with irony that "it would hardly be respectable, on one's return from Egypt, to

present oneself in Europe without a mummy in one hand and a crocodile in the other" (Fagan 1975:11, 13).

With Egypt under increasing European control, much more than mummies was removed from the country. Major prizes taken from Egypt include a large head of Ramses II, the Table of Kings of Abydos and another from Karnak, and, perhaps most famously, the spectacular Zodiac of Dendera, which was removed in secret by Lelorrain and Saulnier, two Frenchmen who were racing against Lepsius, a German, to take the Zodiac. Lelorrain actually used gunpowder to dynamite the Zodiac from the ceiling of the temple because there wasn't time to cut it from the stones using regular cutting tools. Lelorrain and Saulnier sold it for a huge profit to King Louis XVIII. Today, the hole in the ceiling of the temple left by Lelorrain has been filled with a plaster replica of the Zodiac; the original Zodiac stands in the Louvre.

Figure 2.4. A painting of an ancient Egyptian zodiac done on papyrus for sale to modern tourists. Photograph by Danis Derics.

Figure 2.5. A Victorian engraving of one of Cleopatra's Needles, the obelisks of Alexandria, which were removed from Egypt and now stand in New York City and London.

Obelisks were a favorite prize. One of the two Luxor obelisks was given by Muhammad Ali to the French in 1819, and taken more than a decade later by the engineer Lebas to Paris, where it was erected in the Place de la Concorde. (More obelisks were offered to and claimed by the French, but the difficulty and immense cost of transporting the Luxor obelisk dampened the French government's ardor for funding further large-scale acquisitions.) The obelisks of Alexandria, nicknamed "Cleopatra's Needles," were claimed by different countries; one eventually went to London, while the other was raised in New York City's Central Park in 1880 accompanied by Masonic rites.[9] In all, there are two Egyptian obelisks in England (in Dorset and London), one each in Istanbul, Paris, and New York City, and thirteen in Rome, where they adorn numerous city squares (Habachi 1988).

The rivalry for Egypt's treasures was fierce and nationalistic, as this quote by the artist David Roberts, who traveled through Egypt making drawings of monuments during the nineteenth century, makes clear, when he describes the removal of the Luxor obelisk to be raised in Paris:

The Obelisk which has been removed required a series of operations which employed five years, from July 1831 to October 1836, between its disturbance at Luxor and its erection in the Place de la Concorde at Paris; where it became the sixth object that has occupied or been prepared for the same spot within fifty years. A statue of Louis XV was there during the old regime; a statute of Liberty (with the guillotine before it) during the Revolution; a column of wood during the Empire; which was removed at the Restoration, and arrangements made by Louis XVIII to replace Louis XV; but an order of Charles X substituted a statue of Louis XVI. This was not, however, carried into effect before the Government of the last Revolution adopted the Obelisk of Luxor. The traveler who now looks upon the ruins of the Temple feels a deep regret that the completeness of its glorious façade should have been destroyed to gratify such a frivolous national vanity. The French obtained leave from Mahommed Ali to remove it; and erected it, at enormous cost, in their capital. *Cui bono?*—not to preserve it from destruction, but to commemorate a victory, or to mark an era in the history of France; but it was removed from its place of honour, where it had stood for thirty-three centuries only to decorate, with the help of bronze and gilding, a spot in Paris which has been stained with a thousand crimes! (Roberts 2000)

Roberts was irked by the removal of one of the two obelisks which stood as twin sentinels at the pylon gate which approaches the Temple of Luxor, leaving the remaining obelisk solitary and asymmetrically placed. (France was also offered the other obelisk, but, as noted, the cost and effort involved in removing the first was prohibitive enough to discourage them.) Yet Roberts's sharp criticism of France is somewhat ironic, given that England also took two obelisks from Egypt.

A strong sense of national pride was involved in the race to obtain the finest treasures and the richest excavation sites. However, the consuls, although using their countries' power to further their hunt for antiquities, were not acting on behalf of France and England to fill national museums. Salt and Drovetti personally funded their excavations, used the political strength of their own countries to shield themselves from interference, and then sold the booty to the highest bidders to make their own fortunes and glory. Other collectors quickly entered the fray, finding various means of working around Salt and Drovetti's monopoly. Embassies, missionaries, and independent adventurers collected for the noblemen and kings of Europe, whose collections served to fan the flames of interest in Egypt, and were the basis for international collections of Egyptian antiquities that eventually ended up in European museums. By the early 1800s, European travelers were already complaining that better artifacts were to be found in London and Paris and Rome than in Egypt itself (Greener 1966:108).

Figure 2.6. A 1908 postcard by Max H. Rudmann, mailed from Aswan to Belmont, Massachusetts. Collection of L. L. Wynn.

All this scavenging and treasure hunting, it is often said, may have prevented the monuments from facing worse fates. The Ottoman rulers had been grinding down stone from temples and monuments for saltpeter. Many temples and tombs were thus completely wiped from the historical record (Walz 1996:70).

But while these early adventurers may have saved some monuments for posterity, their work could hardly be called archaeology. It was treasure hunting. Even after Champollion had learned how to decipher hieroglyphs (some twenty years after the Rosetta Stone was found) and scholars were using papyri and tombs to reconstruct ancient Egyptian history, the treasure hunters were racing against each other to amass collections, gathering together all their treasures haphazardly, blasting them out of tombs in some cases, and pocketing scarabs and figurines, without a record of where they came from, how they were found, or what they were found with. Papyri were bought and sold without any record of what tomb or mummy they came from.

The mid-nineteenth century saw a gradual change in attitudes toward preserving Egypt's antiquities, how excavations should proceed, and who had rights to the finds. In 1858, a Frenchman named Auguste Mariette, who had made his fame uncovering the Serapeum at Memphis, the avenue of sphinxes in Saqqara that Strabo had written about, was appointed first director of the country's antiquities service. He established a new museum in Bulaq, and Said Pasha supplied him with labor for his archaeological excavations to gather material for the new museum. He could requisition the labor of an entire village if he wanted to—and he did, employing some 2,780 laborers in total (Fagan 1975). It was still a treasure hunt, although the treasures were now meant to stay in Egypt instead of going to Europe. Mariette sought to keep a rapid flow of attractive antiquities coming, both to fill the museum and to keep the interest of the Pasha, on whose goodwill he depended for funds and labor. A later Egyptologist despaired of Mariette's excavating techniques, which included the use of dynamite:

> Mariette most rascally blasted to pieces all the fallen parts of the granite temple by a large gang of soldiers, to clear it out instead of lifting the stones and replacing them by means of tackle. . . . It is sickening to see the rate at which everything is being destroyed, and the little regard paid to preservation. (Cited in Fagan 1975:332)

Mariette's appointment by Said Pasha angered consuls and treasure hunters who objected to state control over archaeological finds. But while he managed to keep finds in Egypt in the Bulaq Museum, the French used Mariette for political and diplomatic purposes. He was pressured to accompany Said Pasha to France in connection with a financial loan the French wanted Egypt to take; the debt that resulted from such European loans later provided the excuse for the British and French to depose Said's successor, the Khedive Ismail, in 1879. Again, we see how antiquities were tied up with European imperialism in Egypt. The British controlled the country's politics through their puppet leaders, but the French maintained a presence in the country as well, and continued to direct Egypt's antiquities service until the Free Officers' Revolution in 1952.

ARAB AND EGYPTIAN (DIS)INTEREST IN ANCIENT EGYPT?

The fact that few Egyptians attained prominence as Egyptologists in the early days was not due to a lack of Egyptian interest in its pharaonic past. Early Muslims were interested in the pharaonic ruins, seeing them as the remains of an ancient race of giants or magicians. The medieval Arab historian and traveler Ibn Khaldoun had complained that the Arab fad for treasure hunting using magic in Egypt was so widespread that it was a taxed industry (Greener 1966:85). Medieval historians Michael Cook (1983) and Ulrich Haarmann (1980, 1996) have both described how medieval Arab historians portrayed ancient Egypt, its history and monuments. As Haarmann writes,

> Outlandishness, wondrousness and weirdness may well be the dominant qualities attached to Egyptian antiquity in medieval Muslim texts. An-

cient Egypt turned into a land of miracles, magic and treasures, yet also of mathematical ingenuity and scientific wisdom, a double image that is familiar to us from Hellenistic hermeticism and Renaissance as well as Enlightenment Europe. (1996:607)

Medieval Muslims toured the Egyptian monuments, visiting the ruins of Memphis, Saqqara's step pyramid and mummies, the Sphinx of Giza, the mastabas in the Dakhla oasis, Philae, Aswan, Dendera, and Luxor (Haarmann 1996:611, 615). Haarmann reports that the key tourist destination for medieval Arab travelers was the temple of Akhmīm, south of Giza, and located along a caravan route (ibid.:612–613). Like Roman tourists before them and Europeans after them, medieval Muslim tourists left their mark by way of Arabic graffiti on the monuments (Vachala and Ondráš 2000), and, like the Romans and Europeans, they also damaged monuments and tombs searching for treasure.

Rifaʿa al-Tahtawi, the famous Egyptian intellectual, had traveled to Paris in the early 1800s when Egypt was all the rage, thanks to the Egyptian exhibit at the Louvre and the headway Champollion was making in deciphering hieroglyphs, and Tahtawi returned to Egypt with a new interest in ancient Egyptian history (Yared 1996). He had protested when Muhammad Ali offered an obelisk to King Louis-Philippe. Tahtawi was an early progenitor of an Egyptian pharaonic nationalism, later elaborated by figures such as Ali Mubarak, Mustafa Kamil, and Ahmad Lutfi al-Sayyid, which took pride in the great superstate created by the pharaohs and celebrated its pharaonic heritage as the unique distinguishing factor of Egyptian-ness.[10]

Numerous other Egyptian intellectuals took a keen interest in the pharaonic past (see Reid 2002 and Selim 2001). So, while some have claimed that Egyptian or Ottoman disinterest in antiquities was what led to their removal by Europeans during 150 years of colonialism, the statement needs qualification: no doubt some were uninterested, just as plenty of Europeans cared little for monuments, Egyptian or European, but that cannot be the case for all Egyptians of that time. Rather, we should look to structural reasons that encouraged European interest in the monuments of Egypt and discouraged Egyptians and other Arabs from the same. The fact that the supposed lack of Egyptian and Arab interest in monuments coincides with a period of European military conquest in Egypt is instructive.

Likewise, it was not a lack of interest that kept Egyptians from studying Egyptology and made the majority of archaeologists studying ancient Egypt European. Rather, it was French and British Egyptologists who took pains deliberately to exclude Egyptians from the profession. Mariette, who is often revered as the founding father of the Egyptian Antiquities Service, actively fought to stamp out the careers of some early Egyptian Egyptologists. German scholar Heinrich Brugsch had set up a "School of the Ancient Egyptian Language" in 1869 and included ten Egyptians among his students. But Mariette feared losing his monopoly over the country's antiquities if an Egyptian was eventually qualified to take over his post. So he actually conspired to prevent Brugsch's Egyptian students from being allowed to study in the museum or at archaeological sites (Reid 1985:235). The school eventually closed because Mariette refused to hire its graduates in the Antiquities Service; the Egyptian students had to take other jobs outside of Egyptology. Later, British and French archaeologists, who were still fierce rivals for power in Egyptian affairs, nevertheless cooperated to exclude Egyptians and maintain European hegemony over the Antiquities Service. All in all, "in the half century before 1922 Western archaeological interests in the Antiquities Service forced three indigenous Egyptological schools in succession to close by refusing to employ their graduates" (Reid 1985:246).

The discovery of Tutankhamun's almost-untouched tomb by Howard Carter in 1922 became heavily politicized within Egypt and affected archaeological excavations for decades afterward.[11] It also served to strengthen the pharaonic component of Egyptian nationalism. Egyptian nationalism had been on the rise, and just eight months before Carter made his discovery, Britain had granted Egypt a partial independence, paving the way for the nationalist leader Saad Zaghloul's rise to power in 1924. Meanwhile, Carter's discovery of Tut's tomb in October 1922 was making headlines around the world. When Zaghloul's government tried to impose restrictions on Carter's continuing excavation, Carter closed the tomb in protest. Pierre Lacau, the French director of the country's Antiquities Service, seized the tomb for the Egyptian government and declared that nothing in it was to leave Egypt. It wasn't until two years later that Zaghloul's successor, Ahmed Ziwar, readmitted Carter to work on the tomb, and relations between Carter and the Antiquities Service were never really mended (Reid 1985:238). When Saad Zaghloul died, he was laid to rest in a large neo-pharaonic mausoleum that takes up a city block in the al-Mounira district of Cairo, an architectural testament to the increasing symbolic importance of pharaonic history for Egyptian nationalists in that period.[12]

Despite increasingly rigorous archaeological methods and national control over the country's antiquities service, it was still many years before laws would be put into place to keep all antiquities from leaving Egypt. Some very fine pieces were taken out of the country through loopholes in the laws protecting Egypt's patrimony.

The bust of Nefertiti is a famous example. Until less than twenty years ago, Egyptian law permitted foreign archaeologists excavating in Egypt to take abroad some of the portable antiquities they unearthed. After each excavation

Figure 2.7. A group of 1930s Western tourists crowd into the entrance of King Tutankhamun's tomb. Photographer unknown; collection of L. L. Wynn.

was concluded, archaeologists had to present their findings to a representative from the Egyptian Antiquities Service, who would select the pieces he wanted to keep in the country. The remaining pieces were given to the archaeologists to take home with them. Letting the Egyptian inspector take first pick was meant to ensure that the best finds would remain in Egypt, but foreign archaeologists developed clever ruses to keep the best pieces for themselves.

In 1912, a German archaeologist by the name of Ludwig Borchardt led an expedition for the Deutsche Orient-Gesellschaft in Tel el-Amarna. On 6 December, his team unearthed the bust of Nefertiti, an extraordinary piece of sculpture.[13] Laws at that time permitted the division of antiquities between Egypt and licensed foreign excavators. After any excavation period was completed, an Egyptian antiquities inspector was presented with the finds and then had the right to choose the pieces that would remain in the country; the rest became the property of whoever held the excavation license. When the results of Borchardt's excavation were published in 1923, with the bust of Nefertiti the celebrated centerpiece of Borchardt's collection, shortly after the Howard Carter–Tutankhamun affair, the Egyptian Antiquities Service insisted that the head must have been smuggled out of the country by Borchardt and tried un-

Figure 2.8. The bust of Nefertiti. Photograph by Aurelio.

successfully to get it back. How had such an archaeological gem slipped past the Egyptian antiquities inspector?

What is thought to have happened is that Borchardt, recognizing the statue's value, covered it in mud, but carefully cleaned up the other pieces he took out of the ground. When the inspector came to select the pieces that would stay in Egypt, he ignored the mud-covered head and chose from among the cleaned items. Nefertiti's head became the property of James Simon, the Berlin merchant who had financed the excavation; it is now one of the prizes of the Ägyptisches Museum's collection. It was a young Egyptian archaeologist named Tariq el-Awady who told me the story of Nefertiti's bust. Against my protests over Borchardt's ethics, Tariq was philosophical. "Borchardt was very clever," he said with a shrug.

After the Nefertiti and Tutankhamun incidents, which spurred Egyptian nationalists' concern over antiquities leaving Egypt, foreign excavations in Egypt came almost to a standstill for decades, because, without assurances that they'd be able to take substantial treasures home with them, Egyptologists could not drum up funding from supporters (Hoving 1978). The 1952 Revolution in Egypt further limited Westerners from engaging in Egyptian archaeological work. It wasn't until the early 1960s that foreign Egyptologists started returning to Egypt as a result of the Egyptian government's appeal to UNESCO for international support in saving Abu Simbel and the other Nubian monuments, which were about to be drowned by rising Lake Nasser after the Aswan High Dam was built (Wilson 1964:195).

Yet it was not until the late date of 1983 that Ahmed Qadri, then Chairman

Figure 2.9. Abu Simbel, after the monument was moved and reassembled on higher ground to save it from being submerged under Lake Nasser after the High Dam was built. Photograph by Vladimir Pomortzeff.

of the Egyptian Antiquities Organization (EAO, the predecessor of the Supreme Council of Antiquities), successfully fought to rescind the rule that permitted subdivision of artifacts between foreigners and the Egyptian state. Egyptian Law no. 117 of 1983, the Egyptian Antiquities Law, decrees that all antiquities found in Egypt belong to the state of Egypt. Nationalist calls to keep Egypt's treasures in the country had long pre-dated that, but Egyptian lawmakers before 1983 must have reasoned that they would only be letting the less important finds go. Egypt is positively inundated with antiquities, and has not the resources to properly store, much less exhibit, them all. On average, a new archaeological site is uncovered every month in Egypt. At the present time, the Cairo Museum contains some 176,000 treasures, but there is only space to display 40,000 of them. The rest are crowded into storage areas in the museum's basement (Gharib 1997:45–46). (A much larger museum on the outskirts of Cairo is currently in the works.)

My too-brief historical account given here is largely derived from secondary sources, and readers will want to examine more complete and authoritative historical accounts than my own. But it is important to briefly recap this history of Egyptology in order to understand the contemporary politics of Egyptology today (including the conflicts between orthodox Egyptology and "New Age" authors theorizing about ancient Egypt which are discussed in the following chapter), as well as to understand the fascination that pharaonic Egypt holds for Western, but not Arab, tourists.

So let's review some of the key points that this history can tell us about the historical relationship between Egyptology and colonial politics. First, the early collectors used their diplomatic (i.e., political) connections to obtain permits to excavate and remove items from Egypt, ensuring that the majority of the early finds were taken by representatives of the two European countries which held the most power in Egypt: England and France. Even when excavators didn't have diplomatic status, some would feign such by raising their countries' flags to prevent other treasure hunters from taking their spoils. Peter Green aptly describes this as "a series of treasure hunts thinly disguised as 'scientific investigation,' and carried out under the aegis of gunboat diplomacy" (1979:20). Second, the French head of the Egyptian antiquities service, Mariette, was used by the French government to convince Egyptians to take loans, and these loans consolidated European imperial power as Egypt sunk deeper and deeper into debt, permitting its creditors to exert more and more control over the country's finances. And third, some European Egyptologists actively worked to prevent Egyptians from rising in the ranks and threatening their positions, and the French retained control over Egypt's antiquities service until 1952.

THE POLITICS OF EGYPTOLOGY TODAY: LANGUAGE

Today, most foreign archaeologists would never even think of removing antiquities from the country. They are painstakingly careful about following the rules and respecting local excavation laws. The structure of archaeology has changed; the incentives and punishments for removing antiquities have shifted sufficiently that no trained archaeologist would contemplate taking something home as a souvenir of his or her excavation or to sell, as Howard Carter apparently did. There are still treasures in Egypt's sands for foreign archaeologists to find, but now, instead of artifacts of antiquity, their treasure is the work they do, which results in discoveries that make their fame, publications that further their careers, and Ph.D.s earned for their graduate students.

But Egyptology remains politicized, though in different ways. Even today, many Egyptologists complain of a European hegemony over the discipline. The vast majority of the articles and books are published in European languages. When Egyptian Egyptologists publish in Arabic, they risk their articles never being read by the Western Egyptologists who dominate the field, since the vast majority of Egyptologists do not read Arabic. During the Eighth International Congress of Egyptology, held in Egypt in 2000,[14] organizers proudly proclaimed Arabic to be the official language of the Congress for the first time ever. But Egyptian journalist Yousry Hassaan attended the Congress and later wrote that he felt like "a deaf man at a wedding procession,"[15] because virtually all the proceedings were in English and only one of the four hundred papers was delivered in Arabic. Minister of Culture Farouk Hosni delivered his opening address in Arabic, but while it was translated into English afterward for members of the audience, none of the English-language speeches was translated to Arabic—in spite of the fact that Arabic was supposedly the official language of the Congress. "Egyptologists speak all languages—except Arabic," complained Hassaan.[16]

Hassaan attacked the organizers in the press.[17] When Congress organizers recruited young archaeology students to work as ushers dressed in retro khaki field suits and pith helmets, Hassaan snidely commented that "the Congress's president proved his good taste by gathering together a group of pretty girls to work as ushers, wearing extremely peculiar hats on their heads." Hassaan also produced conspiracy theories about control of information. He claimed that the use of European languages and English in particular, rather than Arabic, was designed to exclude outsiders and ensure that no Egyptians could get any news from the Congress except what the organizers wanted them to have.

The Congress was extremely well organized, thanks to the efforts of a largely Egyptian organizing committee. The pith helmets were intended to be tongue-in-cheek and were worn by both male and female ushers (who were all Egyptology students in Egyptian universities and not selected for any particular aesthetic characteristics) with a sense of humor. Each day, a special team of organizers translated into Arabic summaries of what they considered the most important papers and news of the day and distributed them to the local Arabic-language press. Organizers could not provide simultaneous translations into Arabic of the vast quantities of materials, but there was no control of information. There were many Egyptians who delivered papers at the Congress; the fact that they delivered them in English merely reflected the reality of the profession. If they had delivered their papers in Arabic, they would have excluded all of their European and American colleagues from comprehension, while delivering papers in English ensured that they would reach both Westerners and Egyptian Egyptologists, all of whom have to learn European languages to succeed in their profession.[18]

Hassaan's press attack reflects a nationalist consciousness of the irony that the profession of Egyptology, the center of which, naturally, is Egypt, is dominated by Westerners, the majority of whom are not fluent in Arabic. That is a pity, and not just for the sake of cultural politics, but also for the sake of scholarship—both Ahmed Kamal in the late 1800s and Abdel Mohsen Bakir nearly a century later independently recognized the affinities of Arabic with ancient Egyptian (Reid 1985:237, 245), a socio-linguistic connection which Egyptian Egyptologists often remarked upon in conversation with me, but which non-Arabic speakers will never be able to appreciate firsthand.[19]

THE POLITICS OF EGYPTOLOGY TODAY: SITE MANAGEMENT

Another issue in the politics of Egyptology today that was frequently raised during my fieldwork by Egyptian Egyptologists working on the Giza Plateau was the lack of effort expended by foreign Egyptologists on restoration and preservation of decaying monuments. Members of Egypt's Supreme Council of Antiquities (SCA) complain that foreign excavating teams come into the country and spend much more energy and funds excavating new sites than they do consolidating and restoring old sites, many of which were left exposed to the elements by previous archaeologists' shoddy excavating techniques, and are being slowly eroded. Egypt's antiquities are in real danger. John and Elizabeth Romer (1993) argue that more damage has been done in the last one hundred years than in the previous four thousand, and more damage is threatened by the work of modern Egyptologists. Ancient Egypt is a profitable business for many, from those who legally trade relics of the past (as when the Metropolitan Museum of Art in the early 1970s sold off thousands of the smaller items in its Egyptian collection) to the blockbuster money-making exhibits of Egyptian antiquities in contemporary museums. And yet, according to the Romers, "of the tens of millions earned by ancient Egypt in the West, barely one per cent has gone back into its conservation on site."

In Upper Egypt, for example, the Valley of the Kings is subject to periodic flash flooding, and all but nine of the tombs in the Valley have flooded, while many have been completely filled by flood debris. The Romers hold that archaeologists are responsible, since the majority of these tombs filled with water after archaeologists opened the tombs, leaving them exposed to the elements. Archaeological excavations, particularly the excavation of tunnels in the tombs, have further weakened the structural integrity of the tombs, many of which have started to collapse. In 1991, a part of the ceiling of the tomb of Tutankhamun, painted with beautiful astronomical scenes, collapsed, as well as part of a wall. The Romers blame most of the damage in Tut's tomb on archaeological excavations, not tourism, pollution, Egyptians living nearby, or any of the other factors usually deemed the culprits.

And yet, at the Sixth International Congress of Egyptology in 1991, out of 340 papers delivered, a mere 3 of them were about site preservation. When the head of the Egyptian Antiquities Organization addressed this issue of the urgent need for conservation and called for action,[20] he was scolded by the president of the Congress who reminded him that the Congress was dedicated to Egyptology, not archaeological conservation.[21] Despite the fact that Egyptologists are the ones who are most invested in antiquities and therefore have the greatest responsibility to protect them, little has been done to restore and conserve monuments. Hawass (2003), the Romers (1993), and others complain that archaeologists are far more interested in making new discoveries and continuing to excavate than they are in paying for restoration or even for glass to protect tomb inscriptions from the hands and breath of tourists.

Many of the archaeologists interviewed for the Romers' book privately complained that Egyptian officials were responsible for damage to and decay of tombs; others evoked tourism as a leading culprit. But "in reality, the Egyptian officials are the only people who concern themselves, day-by-day, with the salvation of the monuments. Their constant requests for co-operation in what is now the high-tech industry of conservation are, with few exceptions, ignored" (Romer and Romer 1993:1).

Many archaeologists don't have the techniques necessary for restoration of tombs. There is great danger in making mistakes in a restoration project. For example, incompetent restoration of the Sphinx in the early 1980s used thick layers of cement (which seals in moisture and pollution without allowing the rock to breathe) to attach stones to the Sphinx's body, further damaging the structure (Stille 2003). But even for those who could marshal the resources and expertise for restoration, there is little incentive; most archaeologists are more interested in the short-term boost to their careers to be gained by publishing a new discovery, and less invested in the long-term preservation of Egypt's patrimony. Preservation and restoration projects are costly and are mostly undertaken as large institutional projects.[22]

Dr. Hawass is one of those archaeologists who express frustration about this situation (Hawass 2003). He points out that to date there is still no archaeological map of Egypt, and not all excavations result in publications, which are necessary to make the archaeological record available to generations to come. This is especially important in the case of those sites that are disintegrating and may soon be lost. In particular, the Valley of the Kings in Upper Egypt is in danger. Tombs visited by masses of tourists are eroding at a phenomenal rate, especially those with paintings on the walls, as they are exposed to air and wind, sunlight and camera flashes, salt in the sweat of tourists, vibrations from heavy tour buses moving overland near the tombs, and of course tourists who touch the walls to experience the carved hieroglyphic reliefs. Some archaeologists predict that many tomb paintings, particularly those in the Valley of the Kings, will be completely lost in two hundred years or less at the rate they are being eroded (Sadek 1990:16–17). At the time I did my fieldwork, Hawass was lobbying for a ten-year moratorium on excavating in Egypt, with the exception of the Nile Delta, where little excavation has been done, historically, but where water and humidity are eating away at the monuments so quickly that many are in immediate danger of being lost. After I finished my fieldwork, Hawass was promoted to Secretary General of the SCA, and shortly thereafter the SCA issued a new regulation banning all new excavation projects from Giza to Abu Simbel, allowing only restoration and epigraphical work in this area, while the Delta and the desert oases remained the only places where new excavation permits would be issued.

Hawass complains that all that many archaeologists are interested in is fame. (Other archaeologists accuse him of the same.) Hugely expensive restoration projects have been undertaken, usually with foreign aid money, to clean up and restore the most visible and famous of monuments, such as the Sphinx and the inner chambers of the Giza pyramids. But thousands of other excavated tombs and monuments are in just as much need of preservation but are neglected, because there simply aren't enough funds or people to conserve them. "We don't need more excavations," Hawass argues. "We need to preserve what we have." But great discoveries still make an archaeologist's fame, and most archaeologists—Egyptians as well as Westerners—would rather discover a thrilling new site full of archaeological prizes than restore an old tomb whose discovery made another's fame in years past.

Yet such debates about excavation and preservation of monuments beg the question of consumption: for whose enjoyment are the monuments being excavated and preserved? (Colli 2002). For the most part, it is for foreign tourists. Egyptians are charged a token entrance fee for visiting the pyramids that, at the time I did my research, was about one-twentieth the fee charged foreign tourists. But in recent years, a ruling closed the pyramids to Egyptian (but not foreign) visitors during Egyptian national holidays. When I asked Dr. Hawass about this ruling, he said that, during school holidays, tens of thousands of Egyptian students and families would converge upon the pyramids for picnics, perching on the lower stones of the pyramids to have their lunch. It was necessary, he argued, to close the pyramids to Egyptians during these holidays to prevent the large numbers of visitors from causing damage to the pyramids. Limiting the number of people at the pyramids was a practical decision made in the name of site preservation, he explained. After the site was closed to Egyptians on holidays, guards were berated by irate Egyptians protesting the fact that they were not permitted to enjoy what was, supposedly, their own patrimony.

Egyptologists and local Egyptians are also opponents in debates over excavation rights. Many of Egypt's archaeological sites lie beside or under the homes of living Egyptians.[23] The Egyptologists I interviewed longed to excavate under the village of Nazlet el-Semman, bordering the pyramids, where they suspect important temples connected with the Giza pyramid complex are buried, and they frequently complained that villagers were squatting on historical sites. In an effort to eventually drive villagers out of their homes, a complicated law was enacted that divides up the village into zones (designated A, B, and C), according to their suspected archaeological value, and prohibits villagers who live in prime archaeological Zone A not only from building new homes but even from making the slightest repair to existing homes. The idea, Dr. Hawass explained to me, is that, as their houses gradually fall apart over time, the villagers would abandon them for better properties elsewhere, and the land would be reclaimed for archaeology. Villagers complain bitterly about the archaeologists' interest in abstract and ancient history and the way they conveniently ignored the residents of recent centuries, of whom they were the descendents. One villager that I interviewed wryly observed that artifacts of the past were to be found under every Egyptian home, including President Mubarak's in Heliopolis, and that it was curious that the archaeologists weren't interested in digging under Mubarak's home, focusing instead on poor villagers who had less political clout.

This is a hotly contested arena where what is being debated is the worth of the remains of the past relative to the existence of contemporary Egyptians, and is reminiscent of some of the colonial era of Egyptology reviewed above.

The fact that the archaeological prize is no longer a treasure-filled tomb that can be carted off to a museum means that villagers cannot take their revenge by finding the objects first and selling them off before the archaeologists get to them (though I frequently heard archaeologists gossiping about holes being dug in the courtyards of village homes in the hopes of unearthing something that could be sold on the antiquities black market). Now the archaeological prize is the knowledge to be gleaned from meticulous excavating, and villagers complain that some Egyptologists will be content with nothing less than the complete expulsion of modern residents so that they can divide up the land into grids and dig for years on end.

There is another way that this issue links up to the history of European imperialism in Egypt. As Silberman (2000) has argued, archaeology throughout the Middle East has focused on the distant past while completely ignoring the more recent past, which, if addressed at all, was usually described as a hindrance to efforts to excavate, since people have tended to build over older sites again and again (see also Abu El-Haj 2001). Describing the excavation of the biblical site Tel Taanach in the West Bank, Silberman points out that excavators have had almost nothing to say about the post-biblical history of the site. "It was almost as if the lives and culture of the modern villagers (who incidentally served as the excavation laborers) were utterly inconsequential to *anyone's* history" (Silberman 2000:245, emphasis in original). What Silberman describes as the "Golden Age myth," the idea that archaeology's concern should be with a very ancient past, long gone and holding clues to the great history of humankind, makes contemporary archaeologists heir to the ideologies of imperialism that were so much a part of the history of Egyptology, by elevating ancient Egyptians while simultaneously declaring the irrelevance of modern Egyptians to world civilization (ibid.:249). And Reid (2002) finds it particularly noteworthy that the field of "Egyptology" is devoted only to the excavation of pharaonic remains, and not the more recent archaeology of Coptic and Islamic periods in Egypt; the naming of the field implicitly defines the real Egypt as that of the very distant past.[24]

WHOSE HISTORIES?

Revisionist histories such as Fagan's (1975) and France's (1991), instead of celebrating the history of Egyptology and the "treasures" that it brought to U.S. and European museums, portray it as the large-scale looting of ancient Egypt by European treasure hunters and locate that within the historical context of European imperialism in the Middle East.[25] But these revisionist accounts still portray the history of Egyptology as a largely European endeavor. The fact that insufficient attention has been paid to Egyptian archaeologists by historians of the discipline produces the impression that somehow Egyptian history belongs to the Westerners who have long been fascinated with it (Colli 2002). With *Whose Pharaohs?* (2002), Reid has rewritten the history of Egyptology, focusing on the numerous Egyptian archaeologists and actors who are often neglected in the historical accounts of this history.

These revisionist accounts also privilege the monuments and artifacts and tombs, mute objects whose desecration offended no surviving Egyptian religion. At the same time, these histories treat matter-of-factly the conscripted (corvée) labor of the Egyptian peasants who were forced to dig sand in the heat under the direction of the European (and, as Reid would remind us, Egyptian) excavators, who got all the glory for their discoveries without the backbreaking labor of digging them out from under tons of sand.

Now, for modern-day Egyptians who celebrate their pharaonic past, looking back at the history of Egyptology and the way some of Egypt's finest historical art objects were removed from the country may indeed feel like a violation. But this is an elite view that privileges objects and "heritage" over people (Meskell 2005). How different might the history of Egyptology look if seen from the perspective of Christian villagers who had erected houses and places of worship over an ancient pharaonic tomb and then were forced to move their homes by a united front of excavators and local or colonial authorities who described them as "vermin" (the illustrator David Roberts uses this and other choice terms to describe villagers who lived around and on the half-buried monuments) that had no right to live there (Roberts 2000)? Or if it were described from the perspective of one of the several thousand Saqqara villagers who were forced to dig out the Avenue of Sphinxes in "Memphis" for Mariette, who thus made his fame as an "excavator"?

The histories of Egyptology that have been written remain elite histories, and accounts that portray the exploitation in the history of Egyptology as residing primarily in the removal of antiquities from Egypt are leaving out an important story about the ways that Egyptology, both European and Egyptian, were and are founded on the labor of Egyptian peasants.[26] As Taussig observes (2004), the celebration of objects and materials in museums reifies them as the embodiment of a culture while simultaneously effacing the relationship between those objects and people, and the labor that produced those objects. The focus on spectacular objects both in Egyptological histories and in contemporary patterns of Western tourism in Egypt is a legacy of the relationship between Egyptology and colonialism's treasure hunt.

Egyptology used conscripted labor, just as did many other large-scale state projects, such as digging the Suez Canal (Beinin 1998). But what is celebrated

Figure 2.10. The mosque of Abu Haggag which stands on the ruins of the Luxor temple. Photograph by Bill McKelvie.

in history books is the glorious historical objects that these laborers' digging revealed, or even the efforts of the archaeologists in directing the excavations, but not the scorching, backbreaking labor of digging vast quantities of sand for no (or paltry) remuneration. Perhaps sweaty shoveling doesn't make for as interesting a historical account as the narrative of a treasure hunt or a great discovery, and it certainly doesn't make for blockbuster museum exhibit tours, like the King Tut tour in the late 1970s (which started to tour again in late 2005 and earned even more than the millions it did on its previous run).

In these histories of Egyptian antiquities and their discovery, the Egyptian peasant lurks in the margins, rarely the star of the story (except when depicted as the hapless accidental discoverer of some treasure that an archaeologist later excavates—see Hawass 1997, 2000a), though often the villain (as when they are described as tomb robbers or squatters—see Hawass 2002b, El-Wakil 1988), but everywhere touching on the outcome featured in the heroic accounts of discovery, history, civilization, and the discipline of archaeology. There are reasons why it is important to examine the role of less privileged groups and individuals in a study of Egyptology: not just for some abstract and elusive goal of "helping the subaltern to speak," but because these people have a role and an impact on the discipline, though this role is hidden in most historical accounts. The obvious example is that the uneducated Egyptian workers working on digs do most of the digging and actual hard labor. While they may not be university-educated archaeologists, they are trained and skilled in excavating techniques. I recall a time that I was visiting the excavations of the tombs of the pyramid builders at Giza in 2001. The Egyptian archaeologist supervising the dig wanted to show me a recent find. "Show her the skull," he said to one of the workers, barefoot and clad in the traditional *galabiyya* of an Egyptian villager. The worker knelt down in the sand and started to draw a circular line in the sand with his fingers. As he repeatedly traced this line, pushing back the sand away from the center of the circle, the sand trickled away to reveal a 4,500-year-old skull that they had unearthed and then re-covered to protect from the elements. This laborer, with no formal archaeological training, knew exactly how to reveal the find without touching the skull and risking any damage, while the archaeologist stood above him, watching his work. That moment promptly reversed my assumptions about the "unskilled" labor used in excavations. Yet the work of these laborers is hidden while archaeologists build fame and careers on the excavations that they direct.

A less obvious example of labor that most accounts of archaeology neglect is that of the tourism police who guard the monuments.[27] They are paid very low salaries of a few dollars a month. The incentives are strong to either steal antiquities or look the other way while others hunt for antiquities to sell on the black market, and items have occasionally gone missing from the storerooms on the plateau, though this is infrequent, since the punitive disincentives for getting caught are also powerful. But guards are also bribed by those who want to get unofficial access to the monuments, such as tourists who want to climb the pyramids, or enter tombs after hours. Accounts frequently surface in books and on Internet sites of tourists who find an Egyptian tour guide who knows how to slip a hundred pounds to the nighttime guards so that they will patrol a different area of the plateau while the tourists scramble up one of the pyramids before dawn.

While the salaries of the tourism police are incredibly low, so are the salaries of most Egyptian bureaucrats. The Egyptologists and antiquities inspectors working on the plateau that I mentioned at the beginning of this chapter also work for wages that scarcely cover the cost of the bus ride to and from work, and perhaps a bean sandwich for breakfast. But some—though not all—of these archaeologists have other options for supplementing their meager salaries, licitly, by moonlighting in the afternoon as tour guides for local tour agencies, or, with luck, by publishing books on the monuments (as Hawass has successfully done). Tourism police and storeroom guards have no such opportunities.

Mounting the Pyramid.

au revoir

Figure 2.11. A 1906 Lichtenstern & Harari postcard mailed from Alexandria to Greece (the writing on the back of the postcard is in Italian, Greek, and French) depicts Egyptian guides helping Europeans climb the pyramid, a popular but risky tourist activity. Climbing the pyramids is now officially banned. Collection of L. L. Wynn.

To understand why not, a digression is necessary to briefly explore the factors that determine who benefits from tourism to archaeological sites in Egypt. First and foremost are the multinational corporations and the few wealthy Egyptians who own the luxury chain hotels that host tourists and Nile cruise liners; Mitchell (2002:179–205) has discussed this profit network. On-site, it is the tour guides working for travel agencies who show tourists around. There are many travel agencies in Cairo and Giza owned and operated by Nazlet el-Semman villagers; their success in gaining clients partly depends on their connections with hotels where tourists stay, which advertise half- and full-day tours with tour agencies (with which the hotels negotiate exclusive arrangements in exchange for a percentage of the profits). The tour guides earn a small wage for escorting their tourists all day, plus any tips that tourists give them, as well as a small percentage of any purchases made by their tourists at souvenir and gift shops during the tour. The so-called "tourist hustlers" or, in local parlance, *khurateyya* (sing., *khartī*),[28] who often come from the villages bordering tourist sites and who have sold souvenirs and postcards to tourists from the time they were children (in Giza and Cairo these are often but not exclusively from Nazlet el-Semman), also earn a percentage of any purchase a tourist makes while accompanied by the *khartī*.[29]

However, only licensed tour guides are permitted to guide tourists through museums or state-designated heritage sites such as the pyramids and the Sphinx. An Egyptian needs a university degree in Egyptology or archaeology to work as a guide, in addition to a guide license, for which she or he must pass a state-administered exam. Guards often prevent *khurateyya* from entering museums or sites with tourists. Non-Egyptian scholars of Egypt who bring tour groups to Egypt must partner with a local guide and defer to the Egyptian guide to lecture while on-site; some of the foreign Egyptologists who were working on digs in Egypt during my fieldwork described being chastened and silenced at museums by licensed guides or guards, even when walking through the museum with friends, because without a license, they are not permitted to lecture about antiquities at sites or museums, no matter what their expertise.

There were two principal reasons given me to explain these restrictions. First, ensuring that only trained and licensed guides lecture about the past prevents the uninformed from feigning expertise, conveying incorrect information, and even inventing stories about the past. It also attempts to mute alternative views on the past that are not in line with the orthodox archaeological and state-approved narrative of Egyptian history (these alternative views are taken up in the next chapter).

The second reason for these restrictions is that they map ideal paths for tourism revenue to take. They prevent non-Egyptians from taking jobs from Egyptian guides. But they also keep unlicensed Egyptians from making money as guides. Egyptians who work as archaeology inspectors at places like the Giza pyramids receive extremely small salaries from the Egyptian government, but several of the ones I knew worked from morning until the early afternoon at the pyramids, then had afternoon and evening jobs working as private-sector tour guides. By holding two jobs in this fashion, they could barely earn enough to live a middle-class urban life.

The uneducated guards and laborers on the excavations do not have the same opportunities to profit legitimately from the tourism industry as the licensed tourism guides; unless they have learned foreign languages, then they also cannot earn money from the purchases of tourists that they may guide informally. It is no wonder, then, that antiquities sometimes go missing from government storerooms to which such poorly paid guards have keys, or that villagers living near excavation sites are often rumored to make a living as tomb robbers, selling antiquities on the black market, although this trade is usually characterized as taking place "in the past."[30] Such rumors, whether or not they are true in the particulars, truthfully describe the structures that determine how income from the Western fascination with pharaonic monuments trickles, very unevenly, through Egyptian society, by delineating both incentives and opportunities for profit from Western demand for illicit antiquities.

Helaine Silverman (2004) argues that, when examining the archaeological record of a place, it is insufficient to simply examine the history of antiquities looting as a history of "violence done to the . . . archaeological record." Instead we have to take into account the forms of social violence that spur this looting, that is, the poverty that prompts peasants and laborers to "seek extra income by grave robbing for an insatiable antiquities market" (2004:733–734), which pays small profits to grave diggers for objects that sell for many times those sums once they are smuggled out of the country.

EGYPTOLOGY, COLONIALISM, AND TOURISM

Just as Roman, French, and British colonialism in Egypt paved the way for archaeology, so too did colonialism pave the way for tourism, protecting the Roman tourist and, later, Europeans of the Age of Enlightenment. Herodotus, Pliny the Elder, Strabo, and Plato all visited Egypt and wrote about their trips. And, as in modern history, Greek and Roman tourism thrived under colonialism. When Alexandria was held by the Greeks, Greek tourists visited Canopus for sex tourism, but they also traveled further afield, taking in temples and ruins. The Romans occupied Egypt in 30 BCE, and for two centuries after that they made Egypt safe for Roman travelers on the Grand Tour (Greener 1966). The Roman Empire depended on reliable communications and secure routes of travel for its administration; tourism in Egypt thus became widespread during this era for the elite classes. Ships constantly crossed the Mediterranean bringing Roman tourists and merchants to Alexandria (Fagan 1975:20). As in Greek times, Alexandria was still famous for its pleasure resorts, but Romans also visited the Giza pyramids and Memphis, and traveled down the Nile to Thebes, visiting religious shrines and monuments and scratching their graffiti all over the sites they visited. Aristede of Smyrna wrote,

> One need no longer fear the narrow sandy roads of Arabia and Egypt; no mountain or river is any longer inaccessible, [there is] no barbarian nation that one cannot visit. To be secure, one has but to be a Roman. (Cited in Greener 1966:12)

Greeks and Romans were also the first Europeans to cart off Egyptian monuments and use them to adorn their own cities.[31] The fact that Rome contains thirteen Egyptian obelisks, vastly more than any other European city or country, is entirely due to the fact that the Romans had a head start of 1,800 years on northern European collectors.

As in Roman times, nineteenth-century European tourists made the boat trip up the Nile to see the ruins, but modern methods of transportation drastically reduced the time it took for such a tour. Travel agencies such as Thomas Cook paved the way for mass tourism (Hazbun 2006), and the colonial government ensured the safety of travelers. As early as 1737, a European traveler reported that the interior of the Great Pyramid was blackened with soot from the torches of visitors (France 1991:97), suggesting that it was not only the somewhat rare European travelers who were visiting the inside of the pyramids, but, as Haarmann suggests, medieval Arab travelers. But European colonialism facilitated a booming Western travel in Egypt, and by the late 1800s, a Victorian traveler noted that Abu Simbel had become "positively crowded" with European tourists (Edwards 1983).

In Egypt today there is a popular awareness of the links between Egyptology, colonialism, and tourism. One day I was talking to a spice merchant named Mohammed in the Khan el-Khalili about my research project. I told him that it was a comparison of Western and Arab tourism in Egypt. He proceeded to give me a typology of tourists. Arab tourists, he said, came to Egypt for many reasons: for pleasure, for medical treatment, for sports, for religious pilgrimages to saint shrines, and even for magical remedies. As for Western tourists, he said,

There are different kinds of Western tourists. There are cultured people, students of science and curiosity. The majority of them are interested in ancient ruins, pharaonic and Islamic monuments. They're interested in knowing about

Figure 2.12. An ancient Egyptian obelisk that stands in the Vatican, topped by a cross. Photograph by Adrian Pelcz.

the occupation of Egypt by their own countries. The Frenchman asks about what Napoleon did in Egypt and what his ancestors did during the French occupation. It's the same with the English and the Italians. The Italians were the oldest occupiers. Italians today ask about Roman ruins, which came at the end of the pharaonic reign of Egypt. [Fieldnotes, 28 July 1999]

Mohammed made an explicit connection between the history of Western co-lonialism in Egypt and contemporary Western interest in Egyptian ruins (see

Figure 2.2). Similarly, the politics of Egyptology today that I have described in this chapter reflect a modern intellectual and nationalist consciousness of the historical relationship between Western interest in Egyptian antiquities and Western imperialisms in Egypt. Complaints that foreign Egyptologists are too little interested in site conservation suggest that the days of the antiquities treasure hunt are not entirely past; the treasure hunt has simply exchanged the prize of museum artifacts for the prize of publishing a new discovery and the boost it gives to an academic career.

It was not only colonialism that paved the way for mass Western tourism in Egypt. The idea of Egypt was already part of the popular cultural imagination. In modern Europe and America, much of the popularity of Egypt was due to the fact that, though an exotic foreign land, it was at the same time made familiar by the Bible. This was nothing new. The Roman Julius Honorius had theorized that the pyramids were Joseph's granaries used for storing corn in years of plenty, and some medieval Arab thinkers repeated this view (Haarmann 1996). In the early years of archaeological exploration in Egypt (when the treasure hunt was turning into more of a science), a number of excavations specifically aimed at finding archaeological proof for biblical stories. These were popular with armchair Egyptologists and sources of funding back home.[32] Many popular authors today continue to appeal to a similar audience base with books that link ancient Egypt with the Bible and with other important Western cultural symbols of ancient mystery such as Atlantis (see Chapter 3).[33]

Egyptians have had mixed attitudes toward identification with the pharaonic past. The pharaoh of the Qur'an is a symbol of despotism, tyranny, and idolatry who oppressed the prophets of the one true God and was subsequently humbled by Him. And yet the monuments the pharaonic age left behind are undeniably spectacular. In medieval times, both Christian and Muslim Egyptians defaced pharaonic monuments, paintings, and hieroglyphs to symbolize their rejection of the idolatry they supposed these to represent. But others visited them to marvel, to hunt for treasure, and even to pray. Medieval authors such as al-Idrīsī, an Egyptian of Moroccan descent, argued that visiting the marvels (ʿajāʾib) of Egypt was not only Islamically permissible but even recommended for the seeker of knowledge (Haarmann 1996:611).

In the modern period, we see similar Egyptian ambivalence toward the pharaonic past. In the 1920s and 1930s, Egyptian nationalist politicians, authors, and artists celebrated the pharaonic past, fueled by the spectacular discovery of King Tutankhamun's tomb by Carter in the 1920s and the subsequent conflict between the Egyptian government and foreign excavators (see Hoving 1978) which led to the Egyptian seizure of the tomb and the revision of excavation rules. The same intellectuals who championed pharaonic nationalism in the 1930s were, by the 1940s, rejecting it in favor of an Arab Egyptian identity, and

Figure 2.13. The Egyptian 100-pound note. Currency courtesy Rania Salem.

while Nasser briefly flirted with pharaonic nationalism, that was eventually abandoned in favor of the pan-Arab identity that allowed Nasser to challenge Iranian and Saudi attempts at regional leadership on the basis of a pan-Islamic identity.

After the Arab defeat in the 1967 war with Israel, and particularly after Nasser's death, Egyptian intellectuals again turned to pharaonic nationalism, very likely as an expression of the failure of pan-Arabism, and several authors (such as Ni'māt Fu'ād) attempted what critics describe as an almost absurd attempt to reconcile a combined pharaonic and Arab identity for Egypt.[34] Sadat styled himself "the last of the pharaohs," and Selim (2001:14) points out that the specific pharaoh to whom Sadat was likened (or to whom he likened himself) was Akhenaton, who is widely known within Egypt and without as Egypt's "monotheistic pharaoh." (Akhenaton introduced monotheistic worship of the sun god Aton in opposition to the powerful priestly class of the time.) With his innovative and ultimately doomed attempt at spreading monotheistic worship in ancient Egypt, Akhenaton has been popularly interpreted as an early prede-cessor of the monotheistic religions of Judaism, Christianity, and Islam. Thus

Sadat's identification with pharaonic Egypt averted some of the negative connotations of the Qur'anic reference to pharaoh.[35] Yet Sadat, who cracked down
brutally on the Islamists he had previously encouraged (to counter pro-Nasser
sentiment that threatened his leadership), was assassinated by Islamists, who
seized on the negative aspects of this imagery when they reportedly shouted,
"We have killed Pharaoh!" at his assassination. (Sadat was buried under a pyramidal monument in Nasr City.)[36]

Historically, Egypt's pharaonic nationalism has been wielded oppositionally. In the 1920s and 1930s, the discovery and excavation of the tomb of King
Tutankhamun was interpreted by the Egyptian press as a symbol of Egyptian
greatness which Howard Carter (the archaeologist), Lord Carnarvon (the dig's
sponsor), the Metropolitan Museum (which was eyeing the discovery as an opportunity to add to its Egyptian collection), and the London *Times* were stealing away, at the very least figuratively, and perhaps, it was suspected, literally.[37] Pharaonic nationalism also articulates an Egyptian identity distinct from
a wider Arab or Islamic identity, which explains its reemergence after Egypt's
defeat in the 1967 war, when pan-Arabism was perceived as having failed.

Western tourism focusing on pharaonic ruins may not directly affect many
Egyptians personally. But pharaonic images have worked their way into many
symbols of Egyptian identity, from the pyramid logo of the official newspaper
al-Ahrām (which translates as "the pyramids") to the pyramid tomb marker in
Nasr City for those killed in the 1973 war, to drawings of pharaonic symbols on
the Egyptian currency. It is surely no coincidence, though, that in all denomi-
nations of Egyptian currency, the side showing pharaonic symbols (statues of
pharaohs, solar boats, stylized lotus flowers, hieroglyphs, cartouches, ankhs,
Abu Simbel, the Sphinx, and so on) is always the side with English-language
script, while the other side, bearing images of Egyptian mosques and Islamic
geometrical designs, has Arabic script (see Figure 2.13).

Symbols of the pharaonic past are pervasive in contemporary Egyptian material culture. Even when their meaning and import are debated as a source of
Egyptian pride, remains of the ancient past have become an inescapable part
of the vocabulary for discussing Egyptian national identity. The next chapter
discusses a different perspective on the ancient past in Egypt and its relationship with both European colonialism and contemporary Egyptian nationalism:
mystical or "New Age" imaginations of ancient Egypt.

▲ ▲ ▲ ▲ ▲ ▲ ▲ ▲ ▲ ▲ ▲ ▲ ▲ ▲ ▲ ▲ ▲ ▲ ▲

CHAPTER 3

ATLANTIS AND RED MERCURY

As soon as I got to the pyramids [this morning], Dr. Hawass gave me something to type up, so I went back into the computer room and started working. It was an article he was writing for al-Ahram newspaper. I had just sat down and written the title when Tarek came in the room and told me that there was a guy here who believed that there was something secreted away under one of the rocks of the Great Pyramid. Stone tablets with ancient writing on them. I got excited and said, "Can I be there when Dr. Zahi is talking with him?" Tarek told me that they'd already sent him in to see Hawass for approximately 30 seconds, then Hawass had quickly passed him off on Tarek who was supposed to accompany him to the Great Pyramid to check out this stone. Tarek said to me, "As long as you're so excited to meet him, what do you think if I tell him that I'm busy and I'm going to send him with another one of Dr. Zahi's assistants: you? We'll get you a car and everything." I said, "Yes, yes!" I was almost beside myself.

So we went in a red car with Mohamed, another one of the archaeologists/antiquities inspectors, over to the other side of the Great Pyramid. Mohamed was very kind and uncomplaining about what must have seemed a ridiculous errand in the sun which he pronounced had reached 40 degrees C. We went there and Felipe brought us to the rock. He had marked it so that he would remember it by leaving a white stone over a piece of paper on the ground in front of it. He pointed out the rock and then while me and Mohamed watched he climbed up a few levels and patted it, just to make sure we knew which rock it was. We asked how he had reached the conclusion that this was *the* rock, and he said because he had counted over approximately 30 blocks and up about 5 to 8 meters (it was about 7 or 8 meters off the ground) and he just had a feeling that this was *it*.

We stood there a few moments looking at the rock, trying to feel the gravity of the moment with him. It was anti-climactic. Felipe was looking at the rock solemnly, Mohamed and I were red and perspiring, and nobody knew what to say or do, so we just returned to the car and drove back to the offices in the pyramids. On the way back, Felipe asked me how long I had been working for Zahi Hawass. I said a few months, and told him that it was only volunteer work, and I wasn't an archaeologist. Then he asked me, "What do you think Dr. Hawass will do now with the information that I have given him?" I said, "Honestly? Nothing at all."

He looked disappointed, and I was a little amazed. Did he think that, just on the basis of his "feeling" (his word) that there was something behind that rock, that the Egyptians were going to rip a hole in the Great Pyramid? Just to investigate his hunch? I said, "You see, it has nothing to do with your particular case. He can't go ripping rocks out of the pyramid, even if he wanted to. For any excavation work to be done here, there has to be permission from the Supreme Council of Antiquities, and you have to submit an application to them through the auspices of an established university or museum, and you have to be an archaeologist with a Ph.D. and you have to have funding for the expedition, and then the application is reviewed by a 30-member committee. . . . So, in short, it's not in Dr. Zahi's hands. It's in the hands of the committee from the Supreme Council of Antiquities and they won't do anything unless you're an archaeologist, coming through a university, with funding for your research."

Back in the offices of the antiquities inspectors, Felipe told me that he thought that the ancient Egyptians were descendents of the people of Atlantis who fled there when their city was drowned and who built the pyramids, hiding under them their records in a secret chamber. I said, "You know, there's a lot of people who have the same theory." He seemed a little put out that I was attributing his ideas to someone else, and he said, "But do you know where the original idea for the people of Atlantis comes from?" I said, "The Cayce Foundation?" He said, "No, Plato. It comes from Plato originally." "Oh, yeah." He said that he found it very difficult to get through the ideas of Cayce because the ideas about Egypt were mixed in with so many other things. I said, "Yes, but I think that Mark Lehner collected all of the Cayce readings that have to do with Egypt and put them together in one book." So I went and got Zahi's copy of *Secret Chamber*, the book by Robert Bauval, which was where I remembered reading about Lehner's compilation of the Cayce readings. Felipe sat down on a couch in the outer office and started flipping through the book, looking content to just hang out there.

He hung around for a couple of hours, and I would see him every time I went from the computer room over to Dr. Zahi's office to let him review a draft of what I was typing. Before Felipe left, I gave him my number and told him to call me some time if he wanted to discuss his theories further.

That night Felipe called me to see if I wanted to meet him for a drink, so I told him he could meet me and my friends. I didn't want to go out with him alone, and I had already planned to meet Nada and Hamada and Nasr, and I figured that Felipe would probably like to meet some more Egyptians. I went to pick him up at his hotel on Pyramids Road, and then we took a taxi to Hardee's (of all places—thanks to Hamada's infatuation with their roast beef sandwiches). The others were late, so while we were waiting, I ate French fries and Felipe started telling me his theories about the pyramids. It was a long story, but what it boils down to is this: The people of ancient Egypt are descended from the people of Atlantis, who are themselves descended from aliens. The Atlanteans built the pyramids. There was some war between the Atlanteans and the Lemurians (two different races of aliens, he was careful to point out, from different planets), which wiped out most of both groups.

Felipe had visited Egypt first about ten years previously, and during this time he was really struck with the power of the monuments, but he said that he only came across this knowledge about Atlantis and Lemuria during a regression some years ago, when he learned this history and also discovered that he was the reincarnation of an ancient Egyptian priest from Atlantis. (Reminded me of what Semasem [a Swedish belly dancer working in Cairo] said about reincarnation beliefs: "I don't have a problem with reincarnation. But why does everybody always think they are the reincarnation of Cleopatra or some ancient Egyptian high priest? You never hear of anybody who is the reincarnation of some ancient Egyptian garbage collector. But those garbage collectors must be reincarnated *somewhere!*") He had had several regressions that made him realize this. I didn't understand what he meant by regression, so I asked, "Did this happen in a dream, or in a trance, or when you were meditating, or what?" He said, "No, this happened during regression hypno-therapy in Australia, it takes a trained person to help you through this." So he came to Egypt where he believed that there was a secret chamber in the Great Pyramid behind one of the rocks which holds stone tablets with this informa-tion which will prove his belief. His goal [was] to get someone to dig behind that rock, find the chamber, and vindicate him.

Thus, he told me, he has come here on a specific mission, not just as a tourist for sightseeing, but to try to uncover this information that will vindi-cate his beliefs. I asked him, "So what are you going to do now that you know that Dr. Zahi will not act on your knowledge?" He gave me an elusive smile and said, "I'll just wait and see how things develop." He told me about these beliefs before Nada and Hamada and Nasr arrived, and then again when they were talking amongst themselves and he had a moment to draw me aside and speak to me privately. However, to them, Felipe said nothing about his purpose here in Egypt. When Nasr kept politely probing into his interest in Egypt (since I had told Nasr previously the circumstances under which I met Felipe at the pyramids), he doggedly revealed nothing, just told them that he's a tourist here, and gravely consulted Nasr for his advice about whether it would be more worthwhile to visit Siwa Oasis and the temple of Alexander the Great or to go to Abydos.

Nasr later told me that what primarily struck him about Felipe was the fact that, despite his fascination with Egypt, he seemed to know absolutely nothing about the contemporary Middle East. He didn't know anything about Islam, about Coptic Christianity, about politics, or even about basic geography. "He didn't know anything about the Palestinian-Israeli conflict, he didn't know where Kuwait is located . . . he didn't even know how to attach the mouthpiece to the *shisha!*" Nasr said, incredulously. "All Americans know how to do that. That's the first thing they learn, is how to smoke *shisha*" [the water pipe].

Back to the pyramids. The same day that I met Felipe, towards the end of the day, I had finished all my typing, so I was sitting in Dr. Zahi's office, just reading quietly one of the archaeology books from his library, when Dr. Zahi said that an Arab prince from one of the Gulf states was coming to see him. I asked if he wanted me to leave the office and he said, apologetically, "Yes: this person is politically important." The office manager came in to straighten everything up in his inevitably dusty office, and I took my book and went to sit in the other room. A man in a dark suit came walking up the path with another man. Both were quite nondescript, there was no entourage, no sirens, just one black Mercedes with a driver—none of the impressive trappings of royalty that I expected. They went directly into Dr. Zahi's office, while I and the archaeologists in the outer office all craned our necks to see him going in. He left, twenty minutes later, with similar lack of pomp. Shortly afterwards, Dr. Zahi asked me if I was ready to leave for the day. He was going to give me and another archaeologist a ride home, since we all lived in the same part of town.

In the car driving back to Mohandiseen, he started to tell us about the prince's visit. He said that the prince told him that his mother had been very ill and had gone into a coma some six years ago. She could not see, talk, or communicate in any way. Since that time her son had traveled all over the world looking for someone who could help her. He'd spent millions and nothing had worked so far. He'd exhausted medical science and started to consult *shuyūkh*, popular religious healers. They too had taken a lot of his money and sent him on a lot of wild goose chases, and still nothing had healed his mother. Finally, one *sheikh* (a religious healer) in Saudi Arabia had told him, "There is a famous man in Egypt named Zahi Hawass. You must go to Zahi Hawass and he will give you a bottle which he has found in one of the tombs he has excavated, a bottle of *al-zī'baq al-ahmar*, red mercury, from a mummy. This bottle will contain in it an essence which will heal your mother." So he came to Dr. Zahi and told him this.

Dr. Zahi told him, "Look, I don't have a bottle of red mercury or a bottle of anything else for your mother. I don't know anything about this, I don't know how to help you. You will find a lot of people in Egypt who will kiss your ass and run after you for money, but I'm not one of them. I don't care about your money. I'm sorry about your mother but there is nothing I can do for her." The prince told him that he had someone (the man with him) who would just shake his hand and perhaps there would be something in his (Dr. Zahi's) aura that even Dr. Zahi himself didn't know about which could help his mother. Dr. Zahi used the word *aura* as he was recounting the story to me in English. I thought it was interesting that he used *aura* to translate the word the prince had used in Arabic, which I assume was *baraka*. I had never thought of such a translation before, but it made perfect sense in this context. Also showed that, mentally, Dr. Zahi was classifying the prince in the same category as the New Age people like Felipe who meditate in the pyramids.

I asked him about this "red mercury." It is the Arabic word for some radioactive substance, but there is also a popular belief among Egyptians and Arabs in something called "Egyptian red mercury" or just "Egyptian mercury" (*al-zī'baq al-masrī*) which is said to be a very rare substance that was created magically by ancient Egyptian priests and buried in bottles with the mummies of royal personages. Of course, Dr. Zahi said, he's never found any such substance or bottle in the mummies he's excavated.

After relating all of this to me, Dr. Zahi said, "What do you think about this story?" I said, "I think it is very interesting for my research!" A strange coincidence to have Felipe and the prince appear on the same day in Dr. Zahi's office. I guess it just goes to show that the Westerners aren't the only people with alternative histories and non-scientific theories about ancient Egypt, whether it's a "sheikh" in Saudi Arabia or a regression-hypnotist in Australia. But while such Westerners tend to think they're the reincarnation of an ancient Egyptian, the belief in this red mercury seems to be a particularly Arab imagination of the legacy of ancient Egypt. [Fieldnotes, 27 July 2000]

The meeting of both Felipe and the prince in Zahi Hawass's offices on the same day reminded me that both Arabs and Westerners have mystical imaginations about ancient Egypt. However, this kind of imagination about ancient

Egypt is more prevalent among Westerners, to the extent that a small industry catering to these groups has sprung up in Egypt. New Age tour groups are considered a prime market for travel agencies, and even tourist hustlers are said to specifically target the gullible (or so it is thought) "worshippers," as they are called, because they are thought by many Egyptians to worship the pyramids.[1]

Some historians of the New Age movement trace its inception back to the 1960s and 1970s hippie counterculture (Danforth 1989). But the roots of the tradition go back to the Spiritualist movement of the nineteenth century, and perhaps can be traced even further, back to the eighteenth-century Enlightenment critique of established religion (Melton 1988). In the sense that it is a tradition of bridging the scientific and the spiritual that seeks "alternatives to conventional knowledge and faith," the New Age movement is really not very new at all (Hess 1993).

This is nowhere truer than with New Age imaginations of ancient Egypt. Two of the most prominent movements active on the Egyptian scene that I introduce in this chapter, Rosicrucians and the Association for Research and Enlightenment (ARE), predate the baby boomers. The Ancient Mystical Organization of the Rose Cross (AMORC, or the Rosicrucians) was organized in America in 1935 by J. Spencer Lewis; the ARE is a foundation dedicated to promoting the thoughts of Edgar Cayce (1877–1945), a famous American psychic who believed that Egypt was an ancient colony of the lost civilization of Atlantis.

Orthodox Egyptology and alternative, mystical interpretations of ancient Egypt converged at several points in the nineteenth century, when there were multiple links between the gradual development of Egyptology as a science (from an organized campaign of treasure hunting and looting, as described in Chapter 2), mystical imaginations of Egypt, and religious imaginations of Egypt. The first organization to fund archaeological investigations in Egypt, the Egypt Exploration Fund, sponsored some early Egyptologists who sought to find archaeological proof of biblical stories. Charles Piazzi Smyth, an Astronomer Royal of Scotland, became deeply interested in Egypt late in his career and proposed the theory of the "pyramid inch," a special measure unique to the pyramid (which he regarded as divinely inspired) that was unlike any other Egyptian measurement. Flinders Petrie, considered by many the father of modern archaeology, first came to Egypt in search of Smyth's "pyramid inch," and wrote of his disappointment at finding the theory untenable (Fagan 1975).

With time, Egyptology moved away from mystical, biblical, and spiritual explanations of ancient Egyptian history. But among Western tourists, such imaginations of ancient Egypt remain popular. New Age tours of Egypt are a booming business for tour guides, and respected Egyptologists often give lectures to tour groups alongside their theoretical opponents in the New Age community. Tourism provides a continuing link between these different groups.

This chapter traces the historical development of a few trends in the alternative imagination of ancient Egypt, from theories of Atlantis to the Hermetic traditions underpinning movements such as Rosicrucianism. It then examines their links, both historical and contemporary, with orthodox Egyptology and with Western imperialism in Egypt. Finally, it shows how the dispute between Egyptology and "New Agers" is not only about the politics of academe, but about Egyptian nationalism as well.

I make no attempt to exhaust the history of mystical imaginations of ancient Egypt, and this chapter makes only a partial pass at the literature, which is vast. There are countless original appropriations of ancient Egypt that I could explore, from Afrocentric histories of Egypt to Joseph Smith's purchase of ancient Egyptian papyri to the American Nuwaubian cult in Georgia; this work, however, focuses only on a small group of mostly European alternative theorists of ancient Egypt.[2] How, then, did I select the group of theorists and writers that I discuss in this chapter? I was led to each one of them, in one way or another, through my fieldwork site, namely the offices of the archaeologists at the pyramids. Some I first discovered by reading their books that I found on the shelves of Zahi Hawass, who has an extensive collection of books by Robert Bauval, Graham Phillips, Graham Hancock, and other "New Age" writers in his library. As I read the books by these authors, I was led to Rosicrucianism and the Cayce Foundation. Other authors and theories came up in conversations with a New Age tour guide, Mohamed Nazmy, to whom I was referred by Dr. Hawass. I first met John Anthony West and Robert Schoch in Dr. Hawass's office. And, in turn, all of the theorists I cover in this chapter have shown in their writings an intense interest in Zahi Hawass, Mark Lehner, and their archaeological investigations on the Giza Plateau. Indeed, the truth is that I never originally thought of looking at New Age theorists of ancient Egypt until I started working in Dr. Hawass's office and found it necessary to familiarize myself with their theories. Dr. Hawass talked about them frequently and brought them up in the lectures he occasionally gave to New Age tour groups. Thus these theorists were very much a part of Dr. Hawass's consciousness in his work on the Giza Plateau.

But first, a note on terminology: I have struggled to find a word to describe people who have positions on the history of the Egyptian monuments that do not coincide with the archaeological standpoint. *Non-Egyptologist* doesn't work, since a number of these theorists consider themselves Egyptologists, whether or not they are accepted by the orthodox Egyptological community. Sometimes *New Agers* is appropriate, but for the most part I avoid the term because it is vague, it is not value-neutral, and in any event, some of these people do not consider themselves New Agers at all. *Pyramidiots* is the term privately given to them by many Egyptologists, but of course that is unacceptably demeaning. Finally I settled on *alternative theorists*. Even that term may be unacceptable to some, since it lumps together such wildly different groups—and, as John Anthony West pointed out to me (West 2000), it is a convenient trick of Egyptologists to dismiss anyone who doesn't agree with them by lumping them all together in the category of "pyramidiots" like von Däniken (who famously theorized that the pyramids were built by roving extraterrestrial astronauts), when in fact other authors have well-researched theories for which a scientifically solid case could be made, even if they are not accepted by Egyptologists. However, "alternative theories" does express a fundamental division between orthodox Egyptology and all others, a division that even "alternative theorists" like West recognize as a powerfully exclusive process to which they are subjected by academia.

> Whoever explains ancient Egypt can claim to command the gates to Western culture itself. That might be why mavericks with abstruse theories about pyramids and pharaohs have flourished ever since. (Tonkin 1996)

In recent years, a number of best-selling books have popularized theories linking monuments with astronomy and astrology, biblical stories, and the myth of Atlantis. Their theories are grounded in pharaonic ruins, but they diverge in key respects from the orthodox archaeological narrative of ancient Egypt. A number of these people are on a quest for a secret chamber buried in the sands of Giza, a "Hall of Records" of some mysterious Lost Civilization that predates the pharaohs. Their theories are based on various Western myths and legends and fueled by archaeological discoveries, such as the infamous "door" with the copper handles within the Great Pyramid, and the symbolic tomb of Osiris that was excavated in 1999. The books are extensively researched and footnoted, but unlike most archaeological accounts, they are also packed with sensationalist prose and attention-grabbing (and book-selling) conspiracy theories. Take, for example, the opening paragraphs of Robert Bauval's (1999a) book *Secret Chamber: The Quest for the Hall of Records:*

> The story that I am about to tell is as strange as it is controversial. It is the story of an age-long mystery. A mystery which has haunted the imaginations of seekers from generation to generation. . . . For deep inside the oldest, the largest, the tallest, the most tremendous and sacred monument on this planet, is a heavily guarded secret. Inside the Great Pyramid of

Giza, wrapped in unearthly darkness and standing in hallowed stillness, could lie a secret chamber, waiting any minute now to be opened. It could be the supreme archaeological prize. Since March 1993, an entrance which may lead to such a chamber has been known.

Yet there is more.

The Giza necropolis, it seems, has finally decided to discharge all its secrets at once. For not far from the Great Pyramid, in a shallow enclave to the east, is the Great Sphinx. It, too, may be guarding a treasure-trove under its belly: a "Hall of Records" of a civilization long lost in the mist of time. There, too, with amazing synchronicity, an entrance to such a vault has been known since 1993.

Why have these "chambers" not yet been opened?

What could be within them?

Could the Egyptian authorities know more than they are letting on?

Is there a "conspiracy" here, one that might involve not just Egyptology but other, more sinister, institutions? Or is there "something else"?

We shall return to the works of these contemporary popular authors. For the moment, though, I invoke Bauval's work as an example of one distinctly Western way of imagining Egypt which links ancient Egyptian monuments, secret tunnels, buried chambers, and the mystical records of a long-lost civilization. Not all Western tourists are interested in an Atlantean Hall of Records and "sinister" conspiracy theories. However, what this particular imagination of Egypt has in common with more mundane versions of Western tourism in Egypt is that both center on the monuments of a pharaonic past.

ANCIENT EGYPT, LOST CIVILIZATIONAL KNOWLEDGE, AND SECRET CHAMBERS: ATLANTIS

Of course, Felipe was right—the concept of Atlantis originated in Plato's writings. Plato's description of the wars between Athens and Atlantis in *Timaeus* and *Critias* is an allegorical tale of the struggle for Liberty. The story is seen by many as representative of the conflict between Persia and Hellas. The island of Atlantis, once pure and beloved of Poseidon, has degenerated into corruption and failed to worship the gods.[3] In Atlantis, Plato describes a splendor of Oriental wealth that most commentators believe to be an allegorical description of "a Babylonian or Egyptian city, to which he opposes the frugal life of the true Hellenic citizen" (Jowett 1953:787). Plato gives the same date—nine thousand years before Plato himself was writing—for the foundation of Athens and for the repelling of the invasion from Atlantis.

According to Plato, Solon's tale of Atlantis originally came from Egyptian priests. This is probably the basis for later theories that connected Egypt's monumental architecture with fleeing Atlantean colonists. It has also led some academics to look for the Egyptian mythical origin for Plato's Atlantis. Griffiths (1991:11) argues that Solon's visit was a historical reality and finds parallels between the Atlantis myth and various Egyptian ones. M. Martin suggests that the tale actually did come from the Egyptian priests, but that "the Egyptian priests took a pleasure in deceiving the Greeks" (cited in Jowett 1953:787). Jowett, though, sees Plato's Atlantis story as pure myth, and in response to Martin, argues that "there is a greater deceiver or magician than the Egyptian priests, that is to say, Plato himself" (ibid.).

Whether Plato had an Egyptian source for his story or not, he certainly had a more immediate Greek source: Herodotus. While the first recorded mention of Atlantis is Plato's, it is Herodotus who first speaks of Solon's travels to Egypt, and there are substantial similarities between Herodotus's Ecbatana, capital of the Median Empire, and Plato's Atlantis: both cities are constructed as several concentric rings within rings, for example (Griffiths 1991:5–8). There are also a number of parallels between Plato's Atlantis and Herodotus's account of Egyptian kingship rites. Griffiths wryly notes, "Plato was supremely original in many aspects of his thinking, but during his visit to Egypt he was perhaps content . . . to use Herodotus as his *Baedeker*" (ibid.:19).

Contemporaries of Plato such as Strabo and Longinus evidently saw his Atlantis as a parable. But later neo-Platonists regarded it not only as allegory but also as historical fact (Jowett 1953:703). Jowett calls it a world-famous fiction,

> second only in importance to the tale of Troy and the legend of Arthur. . . .
> As many attempts have been made to find the great island of Atlantis, as
> to discover the country of the lost tribes. Without regard to the description
> of Plato, and without a suspicion that the whole narrative is a fabrication,
> interpreters have looked for the spot in every part of the globe, America,
> Arabia Felix, Ceylon, Palestine, Sardinia, Sweden. (Ibid.:781)

The myth of Atlantis was revived with the European discovery of America. America fit Plato's description of a massive landmass equivalent in size to Libya (by which the Greeks meant Africa) and Asia combined, located beyond the pillars of Heracles—that is, the Straits of Gibraltar. (It was hardly a sunken island, however.) Yet when Sir Francis Bacon wrote *The New Atlantis* and Sir Thomas Moore drew on the idea in the construction of his *Utopia*, they were not so much reviving the myth of Atlantis as they were writing in the Platonic tradition of an imaginary state.[4] In the seventeenth and eighteenth centuries, the myth of Atlantis was combined with Old and New Testament narratives (most enduringly identifying the story with that of Noah's flood).[5]

The idea of Atlantis was dramatically revived in 1882 with the publication of Ignatius Donnelly's book *Atlantis: The Antediluvian World*. It was an instant best-seller that fired the imagination of a generation. Donnelly reviewed legends of the flood from diverse cultures, noted similarities, and suggested that all these groups were descendents from one ancient super-culture, that of the Island of Atlantis, which had sent out colonists who reached the shores of virtually every land where there is evidence of ancient civilization. According to Donnelly, the oldest colony of Atlantis was Egypt. Atlantis was the source of the original Phoenician and Mayan alphabets. It was the original biblical Garden of Eden and the Mount Olympus of the Greeks. The actual kings, queens, and heroes of Atlantis became mythologized as the gods and goddesses of the ancient Greeks, Hindus, Egyptians, and Scandinavians. It was the land where man progressed from barbarism to a state of civilization. As Richard Ellis notes, "in Atlantis, Donnelly had found the cause of almost everything" (Ellis 1998:41).

Donnelly inspired many later writers—too many to list here. But one worth noting is Madame Helena Blavatsky, a Russian spiritualist who was a founder of London's Theosophical Society and who, not long after Donnelly's book came out, published *The Secret Doctrine*, which claimed to be based on an At-lantean record called *The Book of Dzyan*. Donnelly's writings about Atlantis also inspired writing about another mythical lost continent. He had observed that Australia was the remains of another geologically ancient continent in the Pacific. Zoologist Philip Sclater, in the 1870s, noted the presence of lemur fossils in Africa, though the creature now is found only in Madagascar, so he hypothesized about a now sunken Indo-Madagascan land bridge and called it Lemuria. Madame Blavatsky appropriated the name and suggested that the Le-murians, a race of ape-like hermaphrodites, had pre-dated the Atlantean races on the earth (Ellis 1998:65). The idea of Lemuria was later appropriated (as that of Atlantis) by Rosicrucians (Cervé 1963:11).

In contemporary times, Donnelly is the spiritual ancestor of authors such as Graham Hancock who continue to link the myths and the monuments of different world cultures to find evidence of one original ancestor civilization. (In this, they are not far removed from the goals of some early anthropolo-gists.) In Hancock's *Fingerprints of the Gods* (1995), the thesis is advanced of an evidently Atlantean civilization that flourished before 10,500 BCE and later vanished in "the great cataclysm that shook the earth at the end of the last Ice Age." Settlers from this lost civilization spread throughout the world, estab-lishing "wisdom cults." And in *Heaven's Mirror: Quest for the Lost Civilization*, Hancock argues that, from the step pyramids of the Mayans and Incans to the

Cambodian temples of Angkor to the pyramids of Egypt, all "clearly bear the imprint of a common purpose, and were designed to serve a common spiritual idea" (1998:313). Hancock also takes from Bacon the idea of a secret society "dedicated to the preservation of a mysterious legacy of knowledge from before the Flood" (1998:315).

It is clear that, from the beginning of the Atlantis legend, important links were made between Atlantis and Egypt. Less clear are the origins of the idea of a secret chamber hidden under the Giza pyramids or the Sphinx containing the records of lost civilizations. Although later the idea was associated with an Atlantean Hall of Records (detailed below), historically, the idea that mystical, magical knowledge from a lost civilization was interred beneath the sands of Giza appears to come from a different tradition in the European imagination of ancient Egypt: the Hermetica.

THE HERMETICA AND THE ROSICRUCIAN ENLIGHTENMENT

The Hermetic texts are a body of writings (mostly in Greek) that were probably compiled sometime before the second century CE by unknown authors and attributed to Hermes Trismegistus. Hermes Trismegistus (Hermes the Thrice Great) is a syncretic combination of the Egyptian god Thoth and the Greek Hermes that was a result of the Greek colonization of Egypt. But the Corpus Hermeticum, a group of seventeen texts compiled at an unknown date, is not mentioned as a body of texts until the eleventh century. The texts are subdivided into two categories: the technical Hermetica, which cover topics of magic, alchemy, astrology, astrological medicine, and astrological botany; and the philosophical Hermetica, which consist of "*Discourses* addressed by Hermes to Tat, Asclepius and Ammon, and by Isis to Horus" (Fowden 1993:4).[6] These astrological and alchemical texts were preserved thanks to the fashionableness of their subject matter in Byzantium; even some of the philosophical Hermetica were popular with certain Christian Byzantine writers, such as Lactantius, but the latter drew from those which fit his understanding of the nature of Christianity, while editing out other aspects of Hermetic mystical teachings (ibid.:8). The few philosophical texts that were preserved were substantially added to when, in 1945, a body of philosophical Hermetical papyri written in Coptic was found near Hamra Dum in Upper Egypt (ibid.:4–5). Drawing on the work of historian Garth Fowden, Robert Bauval proposes that the idea of *buried records* of magical wisdom first appears in the Hermetica, an important point to which we shall soon return (Bauval 1999a:11–30; see also Fowden 1993:27–41).

Medieval Egypt also had its own Hermetic texts and histories of pharaonic

Egypt, which date back to at least the early eleventh century CE. Cook argues that these were probably not the survival of an authentic, native Egyptian tradition throughout the centuries, but rather one that was reintroduced to Egypt from Iraq, while Haarmann (1996:620) suggests that it came from Iran. Cook argues that the authors of the Arabic Hermetic texts merely invoke ancient Egyptian sources to lend their histories authority, but do so fraudulently (Cook 1983:93). One ancient Arabic tradition holds that Hermes Trismegistus was responsible for building the pyramids; this Hermes is identified with historical figures of several religious traditions, including Idrīs of the Qur'an, Enoch of the Bible, and the Egyptian god Thoth (Dykstra 1994:58, Fowden 1993).

The Greek Hermetica became fashionable in sixteenth-century Italy, well before the modern European colonial incursions into Egypt. Giordano Bruno, a Hermetic philosopher, "propagated throughout Europe in the late sixteenth century an esoteric movement which demanded a general reformation of the world, in the form of a return to 'Egyptian' religion and good magic" (Yates 1986:216). Bruno may have formed a secret society in Germany, and he and other Hermetic philosophers were an important factor behind the "Rosicrucian Manifestos" which were published in Germany in the early seventeenth century. Francis Yates proposes that the Hermetic alchemical tradition was a critical impetus for the European Enlightenment. The Hermetic texts' treatment of alchemy, with its proposition that chemical processes were attainable through experimentation, provided a critical bridge between medieval magical mysticism and science, the Renaissance, and the scientific revolution of the seventeenth century (see also France 1991).

The Rosicrucian Manifestos were "proclamations of enlightenment in the form of an utopist myth about a world in which enlightened beings, almost assimilated to spirits, go about doing good, shedding healing influences, disseminating knowledge in the natural sciences and the arts, and bringing mankind back to its Paradisal state before the Fall" (Yates 1986:207). They were tremendously influential in Europe at the time. The Manifestos speak of a secret fraternity founded by Christian Rosencreutz. Yates argues that no serious historian can believe that the Rosencreutz story was anything but an allegorical fiction, but she points out that, even if there were no such secret societies at the time of the publication of the Rosicrucian Manifestos, these certainly did inspire the formation of a real secret society at some later date (ibid.:206–208). These European fraternities were the ancestors of today's AMORC Rosicrucian Order, which was established in the U.S. in the early 1930s by Dr. H. Spencer Lewis.[7]

Though Rosicrucianism and Freemasonry are two distinct traditions, there are also many critical historical, as well as structural and symbolic, links between them.[8] A famous early Masonic initiation was that of Elias Ashmole in 1646; Ashmole, Yates documents, was profoundly affected by the Rosicrucian Manifestos, copying them out in his own hand (ibid.).[9] In the middle of the eighteenth century, a new grade of Freemasonry called the Rose Cross grade was adopted within France. "This would seem like an acceptance, within Masonic tradition itself . . . of the idea of a connection between Rosicrucianism and Masonry" (ibid.:211–212). The Rosicrucians and Freemasons also use much of the same mystical Egyptian symbolism. Both Rosicrucians and Freemasons claim a philosophical heritage in ancient Egypt, and both have legendary histories that trace their secret fraternities back millennia to ancient Egypt. Rosicrucians claim that theirs dates to the time of Pharaoh Thutmosis III in 1489 BCE.[10] And, according to Masonic legend, the brotherhood dates back to the origin of architecture itself, and is thus associated with the Egyptian pyramids, the most ancient remaining specimens of monumental architecture.

As noted, historians of the movements point out that these histories are purely legendary. In 1818, Thomas Paine cited an essay written in 1730 by Samuel Pritchard (a Mason), who wrote that "at the building of the tower of Babel, the art and mystery of Masonry was first introduced, and from thence handed down by Euclid, a worthy and excellent mathematician of the Egyptians; and he communicated it to Hiram, the Master Mason concerned in building Solomon's Temple in Jerusalem" (Paine 1818). Paine points out that "there is a glaring contradiction in point of chronology in the account [Pritchard] gives. Solomon's Temple was built and dedicated 1,004 years before the Christian era; and Euclid, as may be seen in the tables of chronology, lived 277 years before the same era. It was therefore impossible that Euclid could communicate any thing to Hiram, since Euclid did not live till 700 years after the time of Hiram" (ibid.).

Certain authors (see Bauval 1999a) cite the Egyptian inspirations behind the European Hermetic trend of the late Renaissance/early Enlightenment (as documented by Fowden and Yates) as evidence of an unproblematic historical trajectory of ancient Egyptian knowledge that has been passed down from generation to generation from the times of ancient Egypt until today. But there are problems with this reasoning. While contemporary Rosicrucian literature cites the Rosicrucian Manifestos of seventeenth-century Germany as the inspiration behind their movement, their source for information about the Egyptian history of their movement is modern-day archaeology (Pharaoh Thutmosis III was certainly unknown to Renaissance and Enlightenment Europe). And as Yates (1986:206–207) points out, there is no historical evidence that points to an existing Rosicrucian society at the time that the Rosicrucian Manifestos were published; instead, evidence supports the thesis that the Manifestos' fictional story of Christian Rosencreutz inspired, rather than documented, the formation of secret fraternities which were the forerunners to modern Freemasonry and Rosicrucianism.

What the links between contemporary Rosicrucianism and the Hermetica do point to is a history of European appropriation of Egyptian myth and mysticism that dates back to the Greek colonization of ancient Egypt and the ensuing syncretism of Egyptian and Greek religion. Hermes Trismegistus is the embodiment not only of the ancient wisdom of a lost civilization passed down through the generations, as Bauval and others would have it, but also of a European tradition of imagining ancient Egypt as the repository of the ancient wisdom of a lost civilization.

BURIED TREASURES OF KNOWLEDGE

At some historical point, the two myths—that Egypt was a colony of the lost civilization of Atlantis, and that records containing the lost wisdom of Hermes Trismegistus (Thoth-Hermes) were buried beneath the sands of Egypt—became conflated in the Western imagination. Rosicrucians, who, we have noted, trace their roots to a European Hermetical tradition, adopted the myths of Atlantis and Lemuria as part of their fund of mystical beliefs (see Cervé 1963). But perhaps most famously, Edgar Cayce linked the ideas[11] with his belief that the records of the lost civilization of Atlantis were buried below the Giza monuments—beneath the paws of the Sphinx, to be precise.

Edgar Cayce, a psychic visionary who was born in Kentucky in 1877, rose to fame on the basis of his ability to heal people by going into trances in which he would diagnose ailments and prescribe cures which, in many cases, were effective where conventional medicine had failed. During his trances, he would also speak about past lives and historical moments, for which he earned the appellation "the sleeping prophet" (Cayce 1968).[12] Although a Christian, Cayce believed in reincarnation—believed, in fact, that he himself was an Egyptian high priest named Ra Ta in a previous incarnation.

During a number of his trances,[13] Cayce spoke about Atlantis, which he believed was a civilization that dated to some ten million years ago, when the Atlanteans arrived on earth (Cayce, Schwartzer, and Richards 1988:xxi). When their island sank around 10,000 BCE, survivors from Atlantis fled to ancient Egypt. The pyramids and the Sphinx, Cayce believed, were built by these Atlanteans between 10,490 and 10,390 BCE, when they took refuge in Egypt.[14] According to Cayce, they built a secret chamber under the paws of the Sphinx called the Hall of Records, which contains information about their lost civilization. He further suggested that this Atlantean Hall of Records would be rediscovered in or around 1998 and that this would bring about the Second Coming and the dawning of a New Age. Cayce died in 1945, and his children and followers established the Cayce Foundation, as well as the related Association for Research and Enlightenment (ARE) and the Atlantic University, in Virginia Beach, which promote his thoughts and which remain very much interested in ancient Egypt. They have, as we shall see, been active in supporting a number of recent archaeological and geological investigations devoted to the search for this Hall of Records.

SECRET TUNNELS, ASTRONOMY, AND THE AGE OF THE SPHINX

Seeking to prove Cayce's predictions, the Edgar Cayce Foundation (ECF) started, in the 1970s, trying to find ways to fund archaeological searches for evidence of a chamber—the Atlantean Hall of Records—hidden under the Sphinx. They sent an American graduate student to study Egyptology at the American University in Cairo, with the aim of eventually making contacts on the Giza Plateau,[15] and in 1978 they teamed up with the Stanford Research Institute (SRI) to help fund an electrical resistivity survey of the Sphinx enclosure and Sphinx temple to try to map out possible anomalies in the ground in the hope of finding a hidden buried chamber. In the early 1980s the ARE and ECF also helped to fund several projects on the Giza Plateau, including the Giza Mapping Project in 1979 and 1980, and the Pyramids Radiocarbon Project in 1983 to 1984, an attempt to carbon-date the mortar used in the Great Pyramid.[16]

All of these expeditions were fruitless. They found signs of holes in the rocks, but there was no evidence that these were anything but natural anomalies in the limestone. The attempts to date three samples of mortar from the pyramid produced widely varying results, with a range of dates all several centuries prior to the standard Egyptological dating of the Giza pyramids, but nowhere near the 10,500 BCE date proposed by Cayce.

But then in the late 1990s, the Egyptian archaeologists on the Giza Plateau rediscovered a water-filled deep well shaft on the plateau, located between the Sphinx and the second pyramid, about 250 meters from the base of the Great Pyramid. It had actually been documented in the 1930s by Egyptologist Selim Hassan but not fully excavated because of the water filling it. Under Dr. Zahi Hawass's supervision, the well shaft was drained and explored. It had three levels, the bottom of which was about 90 feet below ground level. The second level contained six rooms cut into the rock, and two large granite sarcophagi were found in two of the chambers. The third or lowest level, which was full of water, contained another massive stone sarcophagus, the lid of which, like those in the second chamber, had been pushed aside. All were empty.

Figure 3.1. An American tourist (my mom) poses next to one of the paws of the Sphinx. Photograph courtesy Louise Wynn.

The discovery excited ARE, Rosicrucians, and others who thought it might be the beginning of a series of underground passageways that would lead to secret chambers under the Sphinx and/or the pyramids. Indeed, a small tunnel-like passage seemed to lead off from one corner of the tomb, raising more hopes. The archaeologists investigated the lead but found that the tunnel ended after several feet. Basing his conclusions on pottery shards found in the shaft and a hieroglyphic inscription found on the wall next to one of the sarcophagi, Hawass dated the well shaft to the Saite period, some two millennia after the Sphinx was carved and the pyramids were built. He hypothesized that it was a symbolic tomb and cenotaph dedicated to the god Osiris, Lord of Rasataw, and so he nicknamed the discovery the "Tomb of Osiris." (A 1999 Fox Television special starring Dr. Hawass was devoted to the discovery.) But the dating is not undisputed; Robert Bauval and others, seeking to hold on to the hope of secret underground tunnels, argued that Hawass's dating of the tomb was flawed (see below).[17]

Also in the 1990s, Cayce's theory about a sophisticated Atlantean civilization coming to Egypt about 10,000 BCE received unlikely support from two separate theories that challenged the Egyptological dating of the monuments on the Giza Plateau. First Robert Bauval and Adrian Gilbert wrote a book called

The Orion Mystery (1994), which proposed that the Giza pyramids reproduced the position of the three stars in the belt of Orion. Using precessional astronomy—or "the science of archaeoastronomy" (Bauval and Hancock 1997:62)—Bauval and Gilbert proposed that the three pyramids on the Giza Plateau (Khufu, Khafre, and Menkaure) precisely match up with the three stars on the belt of Orion (al-Nitak, al-Nilam, and Mintaka)—but not in 2,500 BCE, the approximate date Egyptologists give for the building of the pyramids. Going against all archaeological evidence that the Great Pyramid was built in the Old Kingdom 4th Dynasty, Bauval and Gilbert claimed that the "archaeoastronomical evidence" proved that the pyramids could be dated to the early Stone Age of 10,500 BCE.[18]

At around the same time, John Anthony West was developing his own theory about the dating of the other great monument on the Giza Plateau: the Sphinx. West had been reading *The Temple of Man,* the work of a French scholar of ancient Egypt[19] by the name of Rene A. Schwaller de Lubicz (1998 [1957]), who suggested that the Sphinx showed signs of being eroded by water and not by wind. Excited, West took the theory to Boston University geologist Robert Schoch in 1989, and Schoch, though initially reserving judgment, after examining the body of the Sphinx, agreed. Because Egypt was a desert climate long before the Dynastic period, and because, Schoch felt, the erosion in the Sphinx had to have been caused by precipitation (not flooding), the date for when the Sphinx was carved had to be much earlier than the traditional Egyptological dating of the monument. Basing his claims on the paleoclimatology of the region, Schoch argued that the Sphinx's body had to have been carved sometime between 5,000 and 7,000 BCE at the latest, a minimum of some 2,500 years before the date Egyptologists give for it (see Schoch 1992a, 1992b, 1993). Marshaling the expert testimony of Schoch as well as that of a seismologist, a paleoclimatologist, and a forensics expert,[20] West produced a film presenting his theory called *The Mystery of the Sphinx* (West and Heston 1993). Narrated by Charlton Heston, it aired on NBC in November 1993 to a record 33 million viewers (Bauval 1999a:203).

Then, in 1996, Bauval and Hancock (remember that Graham Hancock had in 1995 published *Fingerprints of the Gods,* proposing that some kind of lost Atlantean super-civilization had antedated the pyramids in Egypt, Mexico, and Peru) produced *Keeper of Genesis* (1997), which drew on West's theory and used the principles of precessional astronomy to date the Sphinx to 10,500 BCE. It also expanded on Bauval and Gilbert's *Orion Mystery* (1994) by using computer charts of the skies to match up the Giza monuments and the constellations at 10,500 BCE.

Bauval, Gilbert, Hancock, and West are neither members of ARE nor Cayce believers, although they are occasionally asked to speak about their theories at ARE meetings. But they found a ready audience for their theories among people willing to believe that the monuments of the Giza Plateau had more mystery than the standard Egyptological story portrayed.

So how were these theories received among archaeologists? In general, the Egyptological community is not particularly fond of mystical theories of ancient Egypt, but neither, for the most part, does it perceive them as a threat. Egyptologists tend to either ignore them or laugh at them, as the following encounter from my fieldnotes describes.

[Sitting outside Dr. Hawass's office, I was chatting with A., a British Egyptologist. We were looking through some material sent to me by Elizabeth Mazucci, who had written a very interesting undergraduate honors thesis on the Nuwaubians, a cult group in the southern United States that believes that black Americans are not descended from Africa at all, but from aliens from outer space, via ancient Egypt.]

I started showing A. the Nuwaubians material and she was amused. We looked at a picture of Malachi York, founder of the Nuwaubians, dressed up in a pharaonic costume with headdress, flanked by two statues loosely interpreted from some Tutankhamun exhibit, and she said, "Look at that! Did you notice his shoes? Look! He's all dressed up in this outlandish outfit, and then underneath, you can just see his lace-ups. It's the one thing that pulls the picture back to reality." She couldn't stop laughing at his shoes.

We kept flipping through the material. "Look, here they have a pyramid and they're carrying along an Ark of the Covenant," I said.

"But where did they get the Ark of the Covenant from?"

I looked at her and said, laughing, "Well, it's not really the Ark of the Covenant!"

She laughed. "No, I mean where did they get the idea? What brought together these Egyptian symbols, the Islamic words and the Arabic, and the Ark of the Covenant?"

She then looked at their invented hieroglyphic language, said that some of them are real hieroglyphs, some seem to be related to hieroglyphs but are not quite, and other symbols are not hieroglyphs at all and are either taken from other sources or are invented. What she told me, however, is that none of the characters in the Nuwaubian legend, even the ones that are real hieroglyphs, are given their actual corresponding sounds that they have in the actual Egyptian language. "And look at this symbol! It doesn't even have phonetic value at all!"

B., an American Egyptologist, came into the office, sat down, and told A. about a recent find on his nearby dig. . . . A. got excited and said that she wanted to go out and have a look at what he was finding. A. asked B. to ask Zahi, when he went in to see him, if he [could have] Zahi's permission for A. to visit B.'s site. I asked A. why this was necessary—"Do you have to get permission just to go visit another archaeologist's dig?" She said, "Well, maybe not to visit, but because I want to have a look at what they're finding, and when you do a dig, you have to submit a complete list of the people on your team and get security clearance, which takes about three months. So I think at least we should probably inform Zahi if I'm going out there to have a look, since I'm not part of the official team. Zahi would almost certainly never say no, but still it's good to inform him."

B. came back in after being admitted to see Zahi, and encouraged A. to get out to his site as soon as possible. He was about to leave when I jumped up to show him the Nuwaubian material. He glanced at it, incuriously, then started to leave. "I just find all that stuff so boring, I can't stand to look at it."

"Not even funny? You don't even find it funny?"

"Not even funny, not anymore. Some of my colleagues find it 'cute,' but I just find it boring, I can't stand it at all." [Fieldnotes, 22 January 2001]

But when *Mystery of the Sphinx* was aired on NBC and presented to an enormous audience as a plausible scientific method of dating the Giza monuments, Egyptologists could neither ignore it nor dismiss it as "cute" or "boring." It was no longer a trivial theory published in obscure books that were read by a New Age audience; this was a theory that directly contradicted the Egyptological dating of the Giza monuments, and it was airing on American primetime television. Egyptian Egyptologists were particularly incensed. A reporter for *Akhbar al-Yom* wrote an article (8 January 1994) headlined "Stealing Egypt's Civilization" which quoted Dr. Hawass as calling West's theory a "cultural invasion" and a "kind of Zionist penetration" (see note 40 below for an explanation).

Egyptologists closed ranks in the face of West and Schoch's challenge, and mustered their own experts to examine the geology of the plateau. In two separate articles that appeared in the Egyptological review *KMT*, geologist James Harrell (Harrell 1994) and Egyptologist Mark Lehner (Lehner 1994) rebutted Schoch's argument point by point.[21] And Lehner concurred with Hawass's reaction, namely that the theory was an insult to Egyptians. He argued that it was a matter of principle to defend the Egyptological interpretation of ancient Egypt, not just for the sake of science, but for the sake of Egyptians themselves. "I believe we have a professional responsibility to respond to notions—like those of Cayce and West—that would rob the Egyptians of their own heritage by assigning the origins and genius of Nile Valley civilization to some long-lost agent like Atlantis" (Lehner 1994).

West, accustomed to skepticism and scorn from the Egyptological community, took the criticism in stride, but Boston University geologist Schoch was surprised to find himself summarily dismissed as a New Age purveyor of a crackpot theory. Even in the film, it was apparent that West and Schoch disagreed over certain points. Schoch had always favored the most conservative date possible for the Sphinx, leaning toward 5,000 BCE, and he didn't deny that the head of the Sphinx was a dynastic sculpture of King Khufu, but suggested that it had been recarved. "In my mind, clearly the dynastic Egyptians, which I believe inherited this structure, to use colloquial terms, mucked about with it quite a bit, recarved the head," he says (Schoch 2000). West is still not convinced that the head is Khufu's, and he proposes a much earlier date for the body of the Sphinx—pushing it back to 36,000 BCE—a far cry from Schoch's comparatively modest 5,000 BCE date.

In July 2000, I interviewed West and Schoch after meeting them in Zahi Hawass's office. Their meeting marked a new trend in relations between Hawass and those with alternative theories, such as West, Bauval, Hancock, and others. After almost a decade of bitter name-calling, and having been expelled from the plateau while doing research in the early 1990s, West and Schoch had finally met with Hawass on a friendly basis and agreed to cordially disagree. They had even given lectures together to the same audience, each presenting his own theory. It was tourism that brought them together: not only were they linked by the lectures they jointly gave to tourist audiences, but their first meeting was mediated by Mohamed Nazmy, a tour operator who caters to the New Age crowd and is a good friend to Hawass as well as to West, Bauval, and other alternative theorists.

Yet despite the détente with Hawass, the fact that their theory was summarily dismissed by the Egyptology community still rankled with Schoch, a friendly and mild-mannered man. "I'm not 'alternative,' I hope you appreciate that," he said by way of prefacing his remarks to me. "I'm a B.U. faculty member since 1984—you know how faculty members are, they're part of the establishment!" he said with a smile. "But on the other hand, I'm going to call it the way I see it, and this is a very clear case of where there is water-weathering, precipitation run-off."[22]

Before the NBC movie was made, Schoch and West had delivered a scientific paper at the 1991 meeting of the Geological Society of America presenting their theory, which was well received among geologists, none of whom disputed their conclusions, and many of whom, according to Schoch, were "very enthusiastic about it."[23]

Everything was fine until the papers got a hold of it and started calling Egyptologists, who immediately [said], "This is crazy, this is nonsense, we know how old the Sphinx is"—and of course they've seen none of the data whatsoever, they haven't been at the presentation. . . . And they're not geologists, and they're just [going on] this instinctive gut-reaction which I was not used to! I was not expecting that. (Schoch 2000)

But, according to Schoch, the Egyptologists were so invested in one version of ancient Egyptian history that it blinded them to other possibilities. Even the geologists who agreed with the Egyptological dating were "geologists who have been working on the plateau with Egyptologists, and . . . basically they're as much Egyptologists as Egyptologists are . . . I mean they have a vested interest already. . . . Basically, they were not doing good geology, but you know, they already knew what they wanted to get to, which is that the Sphinx is only 2500 BCE, so they're trying to explain away my data."

In short, concluded Schoch, Egyptologists weren't being good scientists, because they weren't willing to look at any new ideas and evaluate them on their merits; instead, they dismissed out of hand anything that didn't already conform to their preconceived notions about dating the Giza Plateau. "Essentially to me it's a very circular argument: 'We don't know that they were doing any monumental stone architecture in Egypt before a certain date, therefore, this can't be before that certain date'—it's basically saying we can't discover anything new in that realm," he said.

Schoch measured up the Egyptologists against his criteria for good science and found them lacking. West, on the other hand, had different standards. In his opinion, the official credentials flouted by Egyptologists counted for little. At our interview, he prefaced his remarks to me by making it clear that he was not a trained Egyptologist—and proud of it. "Sometimes when people say what are my credentials I say I don't have any, that's why I know something." Establishment archaeologists, in his opinion, were too narrow-minded to entertain a new theory. "In my considerable experience, an open-minded scientist of any kind is about as common as a fundamentalist Christian who loves his enemies," he said with a laugh. He echoes Alvares (1988) who has argued that "[m]odern science makes knowledge scarce because it asserts unrivalled hegemony" (cited in Nader 1996:1).

"New Agers" are not anti-science. Loring Danforth points out that "where the New Age movement does differ from other more clearly religious movements is the degree to which it draws on areas of American culture that would be considered not only secular but scientific as well. . . . Paradoxically, then, although much New Age thinking is characterized by a lack of faith in science, it would not be an exaggeration to say that in the New Age science has become a sacred symbol" (Danforth 1989:254). This certainly holds true for alternative

Figure 3.2. The Sphinx in 2006, with scaffolding for ongoing restoration of the right shoulder, part of which fell off in the late 1980s. Photograph by Mahmoud Abbas Elbadawi.

theorists of ancient Egypt. While theorists like West and Bauval set themselves up in opposition to the orthodox Egyptological community, they also muster what scientific evidence they can. West, dismissed by Egyptologists, surrounds himself with a posse of scientists from other disciplines to provide validation for his theory. His film, *The Mystery of the Sphinx,* lists a "scientific team" of experts, including Schoch, as well as another geophysicist/seismologist, a paleoclimatologist, and a forensics expert, and the film describes West himself as an "Egyptologist."

And Bauval and Hancock (1997), to take another example, keep abreast of new developments in Egyptology, and sometimes try to reconcile their theories with those of Egyptologists. They are aware of Hawass and Lehner's research on the workmen's community in Giza and the tombs of the builders of the pyramids, and they accept the orthodox premise that the pyramids were probably built around 2,500 BCE by Egyptians. But they still assert that the *design* for the monuments was made in 10,500 BCE by an earlier sophisticated civilization, the evidences of which have been destroyed, and suggest that this knowledge was preserved and passed down by a priestly caste until the time when the Giza pyramids were actually built in the Fourth Dynasty.

Part of the difference between the two camps is the way Egyptologists and alternative theorists approach Egyptian myths. West says that the reason he can entertain a date for the Sphinx of 38,000 years ago is that ancient Egyptian mythical histories support such a date. As West explained it to me,

> The Egyptians themselves in several texts . . . talk about earlier long periods . . . long periods of time in which Egypt was ruled by, first, the Neche, effectively the gods themselves, and then by long reigns of kings who were called the Shems Horus, semi-divine beings. And the dating, they disagree between themselves, these separate texts, but they're talking about a tremendous amount of time, they're talking about thirty-four to thirty-six thousand years. And of course, it's dismissed out of hand by orthodox scholars. Now . . . I'm inclined to believe that the Egyptians knew what they were talking about. In any case, I'm inclined to think that maybe the Egyptians knew more about their own history than modern Egyptologists.

The "Tomb of Osiris" controversy presents another interesting example of how differently Egyptologists and alternative theorists approach ancient Egyptian myth. As noted, Osiris was called "Lord of Rasataw," and the literal meaning of Rasataw is "underground tunnels" or cemetery. Specifically, it was used in the New Kingdom period to refer to Giza. Egyptologists take this to mean that, by the New Kingdom and especially the Late Period (nearly two millennia after the pyramids were built in the Old Kingdom's Fourth Dynasty), the ancient Egyptians had themselves come to mythologize the Giza Plateau as a place of hidden underground tunnels and had dug this well and placed in it a symbolic cenotaph for Osiris, deity of the underworld. Bauval, on the other hand, insists that, rather than seeing it as mythology, the New Kingdom use of the term *Rasataw* (Bauval spells it Rastaw or Rostau) to refer to Giza occurs because they had information handed down through the generations that the Giza Plateau sat over a series of underground tunnels and chambers in which sacred texts had been buried of old. So Bauval and West take literally what Egyptologists take as myth. It is also interesting to see the different ways that Bauval and Hawass reach their conclusions about dating. While Hawass dates pottery and a hieroglyphic inscription and correlates them with the New Kingdom and Late Period myth of the Giza Osireion, Bauval insists that "intuition" tells him that the well is much older than the Saite period to which Hawass attributes it. He says, "My intuition told me that Hawass could be wrong. This place felt old, very old—perhaps as old as the Sphinx itself" (1999a:298).

This is not just a different approach to myth—it's a different attitude toward what constitutes acceptable ways of knowing. No archaeologist would defend the dating of a site based on "intuition," as Bauval does. But that's precisely the appeal of these theorists: they argue that there is another way of knowing that is not mechanical and scientific but rather intuitive and mystical. As Hess notes, "The New Age movement represents a deep interest in alternatives to conventional knowledge and faith" (1993:3). Both Bauval and West accuse Egyptologists of neglecting key aspects of ancient Egyptian beliefs:

> The modern Egyptological establishment, since the 1940s or so, has cut itself away from the magical and mystical tradition of ancient Egypt. Regarding themselves as "scientists," they feel uneasy and somewhat polluted when confronted with the intense esoteric aspects of the very "science" they have declared themselves the custodians of. . . . This is like a surgeon trying to find the soul of a person by dissecting his body. Sadly, this is the very thing that has been happening to the scholarship of ancient Egypt—and indeed to other ancient cultures—when left in the hands of "scientists" alone. Egyptology is not a "science," it is a *sacred science.* The Great Pyramid is not only an engineering structure conforming to clear geometrical rules, but a sacred temple of initiation into the mysteries of cosmic existence. (Bauval 1999a:41–42)

And West argues that, in his study of ancient Egypt,

> the deeper I got into it, the more I realized that actually the ancients had been egregiously misrepresented by modern history, actually, and Egypt in particular. . . . According to orthodox Egyptology—and it's a strange position to take in the midst of the most fabulous art and architecture in the world—the Greeks really invented civilization, and before that Egypt was a kind of magnificent dry run, but they had no real philosophy, they had no real coherent religion, they had no science to speak of, they had a primitive mathematics. This is all [the] orthodox [position]. And my conviction was, to begin with, that not only that history was being misrepresented, but that Egypt represented not the beginnings of civilization, but in a way, the end of great civilization, and it's been a downhill trip ever since. (West 2000)

Mark Lehner retorts, "So a John West can blast Egyptologists for suppressing the sacred science inherent in Egyptian culture without being able to read Egyptian language—a little like saying one knows Shakespeare's real meaning without reading English."[24]

On some important level, Egyptologists and alternative theorists are not studying quite the same thing. As Bauval and West both argue, "Egyptology is not a science, it is a *sacred science*" (Bauval 1999a:42). Alternative theorists define their object of study as a mystical one, not a mere sortie into secular history that can be achieved by sifting through rubble in the sand. Egyptologists and alternative theorists have different objects of study, and their respective methods flow from those different definitions, so that, speaking of the Osiris well, Bauval can say that he knows it's old because of "intuition." The mysticism of the object authorizes the mysticism of the method.[25]

More broadly the dispute is about the canon and a willingness to engage with a body of texts and of knowledge. There is a fascinating exchange between Lehner and Bauval and Hancock published in *Keeper of Genesis* (Bauval and Hancock 1997). Lehner, after dismissing West for not knowing ancient Egyptian, continues,

> Another pyramid theorist said, in an animated dinner conversation, "Where's the evidence? The pyramid stands out there with no evidence of how the ancient Egyptians could have built it." I ticked off four Egyptological titles—all in English—devoted to ancient Egyptian tools, technology, stone building, and materials and industries. Although he had published a widely acclaimed book with a new theory on the pyramids, he admitted to not having read a single one of these basic works. It would be so much more fun and challenging if such theorists did actually read and absorb such primary sources, and then launched the dialogue. (Bauval and Hancock 1997:311)

Bauval and Hancock respond:

> We remember one Egyptological title (not four) that you "ticked off" during a certain "animated dinner conversation." The one title was Clarke and Engelbach's *Ancient Egyptian Construction and Architecture*. We've both read it since and weren't overly impressed. Robert Bauval, as you know, is a construction engineer by training and spent twenty years actually *building* enormous buildings in the Middle East. In my opinion—Clarke and Engelbach notwithstanding—this gives him a rather good basis from which to engage in "fun and challenging" dialogue about the construction logistics of the Great Pyramid. There's no substitute for real experience no matter how many "primary sources" we "read and absorb." (And by the way, in what sense are Clarke and Engelbach a primary source? Were they present when the Pyramid was built? Did they build it?) (Ibid.:314, emphasis in original)

This exchange is profoundly telling. Lehner is not unwilling to engage in dialogue, but he asserts that, to engage him in debate, one must first speak the same language of Egyptological literature. The primary sources are, for him, self-evident. But Bauval and Hancock refuse to engage him on his terms, challenging the nature of the canon and the definition of a primary source.

A battle is being fought over what is science and what is Egyptology. West musters a "scientific team" to validate his Sphinx theory; Bauval calls his research "the science of archaeoastronomy," yet no degree-holding Egyptologist I have interviewed considers Bauval's methods or conclusions scientific. West calls Schwaller de Lubicz a "renegade Egyptologist," while an Egyptologist that I interviewed dismisses him as a New Ager.

Looking at how these alternative theories have been received within academia reveals a great deal about the ways that Egyptologists know what they know and the process by which scientific work is validated. It also reveals the politics of Egyptology and professional boundary marking. To set a boundary—to call something "Egyptology" and something else "New Age"—is also to establish a hierarchy, to buttress one mode of knowledge production by contrasting it unfavorably with another. Science is both social and political, because in the end, as Laura Nader reminds us, it is "an institutional setting, . . . a group of people united by a common competence. Science is systematized knowledge, a mode of inquiry, a habit of thought that is privileged and idealized" (Nader 1996:1).

And this is why such authors are fascinated with Dr. Mark Lehner: because Lehner embodies in his career a crossing over from the New Age camp to that of orthodox Egyptology.[26] An Egyptologist who has a visiting assistant professor appointment at the University of Chicago's Oriental Institute, Lehner originally came to Egypt in 1972 as a Cayce disciple, funded by the ARE, and bent on proving that the Sphinx was carved by Atlanteans.

After that first visit to Egypt, Lehner returned to the American University in Cairo to study anthropology, again, funded by ARE members. In 1977 and 1978, the Stanford Research Institute obtained clearance to do an electrical resistivity survey of the ground under the Sphinx, to look for cavities in the rock. The project was partially funded by the Cayce Foundation, which hoped the research would reveal evidence of a subterranean Hall of Records, and Lehner participated as a member of the field team. They drilled fine holes into the ground where electrodes had indicated cavities in the rock, but instead of finding a buried chamber, all they found were apparently natural geological anomalies in the rock.

According to Lehner, that point marked the beginning of his doubts about finding the Hall of Records. Working with Zahi Hawass, then a young Egyptologist, to clear the ground around the Sphinx in preparation for SRI's resistivity survey, they found fragments of tools and Old Kingdom pottery, which had obviously been left by the people who built the Sphinx. He became fascinated with the facts about ancient Egypt that archaeology was revealing, rather than mystical predictions about a mythical Egyptian past.[27] Now, after almost thirty years of working in Egypt, Lehner is known as one of the world's experts on the Sphinx. He spent five years as field director of the American Research Center in Egypt's (ARCE) Sphinx Mapping Project, a project that paved the way for restoration efforts by using photogrammetric cameras to document the volume and precise dimensions of the Sphinx. Lehner did much of the mapping by hand. As he tells the story, when he was confronted by the actual history of the place, the mysterious, exotic notions of Atlantis, aliens, secret chambers, and the Hall of Records no longer had any hold over him.

Lehner went back to school in 1986 to do a Ph.D. in Egyptology at Yale. The work he was interested in doing was different from the bulk of traditional Egyptology, much of which has relied on studying elite objects that were unearthed from royal and noble tombs. Little was known about everyday life and common people in Egypt. Instead of looking for art objects and undisturbed tombs, Lehner looks for clues that weren't deliberately left for posterity (or for eternity); instead of looking at tombs, he sifts through the dirt near them to look for tool fragments, he examines tool marks in stone, he collects mud samples and has them chemically analyzed for traces of metals. High levels of copper in one area, for example, tell him that copper tools were used for cutting stone; because the metal is so soft, it is quickly ground down with use. He then reconstructs possible copper tools and drills that the ancient Egyptians may have used, and uses them himself to measure at what rate the tools were worn down. Then, based on the quantities of copper found in the dirt, he can infer a great deal of information about what kind of cutting, and how much of it, took place in a certain area, which is helping to solve mysteries of how ancient Egyptians cut stone in the Bronze Age. In short, instead of looking for secret chambers with spectacular caches of treasure, Lehner does extremely mundane, tedious, absolutely unspectacular work, sifting through dust and slag and analyzing it for its chemical content.

Lehner provides a compelling account of his conversion to orthodox Egyptology in his letter to Bauval and Hancock, published in *Keeper of Genesis* (1997).

> During my two years at the American University in Cairo I majored in anthropology, and took my first courses in Egyptian archaeology and prehistory. I also spent most of my free time at Giza, and I visited other

ancient sites and archaeological projects. I did not "find footprints of the gods." By becoming acquainted with a vast amount of previous archaeological research with which the Cayce community and like-minded Egypt-enthusiasts are only minimally familiar, I found the "footprints" of people—their tool marks, names, family relationships, skeletons, and material culture . . .

I began to suggest to the Cayce community that they look at the Egypt/ Atlantis story as a myth in the sense that Joseph Campbell popularized, or that Carl Jung drew upon in his psychology of archetypes. Although the myth is not *literally true,* it may in some way be literarily *true.* The Cayce "readings" themselves say, in their own way, that the inner world of symbols and archetypes is more "real" than the particulars of the physical world. . . . In archaeology, many dilettantes and New Agers want to be on the trail of a lost civilization, aliens, yes, "the gods," without having to pay attention to the real people behind time's curtain and without having to deal with the difficult subject matter upon which so-called "orthodox" scholars base their views. (Cited in Bauval and Hancock 1997:310; emphasis in original)

There are some important insights to be gained from this brief review of some of the theorists of ancient Egypt. West, Bauval, and others in the "New Age" camp accuse Egyptologists of having too narrow a vision of what ancient Egyptian mysticism and religion looked like. Egyptologists accuse the New Agers of having no real scholarly grounding in the study of ancient Egypt, and of adopting a cut-and-paste approach to Egyptology—choosing the material that fits their theories, and discarding what doesn't. Robert Schoch finds himself in an uncomfortable situation. On the one hand, he views himself as a scientist, committed to testing theories without preconceived notions. Yet Egyptologists dismiss him out of hand, because he's not coming at it from an Egyptology background, and because he partnered with the "wrong" person. So he finds himself in the same camp with West, who has the same idea as Schoch does about water erosion and an earlier date for the Sphinx, but who goes way beyond him, dating the Sphinx to 36,000 BCE based on his calculations of precessional astronomy.

Egyptologists concede that some of the work of alternative theorists involves extensive learning and research, but argue that when such theorists use scientific data to support their theories, they just pick and choose, rather than taking in the whole and trying to work back from there to a historical vision that is not predetermined by their esoteric ideas. But also it is clear that they are excluded from being taken seriously by Egyptologists because they are not engaging on the same terms, working from the same language, the same cor-pus of literature, the same vocabulary of shared reference points.

Archaeology is a science, and like any science, it has its own culture and social procedures for validating a theory and excluding outsiders.[28] As Lehner's comments indicate (when he said that he and other Egyptologists have a pro-fessional responsibility to respond to theories "that would rob the Egyptians of their own heritage"), there are clear political aspects to this debate that is being waged in terms of scientific credentials.

CONSPIRACY THEORIES

On the Internet, Gary Val Tenuta claims that Hawass is the spiritual descen-dent of a "non-human entity" channeled by occult writer Aleister Crowley, and insinuates that Hawass is an "emissary of the Dark Side."[29] Richard Hoagland (whose website includes doctored photos of hieroglyphic spaceships on the wall of the Temple of Abydos) alleges that, not only is Hawass doing secret and illegal excavations under the Great Pyramid, he also chooses all of the landing sites for the NASA planetary exploration missions.[30] Hawass's favorite Internet rumor is the one that claimed that there was a secret passageway running be-tween his bathroom and the Great Pyramid which he uses to go to the pyra-mids to squirrel away secrets of "lost civilizations."

Egyptologists have long referred to these types as "pyramidiots" among themselves, but the director of Giza antiquities delights in calling them such openly.[31] Dr. Zahi Hawass has been the target of numerous rumors and con-spiracy theories that are spread over the Internet and in the media, both in Egypt and abroad. While many have been of the above sensationalist variety and brushed off by Hawass with a sense of humor (he shows a picture of his office bathroom as part of the slide show he gives to tour groups to make the point that it contains no secret tunnels), others have hit closer to home and smart a bit more. Hawass often speaks indignantly of the time when Internet conspiracy theorist Larry Hunter teamed up with a group of Hawass's enemies in the village of Nazlet el-Semman to attack him in a smear campaign in the local press when a portion of the Sphinx's shoulder fell off.[32]

Hawass is not hostile to New Age groups. In fact, he claims to be the first to have allowed these groups to meditate in the pyramids after hours, until Internet rumors prior to Y2K started circulating about a group planning to commit suicide in the pyramid on the eve of the millennium. (At that time the authorities closed the pyramids to after-hours groups, who previously had paid a hefty sum for the privilege of spending two hours in the pyramids at night.) A great deal of Hawass's job as Undersecretary of State for the Giza

Monuments[33] centers around public relations—he gives newspaper and television interviews nearly every day on various subjects—and much of this PR work is structured as a response to the claims of these "pyramidiots." That is, he said, what prompted him to write more popular articles and books on Egyptian archaeology—so as to be able to compete with the "pyramidiots'" monopoly over the layperson audience interested in ancient Egypt. And he started his own website (http://www.guardians.net/hawass/) in order to compete with the Internet conspiracy theory rumor mill and to counter accusations that the Egyptian government and SCA were black boxes of information.

"I decided to not spend my time writing articles that no one would read, and instead to keep in contact with the public, especially since there is such a large number of people obsessed with the pyramids and ancient Egypt," he told me. And his campaign has been largely successful. In 1992 he invited Art Bell, who has a popular radio program in the United States devoted to paranormal phenomena, to witness Egyptian stoneworkers cutting and dressing stones for restoration work. Bell had been among those who had been propagating the idea that the pyramids could not have been built by ancient Egyptians without modern tools, and he had hosted several authors who favored theories that the pyramids had been built by aliens. When Bell saw how contemporary Egyptian laborers cut the stones with very simple tools using the same techniques that must have been used in ancient times, Bell broadcast to his listeners that he'd been converted to Hawass's camp.

Another time, Hawass gave a lecture to a group of tourists who were all wearing pyramids on their heads. He asked the audience what they were for, and they told him that it was because of "pyramid power"—a belief that anything that is kept under or within a pyramid is preserved. So Hawass took some raw meat and left half of the meat in his office for three days and the other half of the meat inside the Great Pyramid. At the end of the three days, he checked on both of them. The meat that was left in the pyramid was, he says, more rotten than the meat in his office. He invited international reporters to examine the two meat samples, and told them, "Maybe *our* pyramids don't have power and your pyramids in Virginia Beach and California have power."[34]

Each time I saw Hawass give interviews to Egyptian television on the Giza Plateau, a large segment of his monologue pivoted around refuting foreign imaginations of Egypt that, he claimed, sought to "take away Egypt from Egyptians" and efface the monuments' meaning as a component of Egyptian national identity and pride. What this drives home is that these alternative theorists are not marginal; they are a significant part of the consciousness of the Egyptian team of archaeologists at the pyramids. The Egyptian government is very much aware of, and actively engaging with, these Western imaginations of ancient Egypt.

SECRET DOORS IN THE PYRAMIDS

And yet the conspiracy theories still flourish. Despite the détente between Hawass and alternative theorists such as Robert Bauval, Bauval can still tantalize readers, in his latest book, by asking, "Is there a 'conspiracy' here, one that might involve not just Egyptology but other, more sinister, institutions?" (1999a:xvi). The case of Gantenbrink's Upuaut robot was a prime example of an enduring focus for conspiracy theories on the Giza Plateau.

In 1993, the German (Deutsche) Archaeological Institute (DAI) was commissioned by the SCA to clean the "ventilation shafts" in the Great Pyramid and install fans. This pyramid is unique in having four narrow shafts (about eight inches in diameter), two coming from the northern and southern walls of the so-called "Queen's Chamber" and two from the northern and southern walls of the "King's Chamber." The two coming from the King's Chamber run to the outside of the pyramid, but the two in the Queen's Chamber do not exit the pyramid, and it is unknown just how far they extend. Originally, the openings were not exposed in the Queen's Chamber itself; they were discovered in the 1870s by an explorer, Wayman Dixon, who broke through the five or so inches of stone that blocked them off. Egyptologists do not know what purpose these closed-off shafts served, but Bauval and Gilbert (1994) have speculated that they were designed to provide a pathway for the pharaoh's soul to the stars above.

In any event, the SCA decided that the passageways in the King's Chamber should be cleaned out and fans installed to renew the air inside that was breathed by hundreds of tourists each day. Besides the problem of stale air inside the pyramid, condensation from the sweat and breath of tourists had led to thick layers of salt deposits building up on the inner walls of the pyramid.

The DAI brought in a German engineer by the name of Rudolph Gantenbrink to perform the cleaning work. He used primitive techniques to clean out the already open shafts coming from the King's Chamber and installed ventilation fans, but then designed an ingenious robot equipped with a video link to explore the small unopened shafts coming from the Queen's Chamber. The robot, which he named Upuaut II, penetrated the shaft to a distance of some two hundred feet, at which point its progress was halted by what appeared to be a portcullis door with two copper handles.

Gantenbrink was excited. Could it be a door hiding a previously unknown secret chamber in the pyramid? Eager to exploit the opportunity, he brought in a television crew to film the further exploration; apparently he was planning to produce and commercially market a documentary film about the robot's exploration of the shafts. He was stopped by the DAI, which told him that he couldn't film without a permit from the SCA. All filming of archaeological investigations

Figure 3.3. The interior of one of the Giza pyramids. Photograph by Elias H. Debbas II.

in Egypt requires a government permit separate from (and in addition to) the research permit. Gantenbrink didn't want to wait around the several months that it would take to get the permit, so, claiming that he'd been given the verbal go-ahead from Zahi Hawass (a claim which Hawass has vehemently denied), he proceeded with the filming and the exploration.

In April 1993, the news started to break to the world press. The *Times* of London proclaimed, "Secret Chamber May Solve Pyramid Riddle," and the *Age* in Melbourne headlined its article, "Pyramid May Hold Pharaoh's Secrets."[35] And abruptly, a backlash ensued. The SCA and the Ministry of Culture were furious that Gantenbrink had gone to the press directly and not through them. And the fact that he had been filming without an official license and planning a money-making commercial film sealed his fate. Gantenbrink was banned from further research, the DAI abruptly disassociated itself from him, and the Egyptian authorities vaguely promised that the exploration would go on at some indefinite time in the future under the sponsorship of a responsible organization, probably the National Geographic Society.

After that, conspiracy theories ran wild. Larry Hunter, for example (who had attacked Hawass after a shoulder of the Sphinx fell off), was among those who accused the Egyptian government of secretly carrying on with Gantenbrink's exploration in the year that the pyramid was closed for cleaning.[36] *Stargate* authors Lynn Picknett and Clive Prince (1999:78) attributed Gantenbrink's losing his research permit to some kind of conspiracy, and mocked the idea that a mere breach of protocol would be enough for the Egyptian government to stop his work.

One of the reasons that conspiracy theories flourish, of course, is that they attract an audience and sell books. But there is another, legitimate reason for the conspiracy theories. Foreigners who are not trained in the bureaucratic procedures of Egyptology imagine that there must be some conspiracies at work, since they simply cannot imagine that the workings of the Egyptian government would be so arcane and obscure. Why, they wonder, would the Egyptian government stop Gantenbrink's work just because he followed incorrect procedures for reporting and advertising his discovery?

First of all, it is worth noting that most Egyptian government officials are extremely nervous about any press attention that involves them. Bad press puts pressure on them, and many fear losing their posts to a public scandal. There is a long history in Egypt, dating back to Carter's discovery of the tomb of Tutankhamun in the 1920s, of the media influencing public opinion with its reports on archaeological excavations and prompting interventions by the Egyptian government (see Hoving 1978). Conspiracy theorists, working from the outside and without an understanding of the internal politics of Egyptian bureaucracies and ministries, simply cannot understand how press reports make bureaucrats nervous. What looks like a conspiracy at work may just be someone trying to save his job.

But what outsiders also fail to appreciate is that the breach of protocol entailed in going over the Ministry of Culture's head and broadcasting the discovery is considered extremely serious by the Egyptian authorities. It is an affront to national control over the monuments that recalls the days when adventurers and consuls did what they liked with Egypt's pharaonic heritage without deference to any local authority (see Chapter 2). The Gantenbrink episode was not the first time that the Egyptian government stopped work over procedural issues relating to publicizing discoveries. In the 1930s, Egyptian Egyptologist Selim Hassan was dismissed from his post and a lawsuit brought against him by Dean Taha Hussein for going directly to the press with his discoveries instead of going through his sponsors at the University of Cairo (Reid 1985:243). More recently, an American paleontologist who discovered the bones of a large previously unknown species of dinosaur in Bahariya Oasis went directly to the press without going through the Egyptian authorities, and he too lost his research license ('Amrān 2000). Likewise, Dr. Joann Fletcher, a British Egyptologist from York University who publicized the discovery of a mummy in the tomb of Amenhotep II and claimed it to be the mummy of Queen Nefertiti, was banned from excavations in 2003 for going directly to the press and not publicizing her discovery through the SCA.

Sufficient press attention had been generated by Gantenbrink's discovery that the SCA realized there was a potentially large audience for further investigation, which would make money and help promote tourism in Egypt. The SCA decided to sponsor its own investigation into the shaft, and they worked out an arrangement with National Geographic to design a robot that could penetrate the shaft and insert a camera under the gap in the "door" to film what lay beyond it. Zahi Hawass would promote and host the television event called "Pyramids Live: Secret Chambers Revealed," which National Geographic would film and broadcast live on the National Geographic Channel and on Fox Television in the United States. This finally took place on 16 September 2002, nine years after Gantenbrink's original discovery. What did they find behind the stone door with copper handles? Another limestone block, almost exactly like the first one, several inches behind it, with similar copper "handles" (National Geographic News 2002).

ALTERNATIVE THEORIES OF ANCIENT EGYPT AND EGYPTIAN NATIONALISM

There is a complex relationship between these alternative theorists, tourism, and archaeology in Egypt. Organizations such as ARE have sponsored important archaeological work in Egypt; mysticism propagated by ARE and by best-selling authors such as Bauval, Hancock, Phillips, and West have in turn spurred on Western fascination with Egyptian antiquities. And that of course leads to tourism; touristic interest in pharaonic monuments provides a key source of funding for the Egyptian archaeological teams, whose work on these sites is funded by admission fees to monuments and museums.

"New Agers" are good for the economy. Yet these groups continue to draw fire in the Egyptian press.[37] So why do New Age theories stir up so much antipathy?

Of course, one reason is a common misconception among Egyptians that the groups who come to meditate in the pyramids are actually worshiping the monuments, which carries distasteful connotations for religious Egyptian Muslims and Christians alike. One Egyptian official on the Giza Plateau who was a personally devout Muslim told me that he was pleased that the pyramids had been closed to meditation groups at night, because he felt that letting such groups in encouraged idolatry.

They have their beliefs, and I have mine, and I'm not saying that they have to believe what I believe, but at the same time I don't have to encourage them, either. They worship in the pyramids, and this isn't the way to wor-

ship God, and if I encourage them or make things easy for them, then I
am partly guilty too.

Another antiquities inspector showed me a photo he had obtained of a *gal-abiyya*-clad Egyptian guide being made by a group of New Agers to stand inside the pyramid with his bare feet on the ground and hands pressed to the
walls of the passageway; the inspector explained to me that the New Agers believe this is a way of drawing ancient energy from the pyramid, but he pointed
out that they had effectively caused the Muslim guide to make the shape of a
cross, which was offensive to his beliefs and religion.

Tour guides commonly describe New Age groups in Egypt as "the worshippers," because it is popularly believed that they worship the pyramids. Not
every Egyptian believes that they "worship" the sites, though. I interviewed
several tour guides who specialize in such groups and they were at pains to
emphasize to me the difference between worship and meditation. Many Egyptians working in tourism accommodate the New Agers, affecting a tolerant,
you-have-your-beliefs-and-I-have-mine attitude when lecturing them about the
history of the pyramids. They even collect the writings of popular New Age
authors in an attempt to understand the beliefs of those they are hosting. (Mohamed Nazmy, for example, the tour guide who mediated a détente between
Hawass and authors such as Bauval and West, has an extensive library of New
Age literature.)

But while this may be one reason for why they're not well regarded in Egypt,
the most significant reasons are more political. These theories are offensive to
Egyptians because they attack Egyptian national pride in its pharaonic legacy.
For Egyptians who pride themselves on being the descendents of a great civilization whose monuments have survived six thousand years, when people
claim that aliens or Atlanteans were the ones who built those monuments,
this is seen as an attempt to deprive Egypt of its glorious ancient history.[38]
Farouk Hosni, the Minister of Culture, has likened this to Israelis attributing
the building of the Great Pyramid to Jewish slaves.[39] And hence the Egyptian
newspapers often spout out that these theories are "a sort of Zionist penetration."[40] It denies Egyptian intelligence and greatness when people claim that
ancient Egyptians couldn't have built the pyramids, and smacks of the dregs
of colonialism.

New Agers insist on claiming the Egyptian monuments as a world heritage,
emphasizing the unity of all humankind. At the same time, this implies that
the monuments, if they belong to the "world" at large, are not Egyptian, thus
challenging pride in the nation-state, and denying the Egyptian appropriation
of the pharaonic past as a means of shoring up the timeless identity of Egypt

as a national entity. Yet the same Westerners who like to claim the pyramids as their own do not abandon their own nationalism and national boundaries when it comes to the world economy. They don't, for example, open their doors to let in an influx of poor Egyptians seeking work and better standards of living like their own. They want to overthrow some national boundaries but not others, taking all the best parts of Egypt for themselves and discarding the rest to return to their comfortable lives back in their own countries.

In a talk he gave to a group of American tourists at the Mena House Hotel (22 February 2000), Hawass asked rhetorically, "Why do Americans like to obsess over 'pyramid power'? Because Americans have two days off each week. Here in Egypt, everyone is so busy, fighting the traffic—there's no time to think about 'pyramid power.'" Hawass insinuates that New Age beliefs are the pastime of comfortable bourgeois elites who have time on their hands and aren't struggling with the demands of everyday life.

Cayce believers are also irritating to Egyptian (and foreign) archaeologists who see just how much money is being funneled into what they consider fruitless searches for a non-existent "Hall of Records" when the money would be better devoted to site management and preservation. In the same lecture, Dr. Hawass said wistfully to the group of tourists, "Imagine if all the money used in arguments about and investigations into secret passages was used for preservation and research!"

But perhaps most important, the search for spectacular, new archaeological finds, like a fabled secret chamber in the Great Pyramid or under the paws of the Sphinx, recalls the early days of archaeological exploration in Egypt, when tombs were hacked into, looted, plundered, and sometimes destroyed in the search for fabulous new finds, wealth, and fame—fame both for the archaeologists and for the countries sponsoring them. That is why Gantenbrink's publicity stunt irritated so many people—and what seems to have been most offensive to Egyptian observers was the fact that he was filming with the intent of producing a commercial film; that is, he was intending to profit off the discovery to the exclusion of the Egyptians. Recall the words of Robert Bauval that I quoted at the beginning of this chapter, when he writes of this fabled hidden chamber as "the supreme archaeological prize" and suggests that "the Great Sphinx . . . too may be guarding a treasure-trove under its belly." Such language—"archaeological prizes" and "treasure-troves"—very much reflects the treasure hunt that was Egyptology's past.

There is still a mystique and appeal to the daredevil, swashbuckling, Indiana Jones image of archaeology. How else to explain that Bauval writes in a sensationalist newspaper article promoting his new book (1999b) that he "sneaked" in to the so-called Tomb of Osiris well shaft to investigate—when in his book *Secret Chamber* (1999a) it is clear that he entered the well shaft after having obtained permission from Dr. Zahi Hawass and was accompanied by Egyptian antiquities inspector Esam Shehab (Bauval 1999a:296)—the same procedure which anybody, Egyptologist and layperson alike, must use to obtain access to archaeological sites that are not open to the public?[41] And Zahi Hawass himself is famous for wearing a hat that people often refer to as his "Indiana Jones hat," whether he is on a dig or posing for his National Geographic "Scholars-in-Residence" portrait. Hawass could choose a number of different head coverings to protect him from the sun while working, such as the wrapped turban that workers digging on the plateau often wear, but he chooses to wear his khaki Stetson for the image it connotes of a romantic adventurer-explorer.

TOWARD AN ANTHROPOLOGY OF ARCHAEOLOGY

The pyramids are such marvels, both in their sheer enormity and in the geometrical precision of their lines, that they are a feat of architecture and engineering that would challenge builders using today's technology. The Great Pyramid is almost five hundred feet tall. Originally cased in hard limestone, it was meant to blaze in Egypt's intense sun, reminding viewers of the connection between the pharaohs and Ra, the sun god.[42] Yet the pyramids were built some 4,500 years ago, during the Bronze Age, by a people who did not even use wheels. Using such basic technology, the Great Pyramid was completed—so Herodotus says—over a period of just about twenty years. Archaeologists still do not know exactly how the stones were raised by workers, though they have many theories. So it is not surprising that, with such majesty and mystery, people should invent stories and fill the gaps with fabulous origins.

As noted in this chapter's anecdote about the Gulf prince who visited Dr. Hawass seeking a cure for his comatose mother, Westerners are not the only ones to do this. Arabs have different mystical imaginations of pharaonic Egypt. Among Egyptians and Arabs, rumors abound about the mythical "red mercury" (*al-zī'baq al-ahmar*) that is said to have been buried with royal mummies. Hawass traces the origin of the red mercury mystique to Alfred Lucas's excavations in Saqqara some sixty years ago, which produced a bottle of some unknown reddish-brown substance that went on display in the Luxor Museum, where it has proved to be the biggest draw for Egyptians visiting the museum. Notably, when Hawass started investigating this rumor, he found that the concept of "red mercury," while surprisingly common "knowledge" among the Arabic speakers he knows, is unknown to Western tourists and archaeologists alike (Hawass 2001a).

Nor are Westerners the only ones to harbor myths of buried treasure on the Giza Plateau. In the Middle Ages, books were published in Arabic for treasure hunters which gave explicit instructions for how timely fumigations and magic incantations would reveal the secret caches of ancient treasure (see Chapter 2). And the early Islamic conquerors, impressed by the colossal statues and temples, but unable to make any sense of the hieroglyphic inscriptions they found, believed that Egypt had been occupied by a long-dead race of giants and magicians—not so far from Western beliefs in aliens or Atlanteans. The myth about red mercury that Hawass connects with Lucas's excavations in Saqqara and the Luxor Museum can actually be traced much further back: the eighth/ninth-century alchemist Jābir ibn Hayyān wrote that "the most precious elixirs to ever have been blended on earth were hidden in the pyramids" (Haarmann 1996:610).

One key difference between Arabs and Westerners who have mystical imaginations of Egypt is that the Westerners tend to be far less informed about modern Egypt. For them, Egypt is an ancient and "antique land," to quote Shelley. After meeting Felipe, with his belief about Atlantis and Lemuria and aliens, my Egyptian friend Mohamed Nasr observed that the single most fascinating aspect of Felipe was that his detailed and profound knowledge of a mystical Egyptian history was coupled with a complete lack of knowledge about the modern Middle East—politically, culturally, historically. This is one explanation for why these alternative imaginations of ancient Egypt can work so powerfully: because Egypt provides a blank slate for projecting ideas unencumbered by knowledge of actual history.[43]

The roots of the European imagination of Egypt go back very far indeed. This is as true for the mystical imagination of ancient Egypt as it is for the Egyptological one. Strange parallels thus emerge between orthodox Egyptology and alternative beliefs about ancient Egypt: just as the Egyptological imagination of Egypt was jump-started by French imperialism, but has its roots in a much earlier Greek and Roman fascination with Egyptian pharaonic monuments and temples, so too does the modern New Age imagination of Egypt trace its own heritage back to Napoleon's expedition, but it is more deeply rooted in a Greek tradition (also born of colonial encounters) of appropriating Egyptian religion: the magical wisdom of Hermes-Thoth.

In tracing back the roots of these societies and organizations and their beliefs, it is important to distinguish between the legendary pedigrees that they create for themselves (the Freemasons claim that their society goes back to Abraham and the ancient Egyptians; the Rosicrucians claim that theirs dates to the time of Pharaoh Thutmosis III in 1489 BCE) and the actual traceable histories of their organizations (which are not nearly as ancient). Yet the intellectual roots of these movements are indeed older than their organizational genesis: the Rosicrucian Enlightenment (as Yates calls it) was rooted in a Hermetic-Cabbalist tradition of the late Renaissance inspired by the Hermetica, a body of syncretistic Greek-Egyptian philosophical, alchemical, astrological, and magical texts that were a product of the Greek colonization of Egypt. And the idea of Atlantis comes from Plato, who in turn seems to have been inspired by reading Herodotus's account of Solon's visit to Egypt.

It is not so very strange, after all, to find links and parallels between orthodox Egyptology and various New Age movements. It only seems so from the perspective of today, when there is a carefully guarded disciplinary fence between Egyptology and alternative theorists of ancient Egypt. But perhaps that explains *why* that fence is so carefully guarded: Egyptology has spent decades trying to *discipline* itself into a rigorously scientific enterprise and distance itself from its speculative, myth-making, swashbuckling, treasure-hunting origins.[44] On several levels, New Agers and alternative theorists are the living incarnation of the skeletons in the historical closet of Egyptology.

It is because of these historical links that orthodox Egyptology and alternative theorists remain dialectically bound together, despite all their differences. Refutations of the pyramid inch, Pyramidology, and other such theories became—and remain—defining moments in the development of the profession of Egyptology. And for all that the alternative theorists of ancient Egypt complain that Egyptologists are too exclusive, too closed-minded, and too quick to dismiss any idea that does not conform with the narrowly defined parameters of their profession, these alternative theorists also remain fascinated by the science of Egyptology and keep a close eye on the discoveries and theoretical developments in the field. Neither Egyptology nor the New Age can quite shake the other.

Science is a knowledge system that defines itself as neutral, objective, and rational.[45] Science and technology studies (STS) is a relatively new and interdisciplinary field that was launched when philosophers of science such as Kuhn (1962) and Feyerabend (1975) challenged the premise that science was a progressive movement toward the objective and rational description of physical reality, by showing how science resists changes to the status quo, regardless of whether or not the proposed changes are improvements on current authoritative theories.[46] STS theorists have subsequently gone on to examine the cultural and social specificity of any description of the physical world. Variations entail not only how different disciplinary fields and world cultures construct that world but also physical sites where knowledge is constructed and authorized, including the laboratory (e.g., Knorr Cetina 1995, Traweek 1988), the medical textbook (Martin 1987), museums (Bennett 1988, Haraway 1994, Castañeda

1996, Silverman 2004), and the archaeological field site (Abu El-Haj 2001, Silberman 1989, Castañeda 1996, Meskell 2001, Hodder 2003), as well as less physically bounded ways in which knowledge is constructed, such as through the negotiations between scientists over how to interpret an experiment result (e.g., Lynch 1985), or in literary techniques adopted by scientists in their writing (e.g., Knorr Cetina 1995; Silberman 1995).

The STS approach demonstrates that scientists define their work as neutral, objective, and rational in order to shore up their own authority.[47] In examining the conflict between West and Schoch and orthodox Egyptologists such as Mark Lehner and Zahi Hawass over dating the Sphinx, we see a constant battle over methodologies, but the real battle is over authority and who has the right to date the Sphinx. The study of scientific controversies has become a method for understanding the way scientific knowledge is socially constructed. "During controversies, knowledge is deconstructed by practitioners themselves, and, as it comes apart, analysts can examine the functioning of the standards that are normally thought to hold it together and the contextual influences that inform the opponents and their work" (Knorr Cetina 1995:163). In Egypt, we see how Western tourism is implicated in these debates. As we saw above, Egyptologists engaged with the New Agers' theories after West and Schoch managed to air a special program on their dating of the Sphinx on television to an audience of millions of viewers. This and subsequent battles over who would investigate and publicize the secret "door" in the Great Pyramid shows that Hawass (in particular), other Egyptian Egyptologists, and the Egyptian government are aware of the potential market value of their research, given ancient Egypt's incredible draw to tourists, and they decided to compete in that market.

Critics tend to reduce STS theorists' arguments to the position that, since all science is social construction, there is therefore no reality at all. They also portray it as a nihilist trend in scholarship, as though it implies that all scientists must accept the hopelessness of objectivity, rationality, science, and truth. (Both sides would do well to remember Geertz's medical analogy regarding postmodern deconstructions of science, when he dryly observes that just because it is impossible to achieve a completely antiseptic hospital environment doesn't mean that physicians will decide to relocate their surgery theaters to the sewer [Geertz 1973:30].)

There are obvious parallels between these "science wars" and the challenge posed by Edward Said to Orientalist scholarship (1978). Said, following Foucault, argues that there is no "pure" knowledge about the Orient, but all is grounded in specific historical and political relations of power. Said's influence throughout the social sciences has been profound, and has created a deep schism in some Near Eastern Studies departments. Said's adherents sometimes portray modern-day Orientalists as reactionary traditionalists. But these "traditionalists" have a complaint about the new trend: namely, that it privileges a political argument or position over a scholarly one, and thus threatens to authorize a generation of scholars whose work is not rigorously grounded in knowledge of historical sources and languages. In short, some worry that when objectivity is put into question, then the goal of objectivity will be abandoned, and with it, rigorous intellectual standards.

The criticism is one that has to be taken seriously in science studies, particularly when non-scientists are studying fields that they may or (more often) may not know as well as the scientists they are studying, and publishing for an audience that largely does *not* know the scientific field about which they write. Alan Sokal raised the issue in a particularly poignant way when he wrote a parodic deconstruction of the social construction of quantum physics ("Transgressing the Boundaries: Toward a Transformative Hermeneutics of Quantum Gravity") and submitted it to the journal *Social Text* (Sokal 1996a). Sokal describes his own submission thus: "Nowhere in all of this is there anything resembling a logical sequence of thought; one finds only citations of authority, plays on words, strained analogies, and bald assertions" (Sokal 1996b:63). The article was published, and Sokal gleefully followed up in the journal *Lingua Franca* with a deconstruction of his own piece (Sokal 1996b), as well as the journal's decision to publish it, apparently without a fact check.

Sokal went on to conclude, in his follow-up article about the event, that it proved that "the problem with such doctrines [i.e., "subjectivist thinking"] is that they are false. . . . There *is* a real world; its properties are *not* merely social constructions; facts and evidence *do* matter" (ibid.:63, emphasis in original). Yet this is a serious misreading of the field of science studies. Few authors claim that there is no real world and that facts and evidence do not matter. But while a physical object may really exist, the vocabulary in which it is described is a social construction, and the scientists who describe it do so on the basis of the authority of their degrees, their universities, and their departments, all of which are part of a social world (Knorr Cetina 1995:161).

But the publication of Sokal's parody piece raised other serious issues about the credentials of authors, publishers, and audiences of science studies. Why, indeed, did the editors of *Social Text* publish Sokal's piece? Obfuscating jargon and citations of authority aside,[48] it seems clear that the editors did not have enough knowledge of quantum physics to be able to spot the parts of his article that were obviously (to a physicist) bogus, and yet the deconstructivist nature of the article was so foreign to the world of physicists that the *Social Text* editors surely doubted they would be able to send Sokal's article to a traditional physicist for review and then effectively evaluate that physicist's response.

The point has relevance for this chapter: having confessed my own lack of Egyptological and geology credentials, I have to rely on the accounts of other authorities, and in the absence of agreement between these authorities, how am I to decide which account of the history of the Giza Plateau is the most valid? I lack the credentials to make that decision. Further, lacking the sufficient knowledge to make an "objective" decision about dating the monuments, there are several personal motivations that might influence my decision: I am an anthropologist, so I identify with archaeologists, who usually are considered part of the same discipline as myself (even though I do not come from a four-field anthropology department),[49] and I spent nearly a year in the company of the Egyptologists who were my informants and who were some of the kindest people I worked with in Egypt and extraordinarily generous with their time and knowledge. On the other hand, my father is a geophysicist, which might incline me toward siding with geologist Schoch, who proposes a dating of the pyramids that challenges the Egyptological one; and what's more, I am Mormon, and Joseph Smith published an interpretation of some Egyptian papyri that he purchased back in the 1800s that is dismissed by Egyptologists,[50] so I might have another personal incentive for proving that Egyptologists don't really know as much as they think they know.

And yet my refusal to take sides in the debates I describe is sure to rankle other readers, from traditionalists who believe that there is an objective account of ancient (and modern) Egypt to which we should at least aspire, to Egyptologists who might feel that by not summarily dismissing the alternative theorists, I am thereby validating them and attacking Egyptologists. But "taking sides" in the debates between New Agers and Egyptologists would not only be a strikingly unoriginal approach (since most accounts of the conflict between Egyptologists and alternative theorists take one side or the other), and possibly impossible (given the personal reasons why I might not be able to objectively take sides)—it is also irrelevant to the task at hand. My goal here is not to resolve the conflict between New Age and orthodox Egyptology perspectives on ancient Egypt by explaining to the gentle reader that the Egyptologists' account of Egyptian history is more valid and compelling. Nor is the point to resolve which approach is "science" and which is not. I set aside my opinions on the validity of the New Age and Egyptological theories on the dating of the Giza monuments not only because of my lack of qualifications but also because ultimately I am more interested in using this conflict to understand something about the way science (Egyptology) works, how scientists establish their authority, and how the social, political, cultural, and historical contexts in which scientists work shape that work and the theories they produce. (On the other hand, while I do not offer a position on which approach is more *valid*,

I do argue that each is, in fact, equally *compelling* in its own way.) By looking at Egyptology and its relationship to alternative ("New Age," by some people's terminology) accounts of ancient Egypt, we can shed light on the relationship between history and politics and the construction of a field of knowledge, and the relationship, in turn, between that history and each field's accounts of the past.

The struggle for authority that we see at work in contemporary Egyptology is not just limited to a scientific or academic arena, nor even to the money-making enterprises of tourism and television documentaries. In Egypt, this scientific boundary work (Gieryn 1983) is at one and the same time a struggle over academic authority—with all that that entails in terms of funding, administrative support, tenure, personal fame, and power—and also a struggle over broader historical and cultural forces of the sort that nationalism is. And just as Egyptology is politicized as a result of its historical linkage with imperialism, so too are the alternative theorists of ancient Egypt. With their search for fantastic new archaeological discoveries ("the supreme archaeological prize," as Bauval phrases it) that will force historians to rethink their theories about the development of civilization, and with their occasional disdain for government protocols for announcing discoveries and publicizing their research, both scientists *and* alternative theorists reproduce the language and methods of the nineteenth century adventurers and treasure hunters who were the fore-runners of contemporary Egyptology.

But while Egyptology has been able to mostly shake off the taint of its imperialist past and integrate itself with current Egyptian nationalist policies, alternative theorists of ancient Egypt continue to be a thorn in the side of Egyptian nationalists. A powerful strain in Egyptian nationalist thought posits the civilizational uniqueness of Egypt, distinct from all its Arab and African neighbors by virtue of its heritage in the great pharaonic nation-state of old. But one thing that almost all of the alternative theorists have in common is that they challenge that Egyptian claim to greatness in various ways. Despite the vast differences in their theories of Egyptian history—whether it is von Däniken with his theory of laser-wielding extraterrestrial astronauts or Hancock with his theory of some ancient (possibly, but not necessarily, Atlantean) super-culture spreading out over the Americas and Asia—what all these theorists have in common is that they locate the genius that built the pyramids outside of the niche of a scientifically established and state-approved pharaonic dynastic history. It doesn't matter if these alternative theorists also argue that these ancient people were far more spiritually, intellectually, and scientifically advanced than Egyptology gives them credit for. What matters is that they aren't treated as ancient *Egyptians.*

ARAB IMAGINATIONS OF ANCIENT EGYPT

Western tourists are not alone in engaging with a view of Egypt that focuses on its ancient, pharaonic past. Arabs, too, have mystical imaginations of pharaonic Egypt. The obvious contemporary example is the mythical "red mercury." Seeing the Saudi prince and Felipe visit Zahi Hawass's offices on the same day was a reminder to me that both Arabs and Westerners engage with mystical imaginations about ancient Egypt. However, interest in ancient Egypt is much more prevalent among Westerners, to the extent that the ancient Egyptian monuments are considered to be the primary draw for Western tourists. This is not so for Arab tourism in Egypt. Why?

The reason, I argue, is that Western tourism in Egypt today is the legacy of European colonialism. It directs tourists toward a vision of Egypt as an ancient pharaonic land, scattered with the remains of antiquity, monuments to gods and to the dead. The pharaonic age produced some of the greatest art of human history and erected monuments that defy even modern technology's skills. The pyramids and the Sphinx and the splendors of Luxor are what an official in the Egyptian Tourism Development Authority calls "absolute merit"—intrinsic tourist draws that will always be attractions, regardless of the country's overall progress in tourism development.[51] Perhaps it seems self-evident, to both Westerners and Egyptians, that tourists should come to visit Egypt to see pharaonic monuments.

But, as we will see in Chapters 4 and 5, contemporary Arab tourism in Egypt is not primarily a monuments-oriented tourism. Egyptian antiquities inspectors say that (non-Egyptian) Arabs are the fewest in number of the visitors to the pyramids, and a former director of the Cairo Museum says that the same is true of nationalities visiting the museum.[52] When we compare the different goals of Arab and Western tourism in Egypt, it suddenly becomes apparent that the pharaonic monuments of old are not the only intrinsic touristic treasures of Egypt. Their value is itself a product of a long chronicle whereby historical circumstances—politics, war, occupation, colonialism, economic exchanges, culture, and philosophy—shaped one people's imagination of another in very specific ways. The legacy of Western colonialism in the Middle East continues to resonate in the contemporary politics of archaeology and patterns of tourism in Egypt today.

▲ ▲ ▲ ▲ ▲ ▲ ▲ ▲ ▲ ▲ ▲ ▲ ▲ ▲ ▲ ▲ ▲ ▲ ▲ ▲

CHAPTER 4

SEX ORGIES, A MARAUDING PRINCE, AND OTHER RUMORS ABOUT GULF TOURISM

The third summer I was in Egypt, I moved from my shabby apartment in al-Mounira, near downtown Cairo, to a smaller (but blissfully air-conditioned) flat in Mohandiseen, an upscale Cairo suburb full of shops, restaurants, and fast-food joints. One morning shortly after I had moved in, I was at home writing fieldnotes on my laptop when I heard the sound of music from outside. I went over to the bedroom and opened the wooden shutters onto the small balcony. In the street below, facing the building opposite mine, were a group of three men and a little girl, about eight years old, dressed in a frilly white dress. Two of the men were playing instruments: one had a *kamanga,* a kind of violin, and the other was beating on a *tabla,* a drum. The little girl was belly dancing with a skill beyond her years. The third man held a tambourine in his right hand, which he shook from time to time, and in his left hand he was waving around a long green garden snake which swung back and forth stiffly, petrified with fright.

They played their music, danced, and waved their snake for a few moments; then they stopped playing and the man holding the snake called out, "Saudi Arabia! Kuwait! The Arabian Gulf!" The violin played a few more bars. Someone came to the window and looked out. The little band struck up and the girl resumed her dancing. The man in the window lit a cigarette and leaned on the windowsill, watching. After a few moments they stopped the music and the snake holder called out, "Riyadh! Kuwait City! The Emirates!"

The man in the window said, with some disdain, "Oman."

The snake holder cried out with new enthusiasm, "Oman! Muscat! The Arabian Sea!" He shook the tambourine for emphasis. "Oman! *Ahsan nās*—the best people!"

Figure 4.1. A 1930s snake charmer in Luxor. Photographer unknown; collection of L. L. Wynn.

The man in the apartment walked away from the window. The musicians stood in the street, shuffling their feet. I watched, wondering what they would do next. A few minutes later the man reappeared at the window of the apartment. He dangled a couple of Egyptian five-pound notes tantalizingly. The men waited expectantly, and then the man in the apartment gestured his head in the direction of the little girl. Quickly the musicians started to play, and the girl started dancing again. After a few moments, the Omani man threw down the bills onto the street. The musicians stopped playing, and the leader, still holding the now-limp snake, transferred the tambourine to the crook of his left arm and bent down to pick up the money with his right. Putting it in his pocket, he shouted out a final salute: "Our brothers from Oman!" The troupe turned and moved on down the street, the drummer beating a light rhythm as they walked. The violin player glanced up at me, watching from my balcony, and for a minute I wondered if they would come over to do a performance and shout greetings to the foreigner, hoping for another tip, but they just walked away, heading for the next building.

This scene was repeated numerous times over the course of the summer, and the "snake charmers," as I liked to ironically think of them (since their snakes seemed far from charmed), always performed under the same windows in the same buildings—"furnished flats" that were known in the neighborhood to be rented out to vacationing Arabs. They shouted out their *taḥīyyāt,* or salutations, performed a little song and dance, and hoped that someone would throw money down at them.

I came to expect to hear the musicians play in the street every morning, just as every night the *rabāb* seller would walk up and down the street, playing a sweet tune on his brightly colored plastic stringed instrument, a couple dozen other *rabāb*s tied together and slung over his shoulder to sell to Arab children on holiday. In other parts of Mohandiseen where there was heavy automobile traffic, beggars would wander through cars stopped at an intersection, calling out *"yā rabb"*—"O Lord"—to ask for alms; one particularly clever man would pose by the side of the road next to a spilled tray of eggs, striking his brow for hours with an expression of dismay on his face, as if he'd just lost his life's work. Local residents had seen him at it a hundred times before, but his target was outsiders: sympathetic Arab tourists who would give him money to replace his smashed eggs.

The arrival of the summer Arab tourism season transforms the urban landscape of Cairo. Starting in June, Arab tourists from the Gulf states pour into Cairo for their summer vacation. Some own apartments in Cairo; many rent rooms in hotels at extended-stay rates, while others rent furnished flats for weeks or even months.

In the 1970s and 1980s, during the height of the oil boom which brought newly wealthy Gulf Arab tourists to Cairo in droves, their favorite place to reside and hang out was said to be Pyramids Road, a long street leading to the pyramids and lined with cabarets and nightclubs. But in 1986, a mob of Egyptians set fire to several of the nightclubs (see van Nieuwkerk 1995), and between that and the simultaneous downturn of the oil economy, the area had never quite recovered. At the turn of the millennium, even though Pyramids Road was still popularly associated with Arab tourism for many Egyptians,

Figure 4.2. El Leil, a nightclub on Pyramids Road. Photograph by Mahmoud Abbas Elbadawi.

previously luxurious nightspots, appointed with mirrors, plush carpeting, and all the accoutrements of 1970s disco décor, now looked seedy and run-down, and by 4:00 A.M. were only a quarter full most nights. During the 1990s, the center of Gulf tourism seemed to be moving toward the center of Cairo, to the five-star hotels around Tahrir Square, Garden City, and Doqqi, and to the Marriott on the island of Zamalek in the middle of the Nile.

By the end of the 1990s, when I was conducting my fieldwork, Mohandiseen had become the part of town most famous for Gulf Arabs to rent flats in, and the streets of Mohandiseen were a locus of nighttime social life for Arab tourists. The appropriately named Arab League Street (*Game'at al-Dawal al-'Arabīyya*) was a central hangout. An eight-lane road divided by a wide swath of benched plazas and greenery, it was lined with shops, cafés, and virtually every international fast-food chain restaurant: McDonald's, Hardee's, Bob's Big Boy, Subway, Baskin-Robbins, Wimpy, Pizza Hut, Kentucky Fried Chicken, House of Donuts, A&W, and Taco Bell (but with no beans in any of the dishes, since beans were considered too déclassé for an upscale chain restaurant). Egyptian as well as Gulf Arab couples would stroll along the wide sidewalks, gazing at the shops of clothing, shoes, electronics, perfume, and gold; street vendors sold cheap watches, sunglasses, and children's toys. On summer nights, on the island in the middle of the street, there would be donkey rides for little kids and not-so-little kids, and Arab youth would throw firecrackers onto the ground and at each other, making incessant popping sounds that lasted all night long. By day, peddlers would roam the streets selling toy stringed musical instruments and flutes, cotton candy, and *libb*, bags of roasted seeds and nuts.

By the middle of September the tourists would leave. The musicians stopped playing under people's windows, the egg-spilling beggar disappeared, and the *rabāb* seller would only pass through every couple of weeks instead of nightly. Nine months later, the same characters would reappear on the scene.

I quickly learned that the arrival of Gulf tourists in the summer changes not only the visual but also the moral landscape of Cairo. During the summer I often got warnings from friends, couched as brotherly or sisterly advice, not to be out late on the street, "because the Arabs are here." The warnings didn't seem to indicate that they thought I'd be assaulted by an Arab—it was more a question of the possibility of harassment, or general concern for my respectability, since any woman hanging out late at night in a place full of Arabs might be thought a prostitute.

This association between Gulf tourists and illicit sex was explicitly stated again and again during the course of my research. One officer in the tourism

Figure 4.3. Street vendors on Arab League Street in Mohandiseen. Photograph by Mahmoud Abbas Elbadawi.

police stated, matter-of-factly, "Look, Gulf Arabs come here for sex. As for their women, they come to get away from cultural traditions in their own country—so that they can wear normal clothes for a change." And one assistant manager at a five-star hotel who fancied himself a bit of a Don Juan insisted that all Gulf Arabs came to Egypt for sex and to drink alcohol—and even went so far as to claim that Gulf women constantly tried to seduce the men who worked at the front desk (including, of course, himself), calling down and inviting the men up to their rooms. Three hotel managers (out of four interviewed) asserted, without my prompting, that Gulf men brought prostitutes back to their rooms in the hotel, and this caused problems because the prostitutes would often steal from them, and the men would then complain to the hotel that a member of the cleaning staff had stolen from them.

"The single men don't usually report the theft, because they know it's their fault for having brought such a woman up to their room; but the married ones report this because then, when their wife asks, 'Where is your watch?' they can claim that it was stolen and say that they reported it to the hotel." [Fieldnotes, 18 August 1999]

The assumption of a link between Gulf tourists and prostitution was also widespread among those who were not directly working in the tourism industry. In a disco, if an Egyptian woman danced in the *khalīgī*, or Gulf, style, my middle-class Egyptian friends would immediately brand her a "prostitute," since, they said, she must have learned how to dance that way by dancing for Gulf Arab men. (They apparently never considered the notion that she might have learned the dance from Saudi female friends.) And one professional belly dancer told me that, as far as she was concerned, any dancer who dated Arabs must be a prostitute.[1]

There was a clear assumption that Gulf men were predatory, especially with Egyptian women. A Mohandiseen resident said to me,

"You know, they are very destructive to our country. They come here to do things they can't do in their own country. You see, Americans and Europeans can do whatever they want, they can drink or take drugs if they want, they can have relationships with women before marriage, so they don't feel that they have to go to extremes; it's nearly the same in Egypt, there is everything and you can lead whatever kind of life you want. But in Saudi Arabia, there is nothing, so they go crazy when they get out of there. They come here to do all the things they can't find there—drinking, drugs, women, nightclubs, etc. And they destroy our country. Why? Because they have fun here, with Egyptian women, and then they safely go back to their own countries. But what about the woman? She might end up pregnant. And then what? Her life is destroyed. What is she going to do? He has gone back to his own country, and she's the one who has to deal with the consequences." [Fieldnotes, 9 August 1999]

Another time I was discussing my research with an Egyptian friend who was a middle-class medical student. He warned me against interviewing any Arab men for my research, implying that they would harass me. I told him that I thought Gulf Arabs were very polite compared to Egyptians, because they never bothered me or said a word to me on the street, unlike Egyptian men, who called out flirtatious or rude remarks all the time. He looked at me with some disbelief and scoffed,

"I don't know where you get these ideas about [Gulf] Arabs. They are *not* nice, they are *not* polite. They are just jerks who come here to chase after women. Maybe they don't talk to *you* because they don't know how to talk to normal women. They just know how to talk to prostitutes on the street. They come here to Egypt to *see* women, since they can't see them in their own countries. And the more ambitious ones come here to *talk* to women. More ambitious than that, they come here to *sleep* with women! They come here to do things they can't do in their own country." [Fieldnotes, 6 August 1999]

In the beginning of my research, I racked my brain for how I was going to be able to ascertain or disprove these rumors about the correlation between Arab tourism and vice. It was not the kind of subject matter that easily lent itself to scientific study, particularly given the strictures of my research permission. I was not permitted to administer any sort of quantitative survey, and even if I were, I could hardly ask respondents, "Do you frequent prostitutes in Egypt?" and expect a candid answer. Asking too much about such a sensitive issue meant risking losing my research permission, and yet, given the regularity with which the topic was spontaneously brought up by my informants, I could hardly ignore it.

A methodological turning point came for me one day when I interviewed two hotel managers from different hotels about the differences between Western and Arab tourism. Saad told me,

"Arab mentalities are not business-oriented—they primarily want to have fun. When a Western tourist wakes up in the morning, he thinks about the plan for the day, what to do, what needs to be accomplished. When an Arab tourist wakes up in the morning, he just thinks: one, 'How will I drink that day?' two,

'How will I get a girl?' and three, 'How will I sleep with her?'" [Fieldnotes, 24 August 1999]

I was fascinated by the way Saad implicitly claimed to be able to read the minds of tourists. Shortly afterward, I interviewed a manager from another five-star hotel who made some fairly fantastic claims about Gulf women indulging in wild lesbian orgies. "There is a recent fashion of lesbianism among Gulf girls, just in the past three or four years. The girls dress up, go out, drink, smoke hash, and then they come home and sleep together with other girls." I asked him how he knew this. "I see them!" he exclaimed. "Room service sees them!"

I thought this was an interesting claim, since it was unlikely that he, as the manager of the hotel, was personally delivering room-service meals. It also seemed unlikely that the hotel staff was catching girls in bed engaged in lesbian acts, since they wouldn't enter a room without knocking first, and presumably even if the women *were* having wild sex parties, they would not be engaged in sex acts while answering the door of their hotel room. So I started to ask myself: where do these rumors come from? Who develops these fantastic imaginations of the illicit activities that Arabs are engaged in? And how are such stories spread?

I came to realize that I did not need to develop and administer some sort of quantitative survey that would reveal the actual activities that Gulf Arab tourists engaged in and break them down according to percentage of tourists who engaged in each act, thereby proving or disproving Egyptian stereotypes about the association between Gulf tourists and prostitution. Rumors, gossip, and urban myths do not have to be proved or disproved to qualify as *social facts*. It may be true that some Gulf Arabs come to Egypt for sex, drinking, and other activities prohibited in their own countries—though it is also certainly true that many do *not* come to Egypt for such purposes. But their actual activities are almost beside the point, since the vast majority of Egyptians who talk about Arabs coming to Egypt for sex and prostitution have not actually *seen* any proof of this themselves. So the question then becomes: in the absence of proof or even evidence that this is what Arabs come to Egypt for, why do these rumors circulate and why are they so widely believed?

In this chapter, then, I want to trace some of the Egyptian imaginations of the Gulf Arab tourist and analyze how these images are transmitted. I then relate these imaginations of Gulf Arabs to broader sociocultural, historical, political, and economic processes that inform the relationships between nationalities in the region, and then I revisit the ideology of Egyptian pharaonic nationalism which figured so prominently in the discussion of the history of Western tourism in Egypt (Chapter 2).

REGIONAL HISTORY LESSONS:
CIVILIZATION, TRAVEL, AND PILGRIMAGE

Before launching into a description of Arab tourism in Egypt, I want to briefly sketch out a "civilizational" history of the Middle East, since, as we will see, the notion of civilization figures prominently in Egyptian portrayals of Arab tourists, and cannot merely be reduced to an imagination of Egyptian national history and identity as pharaonic. Just as European imperialism in Egypt shaped Western imaginations of Egypt as well as the way Egypt presents itself for Western tourist consumption, so does regional Middle East history play into contemporary patterns of Gulf Arab tourism in Egypt. The late-twentieth-century boom in regional Arab tourism can be seen as a distinct contemporary variation on patterns of transnationalism that have characterized the region for centuries, from military conquest to trade to religious pilgrimage.

Pharaonic Egypt is certainly one of the most world-famous ancient civilizations, but the Middle East is known for a number of other great monument-building empires, from Assyria to Babylonia to Sumer. Like pharaonic Egypt, these civilizations developed along fertile river valleys and were initially excavated by Europeans who have long mythologized this part of the world as the "cradle of [Western] civilization." Other Middle East empires and city-states that we have archaeological records for include Najran in what is now Yemen, Palmyra in Syria, and the Nabatean civilization, whose city of Petra in Jordan is well known. It is less known that the Nabateans left another city of carved tombs at Madā'in Sāleh in northwest Saudi Arabia that is very similar to Jordan's Petra. And in southern Arabia, the kingdom of Saba (which is referred to in the biblical story of Solomon and the Queen of Sheba) also had a powerful empire, exporting frankincense, trading in the Indian Ocean, and colonizing parts of East Africa.

Egypt was a Christian country under fragmented Byzantine rule when it was conquered by 'Amr ibn al-'Ās, general for the Caliph Omar. The Muslim conquerors crossed the Sinai and entered Egypt via Gaza, and in 639–641 CE, Egypt was taken with a force of some four thousand cavalry. By 710 Arabic was the language of administration of the government, but conversion to Islam proceeded somewhat more slowly: in 725 CE, 98 percent of the country's population was still Christian.[2] Arab tribespeople settled in the eastern Delta and subsequent governors of Egypt brought their own armies, which settled in Egypt, intermarried, and acquired land. Thus Arab colonization of Egypt and intermarriage played a role in conversion, but increasing religious discrimination and tax burdens on non-Muslims also upped the pressure on Egyptians to convert, so that by 1300, according to Egypt historian Vatikiotis, "Egypt had become the strongest centre of Islamic power and civilization."[3] From the ninth through the nineteenth centuries, the country was controlled by Muslim rulers from a succession of foreign dynasties: the Baghdad Caliphate, a series of Turkish rulers, the Fatimids, the Ayyubids of Saladin (Salah al-Din al-Ayyubi, a Kurd), the Mamluks, and, eventually, the Ottoman Empire.

Napoleon invaded in 1798, taking advantage of the weakness of the Ottoman and Mamluk rulers of Egypt. Though the conquest was short-lived, it brought significant, long-term changes to Egypt: first, it discredited the Mamluk leaders; second, although Egypt long remained a nominal outpost of the Ottoman empire, the European conquest helped to sever Egypt from Ottoman rule, a trend which was solidified by Muhammad Ali's savvy political maneuvering; and third, it marked a new era of increasing European influence, and later control, over the government in Egypt (see Chapter 2).

After the French were expelled by the British in 1801, Muhammad Ali, an Albanian Ottoman, soon emerged as the exceptionally strong ruler of Egypt. Muhammad Ali broke Mamluk power in Egypt and eventually negotiated significant autonomy from the Ottoman Empire. Within Egypt, he developed agriculture, irrigation, and a large number of public works and factories, relying on European advice and technology and installing European advisors in his government. He modernized the army and introduced state education. Most historians of Egypt regard the French invasion and subsequent rule of Muhammad Ali as marking the beginning of the modern period in Egypt, largely because of Muhammad Ali's extensive program of reforms for the country, consolidation of centralized state power, the nascent emergence of a national Egyptian identity independent from the Ottoman Empire, and incorporation into a larger world system, beginning with the increased interaction with European state powers.[4]

Meanwhile, in the late eighteenth century, a new power was rising in the central Arabian peninsula. A tribal ruler from the province of Nejd by the name of Muhammad ibn Saud, allied with a religious reformer by the name of Muhammad ibn Abd al-Wahhab (whence "Wahhabism," the name often applied to the reforming Saudi approach to Sunni Islam), embarked on a campaign of conquest and religious purging of what they considered idolatrous saint worship. Ibn Saud conquered Nejd, Hasa, and Najran, key provinces of central, western, and southern Arabia, before marching on Makkah and Madinah in 1803. His Bedouin warriors, the *ikhwān*, destroyed monuments and graves which had been sites of pilgrimage and prayer (Shiite shrines and practices were a particular target of their Sunni reform), imitating the prophet Muhammad's destruction of idol worship in Makkah in 628. By 1804 ibn Saud controlled the Hijaz, the Western strip of the Arabian peninsula containing the two holy cities. The forces of ibn Saud then proceeded to invade Iraq and Syria.

These military conquests posed a serious threat to the Ottoman Empire, but Istanbul was not in a position to militarily engage this unexpectedly powerful Bedouin tribal leader, so it tasked Muhammad Ali with sending Egyptian forces to drive out ibn Saud's forces and reclaim the Hijaz. Muhammad Ali recaptured lands in the Arabian peninsula between 1811 and 1823, increasing his own authority in the Muslim world vis-à-vis central Ottoman rule. Subsequently he set out on a series of military conquests of his own: in 1820 he set out to conquer the Sudan (he was later driven out by the British), and by 1833 he controlled Syria and Palestine as well, had installed his relatives as rulers of the newly conquered lands, and was effectively independent of the Ottoman Empire, though nominally a subject of it.

Muhammad Ali was on the verge of completely breaking the Ottoman Empire's power when France and England intervened to maintain the status quo and reinstate Ottoman rule. In 1841 Muhammad Ali was forced out of the Levant by the Europeans, but in exchange was named Viceroy of Egypt and secured the right of hereditary rule for his descendents. Egypt remained an autonomous province of the Ottoman Empire until World War I, ruled by pashas, khedives, sultans, and kings of Muhammad Ali's lineage (they were, however, only nominal figureheads during the years of British occupation of Egypt) until the mid-twentieth century, when the 1952 Revolution expelled the British and ended the monarchy in Egypt.

After the Saudi-Wahhabi alliance and their followers were defeated in the early nineteenth century, the Arabian peninsula territories reverted to Ottoman rule, with the exception of the Nejd, which remained independent. Most of the peninsula was sparsely inhabited by Bedouin tribes, with the exception of the merchant classes in the coastal towns and agriculturalists in the western and southern highlands. At the beginning of the twentieth century, Emir Hussein of the Hashemite clan governed the holy cities of the Hijaz, but increasingly itched to be rid of Ottoman control. During WWI, the Hashemites sided with the Allies and led an Arab revolt against the Ottoman Empire, expelling the Turks from the Hijaz and conquering land in Palestine and the Levant. But when the Sykes-Picot Agreement (a treaty signed by France, Britain, and Russia in 1916) was drawn up, it divided the former Ottoman lands into spheres of European control, confining Hashemite rule to the Hijaz. The central Arabian desert was also left independent, though the small emirates to the east (the United Arab Emirates, Bahrain, Qatar, and Kuwait) and the larger southern countries of Oman and the Yemen all experienced various degrees of British intervention and rule in the years to come. In 1914, when the Ottoman Empire went to war against the Allies, Britain declared Egypt a British protectorate; in reality, it had been militarily occupied and its affairs largely controlled by the British since 1882. It remained under British control until 1956.

Meanwhile, in the heart of the Arabian Peninsula, a descendent of the original ibn Saud was setting out to reconquer land gained and lost a century previously. Abd al-Aziz ibn Abd al-Rahman al-Saud rallied together an army of Bedouin to conquer central and eastern provinces.[5] The outside world didn't pay much attention as long as he confined himself to the tribal desert lands. The Hashemites still ruled the Hijaz and Amir Hussein was styling himself the Caliph of Islam, as a descendent of the prophet Muhammad and ruler over the holy cities of Makkah and Madinah. But then, in his biggest conquest to date, Abd al-Aziz al-Saud marched on the Hijaz in 1924, toppling the Hashemite regime and consolidating power over the Arabian peninsula from the east to the west. After taking the Asir, the mountainous agricultural region between the Hijaz and Yemen, his territorial conquests ended, and the Kingdom of Saudi Arabia was established (perhaps better to say finalized) in 1932.

While Muslim lands were ruled from different centers throughout history, the symbolic center (if not the actual administrative center) of the Muslim world remained the Hijaz with its two holy cities of Makkah and Madinah. All Muslims pray toward Makkah and all those who are able are enjoined to undertake a pilgrimage to the city at least once in their lifetime. Rule over the Hijaz was symbolized by which ruler supplied the *kiswah*, the covering for the *ka'aba*, the shrine in the holy mosque of Makkah toward which all Muslims pray and around which the annual (and lesser) pilgrimage revolves.[6] It is replaced each year during Dhul-Hijjah, the lunar month when pilgrimage is undertaken. Thus Muhammad Ali Pasha of Egypt, in an act of independence and asserting his own regional authority, made supplying the *kiswah* the responsibility of Egypt after he seized the Hijaz from ibn Saud in the early 1800s, and the *kiswah* was brought by annual caravan from Cairo. And after Abd al-Aziz al-Saud conquered the Hijaz, he set up a factory in Makkah in 1926 to make the *kiswah*. Makkah and Madinah are not only symbolic centers of power in the Muslim world, but they also provided a source of income for their rulers in the form of tribute paid by pilgrims.[7]

At the time the modern Kingdom of Saudi Arabia was established, prior to the discovery of its vast oil reserves, the country was very poor and minimally governed. The internal economy centered on date farming in the oases and nomadic animal husbandry (goats and camels), and some small-scale agriculture in the Hijaz highlands and the southern province of Asir. Merchants practiced some trade in the eastern and western port cities, and there was pearl diving in the Arabian Gulf in the east. Aside from the tribute paid by pilgrims, virtually all of the country's economy revolved around these small industries.

The discovery of oil in Dhahran and elsewhere in the region changed all of that. By the 1950s oil was the main income source for Saudi Arabia and the other oil-rich states in the region, particularly Kuwait and Iraq. The discovery of oil wrought tremendous change on the cultures of these countries. Abdelrahman Munif's *Cities of Salt* trilogy presents a powerful analysis of this transformation in the guise of fiction; Munif also uses fiction to relate a thinly veiled history of Saudi Arabia's monarchy, particularly the excesses of King Saud bin Abd al-Aziz (son of the Kingdom's founder), which came to symbolize for many the pernicious effects of the sudden oil wealth on desert Bedouin who previously knew only poverty (but see Vitalis 2006).

Meanwhile, the same period saw great change taking place in Egypt's political system. In the 1950s and early 1960s, Egypt's charismatic leader Gamal Abd el-Nasser (usually referred to in English simply as Nasser) rose to regional power as the voice of Arab nationalism. He expelled the British and other foreigners from Egypt and seized their property; he nationalized the Suez Canal; his emotionally moving speeches were powerful rhetoric against both European imperialism and the Zionist colonization of the lands of Palestine.[8] After his defeat in the 1967 war with Israel, however, Arab nationalism was discredited and support for the ideology waned throughout the Arab world; Nasser died in 1970 of a heart attack.

Anwar al-Sadat, Nasser's successor, moved in the opposite direction, abandoning Nasser's Arab socialism and instituting economic reform termed *infitāh,* the "open door policy." A qualified success against Israel in the 1973 war brought Egypt renewed prestige in the Arab world. Egypt's military stretch was aided by the 1973 oil embargo, in which the oil-producing Arab countries cut production, raised prices, and refused to sell oil to the United States and European countries that supported Israel. However, Sadat later used his success in the 1973 war as leverage to make a deal with Israel whereby Egypt signed a peace treaty in exchange for Israel's return of the Sinai peninsula, captured by Israel in the 1967 war. Egypt was popularly scorned and politically and economically isolated by the rest of the Arab world, which expelled it from the Arab League for departing from the unified Arab front vis-à-vis the Zionist state. After Sadat's assassination by Islamic militants in 1981, Hosni Mubarak became president of Egypt, and Egypt was readmitted to the Arab League. In contrast to Nasser and Sadat with their politically charged regimes, Mubarak is often portrayed as the consummate bureaucrat and middle-grounder, continuing the cautious program of economic liberalization launched by his predecessor, formally committed to peace (albeit often a cold peace) with Israel, and allied with the United States. Mubarak has gradually attempted to rebuild Egypt's status as a political leader in the Arab world by acting as mediator in regional disputes and a promoter of the Arab-Israeli peace process.

The other transnational identity in the region that has competed with Arab nationalism is pan-Islamism. Revolutionary Iran has often been portrayed as its ideological center, but a pan-Islamic identity is also associated with Saudi Arabia, and particularly with Saudi King Faisal bin Abd al-Aziz, the second son of the founder of the Kingdom of Saudi Arabia to take the throne. After the reputedly decadent lifestyle of his elder brother, King Saud, had nearly bankrupted the country despite its tremendous increase in oil production, King Faisal, who was known for his personal asceticism, was widely admired throughout the Arab world for the role he played in standing up to the United States and Israel during the 1973 oil embargo (but Vitalis 2006 deconstructs the hagiography of Faisal). And it was under King Faisal that the country vastly expanded its resources for accommodating Muslim pilgrims to Makkah and subsidizing the Hajj. After Faisal's assassination at the hands of an unbalanced relative, the Kingdom was ruled until 1982 by King Khalid and then until August 2005 by King Fahd, who officially adopted the title "Custodian of the Two Holy Mosques" to emphasize the centrality of Islam in legitimizing the Saud family rule.

This brief historical and political sketch has focused largely on Egypt and Saudi Arabia to illustrate some of the contours of the rivalry between Egypt and its neighbor to the east. The attitudes of Egyptians toward Gulf Arab tourism and particularly Saudi tourists has been shaped by, and must be viewed in light of, this political history. Within the Arab world, Egypt's aspirations to political hegemony have met with varying levels of success, from Egypt's role as the center of Arab nationalism under Nasser to its isolation under Sadat, and it is in the political arena that its competition with Saudi Arabia is most apparent. However, Egypt's cultural influence in the Gulf and elsewhere in the Arab world is undisputed. Egypt has the best-known secular and religious universities in the Arab world (from Cairo University to al-Azhar). Egypt long has had the most widely read, viewed, and listened-to news media in the Arab world, although with the huge success of Qatar-based al-Jazeera and other satellite channels, that influence is waning.[9] Egypt still produces the most widely viewed movies and television serials in the Arab world, and despite individual successes from Iraq, Morocco, Algeria, Lebanon, Syria, and Saudi Arabia, Egyptian recording artists are more numerous and their fame the most widespread throughout the Arab world.

While the political history of the region is often portrayed as revolving around the Arab-Israeli conflict, it is at least as important (and for the purposes of understanding patterns of tourism, more important) to appreciate how the oil economy has transformed the region, politically, culturally, and economically. The oil economy has funded the export of political and religious ideologies from Saudi Arabia. It has brought hundreds of thousands of economic migrants from the Middle East, Asia, Europe, and the Americas to work in the Gulf countries (this phenomenon and its relationship to Arab tourism in Egypt is elaborated below). And it has funded leisure travel, as well, on a very large scale. The vast wealth it has brought to the region has funded transnational exchange on an unprecedented scale, but the highly uneven distribution of this wealth has also engendered tensions between nations and people.

The history of transnational exchange is nothing new to the region. Yet when authors writing on the region have made such a comment, it is often editorialized as a novel revelation. Perhaps because the trend in studying transnational movements of people and goods is a recent one associated with a critical turn in anthropology (whereby researchers have rejected the study of supposedly neat, self-contained societies and cultures to focus instead on the way societies are constantly being transformed and cultures re-created through forces of war, migration, trade, and other movements of peoples and goods), it is sometimes assumed that the phenomenon itself being studied is also a new one. Al-Rasheed's recent volume (2005) on transnationalism in the Arabian Gulf is a useful corrective to this assumption, and one which instantly rings true to students of Middle East history who know the region as one that has long been traversed by pilgrims and trade caravans and shaped by religious and military conquests.

Indeed, pilgrimage to Makkah was a powerful force for the transnational movements of people and goods, long before the age of the European world explorations and conquest. With the spread of Islam, pilgrimage motivated the travel of people from regions as far flung as Indonesia, China, and Western Africa to the Arabian peninsula. It spurred the permanent relocation of peoples and cultures, as some pilgrims ended up settling in Makkah, elsewhere in the Arabian peninsula, or other locations along the route of their travel. Both sea travelers and caravans of pilgrims moving over land combined religious duty with trade. Pilgrimage caravans came from Egypt, the Maghreb, Syria, the Sudan, and Persia. Aside from the effects on Egyptians traveling to Makkah, trade and pilgrimage caravans coming from West Africa also passed through Egypt en route.

Yet despite this long history of travel, trade, and pilgrimage, regional tourism and labor migration of the sort described in this chapter are directly related to the oil economy. While transnationalism, therefore, is not a new phenomenon in the region, the scale and the context in which it occurs are new. According to Cole and Altorki (1998:165), the first Arab tourists to come to Egypt on a large scale were Libyans in the 1960s, but worsening political relations between Egypt and Libya led to the closing of the border in the early 1970s. Increasing oil wealth and increasingly large disposable incomes in the Arabian peninsula countries led to the growth of Gulf Arab tourism, and many of these tourists flocked to Lebanon and Egypt in the hot summer months.[10] With the Lebanese civil war from the mid-1970s through the 1980s, tourists abandoned Beirut as a travel destination and Gulf tourism to Egypt, particularly Cairo, soared. Morocco is another popular destination, and since the Lebanese civil war ended, Gulf tourists have started to return to Beirut, and Egypt has seen a corresponding drop in its percentage share of Gulf tourism. The 1980s are widely considered the heyday of Gulf tourism in Cairo, but even as Gulf Arabs have started traveling further afield, to Europe and Asia and the United States (particularly California and Florida) for their holidays, they often pass through Egypt on their way to more exotic destinations.

How do the goals and interests of these Arab tourists compare to those of the Western tourists discussed in previous chapters?

ARAB TOURISM

With tourists as paradigmatic moderns, and modernity generally regarded as a Western phenomenon, sociologists tend to consider tourism an almost exclusively Western category (see Chapter 1). There is a lurking assumption that, while only non-Westerners are authentic *natives*, by the same token, the only authentic *tourist* is the Westerner.[11]

Yet Arab tourists are a powerful economic and social force in Egypt, and Arab tourism is primarily leisure tourism, not a matter of looking for work or visiting relatives. Arab tourists represent some 30 percent of all tourists in Egypt (with Gulf Arabs representing half of that figure); moreover, they stay longer and spend more money per day than their Western counterparts. And their presence in Egypt produces intense cultural debates. For example, during the summer, Egyptian theaters run lowbrow, ribald productions that are designed to cater to Gulf tastes and bring in major tourist dollars, and there are frequent complaints by theater critics that the Gulf influence is corrupting Egyptian culture and engendering a regional elaboration of Egyptian identity as vulgar and immoral.

In a regional context, Egypt is less the Land of the Pharaohs than it is the Land of Umm Kalthoum, Amrou Diyab, Adel Imam, and other famous singers, musicians, actors and actresses, dancers, and comedians. Egyptian films, television shows, and music are broadcast all over the region, and the Egyptian dialect of Arabic is the most widely understood colloquial dialect across the Middle East because of Egypt's hegemony over popular culture in the Arab world. Inas, a receptionist in a Mohandiseen hotel that catered to a largely Gulf clientele, explicitly cited the influence of Egyptian popular culture in drawing a Gulf tourist crowd:

"They come here regularly, year after year, because they have the most free-dom here in Egypt and in Lebanon. In the Gulf, they have more complexes than here—for example, the clothes that the woman wears. Here in Egypt, you wear what you want. Not like those black clothes that *their* women have to wear. And at the same time, for the men, they also can do what they want with absolute freedom. For example, an Arab in the Gulf, he looks around him and all he sees are all these women covered up. And he sees Egyptian television, all the women are uncovered, wearing nice makeup, wearing short skirts, jok-ing and laughing, there are dancers on TV, and I don't know what else, he says to himself, 'I wish I could live there among them for just a while!' [laughs] And when they see foreign films and they see the things they're wearing, they say to themselves, '*Yā salām* [my goodness]! Take me there for a while!' . . . The Egyp-tian videos, you look at anything by Mostafa Amar or Amrou Diyab or any of them, it's full of women wearing short skirts and dancing around—some Gulf man says to himself, 'Wow, I'm going to go to Egypt for a while and see these girls and take a break from the wife . . .' He comes to live his life here. Cairo is like America for them! Walking around gawking, staring at anybody they see . . . wearing sandals, *galabiyyas,* pajamas—they have no idea how to deal here. So that's why they come here, for nothing more than that they want to have a good time, see things, live their lives in freedom. Like here in Egypt, Egyptians, why do you think they like to go to Sharm el-Sheikh and Hurghada? For a change of scene. They'll see foreigners wearing bathing suits, laying out on the beach, they love to see things like that. It has nothing to do with culture! There are no cultures when it comes to this matter. He wants to see something pretty! Pretty ladies! That's it! Right, Ahmed? Men are men. In any time, at any place. Yep! He likes to see all the pretty women and they're all wearing bathing suits . . . and these women might flirt with him. He feels like he's king!" [In response to my laughter]: "I'm serious!" [Fieldnotes, 16 September 2000]

Arab tourists interact with a more contemporary image of Egyptian culture than do Western tourists, one that is grounded in the circulation of a shared language and regional circulation of popular culture. Gulf tourists come to Egypt to see a play with one of their favorite Egyptian actors, or they go to the nightclub of the Semiramis Hotel to see the famous belly dancer Dina, or to be photographed with the pop singer Ehab Tawfiq, who performs there twice a week and whose videos are broadcast on many Arab satellite channels. In the summer, the major five-star hotels in Cairo, Hurghada, and Sharm el-Sheikh hold concerts starring singers from all over the Arab world and charging up to $150 for tickets. These expensive concerts are almost exclusively geared toward a vacationing Gulf clientele, since few Egyptians would pay so much to see a singer. (Even upper-class Egyptians who could afford it usually don't bother,

Figure 4.4. A Cairo street; a billboard advertising a recent Egyptian movie, *Zayy el-Hawā*, named after an Abdelhalim Hafez song. Photograph by Mahmoud Abbas Elbadawi.

since they often see their favorite singers performing at weddings of friends and relatives.)

Gulf tourists do not follow the traditional Western tourist route of visiting pharaonic monuments. An official in the Egyptian Tourism Authority (ETA) told me that Arab tourists rarely visited archaeological sites; the many antiquities inspectors and tour guides I interviewed all made the same claim. A former director of the Cairo Egyptian Museum also told me that Arabs were easily the least represented of visitors to the museum. Figures breaking down attendance at the Sound and Light shows at the Giza Pyramids and Abu Simbel bear out these claims, since attendance at Arabic language shows is a fraction of that at shows in European languages (Egyptian Statistics Yearbook 1997), and that comprises more Egyptian attendees than Arab tourists.

Hotel workers that I interviewed often portrayed Western and Arab tourists as the polar opposites of each other. Their schedules, one hotel manager told me, were completely different. Arab tourism revolved around nightlife, he argued. Arabs stayed up until daybreak, going to nightclubs, discos, or parties, or just hanging out in the hotel lobby, restaurants, or in the streets. They slept most of the day, not waking up until the late afternoon. In contrast, he said, Europeans and Americans woke up early and set out on organized sightseeing tours to visit the Giza and Memphis (Saqqara) pyramids, the Egyptian Museum, and the Khan el-Khalili. They would typically return to the hotel and be

in their rooms by seven or eight o'clock in the evening, and they didn't participate much in the hotel nightlife; the Europeans who frequented the hotel bars
and clubs were usually expatriates living in Cairo.

Several hotel workers whom I interviewed complained about Arab tourists,
claiming that they were more demanding than Western tourists. Nasser, the assistant manager at one five-star hotel, said that Arabs spent much more money
in the hotel than Westerners, but "more money means more headaches. They
complain all the time, they act like they can buy anyone, and they treat hotel
employees arrogantly." Saad, the assistant manager of another five-star hotel,
said,

"Westerners are totally different from Arabs, who have a completely different mentality. For example: a Westerner orders a meal and it is taking a long
time for it to come, so the Westerner will summon the waiter and say to him,
'We've been waiting a long time for our food, why is it late, could you please
hurry it up?'—something along those lines. In contrast, an Arab whose order
is delayed will call over the waiter and complain that he's been waiting 'two
hours' for his food. Also the foreigner knows what he ordered and what he
wants. The Arab doesn't know what he wants—he doesn't even pay attention
to the menu, he just picks something off of it without reading it very carefully,
and then when the food arrives, he complains about what is in front of him
and says, 'This isn't what I ordered!' Even when Arabs and Westerners pay the
same amount of money, tourism workers prefer working with Westerners than
with Arabs."

[Probably you are just saying that because I am a foreigner!]

"I swear I'm not—I'm just telling it like it is, and it's not just me—it's all
Egyptians who work in tourism who feel this way. They are more comfortable
with Westerners. They're more comfortable to deal with, because they are
more predictable, more polite, and they know what they want. Arabs, on the
other hand, treat the Egyptian workers tough. They treat the workers badly and
act as if they can buy anything—including a person—with their money."

On the other hand, a receptionist in a four-star hotel preferred Arab tourists
over Westerners because of their ability to interact with the local culture. According to Inas, Westerners were so isolated that they appeared almost fright-
ened to make any demands at all:

"Westerners, when they come, they don't ask for anything. At the most they
might ask for directions, or ask how much to pay the taxi driver. At the *very*
most, he might call from his room asking for more towels, toilet paper, whatever. He doesn't ask for anything. At all. If he sees anything in the room, he

doesn't say anything about it. I could imagine that they can put up with any-thing! [laughing] I guess they come to enjoy themselves, they don't come with the idea that they're going to be complaining. He doesn't come here to make international calls. He doesn't want room service, either. He comes asking where is McDonald's and Kentucky [Fried Chicken]. He doesn't try any res-taurant. Maybe he's scared of the food, maybe he's scared of the way it's pre-pared. He's afraid of water that it might be tap water instead of bottled water; he's really scared! Also most of the Arabs are afraid to drink the water—Saudis especially are afraid. But the Westerners, not *one* ever drank tap water. They are so vigilant to make sure that it is bottled water, and they are suspicious that we've somehow introduced tap water into the bottle, or in the ice—maybe they got this idea from abroad, God only knows.

"Anyway, dealing with Westerners is very easy. Because there is no dealing! [laughs] Of course there are some who like to get to know Egyptians, who like to laugh and joke. . . . But the Arab is *always* like this. He comes at any time, he has to know what is your name, he likes to chat and so on . . . a European, you don't even feel [his presence]. His requests are very, very few. He practi-cally doesn't ask for anything, and he's always coming through a travel agent and that travel agent is responsible for taking care of everything anyway. The Arab, though, his complaints always precede him. Arabs are always concerned about the air conditioner, they love it, because everything in their countries—car, house, shops—is air conditioned. So the minute something goes wrong with the air conditioning—and that happens to us a lot here in this hotel! [she laughs]—they're ready to start a fight! But in general, Arabs are much nicer to talk to, they like to talk and laugh and joke with you, but Westerners are taking a stand (*wākhidīn mauqif*), afraid to talk to anybody, afraid that someone's going to kidnap him. When you talk to a Westerner, he's always suspicious, trying to figure out what's behind the friendliness, what are you plotting . . ."

One matter on which the tourism workers I interviewed were united, at least, was their opinion that Arab tourists were not interested in ancient Egyp-tian monuments. The stereotype of sex-crazed Gulf tourists was often juxta-posed to the more "cultural" tourism of Westerners. One day I was talking to a vendor in al-Hussein, an area of old Islamic Cairo that was popular among Western and Arab tourists alike. As I asked him about the difference between Arab and Western tourists, he took a piece of paper and started drawing a car-toon Arab wearing a white headdress with a beard, and said,

"Foreigners come here to see the pharaonic sites. They are interested in the old Egyptian history and culture. The Arabs come here for what kind of tourism? Sex. They aren't interested in any sort of history, archaeological ruins [*āthār*], or culture. All they know is Pyramids Road and furnished flats. Do you know what furnished flats are?"

[Yes, like in Mohandiseen.]

"Exactly! They come here for sex." [Fieldnotes, 24 July 1999]

As the vendor's comment suggests, "furnished flats" were, for many, synonymous with illicit sexual (and other) activity, because there was less state surveillance than in hotels. While Mohandiseen was known as the favorite place for Arabs to rent apartments, several Mohandiseen property owners told me that they refused to rent to Arab tourists because of the scandals it caused with neighbors in their apartment buildings. Gulf Arabs were popularly said to drink, hold wild parties, and bring women back to their apartments, which gave a bad name to the apartment and building. Many landlords refused to rent to Arabs, even though they knew they could charge much higher monthly rents to summer Arab tourists than the rents for longer leases charged of Western expatriates. One landlord, a judge, said to me,

"As for Arabs, I would never rent to them. This is a respectable building, and they are known for bringing girls to the apartment. Besides that, they have strange cultural habits! They like to cook and eat on the floor, for example. Once I rented to some Arabs and they were using some sort of coal burner to cook with, and it damaged and burned the floor, leaving it black. I had to replace the whole floor. And they like to eat off the furniture! Yes, indeed! They sit on the living room chairs with their food next to them on the chair, not even on a plate, and they scoop up the rice with one hand to eat directly off the chair. Plus they like to rub their toes. Really! They are insanely fond of giving themselves toe massages at all times! It's disgusting." [Fieldnotes, 17 August 1999]

Those who did rent to Gulf Arabs on short-term leases charged rates often up to three times what a Westerner would be charged for a one-year lease in an equivalent apartment. The apartment owners I interviewed justified this as the cost of sacrificing the respectability of their space to renters. However, it also seemed to be grounded in an exaggerated idea of how much money Gulf tourists had to spend. One landlord named Mohamed Sharabas told me,

"I had a flat in Doqqi that I rented to a Kuwaiti man. It's an average flat that I might be able to rent for a thousand pounds [about $300 at that time], but I rented it to the Kuwaiti for three thousand pounds a month, for three months.

So I had taken from him one month rent, and one month deposit, a total of six thousand pounds."

[But that's an awful lot of money! Three thousand a *month?!*]

"Well, look, the cost of one double room at a hotel like the Semiramis is between US $750 and $800 a night, so of course it makes sense for Arabs to stay in rented flats, even if they're expensive. Anyway, so after that I had no contact with the renter or the flat, until one day, I got a call from one of my neighbors in that building saying that the renter was making a scandal [*fadīha*] in the building, playing loud music and bringing in women at all hours of the night. So I went over to the apartment at night and knocked on the door. As I was climbing up the stairs, I could hear loud Arabic music from two floors below the apartment. I knocked and a woman opened the door. She said, 'Who are you?' and I said, 'No, who are *you?*' So she let me in, and inside the Kuwaiti man was with one Gulf [male] friend, there was one Gulf woman—a Saudi woman, I think—and two Egyptian women. There was food and alcohol and loud music, they were really partying it up. I asked the tenant to leave the apartment and not continue the whole three-month lease. That is why a lot of people won't rent to Arabs, because of the scandals it can cause in their buildings with their neighbors. That's the only time I've rented to Arabs. I learned my lesson after that." [Fieldnotes, 9 August 1999]

The cost of a double room at the Semiramis Intercontinental Hotel at the time of that interview was considerably less than Sharabas imagined—perhaps a quarter of the price he cited to me for a one-night stay, and longer-term rates could be arranged through a travel agent for much less than that. But many Egyptians seemed to exaggerate in their minds the amount of money Gulf tourists had to spend, which justified their hiking up prices. Fantastic stories circulated about wealthy Arab tourists who would drop thousands of pounds on a single night's entertainment, and even middle-class Gulf tourists were thought to live a life of luxury. Inas told me, "In the Gulf states, they are given vacation time and even money to travel! Did you know that? As part of their salaries they get money to take their wife and kids out of the country during the summer!"

This perceived difference in wealth seemed to be resented by many Egyptians who carry in their collective consciousness a memory of the time when Egypt was a wealthy country vis-à-vis the Gulf states, when Egypt supplied the gold-stitched cover of the *ka'aba* in Makkah, when Egypt sent its teachers and doctors to the Gulf to train "uneducated Arabs." I encountered a widespread portrayal of Gulf Arabs as Bedouins without history or civilization, who recently became rich and now lorded it over the rest of the Arab world. One merchant in al-Hussein, a Cairo neighborhood that sees crowds of both Arab and Western tourists, complained about the ill manners of Gulf Arabs, and then said to me, by way of explanation,

"What can you expect? They are primitive. They're Bedouin, they've only recently experienced civilization—only since the discovery of oil. The seventies, eighties. Meanwhile, you know, they still live with goats and sheep. Yes indeed! Once I was in Saudi Arabia, and I saw a man drive up in a beautiful Mercedes, a really fantastic, luxury car, and he got out and took sheep out of the car. I mean, it was a beautiful car, and he's putting sheep in it. I just don't think a new Mercedes is for sheep! But that's how they live, they love their animals, they don't give them up just because of civilization." [Fieldnotes, 30 July 1999]

A taxi driver told me,

"Arabs come here for pleasure; Westerners come here to see the pyramids. The only thing the Arabs do that has to do with the pyramids is ride horses and camels out in the desert around the pyramids—that's where they're from: desert, horses, camels; they don't have any history themselves so why should they be interested in pharaonic history? Arabs don't have civilization. They've just recently been developed; they're still like children. So they just come here, throw their money around on pleasure tourism, they just want girls, alcohol, drugs, etc. But don't get me wrong—the shame is ours as well, because we go running after them—after their money." [Fieldnotes, 25 September 1999]

This is a most peculiar idea that I encountered repeatedly from Egyptians of all different professions and class backgrounds: that Gulf Arabs are without history, and only Egyptians have real history and civilization. It is a construction of the Arab Other that makes invisible a whole host of celebrated historical events, figures, and cultural traditions: from nomadic cultures of desert tribes to long-inhabited urban centers such as Makkah, Jeddah, and Sana'a; from the Queen of Sheba to the caravans of the Frankincense Trail; the Nabatean civilizations of Petra in Jordan and *Madā'in Sāleh* in Saudi Arabia; from *Jahilīyya*-era (pre-Islamic) poetry to the development of Islam, and the subsequent elaboration of influential philosophical and religious traditions in the Arabian peninsula. Reversing Westerners' imagination of an Egyptian civilizational history in the absence of a modern nation-state, these Egyptians imagine contemporary Arab nation-states in the absence of history or civilization.

REGIONAL MIGRANT LABOR

Migrant labor of Egyptian workers in the Gulf is also a major factor contributing to regional social tensions. According to Egyptian economist Galal Amin, prior to the 1970s, emigration had largely been restricted to the elite classes of Egypt, who, displaced by Nasser's revolution, headed to Western countries (Amin 2000:95). But with the sudden and sharp increase in Gulf oil wealth in the 1970s, Egyptian migration took a completely different form. There was new demand for unskilled and semiskilled labor in the Gulf, Libya, and Iraq, and Egyptians started to perceive a short stint abroad as an opportunity to save money and fund important life cycle events: engagement, marriage, raising children and educating them, and building or rebuilding a house, either for oneself or for children (Nada 1991). Labor migration boomed, to the extent that, by the late 1970s, there were between three and four million Egyptians living abroad out of a total population of 40 million (Amin 2000:95–98). Studies of Egyptian labor migration have estimated that, by 1984, between 10 and 15 percent of the entire labor force was abroad (e.g., LaTowsky 1984).

The new phenomenon of labor migration to the Gulf produced substantial social changes in Egypt.[12] Families became willing to endure long separations: husbands left their wives and families behind for years at a time, since unskilled and semiskilled laborers were rarely granted visas to bring their families with them. (Oil-wealthy countries wanted to be certain that the migration was a temporary phenomenon, and blocking workers from bringing their families ensured that the lower-class laboring foreigners would not settle permanently in the host country.)[13] At the same time, travel exposed not only migrants but also their families back home to new lifestyles, commodities, and patterns of consumption. Workers returning from the Gulf would bring back goods unavailable in Egypt:

> After a few years of intensive emigration, Egyptians who had stayed at home started to talk of the migrants having brought on their return home *the* refrigerator, *the* television set, or *the* Japanese fan. Whether this was said with pride, admiration, or envy, such goods were always mentioned with the definite article, indicating that their acquisition had become the goal and purpose of the whole exercise, and that life had become almost inconceivable without them. (Amin 2000:98)

In addition to encouraging the spread of new forms and expectations of consumption, migration facilitated the movement of ideologies and ways of thinking about religion. Egyptian workers returning from the Arabian Gulf brought with them new practices—or, more specifically, new objections to old practices. Migrant labor in the Gulf has been one factor behind the propagation of Egyptian adherence to a more "orthodox" version of Islam (*salafi* Islam or "Wahhabism") in Egypt, which was long accustomed to popular saint worship and other practices considered heterodox by so-called High Islam.[14]

Amin attributes this new willingness by Egyptians to travel to several things: first of all, the shared language, short distance of travel, and improved means of transportation facilitated mass migration by the non-elite. But more important, argues Amin, a shared mass media produced a "revolution of rising expectations." A desire to improve one's standard of living was fed by television, and as a result of both migration and the proliferation of mass-media images of commodity consumption, "goods and services that had been regarded as luxuries were now seen as necessities" (Amin 2000:98).

Recent years have witnessed a reduction in dependence on Egyptian laborers in the Gulf, as they have been replaced by Asian laborers (who are considered to pose less of a threat of permanent migration and political agitation). Rising unemployment among young Gulf Arabs has also led to efforts to indigenize the workforce. Nevertheless, many Egyptians continue to go to the Gulf countries to work as doctors, teachers, drivers, and laborers. For all but the Egyptian upper class, a stint in the Gulf is still considered a chance to make and save money to get married, start a family, or provide for the education or marriage of children. And, as Amin observes, the circulation of labor continues to be intimately tied up with a circulation of pop culture via mass media and the circulation of commodities and new modes of consumption. These flows of people and things have certainly led to a mixing of cultures and to the perception of shared cultural traits, which have in turn contributed to the elaboration of a transnational Arab identity.[15]

And yet the increased contact between nationalities has not proved to be a formula for harmony and greater cross-cultural understanding. The experience of Egyptian workers in the Gulf is not always pleasant. They often are forced to travel without their families, since usually only managerial-level employees can get visas to bring their spouses and children with them. Without their families, it is lonely and hard for them to fit into local social life. But there are other factors that isolate them from the local populations as well. With so many migrant workers moving in and out of these countries all the time, local societies in the Gulf are wary about establishing ties with transitory people. Foreigners are often viewed with suspicion as corrupting influences. In Saudi Arabia, for example, editorials in the local press frequently call for an end to local reliance on foreign nannies, drivers, and other domestic laborers as unhealthy influences on Saudi families (Arebi 1994). The Egyptian author Ibrahim Abdel Meguid has written a novel called *The Other Place* (1997) about the experience of an Egyptian migrant worker in an unspecified Gulf state: it is a surreal, alienating experience of sexual frustration, culture clashes, intrigues, and petty politics.

On a more concrete level, migrant laborers may encounter explicitly racist policies that erode ideologies of Arab or Islamic unity. In Saudi Arabia in the 1990s, for example, some companies (including some state-owned companies such as Saudi Arabian Airlines) had pay scales that set the salary for each position according to the nationality of the employee, not just his experience or qualifications. For example, if there were airline mechanics of every different nationality, each with exactly the same training and experience, the Saudi, American, and Western European mechanics would receive the highest salaries; the Filipino, Pakistani, Indian, and Bangladeshi mechanics received the lowest salaries; and workers from other Arab states found themselves somewhere in the lower middle of the pay scale. The pay scale was based on average wages in the country each worker came from, and was justified on that basis: that workers were all earning more than they would in their countries of origin, and that was considered the relevant point of reference, since it was presumed that the object of working in Saudi Arabia was to remit wages or save them for spending back home.[16] However, the immediate effect of such policies is to discriminate between and reward workers on the basis of their nationality. This creates tensions and resentment that I frequently heard articulated by non-Saudis working in Saudi Arabia.[17]

Of course, many Egyptians have positive experiences living in the Gulf. But the negative aspects of the migrant labor experience generate resentment in Egypt, and are part of what is behind the common statement that I heard again and again, from lower-class taxi drivers to the Egyptian upper-class elite: "Arabs think they can buy anyone and anything with their money."

Mahdi, a Saudi chemical engineer who had been raised in Saudi Arabia but traveled abroad frequently, offered these insights on the phenomenon of international migrant labor in Saudi Arabia:

"Egyptians aren't much liked in Saudi Arabia, in general. I think it relates to the fact that they all go there to work in Saudi Arabia and make money. You feel that that's the primary reason they go, so it's like the fundamental basis of interaction with Saudi Arabia is economic. They're mostly from the lower classes and they're just trying to get money out of us. That's the first reason, it relates to the fact that there are so many Egyptians working in the Gulf. But the second reason is *nifāq*, hypocrisy. The way they speak, they're always saying, '*Yā mu'allam, yā bāsha, yā afendim.*' [Roughly, "sir."] They're always kissing ass." [Interview, April 2002]

He thought about it for a moment, then offered a structural explanation. "Maybe it's because they're poor, I mean the ones who go to work in Saudi Arabia are poor. So they have to always act subservient with the people around them." Mahdi observed that this created a corresponding negative behavior in Saudis dealing with Egyptians: it was too easy to get in the habit of treating Egyptians in a domineering, authoritative, arrogant manner because they were always apologizing and they never stood up for themselves.

"I'm against stereotyping," he continued, "and there are so many Egyptians who are really learned people; the Egyptians have a great civilization, not just a great ancient civilization, but a great civilization *now*. I think that probably we take the wrong impression about Egyptians because it's the lower-class ones, the ones who are more economically dependent on Saudis, who come to work in Saudi Arabia, and as a result, those people have to be ingratiating and subservient. It's like Indians. In Saudi Arabia, Indians are generally considered to be stupid. It's even become an expression: '*Yā ghabī yā hindī inta!*' ["You stupid Indian"]. Or a man can say to his friend, 'What do you take me for, an Indian?' and 'Indian' means 'stupid.' But I think that's because it's all uneducated, lower-class Indians who come to work in Saudi Arabia, they don't speak Arabic and they barely speak English, and they just stand around nodding their heads a lot. So Saudis get the idea that they're stupid. Then when Saudis travel outside of Saudi Arabia and meet other Indians, they realize that Indians are really smart and they have to revise their stereotypes." [Interview, April 2002]

The disdain that Mahdi says many Saudis feel for Egyptians is mutual. During my fieldwork, my Egyptian friends frequently complained about "al-'Arab," as they are referred to in the Egyptian dialect. In August 1999 I was discussing the Arab summer tourism phenomenon with Hamada, a middle-class Egyptian friend.

Hamada said, "I can't understand why Arabs come to Egypt, when they must know how much Egyptians hate them. I mean, okay, I can understand if they stay in the five-star hotels, because then they're paying to be treated well. But I don't understand the ones who stay in Mohandiseen."

"What I think is amazing," I retorted, "is that so many people hate them without even a good reason. I mean, Saeed and Anwar [two mutual friends] both despise them, even though they hardly have any contact with Arabs. I could understand an Egyptian laborer who had worked in the Gulf and was badly treated, coming back here with a negative attitude, but you and Saeed and Anwar . . . ?"

Hamada said, "But that's *why* we hate them, for what they do to other Egyptians." [Fieldnotes, 17 August 1999]

Specifically, the tension that Hamada may have been referring to was related to a 1992–1993 event which was written and editorialized about extensively in the Egyptian press, and which appears to have had a lasting impact on the consciousness of many Egyptians. Briefly, an Egyptian working in Saudi Arabia accused the Saudi headmaster of the school where his children studied of sodomizing his young son. The Saudi, in turn, accused the Egyptian man of slander. The case went to court, where the Saudi judge found the Saudi headmaster innocent and sentenced the Egyptian man to a brutal eighty lashes for false accusation, followed by deportation.

I was living in Saudi Arabia at the time that this case occurred. I was working as a photography teacher in a Saudi girls' school, and I vividly recall one of my Saudi students asking me if I had heard about the case. She informed me that the Saudi newspapers had reported that there had been a number of popular manifestations of anti-Saudi sentiment in Egypt following the man's sentencing. Further, some stores in al-Yamama center, a mall in Zamalek (a neighborhood of Cairo) that was a popular hang-out for both Egyptians and Gulf tourists, had reportedly hung signs in their windows that read, "Arabs not welcome." My student had said to me mournfully, "My parents say that we can't go to Egypt for vacation this summer because it's not safe for Saudis right now." By the time I started doing my fieldwork in Egypt in 1999, Egyptians were still talking about this case (other similar cases have also been publicized in the Egyptian media). Many cited it as a specific reason for why Saudis were disliked in Egypt.

PRINCE TORK AND SUMMER MARRIAGES

But the case that was making the headlines while I was living in Egypt was that of Prince Tork bin Abd al-Aziz al-Saud. This Saudi prince, a brother of King Abdullah, was living in exile in Egypt. He had married a Moroccan woman by the name of Hind al-Fassi, reportedly against the wishes of his family (some Egyptians told me that the union was frowned upon because of the politics of the woman's family; other rumors claimed that the Sauds disapproved of her moral character). Supposedly forbidden to bring his wife home with him to Saudi Arabia, he made his home in Egypt, where he occupied the top floors of the Ramses Hilton, a five-star hotel on the Nile that is a favorite of wealthy Gulf tourists. He lived there with an enormous entourage of servants, cooks, and an international team of bodyguards who accompanied him everywhere he went.

There had periodically been cases reported in the newspapers of skirmishes

Figure 4.5. The Ramses Hilton hotel where Prince Tork formerly occupied the top stories with his entourage of relatives, servants, and bodyguards. Photograph by Mahmoud Abbas Elbadawi.

between Prince Tork's bodyguards and anyone who got in His Royal Highness's way. The bodyguards cleared a path for Prince Tork wherever he went, and they were reported to shove and occasionally rough up anyone who was slow to move aside.[18] But the case that made headlines was that of two Egyptian cooks working for the Prince. After having apparently been held for months without pay in the Prince's Ramses Hilton suites, the cooks decided to escape by tying together sheets and letting themselves out of a window—from more than twenty stories up. One made it down safely; the other fell and broke his back.

The following week Prince Tork was in the newspapers once again when two of the prince's Filipina maids wrote a note on a piece of paper saying that they were being held prisoner in the Ramses Hilton and asking passersby to contact the Philippine embassy. The paper was wrapped with a ten-pound note and tossed down, where it was found and made its way to the Egyptian press. Subsequent articles detailed how the maids had been accused of trying to steal some of the princess's diamond jewelry and how, as a punishment, they were held without pay and beaten.

The cases of the Egyptian cooks and the Filipina maids were covered in all the Egyptian newspapers and were portrayed as an example of the feudal working conditions of laborers in the Gulf. But not long afterward, the Egyptian cooks retracted what they had said, claiming that they'd never been better taken care of than by Prince Tork and that as soon as they had made their accusations, they had been stricken by all kinds of bad luck. Egyptians were disdainful, and popular opinion held that the cooks had obviously been bought off. Indeed, there was a history of cases being filed against Prince Tork and never making it to court; the general assumption by Egyptians was that His Royal Highness avoided them through a judicious application of payoffs, bribes, and pressure.

But finally a case came up that went to court. The prince's bodyguards got rough with an Egyptian police officer by the name of Captain Abaza and beat him, severely injuring him in one eye. Captain Abaza wouldn't be bought off, and the Egyptian authorities could no longer look the other way at this direct attack on the apparatus of state authority. Around this time a new public prosecutor, Maher el-Guindi, had been appointed. El-Guindi was trying to make a name for himself for being intolerant of corruption, and he soared in popularity among the Egyptian public when he charged one of the brothers-in-law of the prince and two of the prince's bodyguards, a Syrian and an Austrian, for assaulting the Egyptian police officer. Court dates were set and one bodyguard, the Syrian, showed up in court and was sentenced. The brother-in-law of Prince Tork, as well as the European bodyguard, simply refused to appear in court, and it was popularly felt that the littlest fish—the Syrian bodyguard— was offered up as a scapegoat to satisfy the public lust for justice.

After that, Tork disappeared from the papers for a while until in 2001, an Egyptian jeweler accused his wife, Princess Hind, of having requested a selection of gold and diamond jewelry worth over a million pounds. The princess did not return the jewelry, nor did she pay for it. Again, the case was covered in all the newspapers and became a popular topic of discussion on the street, as the princess was portrayed as the symbolic representative of exploitative Gulf wealth: so wealthy herself, and yet perfectly willing to cheat Egyptians.

The newspapers took to calling the prince's hotel residence the "Ramses

Emirate," an interesting expression of the conflation between Saudi wealth and political power. One police officer I interviewed commented that the space at the top of the Ramses Hilton was like an embassy: though it did not have official diplomatic immunity, there was a clear sense that this was Saudi space, and inviolable. "He's living in exile, true, but he *is* the brother of King Fahd, after all, and in line to inherit the throne."

By the summer I started my research, the exploits of Prince Tork and his bodyguards had become the common currency of conversation in Egypt; everybody savored his scandals and clucked disapprovingly about the slippery way he always managed to get out of trouble. But what was interesting, I noticed, was that comparisons were often drawn between Tork and the Gulf Arab tourists who came to Egypt in the summer. When being interviewed about Gulf tourists, Egyptians often said to me, "They think they can just do whatever they want here because they have money—just like Prince Tork."

There was a strong element of myth in the stories that circulated about this character. When I interviewed hotel management at the Ramses Hilton about the scandals surrounding Prince Tork, they all refused to speak on record, but among themselves they would gleefully gossip in hushed voices: "They keep rottweilers up there . . ." "The bodyguards play soccer in the corridors; they're bored because the prince does nothing but sleep all the time." "When Tork's granddaughter had a birthday they flew in the Gipsy Kings to perform for her and they rented out forty-five rooms for them at the Nile Hilton." Hotel employees would report sightings of the prince's entourage to each other, anecdotally, with an odd mixture of awe and worldly cynicism.

The "Ramses Emirate" was a mythical world even outside of the hotel. In particular, Egyptians liked to speculate about Tork's wife, Hind al-Fassi. "You know," said Anwar, an Egyptian friend,

"the wife of Prince Tork has a group of Lebanese girls who are with her all the time. They are extremely beautiful, they live with her and they go everywhere she goes. They are *so* beautiful. You know the [Lebanese singing group called the] Four Cats? You know how beautiful they are? Well some people compare these Lebanese girls who are the friends of the wife of Prince Tork to the Four Cats, and these Lebanese girls get angry and say, 'We are much more beautiful than the Four Cats.' So you can imagine how beautiful they are." [Fieldnotes, 20 September 1999]

And Hiba, a young Egyptian woman, said to me,

"Prince Tork's wife is Moroccan and she uses magic. She put a spell on him, that's why he gave up everything in his own country for her. She's an enchantress. Whenever she wants to summon him, she cuts open an apple and says some magic words and Prince Tork comes to her immediately. She is very beautiful," she added. [Fieldnotes, 16 February 2000]

Neither Anwar nor Hiba had any way of knowing such details about Prince Tork and his wife, yet they were declared as facts with conviction. Even the newspapers, supposed sources of fact, offered contradictory information. At the time when the case with Captain Abaza was making headlines, one newspaper said that Tork had resided in the top two floors of the Ramses Hilton for seven years; another said the top three floors; other newspapers cited five, six, and even nine years as the length of time he had resided in Egypt. One newspaper claimed that one of his brothers-in-law who was charged in the attack on Captain Abaza was in custody—a claim which other sources denied.

I spent weeks trying to get the exact facts on Prince Tork, and was frustrated by the apparent impossibility of sorting out fact from myth, gossip, and rumor. At some point, I finally realized that, as with my attempts to locate a factual basis for accusations of the sex orgies of Arab girls, I was chasing after the wrong thing. Gossip does not have to be proved or disproved to qualify as social fact. On some important level, the factual bases for rumors about Prince Tork were beside the point; the contradictory and fantastic stories about power, wealth, exploitation, and even magic *constituted* Prince Tork—that is, Tork as a social phenomenon, an urban myth that is circulated. Prince Tork had become the mythical prototype for the stereotype of the wealthy Gulf Arab who exploits Egyptians.

Prince Tork wasn't the only figure or social phenomenon to take on such symbolic meaning in representing Gulf-Egyptian relations. A few years before the Prince Tork scandals were making headlines, gossip centered around Mamdouh al-Laithy, who was president of the Television and Broadcasting Union, president of the Artistic Production Sector, and one of the highest-ranking officials in the Ministry of Information. He was, in effect, the man who decided who among aspiring actors and actresses was going to be a star, and after a dramatic and much publicized court case, he was convicted of pimping out Egyptian actresses to wealthy Gulf men.[19] It was one of the most famous legal cases in Egypt and became a hot topic for discussion among Egyptians, who were shocked that such a high-ranking government official would sell out to corrupt "Arab" money.

Another issue to receive media attention in recent years has been that of the so-called "summer marriage" phenomenon, in which marriage brokers (semāsera) were revealed to be taking large sums of money to marry wealthy older Arab men to poor, young Egyptian village women. In many cases, the

Arab husband would simply divorce the village girl after the summer tourism season, leaving her in dire circumstances, because now she was no longer a virgin, often pregnant, shamed at being discarded by her husband, and in just as miserable an economic condition as before the "marriage." According to a journalist from *Roz al-Yousef* (the magazine that took the lead in reporting on these summer marriages), these took place in large numbers in the peri-urban village of Hawamadiyya, near al-Mouneeb in Giza, where marriage brokers and Gulf Arabs took advantage of the depressed economic circumstances of villagers. (Many of the girls were underage, and part of the conspiracy involved forging documents to make the girls appear older than they actually were.)

In response to the media blitz and ensuing public outrage, on 10 September 1999, newspapers (such as *al-Wafd*) reported that a law had been passed under Justice Minister Farouq Seif al-Nasr which tried to curb this practice. First of all, the law banned proxy marriages in which a woman could be married to a man who wasn't even present. (Public outrage had been fired up by newspaper accounts of women being married to some appealing bachelor whom they had never met, only later to discover that he was some sick old man who wanted an unsalaried nurse.) The law further regulated marriages between Egyptian women and foreign men by limiting the age difference between the man and woman to less than twenty-five years, and mandating that the man had to put a sum of LE 25,000 (at the time, around US $7,000) in a bank account to be available only to the bride—and not her family—after marriage. The law also required the foreign husband to provide documents certifying his financial and medical status.

The Prince Tork, al-Laithy, and summer marriage cases all revolve around fears of exploitative Gulf wealth subverting the social and moral order in Egypt. Unlike the Prince Tork case, what the al-Laithy case and the summer marriage phenomenon had in common was the fear of predatory Gulf men chasing after vulnerable Egyptian women. This recalls, too, the warnings that I frequently got from well-meaning friends to be careful about staying out late in the summer and to avoid places that were hang-outs for Gulf Arabs. (The specter of sexual predation is an important theme which we will revisit—from a completely different angle—in the next chapter.)

The media contributes by publishing scandals about Tork, al-Laithy, and summer marriages; once a story enters the public domain via magazines and newspapers (like *Roz al-Yousef*, a pioneer in exposing such scandals), it gets mulled over in coffee shops, on the street, and in the home, between friends and relatives who retell and interpret the story until it attains larger-than-life meaning; through such mechanisms, an exceptional phenomenon comes to stand for the whole.

AN ANTHROPOLOGY OF RUMOR

Rumors and urban legends often portray the bodies of a powerless group of society as under attack. For example, authors such as David Samper (2002) and Nancy Scheper-Hughes (1996) have examined rumors about the illegal traffic in the organs and body parts of third world children. Feldman-Savelsberg, Ndonko, and Schmidt-Ehry (2000) have investigated rumors that a tetanus vaccine program in Cameroon masked a plan to sterilize young Cameroonian women. The circulation of these rumors expresses and critiques unequal relationships of economic, political, and social power between groups in society (Turner 1993, Samper 2002). The bodies under attack in these rumors metonymically stand for larger power relationships between local and international actors, or between local people and a distant center of government power.

Stories about Gulf Arabs in Egypt portray the bodies of Egyptian women—whether poor village women, urban prostitutes, or aspiring actresses—as being sexually and morally consumed by wealthy Gulf Arab men. The stories about Prince Tork and his entourage, on the other hand, present both male and female victims. As Egyptians complained about the inability of the Egyptian government to prosecute, the Prince Tork stories came to represent not only the dilemmas of Egyptian migrant workers in the Gulf but also the international power differential between Egypt and Saudi Arabia.

Studies of rumor and urban legends have often focused on rumors that can be proven untrue (as in the case of the vaccine rumors in Cameroon) or which can never be proven to be true (as in the case of rumors about traffic in children's organs). But the rumors about Gulf Arabs in Egypt don't perfectly fit the rumor bill. While some of them (as in the Arab lesbian sex orgies reported by the hotel managers I interviewed) were unprovable, others, like the summer marriages and the exploits of Prince Tork's entourage, were reported by respectable Egyptian media outlets. Indeed, it was this fact that for so long had me confused about how to interpret these stories. I spent hours poring over conflicting newspaper accounts, trying to figure out how I was going to determine which was the correct story and how I was going to verify the claims myself. Even interviewing the hotel management of the Ramses Hilton didn't really tell me much about Prince Tork, and I had no idea how I was going to find an actual victim of a "summer marriage."

Once I finally abandoned the task of separating fact from fiction, I was able to realize that, in certain key aspects, these stories still operated as rumors do. First, even the media accounts about Prince Tork were inconsistent in their descriptions of his lifestyle and residence in Egypt, suggesting that they may have came from sources that were not entirely immune to the mythical component of the Prince Tork character. Second, even if they originated in factual events published in media sources, they continued to circulate by word of mouth by Egyptians who embellished (as did Hiba with her account of Princess Hind's magic apple technique) and added their own personal and social interpretations. Third, like rumors about organ trafficking, they acquired a broader social meaning that made them symbolically greater than any single news event. Each story, in its way, came to metonymically express some larger social, economic, and political aspect of the relationship between Egypt and the Gulf Arab states.

Without doubting that there are indeed a number of wealthy Gulf men who use Egypt as their playground and who prey on economically disadvantaged and socially powerless lower-class Egyptians, especially women, I *do* doubt that such men represent the majority of Gulf Arabs on holiday in Egypt. Most Gulf Arabs who vacation in Egypt are middle class, often travel as families, and probably no more of them frequent prostitutes than do wealthy Egyptians. So why does this minority of cases (Prince Tork, al-Laithy, or the summer marriages) come to stand for the whole?

First of all, these cases express popularly resented inequalities in political and economic power between Egypt and the Gulf. Perceived (and very real) differences in wealth are resented by Egyptians who speak nostalgically of the days when Egypt was a wealthy state vis-à-vis the poor desert Gulf Arab states. Economic difference within a highly interdependent regional economy structures interactions between Gulf Arabs and Egyptians in which, as my Saudi informant Mahdi noted, the majority of Egyptians interacting with Gulf Arabs do so from a position of economic inequality and even dependence. Regional migrant labor also contributes to social tensions. Just as Prince Tork became symbolic of the excesses of wealthy Gulf Arabs in Egypt, so did the case of the Egyptian worker in Saudi Arabia who was beaten and deported after accusing the Saudi headmaster of sodomizing his son get portrayed as symbolic of the abuses and humiliations to which Egyptian workers in the Gulf are subjected.

Perceived Gulf arrogance is mocked and subverted by Egyptians who exchange humorous anecdotes about wealthy Arabs who transport barnyard animals in their luxury cars, who spend money on extravagant meals which they proceed to eat with their hands or off the furniture, and who sit in the cafés of luxury hotels idly rubbing their feet:

I met Zeinab for coffee in the Semiramis. We sat in the coffee shop and watched the people move through the lobby . . . There were lots of Gulf Arabs there and we got talking about the subject of my research. I said to her, "You know, people keep telling me that there is a stereotype about Arabs that they like to play with their toes." I spoke skeptically, but Zeinab leaned forward with wide eyes and said, "Of course! Oh yes! You haven't seen this? They *love* to play with their toes!" A moment later she said to me excitedly, "Lisa, Lisa! Look! Someone is playing with his toes just for our benefit!" I looked over and there was a Gulf man in shorts and sandals sitting at one of the café tables, and he had put his bare foot up on the chair and was holding his ankle. He wasn't then [touching], nor did he at any point in time, actually touch his toes, he was just putting his foot up on the chair with his hand on his ankle to an-chor it there, but evidently that was close enough for Zeinab to categorize his activity as typical Arab toe fondling. She said to me, "He must have heard us and decided to try to seduce us this way. He thought to himself, 'This is the best way to get them back to my room with me, I'll show them my feet!'" Ze-inab was laughing harder than I've ever seen her laugh. [Fieldnotes, 24 August 1999]

Another time I was interviewing a receptionist from a hotel that catered to a largely Gulf Arab clientele. Inas told me,

"They don't order hotel food because there's other specific food they like, there's restaurants here that specialize in Gulf food: *kabsa*, things like that. Yeah, they don't want something nice, they like things down and dirty—if they were to get regular restaurant food, it would be too *chic* for them, and they don't like that!" [Fieldnotes, 29 August 2000]

I was told such anecdotes frequently, reflecting a widespread image among Egyptians of Gulf Arabs as nomadic Bedouins without history or civilization, the nouveaux riches of the Middle East who lord their wealth over the rest of the Arab world but who do not actually know how to behave in a manner that suits such socioeconomic status.

But these stereotypes about class and taste also mask cultural difference. Take Inas's complaint about the way Arabs eat. *Kabsa* is the quintessential Saudi dish, consisting of roasted meat served on a bed of spiced basmati rice. It is a luxury food that is prepared for valued guests in Saudi Arabia. Tradi-tionally it is served out of a common dish to a group of people who eat it with their right hands, and it requires considerable expertise to use just one hand to properly roll up the rice into the right-size ball for putting it in the mouth. But in Inas's opinion, it is a kind of low-class food, "dirty," not "chic," because it is eaten with the hand.[20]

LANGUAGE DIFFERENCES BETWEEN EGYPTIANS AND GULF ARABS

There are also subtle but important language differences between Egyptians and Gulf Arabs that play an important role in transnational encounters between Arabs. In Egyptian Arabic, *inta* (you, masculine singular) and *inti* (you, feminine singular) are used among familiars of equal rank; between strangers, or when someone is addressing an elder or a person of higher status, *hadritak/hadritik* are used instead, similar to the French *vous*. In Saudi Arabia, on the other hand, it is perfectly polite for a person to address a stranger, a child to address a teacher, or a servant to address his or her employer with *inta* or *inti*, and, by contrast, *hadritak* and *hadritik* are used only to denote sarcasm.[21] (It is roughly equivalent to the way Americans use "your highness" sarcastically.) But not all Egyptians realize that Saudis do not use the honorific among themselves, so when Egyptians hear a Saudi addressing them with *inta* or *inti*, it may come off sounding rude, boorish, and even arrogant, since for Egyptians it seems that the Saudi is implicitly putting himself in a relationship of superiority to the person with whom he is speaking.

Likewise, as my informant Mahdi noted, Egyptians come off sounding excessively polite—indeed, obsequious—to Saudi ears. Mahdi argued that this may have been related to class difference and the economic dependence of Egyptians on Gulf money. While that certainly plays a role in determining interactions between Egyptians and Gulf Arabs, the use of honorifics is a general cultural principle among many urban Egyptians, even in interactions among equals. Friends of similar socioeconomic and class backgrounds often call each other *pasha* and *bey* (honorifics from the Ottoman era) as a way of showing a friend honor and respect. Again, what is mere good manners or friendliness for Egyptians can sound fawning to Saudis, and what is a straightforward, honest manner for Saudis can come off as abrupt, rude, or condescending to Egyptians.

Because Egypt is the regional pop culture hegemon, the Egyptian dialect and culture are widely transmitted and familiar all over the Arab world to audiences of Egyptian films, television serials, theater productions, and songs. The corollary of this is that Egyptians themselves do not get as much exposure to other regional dialects and cultures.[22] Egypt is an insulated hegemon, exporting its dialect and popular culture via media productions, but rarely consuming the popular culture of other regions of the Arab world. Most Gulf Arabs I knew were completely familiar with Egyptian Arabic from movies, and many could even imitate it, but for most Egyptians, while the Gulf dialects are comprehensible because of their similarities to classical Arabic, they still sound alien.[23] Even when the dialects are mutually comprehensible, there are other layers of meaning at work; the cultural and social meanings that are coded into the language do not always get translated, or are mistranslated, as in the case of Egyptian and Saudi usages of *hadritak* versus *inta*.

The fact that Egyptians and Gulf Arabs speak a common language (if not dialect) as well as share a common identity as Arabs can be deceptive because it belies important social, cultural, and linguistic differences between Egyptians and Gulf Arabs that can contribute to cross-cultural misunderstandings. In Egypt, despite a shared Arab identity, Gulf Arabs are still cultural and social Others. Rasha, an Egyptian woman who worked in a five-star hotel that catered to a primarily Gulf clientele in the summer, spoke of a substantial (cultural) chasm between Egyptians and Saudis.

"They [Saudis] just don't get us [Egyptians]. You know, you can say something to a Saudi, and he just looks at you . . . either he doesn't get it, or it's something else, cultural, that keeps him from responding. . . . I think probably he just doesn't get it." [Fieldnotes, 4 August 1999]

And in conversations with Inas and Basem, a woman and a man who both worked at a hotel with a primarily Arab clientele, they often related anecdotes to illustrate how culturally different Gulf Arabs were from them.

"Veiled faces for Gulf women don't really mean the same as veiled faces here, it's just part of these women's culture and traditions, but she can take it off and run around half-naked depending on the situation, as soon as she gets out of her own country," Inas told me. Then she started to tell me about one woman who entered the hotel with her husband with her face veiled, went up to her room and changed and came down again wearing tight stretch pants and a tank top. "And she wasn't even nice-looking! The stretch pants looked awful on her! Stretch pants are not for everyone!" added Inas. Basem turned to Inas and told her, "Later she was wearing an evening dress that came up to here!" indicating a level quite high on his thigh. Inas said, "I didn't see that. Too bad I only work during the day." She turned back to me and said, "Yeah, she was half-naked all the time. But then when she had to receive one of her husband's friends, she ran up and covered herself up completely and came down again all veiled." They laughed at the memory. [Fieldnotes, 16 September 2000]

"Once there were 16 [veiled Arab women] staying here with their faces covered. They all went around together, walking in and out wearing all black, you see them coming and you say, 'Here's the black cloud!' They sit here and fill the entire lobby . . ." "And each one looks like the other," interrupted Basem. Inas agreed: "You can't tell one from the other, except to say 'this one is short, and this one tall.' . . . I couldn't tell who was who." [Fieldnotes, 29 August 2000]

In the ways that Egyptians describe how Gulf Arabs dress, eat, and behave in public, or Gulf Arabs criticize Egyptian ways of talking, we see how being confronted with these small markers of cultural difference, among people who are thought to be relatively similar to each other in terms of culture and religion, throws into relief each group's own cultural norms. These differences provoke discussions about what such markers of cultural difference mean—both sides take these differences as evidence of civilization and political histories, among other things. In short, culture gets politicized and tied to civilizational narratives; and so we see how "culture" is tied to "Culture."

The peculiar nature of the otherness of Gulf Arabs is best illustrated by the term Egyptians use to refer to them: ʿArab. "Don't go to that place," friends would tell me. "There are too many Arabs there." "Al-ʿArab garab," others would say, a derogatory rhyme meaning "Arabs are scabies." Such comments confused me when I first started my research, because I had assumed that the term Arab included Egyptians. It took time for me to realize that in such contexts, the term ʿArab referred to non-Egyptian Arabs, and most often denoted Gulf Arabs.[24]

PHARAONIC NATIONALISM IN A REGIONAL CONTEXT

Pharaonic nationalism, or pharaonism, as some have called it (Gordon 1971:126), posits an essential Egyptian national identity dating back to the time of the pharaohs that distinguishes Egypt from the rest of the Islamic and even Arab world.[25] Gordon traces the tradition of pharaonic nationalism back to Urabi Pasha, the revolutionary Egyptian military leader of the late 1800s. Later proponents included Saad Zaghloul, the Egyptian nationalist leader of the 1920s,[26] Mustafa Kamil and Ahmad Lutfi al-Sayyid in the pre–World War I years (Reid 1985:239), and the literary figure Taha Hussein, who, until the 1940s, advocated a version of Egyptian or pharaonic nationalism that claimed that Egypt traced its roots back to Europe, not to the rest of the Arab world (Gordon 1971:126–127). Under the revolutionary leader Gamal Abd el-Nasser, pan-Arab nationalism became the dominant ideology, but both Gordon and Copeland argue that Nasser was originally an Egyptian nationalist and only converted to Arab nationalism after two years in power.[27]

Pharaonic nationalism experienced an upsurge again after Nasser's death, under President Anwar Sadat.[28] The failure of Nasser's Arab pan-nationalism and the Arab defeat in the 1967 war contributed to a rise in the rhetoric of both Islamic and pharaonic identity. Sadat often referred to Egypt's ancient pharaonic heritage in his speeches.[29] By the time of his death, Sadat himself was associated with a pharaonic identity, in a way that had both negative and positive connotations. Sadat famously called himself "the last of the pharaohs" (*ākher al-farā'na*), and Mohamed Hassanein Heikal, a famous Egyptian writer and biographer of Sadat, reinforced this imagery when, in his account of Sadat's life and death, he somberly wrote, "For the first time the people of Egypt had killed their Pharaoh" (Heikal 1983:255). Yet the term has negative, as well as positive, connotations. Sadat's assassins gleefully shouted out, "We have killed Pharaoh!" evoking a religious victory over an ungodly, pagan ruler and illustrating the ambivalence with which Egyptians regard their pharaonic past.

Perhaps the best evidence of the legacy of this pharaonic construction of history is found in the popular use of the word *al-'Arab*—Arabs—in Egypt today. There is ironic significance in the fact that when Egyptians say *al-'Arab*, they are usually not referring to themselves, but to people from the other Arab countries, and particularly from the Gulf—this, in spite of the fact that Egypt is formally designated as an "Arab republic" (*Gomhurīyat Misr al-'Arabīyya*). Similarly, the common statements heard from Egyptians that Gulf Arabs are "not civilized" and that they only encountered civilization starting in the mid-twentieth century when oil money enabled them to enter the "modern world" may implicitly evoke a version of Egyptian history in which Egyptians are descendents of the pharaohs and, in contrast with the rest of the Arab world, have been part of a great civilization for millennia.

Timothy Mitchell (1995) has suggested that Egyptians' identification with the pharaonic past is a product of Western colonialism and, later, Western tourism in Egypt, both fixated on an ancient monumental history, and that is undoubtedly true. He writes about how, when dealing with people who are involved with the tourism industry in Luxor and Aswan, he encountered people who would use "we" when talking about ancient pharaonic civilization. But this identification with ancient Egypt may have as much relevance for Egyptians in setting up an oppositional identity vis-à-vis non-Egyptian Arabs as well.

On the other hand, references to *al-'Arab* and their lack of "civilization" may implicate more recent regional history, in which Egypt was a powerful and even independent outpost of the Ottoman Empire, and defeated the ancestors of the modern ruling Saudi monarchy to briefly rule Makkah and Madinah, the holiest cities of Islam. In this vision of Egyptian and Saudi (or Arabian peninsula) history that is being evoked, the Saudi and other Gulf tourists are portrayed as Bedouin tribespeople who have only recently been transformed and contaminated by obscene amounts of oil money. The use of the term *al-'Arab* to refer to Gulf tourists thus implicitly compares them with Egypt's own internal Other, the Bedouin populations which inhabit the desert outside of the fertile Nile river valley and the Sinai peninsula.

Here I am not arguing for an Egyptian national identity that is exclusively or even predominantly pharaonic, or an Egyptian identity which sees Gulf Arabs as intrinsically other. Indeed, the identification with the Arab world remains strong for Egyptians. Emad, a Coptic Christian who worked in the al-Hussein area of Islamic Cairo in a shop that catered to both Western and Gulf Arab tourists alike, did not much like Gulf Arabs.

"Al-'Arab," he said, "are rude and arrogant. But regardless, we're closer to Arabs than we are to foreigners. The relationship between Egypt and non-Arab foreigners [agānib] is purely utilitarian. At least with Saudi Arabia we share a religion and a language. With non-Arab foreigners, we don't even share that. Look at it this way. With Arabs, Egypt shares fraternal bonds, and with non-Arab foreigners, it's just a friendship."[30]

The difference between non-Egyptians is clearly expressed in linguistic categories, through which Egyptians differentiate Arabs (al-'Arab) from non-Arabs (agānib). In fact, when talking about tourists, Emad and other Egyptians who worked in the tourism industry generally used the term suyyāh (tourists) for talking about non-Arabs, but simply called Arab tourists al-'Arab.

Identity is always fluid, relational, and situational; something which is constantly being assembled from a repertoire of constituent parts (Hammoudi 2002). The final product is never stable but constantly being defined and constructed, and it cannot be predicted merely by looking at all the elements constituting it. Therefore, in looking at Egyptian national identity, the question is not whether Egyptians consider themselves "Arab" or "not Arab." It's a question of when they feel themselves "Arab" and when they feel themselves "Egyptian"—and why. It's not a question of finding one correct identity; it's a question of finding the different layers of identity, and learning the contexts in which each different layer becomes salient. So during the height of Arab nationalism, under President Gamal Abd el-Nasser, or during celebrations of events such as the October (1973) War, and also when Egypt positions itself politically vis-à-vis the United States or Israel, at such times, Egyptians are more likely to feel their Arab-ness. During my period of fieldwork research, the Palestinian intifāda and the media depiction of the suffering of Palestinians at the hands of Israelis bearing U.S.-made weapons fostered feelings of Arab unity in the face of non-Arab oppressors. On the other hand, when Egyptians are confronted with the phenomenon of masses of Gulf tourists hanging out at night on Arab League Street in Mohandiseen during the summer months, Egyptians are more likely to invoke their Egyptian-ness as a mark of difference.

Just as the politics of Egyptology today (see chapters 2 and 3) reflects a history of Western colonialism and travel in Egypt, so does the rhetoric of Egyptian nationalism express complicated historical patterns of Egypt's political, economic, and social relationships with Arab countries. Popular dislike of Arab tourists in Egypt codes resentment over both the exploitation of Egyptian migrant laborers in the Gulf and the inequitable distribution of wealth in the region. The scandals of Prince Tork and his entourage are so popular in Egypt because they have become the synecdochical myth of Gulf wealth and exploitation, just as the "summer marriages" of wealthy older Gulf men to poor young Egyptian village women are seen as the symbolic extreme of the sexual predations of Gulf men, subverting the social and moral order in Egypt. And this is a reminder that it is not just pharaonic nationalism which defines a uniquely Egyptian national identity. The opposition "Egyptian" versus "Arab" may be shorthand for a whole wealth of other distinctions: between civilized urban lifestyle and tribal nomads (as in the use of the term *Arab* to refer to both Gulf Arabs and Egyptian Bedouin), and a host of other references to uniquely Egyptian history, politics, and, indeed, contemporary pop culture.

Cultures encode proprieties by imagining their transgressions. Stereotypes about Gulf Arabs in Egypt are the Egyptian imagination of the Arab Other as the embodiment of the transgression of social proprieties. Seen from that perspective, the question of what Arabs *actually do* in Egypt is a completely separate issue. It is the stereotypes and rumors which themselves are social fact.

That said, what Arabs actually do in Egypt is not irrelevant. In fact, it is fascinating to compare how the actual activities of Gulf vacationers compare to the Egyptian stereotypes about them. The next chapter, therefore, considers Arab tourism in Egypt from the perspective of Gulf (mostly Saudi) tourists.

▲ ▲ ▲ ▲ ▲ ▲ ▲ ▲ ▲ ▲ ▲ ▲ ▲ ▲ ▲ ▲ ▲ ▲ ▲

CHAPTER 5

TRANSNATIONAL DATING

The Egyptian stereotype holds that Arab tourism revolves around drinking and gambling and sex and various other illicit activities. The extremely small academic literature that has reported on sex tourism in Egypt suggests the same. Karim el-Gawhary (1995), for example, has written about the extensive network of real estate agents who double as pimps, supplying "maids" who also work as prostitutes to single Gulf Arab men renting furnished flats in Cairo.[1] More research needs to be done on this phenomenon and on the holiday activities of Arab men more generally.

But for many Saudis, going on holiday to Egypt is about nothing so scandalous. For the Saudi girls I knew in Jeddah, a vacation in Cairo was seen as a chance to meet Saudi young men and hang out with them and maybe date and find a boyfriend. Vacation in Cairo meant being able to go out in a mixed group of men and women to movie theaters (which don't exist in Saudi Arabia); it meant staying out late at night and going to discos, where alcohol might or might not be consumed; it was also about seeing concerts of famous Arab and Egyptian pop singers in the major hotels. For both the Saudi young men and women I knew, a huge part of the appeal of their vacation in Cairo was the chance to hang out with other Saudis in a place which was somewhat—but not completely—free from the social mores restricting interaction between the sexes.

It was my experiences living in Saudi Arabia for two years before entering graduate school that originally led to my anthropological research in Egypt, because I observed the social importance of the Egypt summer vacation in the lives of the Saudi young women I knew in Jeddah. I was interested in generational changes, such as the fact that more and more Saudi young women were

Figure 5.1. Cinema Miami in Cairo. Photograph by Mahmoud Abbas Elbadawi.

dating, in secret, away from the eyes of the older generation, for whom dating before marriage was absolutely taboo.[2] There were certain areas where dating took place, such as the beaches of Obhur and the malls of Jeddah (Wynn 1997). A third such place was while on vacation in Cairo, Alexandria, or Hurghada. I knew several girls in Jeddah who had met boyfriends while on vacation in Egypt and carried on relationships by phone, in secret, once they got back to Saudi Arabia. Some of these relationships led to engagement or marriage. This was one way for both Saudi young men and women to avoid arranged marriages.

I knew how difficult it would be to get a visa to do dissertation research in Saudi Arabia, so I decided to do a research project on Saudi tourism in Egypt. What was fascinating from an anthropological perspective was that here was a social ritual that was very Saudi, but which was taking place outside of the country's borders. To provide a comparative perspective on transnational networks and movements of people, I decided to expand my project into a study of both Western and Arab tourism in Cairo. That was the genesis of the research that eventually led to this book.

When I presented my research project in Princeton, my advisors and colleagues were encouraging. But when I got to Egypt and spoke about my project with other researchers and friends, I was constantly being discouraged from doing research on Gulf tourism in Egypt. One anthropologist who was studying tourism in Egypt herself was automatically dismissive. S. told me that it wasn't important to know what Arabs thought about their experience in Egypt, just what Egyptians thought about Arabs. After living there for five years, S. shared the Egyptian disdain for "Arabs" and didn't think they were worth her time studying. Far from discouraging me, her automatic dismissal fired my interest in this research project, so obviously neglected by researchers.

Likewise, many of my Egyptian friends were discouraging, but for different reasons. First, since they assumed that all Arabs came to Egypt for was to chase women, they thought that my research would expose an Egyptian sex industry. In other words, they assumed that writing about Arab tourism meant writing about Egyptian prostitution. Second, they had reservations about my ability even to gather the data without putting myself in compromising situations. Most of my friends assumed that if I were to approach Arab men for my research, these men would think that I was a loose woman and would treat me disrespectfully.[3]

I agreed with those who pointed out that the research would be methodologically difficult (see Chapter 1) and that there would be severe limitations on my ability to get representative data. But as my fieldwork progressed and I talked to more Arab tourists, I became increasingly convinced that it was necessary to describe Arab tourism in Egypt from the perspective of both Egyptians and Arab visitors to Egypt. First of all, I was struck by the fact that the two groups had such different conceptualizations of the Arab stay in Egypt, and of each other. Second, I realized that the animosity and their stereotypes about each other were a point of entry into some key insights about the political economy of the region, and transnational movements of people, money, culture, and ideologies (see also Chapter 4).

The anthropologist had it right in a sense when she said that the Arab perspective is irrelevant to an understanding of how Arab tourism works in Egypt. That is because the Egyptian stereotype about Arabs is so entrenched that it operates without any reference to what Arabs actually *do* while on vacation. In the beginning, as I listened to Egyptians offer extreme theories about what Arabs do in Egypt (lesbian sex extravaganzas in hotels and old men marrying teenage girls to make them their nurses/sex slaves), I was consumed with the idea that I had to find a way to prove or disprove these theories. How could I find out to what extent Arabs frequented prostitutes? How could I confirm or disprove the stories of Arab lesbian sex orgies in the five-star hotels? Of course it was methodologically impossible to find out how common prostitution was in Egypt, since it is by its very nature hidden, and even if I *were* allowed to distribute questionnaires and surveys (which I was not; see Chapter 1), no methodological techniques that I could think of would allow me to gain reliable quantitative data on such issues. But finally it occurred to me that, on an important level, it was unnecessary to find out how extensive prostitution was in order for me to understand the way Arab tourism is interpreted in Egypt. The way that Egyptians talk about Arabs as coming to Egypt for sex vacations is a social fact in and of itself, and needs to be analyzed. The question becomes not "Do Arabs come to Egypt for prostitution?" but rather "Why do Egyptians believe that Arabs come to Egypt for prostitution?" and "What are the insights that this common Egyptian belief or stereotype can shed on the relationship—economic, political, religious, social, and cultural—between Egypt and its neighboring Arab countries?"

But that was only half the picture. Because regardless of how correct the Egyptian stereotypes about Arab tourists might or might not be (and there is certainly some basis for the stereotype), there is a great deal going on that is *not* sex and alcohol and exploitation. In this chapter, I want to lay out what a vacation in Egypt means to young Saudi men and women by briefly sketching out some case studies taken from my research in both Jeddah and Cairo. I then want to revisit some of the issues discussed in the previous chapter from the "Arab" perspective, and I do this by closely examining the experiences of one Saudi family on vacation in Egypt. I am not taking the Ashour family as representative of Arab tourism as a whole, and so the conclusions I draw are qualified by their specificities (Geertz 1973). But by breaking down and analyzing the activities of this one family and their social interactions with Egyptians, I hope to arrive at some larger insights about cross-cultural contact and about the construction of identities, both of self and of other.

TRANSNATIONAL DATING AND COURTSHIP: MERIAM

Meriam was a fifteen-year-old in the elective photography class that I taught at a private Saudi girls' school in Jeddah.[4] She was bright and outgoing and enthusiastic. One day, we were chatting in the hallway of the school in between classes. Two girls in their senior year passed by and congratulated her. She thanked them, then explained to me: "I just got engaged." She had met her fiancé in a mall in Jeddah one day when she was out shopping with a cousin and a couple of friends. Her father had driven them to the mall, then left them to do their shopping while he sat in a coffee shop by himself. The girls wandered from shop to shop, checking out the clothing and jewelry and knickknacks for sale, and while they were walking, they noticed that a couple of young men had started to follow them around. One of them was particularly good-looking, and Meriam discreetly made eye contact with him several times and discussed him with her companions.

When the girls went to get ice cream from the Baskin-Robbins shop near the entrance of the mall, the men followed. While Meriam's friends and cousin deliberately took their time sampling different ice cream flavors, Meriam stood back a bit to give the man an opportunity to approach her. He tried to talk to her, paying her compliments and asking her name, and she demurely looked down and refused to answer, but he was encouraged because she didn't walk away. In a low voice, so as to not draw the attention of older people around, he repeated a line from a song by Rashed al-Majed, a popular Saudi singer. The song is about a man who pines away for the moon, a metaphor for a beautiful young woman, and the line he recited was *Ama hiya tanzil la, wala huw laha yitla‘* ("Either she must descend to him, or he must ascend to her.") Finally she gave him a small smile. He glanced nervously at an older couple walking toward the ice cream stand. "Quickly, what is your name?" he insisted. "Meriam," she told him shyly. He quickly slipped her a piece of paper with his name and phone number written on it. "Call me," he said, and walked away with his friend.

The next day, when Meriam was at her cousin's house, she called the phone number and talked to Ashraf for almost two hours before her aunt yelled at her to get off the phone. They talked every day after that for at least an hour. Ashraf started insisting that they meet in person. At first she refused, but after a couple of weeks, she agreed to meet him with some of her friends. She arranged to have her father drive her and two of her cousins to the Cheesecake Factory, a popular new hangout on Tahliyya Street. Her father dropped the girls off and went to do some shopping, arranging to pick them up after an hour. Meriam and her cousins ordered some cheesecake and went upstairs to sit in the area reserved for women and families, designed to protect women from the prying eyes of single men. Ashraf, who was waiting for them when they entered the shop, boldly followed them upstairs. The two Filipino men who were manning the store saw him go, but they didn't say anything to him. They didn't bother to enforce the taboo on male-female interaction, which was one of the reasons the Cheesecake Factory was so popular among Jeddah youth.

Upstairs, Ashraf sat across from Meriam "so that he could watch her beautiful face while he was talking to her, for a change." Fifteen minutes into their discussion, Meriam casually let her headscarf slip back from her forehead to reveal her pretty, wavy hair. After a few moments, she made a show of realizing that she was exposing herself, but instead of just readjusting her scarf, she took it off entirely so that Ashraf could see how long her hair was, and then retied it carelessly so that the curled ends stuck out from below the scarf. They chatted and Ashraf said gallant things to Meriam. After forty-five minutes, Meriam's cousin started looking nervously at her watch. Meriam's father would be back soon and they couldn't risk him finding Ashraf there with them, or they'd be grounded from going out without adult supervision. Ashraf took the hint and left.

They met a couple more times in restaurants, always with her cousins and friends in tow, and sometimes with one of Ashraf's friends or his younger brother. Soon she gave up the pretense of trying to keep her head covered, and just let the scarf slip off as soon as they were out of public sight, though she kept it on whenever one of Ashraf's friends was with him. Then they met at 'Obhur beach when the weather was starting to get hot. This was an area north of Jeddah where the wealthy had private houses and docks on an inlet of the Red Sea. Since it was all private property and there were no public beaches there, the *mutawwaʿīn*, representatives from the Committee for the Promotion of Virtue and Prevention of Vice, could not enter the area and monitor behavior like they did in the public places of Jeddah. So the only thing young people had to look out for was their parents. One of Meriam's relatives invited her family to spend the weekend with them in their villa at 'Obhur, and Ashraf's family owned a large villa not too far away from that.

During the day, the adults mostly stayed close to home. Meriam's mother and aunt cooked in the kitchen or sat under an umbrella on the beach, while Meriam's father played with his youngest son. Meriam and her younger brother Abdullah and her cousins wandered down to a dock that was out of sight from her cousin's place, and there they met Ashraf. Meriam and her female cousins were wearing their bathing suits over stretch Lycra shorts that covered their legs to the knee, and they wore sundresses over that. They sat on the pier talking together, and they even swam a little, but not too much—Meriam didn't want to get her hair wet because it would turn frizzy in the water. More than anything she went swimming so that Ashraf could see the shape of her body under the bathing suit and shorts. Then Ashraf took Meriam and then her brother on a ride on his jet ski.

They met several times at the beach that spring, and with Meriam's brother there as her chaperone, she was able to spend time with her boyfriend without her parents ever knowing. Unlike most Saudi brothers, Abdullah wasn't "jealous" and didn't mind Meriam seeing Ashraf. In fact, he loved to ride Ashraf's jet ski. Whenever Meriam's brother was riding the jet ski around, Meriam and Ashraf would take advantage of the opportunity to hold hands discreetly.

They were an exclusive item, and all of their friends knew they were dating. Then in late spring, Ashraf surprised Meriam by going to her parents and asking to get engaged. Ashraf told Meriam's parents that his sister had seen Meriam at a wedding and recommended her as a bride for her brother, and apparently the families were distantly related, but Meriam's mother didn't believe his story. While Meriam's father was in the *sālōn* talking to Ashraf, Meriam's mother excused herself and went and grilled Meriam about whether she knew Ashraf or not. Meriam couldn't stand to lie to her mother, so she admitted that she had met Ashraf out shopping one day and that they'd been talking on the phone since then. She didn't mention all the times she saw him at 'Obhur beach. Meriam's mother did not entirely approve of the phone dating in the absence of an engagement, but she was reassured that Meriam had behaved respectably since their relationship had ended in Ashraf asking for her hand in marriage, so Meriam's mother kept her secret and didn't tell her husband that Meriam and Ashraf knew each other prior to that day.

Both families met each other after that, and they agreed to the engagement. Since Meriam's parents were fairly liberal, they let Meriam and Ashraf sit alone in the *salōn* to talk to each other and get to know each other. They were even allowed to go out with Abdullah in tow. Abdullah liked Ashraf because he bought him cassette tapes and other little presents. Ashraf brought gifts of perfume for Meriam's mother and some pieces of gold jewelry for Meriam. Ashraf was young to be talking about marriage—only in his early twenties—but he could afford to marry young because he was independently wealthy. His father, a rich man, had died some years ago, and Ashraf and his siblings had inherited a lot of money.

The summer came, and Ashraf was planning to spend a couple of months in Egypt with his family. He and his mother came to Meriam's parents and proposed that Meriam come with them. Meriam and Ashraf had signed the marriage contract (*kātib al-kitāb*), and Ashraf's mother assured Meriam's parents that she and Ashraf's sisters would be there as chaperones. Though legally married, without holding the wedding party (*al-dukhla*) they were not socially considered married and there should be no consummation of the marriage yet, which is why it was important to reassure Meriam's parents that the two would be chaperoned.

I heard all these details from Meriam during school breaks. She was just dying to tell someone the story of how she had met her handsome young fiancé. I was a young teacher, only twenty at the time, so she saw me as more of a friend than an authority figure, and since I was American, she assumed that she could talk to me about her love life without worrying about my being judgmental about the fact that she had dated Ashraf before they were even engaged. For my part, I was fascinated by Meriam's story and how she and many other young women at that school managed to circumvent their parents' rules about dating young men. Several of the high school students were dating men that they had met in malls in Jeddah or at the beach in 'Obhur, and a couple were dating men whom they had met while on summer vacation in Cairo. Mai, for example, had met a man from Jeddah in the Cairo Marriott in the outdoor café.

They had quickly found that they had some friends or relatives in common and had spent most of the rest of their vacation hanging out in a large group, going to restaurants and movies and clubs together. Back in Jeddah, Mai carried on a relationship with this man over the phone and occasionally by meeting in restaurants, and she hoped it would eventually end in marriage. Rana had met a Kuwaiti man in Cairo and fallen in love, and they talked all the time on the phone, but she rarely got to see him, and she doubted that her parents would ever let her marry a non-Saudi.

After school let out and my teaching responsibilities were over, I spent the summer working as a freelance photographer for a Saudi woman who photographed Saudi marriages and engagements. In the middle of the summer, Meriam called me and we arranged to meet to go shopping together at Jamjoom Center, a mall near the Corniche. I was surprised that Meriam was back so soon from Cairo. She told me briefly that she had terminated the engagement with Ashraf and come home early from her vacation. At first she didn't want to talk about it, but as we met again and again over the summer, I learned more of the story.

In Cairo, Ashraf's mother had always gone to sleep early and left her children to entertain themselves. Meriam was staying in a room of the hotel with Ashraf's two younger sisters, while Ashraf and his brother shared a room. Ashraf was the eldest child so he could do pretty much whatever he wanted, and his younger siblings all deferred to him. They spent a fairly wild time by Meriam's standards. They slept all day and stayed up all night, going to plays and discos and nightclubs, coming home as late as 6:00 or 7:00 A.M. At first, Meriam was impressed by Ashraf's knowledge of Cairo nightlife. He knew all the cool places to go.

But with time Meriam became disenchanted with Ashraf. He drank alcohol when they were out, something that Meriam never saw him do in Jeddah. He also seemed to know a lot of women at these places and was always leaving Meriam with his siblings to go talk to them. Apparently he spent a lot of time every year in Cairo and had extensive contacts there. He was rich and didn't have to work, so he could spend all his time partying. Meriam was seeing a completely different side of Ashraf's character than she had known in Jeddah. And, as his fiancée, she didn't think he was treating her with the proper respect when he left her alone to go talk to other women he knew in these nightspots. But the final straw came when one day he held a birthday party for a Frenchwoman he knew, and told Meriam to bring the woman a present. Meriam was convinced that this Frenchwoman was Ashraf's girlfriend. She called her parents and told them she wanted to come home. They were supportive and arranged a ticket for her.

Back home, she told her mother what had happened. She didn't know what her mother had told her father, but she was certain that she'd never again be allowed to go on vacation without her family, nor did she ever want to go without them. At home, the engagement was never again spoken of. When she returned to school in the fall, she told her friends that it hadn't worked out, but didn't offer details. She didn't want the fact that she'd been in Cairo alone with a man of Ashraf's morals to compromise her own chances of getting engaged to someone else.

During the school year, Meriam met a new boyfriend, again in a mall in Jeddah, and they talked on the phone and met in malls and restaurants, as she had with Ashraf. They only once met at 'Obhur, though, because Meriam's cousins who owned a villa there were traveling and, though she had friends with villas at the beach, her parents would not let her go to 'Obhur with a family who were not relatives unless her brother came along, which was hard to arrange.

The next summer, Meriam convinced her family to go to Cairo for vacation. Meriam told me that she thought that her parents had arranged the trip as a favor to her, as a kind of consolation for things not working out with Ashraf the previous summer. As for her, she had begged her parents to go to Cairo because her new boyfriend, Saleh, was going. It wasn't just that she wanted to be with him over the summer—she also was determined to see how he behaved in Cairo; after what had happened with Ashraf, she felt it was some kind of crucible of his morals and his behavior toward her.

Of course, she had been dating Saleh for several months already, and had a few opportunities to be alone with him, and even to see him with his friends once, at 'Obhur beach. So he already knew that Meriam wasn't *muhajjiba*—she only wore a headscarf because it was traditional, but not out of personal conviction, since she took it off in front of him when they were out of the public eye. And she knew that his family was fairly liberal, too, since the one time she had seen him at 'Obhur, his sister had been with him and she hadn't covered her head, either. Few Egyptians realize how much dating and other social activity between the sexes occurs in Saudi Arabia, in public places like the mall, in private homes, and at places like 'Obhur beach. Meriam and Ashraf didn't need to go to Cairo to date each other.

But in some sense, Cairo (or any other place outside of Saudi Arabia) really was a crucible of a Saudi's character. So many things were legal there that weren't legal in Saudi Arabia and, Meriam argued, you could learn a great deal about a person by seeing what he would do when the law didn't prevent him from doing it. Of course, alcohol and drugs and sex are all available in Saudi Arabia to the elite whose money and connections and power enable them to flout both social convention and law, but it is still hard enough to get access to them that only a determined delinquent usually makes the effort. Where you really see a person's values, Meriam argued, is in a context where these things become readily available, like at a restaurant in Cairo where cheap beer is on the menu, or at a hotel where a casino is open round the clock and anyone can enter by just showing a non-Egyptian passport, or at a disco where there are plenty of loose women hoping to meet a wealthy Arab man.

Some of Meriam's friends and relatives were going to Cairo at the same time and they planned to meet up there and go out together. Again, Meriam's parents let her go out without adult supervision, as long as her little brother came along, but this time Abdullah was not as easy-going as he had been with Ashraf, whether because his parents had cautioned him to be more watchful or simply because he was growing up and becoming more accustomed to the role of a protective brother, so she was never able to be alone with Saleh. Still, she was able to meet Saleh in a group with her friends, because Abdullah didn't mind his sister going out in mixed groups of men and women. Meriam was pleased to see that Saleh liked to go out dancing and have fun, but he didn't drink alcohol. And Saleh was almost certainly reassured by the fact that Meriam never went anywhere in Cairo without her brother. That let him know that her family was protective of her reputation and her honor. If he had heard anything about her trip to Cairo with Ashraf—she had never mentioned it, but he might have heard from someone else if he was serious enough about Meriam to look into her background—she hoped he would assume that Abdullah had been with her the whole time that summer as well.

Meriam had a serious reason for wanting to go to Cairo, but her female cousins just wanted to have fun. They went to see every movie that was playing in the theaters, both foreign and Egyptian films, and twice they went to the nightclub in the Semiramis Hotel, where they saw the famous belly dancer Dina and one of their favorite singers, Ehab Tawfiq, perform. They had seen his videos on Egyptian television in Saudi Arabia, so it was a thrill to see him in person, and they even got to take pictures with him before the show. During the day, they were sometimes able to get away from their male relatives and go out for a stroll through the lobby of the hotel. They would flirt with other Arab men who were doing the same, just as they did back home on Tahliyya Street and in the malls in Jeddah, and they acquired a few telephone numbers that way. Back in their room, they would call the numbers and talk to the men on the phone.

At night, they would usually meet up with other friends from Jeddah, including Saleh and his friends and relatives, and go out in a big crowd to a bar-restaurant like Los Amigos in the Semiramis, which they loved because every night there was either karaoke or some fun little game or contest run by the Irish DJ. Then they would often go from there to one of the discos in the Nile

Hilton or the Gezira Sheraton. By going out with Saleh's friends, Meriam's cousin Hadile met Hassan, a twenty-two-year-old engineer from Jeddah. They found plenty of opportunities to speak to each other and flirt, and before the vacation was over, Hassan had given Hadile his phone number back in Jeddah so that they could continue their friendship back in Saudi Arabia. Meriam related all these stories to me when she came back from vacation. She was still dating Saleh, and Hadile was dating Hassan. Meriam and Hadile often conspired to evade their chaperones and go to restaurants on double dates with Saleh and Hassan.

ARAB TOURISM FROM A SAUDI PERSPECTIVE

During the summer months, the hotels in Cairo become promenades where men and women parade back and forth, watching each other and flirting. In the summer, the Semiramis Intercontinental Hotel changes the arrangement of the tables in its cafés and restaurants to accommodate the Arab tourists.[5] They move more tables out of the cafés and into the hallways and corridors so that customers can sit and watch others walking back and forth, passing the same place over and over again. The same phenomenon occurs in the café in the Marriott gardens. It's all about seeing and being seen.

Most of the Arab tourists I talked to traveled together in groups of extended family and/or friends, staying together in the same hotels and apartments, and when they didn't actually travel together, they would meet up with friends and schoolmates once in Cairo and go out together. Vacation in Cairo was an opportunity to do fun things that were forbidden back home in Saudi Arabia, but for the Saudis I knew, it wasn't the descent into the pit of vice that most Egyptians imagined it to be. The activities of such groups of vacationers could not be *too* transgressive because they were effectively transplanting a small section of their social world from Saudi Arabia to Cairo, so they couldn't really go very far beyond what was considered acceptable behavior in Saudi Arabia. This kind of activity is not about prostitution; it is about teenagers getting to hang out together, away from the prying eyes of the older generation.

The common stereotype among Egyptians is that Arabs come to Cairo to get away from their own culture and all its restrictions, but that is true only in a very limited sense. For all the Egyptian accusations that Arabs come to Egypt to chase after Egyptian women, or hire prostitutes, what I observed in the course of my research was that Gulf Arabs spent most of their time in Cairo hanging out with other Gulf Arabs. They did not come to Cairo to escape from the society of their countrymen and -women. They might find the social rules about male-female interaction substantially relaxed by virtue of being in a different place with different laws and social norms, but still, the fact that

Figure 5.2. One of several boats anchored on the Nile in Cairo and Giza that feature evening entertainment of restaurants, nightclubs, and luxury shops. Photograph by Mahmoud Abbas Elbadawi.

they were socializing with other Arabs put a limit on deviations from social norms.[6]

In fact, to the extent that dating while on vacation has marriage as a potential motivating goal (which was certainly the case for many of the Saudi young women with whom I spoke), then the people involved have to behave very carefully, and even deviations from cultural norms are limited and strategic. Meriam wanted to find ways to meet with Saleh alone, but at the same time she was always conscious that he would be evaluating her moral character based on how she behaved with him, so she didn't actually mind her younger brother tagging along, since she knew it would give her credibility as marriage material. Possibly Saleh had the same thing in mind when he declined to drink alcohol while he was out with Meriam and her brother. What this illustrates is that vacation in Egypt was not some foreign experience outside of Saudi cultural rules. Meriam, her friends, and her relatives were still very much thinking in terms of not only Saudi cultural rules but also Saudi society, since they traveled expecting to meet up with people they knew from back home.

Further, it is a false assumption that Saudis and other Gulf Arabs come to Egypt to meet women, date, and do other things that they can never do in their own countries. It is true that they come to Egypt to attend musical concerts and go to discos and movie theaters, none of which exist in Saudi Arabia. But the myth that I found current among many Egyptians was that Saudis never get a chance to interact socially with the opposite sex when they are in Saudi Arabia, which simply is not true. In Jeddah, at least, 'Obhur beach, private parties, malls, and restaurants are all sites for male-female socializing—not to mention dating.[7] For many Saudi youth, Cairo is the same type of space as 'Obhur: a place to meet other Saudis of the opposite sex and date. Dating is one of the major ways that Saudi youth evade their elders' control, not only in the short term, by finding small ways to escape the gaze of authority, but in the long term, by seeking their own future spouses and avoiding arranged marriages.

THE ASHOUR FAMILY

Zahra and I were sitting on her bed in her parents' apartment in Mohandiseen. It was a summer day and too hot to go outside so we were lounging around under the air conditioning. Zahra was painting her toenails red, and her seven-year-old brother was sprawled out on the floor with a mess of crayons and a coloring book. I was telling Zahra something that Egyptians say about Arabs. She interrupted me.

"Arabs? You mean Saudis?"

"Arabs, you know . . ." It occurred to me that she might not know how Egyptians use the term. "Well, you know, Egyptians say 'Arab' to refer to anyone from the Gulf. Or even from the Levant, for that matter. Anybody who is not North African and not Egyptian."

Zahra looked at me, somewhat incredulous. "Are you serious?"

"Yeah, didn't you know that?"

"No, I didn't. And what do they call themselves? Aren't they Arab, for God's sake?"

"They're Egyptian. I mean, yes, they consider themselves Arab, but when they're comparing themselves to people from the Gulf, they say that they're Egyptian, and the other people are Arab."

Zahra shook her head in disbelief. "I've been coming here since I was a little kid, and I never knew that. I can't believe it. I mean, I can't believe I didn't know."

I shrugged. "Well, of course they're not going to say it to your face. I'm sure there are similar things that they say about Americans that I never hear, either, because they're too polite to say something like that to me directly."

"Yeah, I guess everyone can see you're a foreigner."

I frowned, annoyed at my own inability to blend in. "Well, sometimes people think I'm Syrian or Lebanese because I don't look Egyptian but I speak pretty good Arabic. If I don't talk too much they can't tell where I'm from.

Or sometimes they ask if I'm an Egyptian who was raised abroad and learned Arabic a little late." I smiled at a memory. "Once I told a taxi driver that I was Palestinian."

"Did he believe you?"

"I don't think so. But he didn't call me on it. He was grubbing for a big tip, and he kept mentioning that I should pay him in dollars. I told him that I didn't have dollars and he looked really skeptical. But he didn't say that I wasn't Palestinian. What, does he think that the currency of Palestine is dollars?"

She laughed and fanned her toenails dry. "Of course he guessed you were American; he just didn't want to be rude and say so, so he was saying it indirectly by talking about a tip in dollars. Arabs are like that." She used the term to encompass Egyptians. "They like to be polite. They don't like to confront you. But that doesn't mean they're going to sit there and pretend that they believe a crazy story. So he had to find a different way to show you that he knows you're lying. Without saying, 'You're a liar.' That was his solution. To ask if you're going to pay him in dollars." She changed her position and started painting the toenails on her other foot.

I stopped to think about that. It was true what she said about Egyptians being polite and not wanting to hurt anyone's feelings with direct confrontation. "But he really was trying hard to get a tip," I said. "I mean, what you say is true, but I don't think he was just using it as an excuse to let me know that he knew I was lying. He asked me if I had children yet, and when I said no, he started telling me about how I would have one soon, he started saying, 'the baby is just over this bridge, it's crawling toward you, it's on its way, it's crawling over the October bridge to find you in Mohandiseen.' It was really a disturbing image, actually. I mean, the idea of some unborn child crawling all over Cairo looking for me, it was like some kind of bad dream. But he figured I must want kids so he was saying it as if he's giving me his blessing, you know, so I'd give him a tip. There are some people who specialize in that, in predicting good fortune for a tip. You know what I mean? It's like a tradition here. Isn't there a special name for those people, or a certain word in Arabic for the way they talk, or something? I learned it once, I think."

She ignored the question. "He sounds really annoying. How did he know that you didn't have children? Why were you talking to him about your private life?"

"He asked. What could I do?" I answered.

She furrowed her brow. "You shouldn't talk so openly to taxi drivers. It's not his right to interfere in your personal life like that. It's none of his business."

"But that's how taxi drivers are. They're always chatty and asking me if I'm married and if I have children. Don't they do that with you?"

"No, they don't. It's probably because you're a foreigner, they think they can do anything and be rude. And because you ride in taxis alone. They never talk to me personally. Also you smile too much. You shouldn't smile at them, they think it's an invitation or something." Zahra frowned. "Actually I can't stand taxi drivers here in Egypt. They never say how much they want to be paid, and then when I give them money, they act annoyed and say 'Ay da?' ["What's this?"], like I didn't give them enough, when I know I gave them a lot, and anyway, why won't they just say how much they want in the first place?"

"Well, the system here is that you just know how much to pay for however far you've gone and then you pay it when you get out of the cab. So the fact that you ask how much they want, they know right away that you don't live here so they take advantage."

"It's so unprofessional. They should have proper meters in the cabs like they do in Saudi Arabia. And so many times I get into a cab and I say where I want to go and they tell me to get out again because they don't want to go where I'm going. I always want to say to them, 'Aren't you a taxi driver? And aren't you on duty?'"

"Do you say anything?"

"No, I never do, I just get out of the cab without saying another word."

I've ridden in taxis with Zahra before and she is generous about paying people. Whenever the driver names a price, she gives him more than he asks for, and when he doesn't ask for a certain sum, she always gives him more than the going rate. When he argues about what she's given him, she gives him more without putting up a fight, even when I protest that it's too much. She doesn't like conflict. "As soon as they hear my accent," she tells me in a tone of resignation, "they immediately double the price of anything." She speaks in a *Jiddāwi* accent, using the hard "g" sound for the letter "*qāf*" instead of for the letter "*jīm*" as the Egyptians do, so she is immediately recognizable as a Gulf Arab. Her cousin Fayga is the opposite. Though Saudi, she can speak in a perfectly Egyptian accent and she tells people off when she thinks they've overstepped boundaries. If anyone harasses the two girls, Fayga puts the fear of God in him and makes him slink away in shame; when Fayga is dealing with the taxi driver, they never get ripped off. "Whenever we go out together, Fayga always tells me to keep my mouth shut and let her do all the talking."

Zahra Ashour is a twenty-one-year-old Saudi girl from Jeddah. She has wheat-colored skin and straight, long, dark brown hair. In Saudi Arabia she covers it up, but that's out of respect for tradition, not her own religious conviction. She says that she's not *muhajjiba,* and she doesn't wear a headscarf when she's in Egypt. In fact, she loves coming to Egypt on vacation because she can wear all her favorite clothes without having to wear an *ʿabāya* over them. Her parents don't mind, as long as she dresses modestly enough to avoid being harassed. When she *does* get hassled on the street about her tight jeans and tops, she generally doesn't tell her parents because she doesn't want to give them an excuse to make her dress more modestly.

The Ashours are a middle-class family from Jeddah's merchant class. Since she was young, her family has been coming to Egypt almost every summer for vacation. Her father retired long ago and her mother is a teacher, so the whole family always had the entire summer off to travel. They have relatives in Egypt and they would sometimes stay with them. Zahra's uncle is married to an Egyptian woman and they live in Alexandria, and Zahra's father loves to stay there because he loves the city of Alexandria and the weather is better there in the summer. Other times they would rent furnished flats (*shuqaq mafrūsha*) in Cairo, because it's a more lively city and Zahra's mother prefers it to any other. In that case, Zahra's father would come ahead of the rest of the family and stay in one of the small hotels that caters to Arab tourists while looking for a suitable apartment for the family to stay in for the summer. He prefers to stay at the Sheharazade, despite its reputation for being a place where Gulf Arabs bring prostitutes. In fact it is unlikely that he knows about the hotel's reputation; he just likes the hotel because it is on the Corniche in Agouza, and that way he can be close to the Nile. He loves the water.

Zahra has a few Egyptian or half-Egyptian friends in Saudi Arabia, and she partly made those friendships through her Egyptian connection (her uncle's wife), which made her and the Egyptians feel like there was some sense of mutual understanding. Zahra loves Egypt. She says that her Egyptian friends from school back in Saudi Arabia are like sisters to her. She says she feels freer in Egypt than she does in Saudi Arabia because she doesn't have to cover up when she goes out. At the same time she says she feels like an outsider—it's not just the lack of friends and the different dialect, but modes of interacting that are sometimes alien and make her confused about how to interpret overtures from people, especially men. She doesn't like the way Egyptian men flirt with her; she considers it too aggressive, even rude. Saudi men are just as flirtatious, but in a way that she considers more polite and deferential.

Zahra likes taking her Egyptian maid out with her because when people harass her or get too close to her, the maid yells at them. The maid is tough with them and knows how to keep them in line, but Zahra doesn't like confrontation. She always says to me, "I don't know how to talk to people here, I prefer anyone else to talk to them for me," and so she almost never goes out alone without either the maid or another relative. Even when we're out together, she waits for me to speak to people, even though I'm American and Arabic is my third language, because I'm not afraid to be assertive in dealing with people

Figure 5.3. Zahra and Sherif bowling together in an Alexandria bowling alley. Photograph by L. L. Wynn.

and I speak in the Egyptian dialect, which Zahra refuses to do. I ask her, "So do you like the maid? You get on well with her?" Zahra shrugs and just says, "Yeah, she's pretty nice, she did *halāwa* on my legs for me the other day," as if that sufficiently explains her relationship with the maid: she trusts her enough to let her sugar-wax her legs, an intimate procedure. But every time she goes out of her bedroom, she locks the door, saying to me, "I don't trust maids." None of her other siblings do this, but then again, they are all boys, so they don't have makeup and jewelry to steal. Zahra also takes the maid out with her to keep her youngest brother, Sherif, in line. I'm relieved to see that the boy isn't so spoiled that he bosses the maid around. He doesn't misbehave with the maids more than he does with anyone else, and she reprimands him when he's out of line.

Most days the family goes to the sports club so Sherif can play tennis. He hits the ball back and forth with a tennis coach. Usually Sherif goes with his father. One day Zahra takes me there with her and we enter the club; she's chatting on the cell phone with her father, who calls every couple of hours to know where she is and what she's doing. We're ten meters inside the club when someone comes after us, swaggering a bit and calling to us, asking what we're doing there. Zahra at first ignores the sound, then turns around and gives the man (a gate guard at the club) a blank look and says into her cell phone, "Talk to him, Papa," and wordlessly hands the man her phone. A short conversation ensues, and then the man respectfully hands Zahra the phone back and says with great deference, "Why didn't you just mention Dr. Abdelaziz's name?" With a small smile, Zahra says politely and distantly, "I didn't know the procedure here."

I am initially surprised at how such a warm person can act the way she does with Egyptians she doesn't know. Zahra isn't haughty or disdainful, but she maintains an absolute distance between herself and the world around her. She behaves in the manner of royalty, schooled to show a politeness that ultimately asserts her superiority. Even when people are rude with her, she shrugs it off without reacting, not even getting angry, and says only, "He doesn't know any better than that; this is how he was raised." We walk into the club and sit down at a table while she carries on talking to her father. The gate guard runs off to find the tennis coach for the boy. Zahra finishes the phone call and turns to me and says, "My dad says I should pay the man fifty pounds for the lesson. Usually the price is twenty or thirty pounds, something like that, but my father always gives extra so that they will treat us well here."

"Oh," I say, "that explains why the gate guard kept saying 'Dr. Abdelaziz' with such reverence."

At home, her father wears striped pajamas around the house half the day, but in the evening he dresses in a plain white *thōb*, no head covering, and takes Sherif out on a long walk of a couple of hours. He does it for his own health and to deplete some of the rambunctious boy's energy. Zahra and I wait until they're gone before we leave so that the little boy (age seven, he proudly shows me, counting on his fingers) won't cry to be allowed to leave with us when we go out at night. Then we slip out the door and take a taxi to a five-star hotel on the water. We sit in the café so we can watch the people walk by, and we order some food. When we're nearly done eating, Zahra's father calls her on the cell phone. He asks where we are, and she tells him. He tells her to be home by 11:00 P.M. She begs to be allowed to stay out later, so he makes it midnight or "12:30 but no later than that."

It's 10:30 P.M. and Zahra and I don't know what to do with ourselves. We've already eaten, the stores have closed, and it's far too early to go to a disco or nightclub. We have a midnight curfew and nobody will even start arriving at the clubs until 12:30 at the earliest. Zahra is pouting about the fact that she never gets to go dancing. I propose that we go to the hotel casino to see what it's like. In Egypt, casinos are exclusively for foreigners (nobody can enter unless they produce a non-Egyptian passport), and they are rumored to be a big hang-out for Arab tourists, especially in this hotel. I've never been to a casino in Egypt, since I could never get one of my Egyptian friends to accompany me, but I've always wanted to go, partly for the sake of my research, and partly out of plain curiosity. "At least we know the casino will be open—they're open twenty-four hours a day."

"Well, but gambling is *harām*," Zahra points out.

"Look, here's what we'll do," I say. "We'll take the amount of money that we would have paid to get into a disco. That's what we'll gamble with. No more than that. Then it's like paying an entrance fee to the place. If we lose, then we just consider that we paid for our own entertainment, and that's no loss since we don't have anything else to do, and anything we do would cost money. If we win, we'll give the money away to charity." Zahra smiles and agrees.

The casino is a large elegant room with lots of chandeliers and drapes on the walls that look like curtains, but there are no windows behind them. There are numerous tables beside which stand men and women in uniform with vacant smiles on their faces. The men wear pants and vests and the women wear short skirts; both wear bow ties. There are only two customers in the place. One is a sluggish-looking man in his fifties who is playing some game I don't know. The other is an obese man who is delicately perched on a stool at the bar. Both look "Arab" (i.e., not Egyptian), and when we eavesdrop on their conversations with the staff, one has a Levantine accent and the other is from the Gulf. Both of them glance at us but neither talks to us.

Zahra and I go to the bar and order pureed strawberry drinks. We try to pay for our drinks but we are told that they are free. We feel pleased with ourselves for getting free drinks. We talk for a while at the bar, drinking our juice, while we try to work up our courage to go explore the rest of the casino. Finally we wander over and have a look at the different games. We decide to play blackjack. We go take our money to the cashier to get chips. They first buy our Egyptian pounds at an outrageous rate and give us U.S. dollars, then we exchange the dollars for chips. We play and win. We play and win again. Then we lose, then we win twice more, and Zahra says, "Why don't we quit while we're ahead? Nobody ever thinks of doing that. They usually just play and play until they lose everything. Let's show that we know when to stop." So we cash in our chips and head out the door. We have made a profit of about $15. We give the money to a beggar on the street. Zahra says she would have liked to give it to the doorman of her building, since he needs the money, but she thinks it would look strange coming from her instead of her father—the doorman might think that she's trying to bribe him to keep quiet about her going out late with me and her cousins, and she doesn't want to give him the impression that she's doing anything behind her parents' backs.

It's only 11:30, and Zahra says we might as well go home. "We might as well, since there's nothing else to do," I agree. "But it's a pity—you got your dad to extend your curfew and then we're not even taking advantage of it."

"I like to do that," she tells me. "I always ask to stay out later, and then I come home before he tells me to. It makes him happy, and it makes him feel like he can trust me."

We go back to her apartment and slip in the door quietly so as to not wake up Sherif. In her room, she turns on the TV and I pull some of her magazines off a shelf to look at. She plugs in her computer and goes online to show me a website that she thinks is an example of really good design. She was just recently taking a class in web design and she wants to model her own web page after this particular site. Her father comes in and asks about our evening. "It was good, Papa." He comments on her coming home early. "There was nothing to do," she tells him. He smiles and wishes us both a good night.

"Oh," he remembers to tell her on his way out the door, "Madame Zeinab called and asked about you." Zahra scowls and says nothing. Her father pretends not to notice and closes the door.

Madame Zeinab is an Egyptian divorcée who lives in the same neighborhood. Zahra suspects Zeinab of having designs on her father, who is temporarily without his wife. Zahra's mother had to teach this summer and so she stayed in Saudi Arabia with two of Zahra's brothers, who both work in Jeddah, and since Zahra doesn't work, Zahra's father took her and her youngest brother Sherif to Egypt for the holidays. Zahra's mother flies over every three weeks or so. Zahra's father met Zeinab at a Saudi embassy reception. Zeinab was once married to a Saudi man and had a daughter with him; she claims that they divorced because her husband was stingy. Zahra thinks that she attends these Saudi embassy functions in the hopes of finding a new Saudi husband to spend on her.

Once she met Zahra's father and found out that he lived so close, Zeinab started visiting him at home all the time, bringing her daughter, under the pretext of wanting her to get to know Zahra. Zeinab covers her head with a scarf when she is outside, but she takes it off when she enters their apartment. Zahra finds this hypocritical. "Does she think she's already married to my father, that she can unveil in front of him?" Zeinab keeps making comments to Zahra that she should consider her like her mother, and tries to foist her daughter upon Zahra as a playmate and someone to show her around town. Zahra at first politely, and then more coldly, declined the offer, and says to me, fuming, "I don't need to think of her as my mother. I *have* a mother!"

With time, and judging by the frequency of the lady's visits to an unrelated man, Zahra became convinced that the woman wanted to marry her father. "She sees a man living alone with a young boy, and she supposes that the man needs a wife, and a mother for the boy. She probably thinks my father is rich. These Egyptian women think that all Saudis are rich and they think it's an excellent catch to get one, even to be the second wife of one. In fact my father doesn't have any money at all, it's my mother who supports the family with her job, and what is he going to do, go to his wife and ask for money to marry another woman? My mother is supporting two houses, one in Egypt and one in Saudi Arabia, and does this [Egyptian] woman suppose that she's going to marry my father and move into the apartment that my mother pays for?" Zahra started acting coldly toward the woman. Zeinab noticed this and complained to Zahra's father, who made excuses for Zahra. Zahra remained quiet while the woman was present, but later complained to her father that he shouldn't make excuses for her. But for the most part, she remains silent about the matter with her father. "I can't talk to him like I can talk to my mother." She called her mother and reported the woman's behavior, and her mother started to worry. She decided to visit more frequently, and now, despite the extra expense, she's going to come to Egypt two weekends every month, just to spend more time with her husband.

I include this extensive description of Zahra's family as a way of understanding something about the experience of Saudis in Egypt. This is not because Zahra's situation is the typical situation of a Saudi on vacation in Egypt. I make no claims to the Ashour family being the prototypical Saudi family. Indeed, in certain ways they are exceptional: Zahra's mother works for the government as a public school teacher and supports her family on her salary. But then, no Saudi family is typical. (Is there one perfectly prototypical Saudi family with 4.53 children? Would we choose a tribal family from Nejd, or a merchant family from Jeddah? Would anyone in the family have studied abroad on government scholarships, or would they be quite provincial and never have left their country except for their vacation to Egypt?) Yet by looking at one case, the details of one single family and the web of social relations in which they are embedded in Egypt, we can understand something about the experience of Saudi travelers in Egypt.

First of all, Zahra is much closer to Egyptian society and culture than most Western tourists. Her family comes to Egypt almost every year for their summer vacation. There is a network of transnational relations by marriage and friendships that connect people from the two countries: Zahra's uncle is married to an Egyptian woman, and Zahra has friends from school back in Jeddah who are Egyptian or half-Egyptian, half-Saudi. She often tells me that she considers the Egyptian girls she knows back home like her sisters.

Nevertheless, Zahra's use of kinship terms to define her relationship with Egyptian friends does not mean that she does not perceive important social and class differences between Saudis and most Egyptians. When I formally questioned her about the experience of Saudi tourists in Egypt, she said, "Well, most Saudis see Egyptians as the servants, the haircutters, the driver, things like that. At best we know them as teachers from school. I mean, *I* don't see them this way, but a lot of Saudis do. I know that there are lots of rich Egyptians, too, but we don't really come into contact with them as much as we do with the poor ones who are working as drivers in Saudi Arabia." She thought for a moment. "Although there are lots of Egyptian doctors, too, so I guess they're not all poor workers." She paused, then said, "I guess you could say that Saudis see Egyptians as people who provide services."

Zahra loves coming to Egypt, but despite her connections with the place, she doesn't feel entirely at home. She feels like an outsider because of her Saudi accent, and she often complains that she is cheated by people who assume that all Saudis are wealthy. As a defense mechanism against these perceived threats, she acts toward most Egyptians in a way that is slightly cold, polite, and detached. On the other hand, her cousin Fayga, who is Saudi and was raised in Saudi Arabia, gets along much better in Egypt. She can speak the Egyptian dialect, which she learned from watching Egyptian films and television shows back in Saudi Arabia, and she feels perfectly at home on the street in Cairo.

Zahra definitely takes advantage of being in Egypt to go out and do things she wouldn't be able to do in Saudi Arabia—walking outside without her 'abaya and headscarf, wearing tight clothes on the street, seeing films at the cinema, and even, once, going to a casino at night with her American friend. But she never ventures too far beyond the social world and cultural rules she was raised with: her parents set a curfew that she sticks to and even tries to beat; she doesn't drink or take drugs; and she doesn't go out alone with any man, whether Egyptian or Saudi. Zahra says that Saudi girls love to come here because they like to date and hang out with Saudi men whom they can't see in Jeddah, and vice versa, because the social rules are so much more relaxed. She has come to know a few Saudi men and women while on vacation and has maintained contact with them when back in Jeddah after the summer. But even when she has met Saudi men on vacation, she always met them through other women—friends or relatives from back home—and they always socialized in mixed groups of men and women.

Perhaps most fascinating about the Ashour family story, though, is the way it illustrates how each nationality claims that the other is a sexual predator. A common complaint among Egyptians is that Gulf men exploit financially disadvantaged Egyptian women (see Chapter 4), whether urban prostitutes or poor village girls. Zahra, in contrast, believes that this Egyptian woman, Zeinab, wants to steal her father away from her mother. She also believes that Egyptian women pursue Saudi men because they think that all Saudis are wealthy and they want to spend their money. So from this Gulf female perspective, the flip side of the wealthy Gulf male predator stealing poor Egyptian women is the cunning Egyptian woman using her sexual wiles to snare a wealthy Gulf man.

CONCLUSIONS: SIMILARITIES AND DIFFERENCE

Saudis and other Gulf tourists come to Egypt for many reasons: vacation, study, medical treatment, business. They escape the stifling summer heat by going to a somewhat cooler clime, where the social rules are a little more relaxed than they are back home. Of course, Gulf tourists vacation all over the world, but Egypt has its own unique appeal. First of all, it is inexpensive, whether one is coming for vacation or for study. It has good academic institutions for those who want to go to university away from home. Many Arabs also prefer to come to Egypt for medical treatment because there are quality medical facilities that are less expensive than in Europe or the United States, and because staying at a hospital in Egypt is culturally less alien than a trip to Europe or the United States. Not only is it easier to communicate with the nurses, but also the hospitals in Egypt make it easier for families to stay with patients and tend to be less rigid about visiting hours and rules than Western hospitals.

A shared language means that it is easier for a native Arabic speaker to get by in Egypt than in Western vacation spots. In particular, the older generation and people who don't have strong foreign language skills prefer to come to Arab countries for their vacation. But even those who spend vacation time in Europe or the United States often pass through Egypt anyway. One Yemeni woman told me,

[My sister and I] visit all kinds of places all over the world. We've gone on vacation to the U.S., Greece, Spain, Italy, England, Syria, and Lebanon. But we always have to return to Egypt, every year, no matter where else we go. It's like the center of the Arab world, and for us it's a place for family reunions. We have family living all over—in Oman, the United Arab Emirates—so Cairo is where we all meet each other. [Fieldnotes, 29 August 1999]

Cairo is familiar territory for Arab tourists, many of whom, like the Yemeni sisters or like Zahra's family, return year after year.[8] But Zahra's story of her awkward interactions with Egyptians shows that there are still moments of culture clash. The shared language, religion, and some shared cultural and social traits can be deceptive, because they lure people into a sense of similarity, and then when differences emerge, they can be jarring. In a sense, it is easier for Egyptians to explain the peculiar behavior of Western tourists who do not speak Arabic: they are wholly different, alien, and whatever they do can just be written off with a shrug and a simple exclamation that in one word encompasses everything that is strange about them—they are *agānib*, "foreigners." But Egyptians never call Gulf Arabs "foreigners," and often they are not even described as *suyyāh*, "tourists."[9] They are, simply, *ʿArab*—a word which both expresses difference, since it implies that Egyptians are *not* Arab, and sameness, since Egyptians are Arabic speakers and are clearly part of the Arab world.

Cultural and linguistic differences are overlaid with other social differences that derive from a regional economy marked by labor migration and extreme differences of wealth. Egyptian migrant labor in the Gulf and both Arab and Egyptian impressions of that experience play an important role in everyday Egyptian-Arab interactions. As Zahra noted, many Saudis see Egyptians as laborers or providers of services. Mahdi, a Saudi man, saw Egyptians as economic mercenaries who came to Saudi Arabia to make as much money as possible (see Chapter 4). He disliked their exaggerated politeness and use of old Ottoman honorifics, which struck him as toadying and insincere. While that is partly an example of culturally and linguistically different styles of address, Mahdi also conceded that it might have to do with the relative economic position of Egyptians vis-à-vis Saudis, since most of the Egyptians he encountered both in Saudi Arabia and in Egypt were economically dependent on himself or on other Saudis or Arabs for their livelihood, which supplied an additional, non-cultural incentive for obsequious behavior.

Many of the Gulf Arabs I interviewed said that they thought that most Egyptians they encountered wanted to cheat them and take their money. The result was that they were wary of Egyptians they encountered on the street, a wariness that could easily have been perceived by Egyptians as aloofness or even arrogance. Here we see the flip side of the various Egyptian stereotypes about Arabs: what might be perceived as Arab arrogance was, in Zahra, a defense mechanism against what she perceived as Egyptian rudeness or aggressiveness. Likewise, the Egyptian image of the Arab male sexual predator has its counterpart in Zahra's belief that greedy Egyptian women sought to steal her father from her mother out of some misplaced dream about Saudi wealth.[10]

Much of the academic literature on tourism (see the Introduction) has observed that one of the primary motivating factors behind travel is a desire to temporarily change one's environment and experience something other than the everyday. It is an intuitive understanding of this aspect of tourism, combined with an exaggerated image of the restrictions of life in the Gulf states, that has produced the Egyptian stereotype about Arabs coming to Egypt to drink, gamble, and chase after women. Yet the cases of both Zahra's and Meriam's families and their several trips to Egypt illustrate that this is not what an Egyptian vacation means for many Gulf tourists.

Meriam's transnational dating experiences, for example, illustrate that Saudis do not necessarily come to Egypt to get away from their own social world. Certainly Meriam and her friends came to Egypt to do some things that they could not do in their own country, such as going to theaters, musical concerts, discos, and bars. But that does not mean that the kinds of social activities that they indulged in while in Egypt were not also found in specific contexts in Saudi Arabia. Satellite television has brought to Saudi homes all of the sights and images they could possibly go to Egypt to see, and more. Alcohol and drugs are certainly available on the black market in Saudi Arabia, and alcohol is legally sold in most other Gulf countries. Further, most Arab youth do not need to come to Egypt to socialize with or date the opposite sex. As I have written elsewhere (Wynn 1997), secretive dating takes place among young adults in Jeddah and 'Obhur beach, and it is safe to assume that the same is true for other cities and countries in the Gulf (Wynn 2006).

Moreover, many of the Gulf Arabs I interviewed either came on vacation with relatives and/or friends from back home, or arranged to meet them while in Egypt. Thus the assumption that "Arabs come to Egypt to do the dirty things they cannot do in their own countries," a belief I often heard expressed by Egyptians, would have to be mitigated by the fact that they often bring part of their countries' social world with them on their travels. In Zahra's case, for example, any inclination to stray too far from her lifestyle in Saudi Arabia was checked by her own moral code as well as her parents' supervision.[11] And Meriam saw her trips to Cairo as a continuation of her social life and dating back home, a different context for exploring and defining those relationships, not a means of escaping Saudi cultural and social mores. One of the most fascinating aspects of the phenomenon of Arab tourism in Egypt is what it illustrates about the transnational nature of culture and society. The case of Saudis using their summer vacation as a way of dating and networking is an example of a quintessentially Saudi cultural phenomenon that takes place *outside* the borders of Saudi Arabia.

In an era of transnationalism, migration, and tourism, it is important to pay attention to the efforts to which people will go to maintain their identities, even in the face of countless opportunities for cultural borrowing and versions of hybridity. Perhaps it is the closeness of Egyptian and Gulf Arabs that brings into sharper focus the differences—cultural, linguistic, and social—between the groups. There is a moral quality to this kind of identity-work that imbues it with almost religious import. It is when one group is confronted with its cultural other, when its life is projected outside of its own culture into a different cultural and social world, that key aspects of people's identity and what they care about are revealed.

AN UNSETTLING POSTSCRIPT

In the fall of 2000, after the summer holidays were over, the Arab tourists had largely left Cairo. The air was starting to get cool and the nights smelled like burning. As farmers burned chaff in their fields after the harvest, the Muqattam Hills to the southeast of Cairo trapped the smoke in a bitter-smelling haze over much of the city.

One evening I went to the Semiramis Intercontinental Hotel to withdraw money from the automatic teller machine in the bank there so that I could pay my rent. As I clattered down one of the long polished granite hallways of the hotel, I heard a tentative, "Lisa?" I had been about to walk past Zayd, a Saudi man I had met that summer. He was the older brother of Bandar, a friend of my husband's from Jeddah. Zayd, a former pilot in the Saudi air force, now worked as the private pilot for some minor princes in the Saudi royal family, and when I asked what he was doing back in Cairo, he said that he had flown there for work and would be staying for a few days. I almost hadn't recognized him because he was wearing a new pair of glasses with electric blue rectangular frames. They looked very expensive, and very chic. He politely asked after my husband, an acquaintance of his, and I asked after his girlfriend, an American woman I knew of but had never met, whom he visited when his work brought him to New York. He told me that they had broken up. "I'm sorry," I told him. He shrugged. We decided to get a drink together at the hotel bar.

Zayd and I sat next to each other on bar stools, ordered juice, and reminisced about the past summer, when Zayd and a group of relatives and friends

Figure 5.4. A postcard of the old Semiramis Hotel in Cairo; date unknown. Collection of L. L. Wynn.

had spent the holidays in Cairo. Zayd, Bandar, and their mother rented a furnished flat in an apartment tower in Lebanon Square in Mohandiseen. In the afternoons, after they woke up, they ordered meals from Maroush, a Lebanese restaurant at the roundabout below their flat, and sometimes they would go shopping at the boutiques in Mohandiseen, but in the main, these just couldn't compare to shopping in Jeddah. In the evenings, they would meet up with other Saudi friends in Cairo. Chief among these were Ahmed and Omar, brothers who had rented a room together at the Semiramis for a full month. Ahmed's girlfriend, Rania, was also staying at the Semiramis with her relatives, and another set of her female friends from Jeddah were also staying there. Omar had just broken up with his girlfriend in Saudi Arabia, and was said to be secretly heartbroken, but was acting very cavalier about it and flirting with all of Rania's friends. Their third brother, Hatim, had stayed at home in Jeddah because he couldn't take time off from his job.

All three of these brothers were handsome, but of the three, Ahmed was the most arrestingly attractive. He was very tall and had brown hair that was tinted almost blond from the sun, and my Egyptian friends, when they had first seen Ahmed, could hardly believe that he was Saudi, because he was clean-shaven and wore somewhat low-rise Levis, and my friends' stereotype of Saudi men was that, because they usually wore *thōbs* and were therefore unaccustomed to wearing trousers, when they wore them on vacation, they usually

Figure 5.5. The Semiramis Intercontinental Hotel in 2006. Photograph by Mahmoud Abbas Elbadawi.

wore them uncomfortably high on the waist, tucking in their shirts to almost absurd effect.

Since Ahmed, Omar, Rania, and Rania's relatives and friends were all staying at the Semiramis, that was where the friends usually met up in the evenings. The group usually visited several places each night and stayed out until five or six in the morning. They would go to hotel nightclubs in the various Hilton hotels for dancing, or to a popular dinner-dance restaurant-bar on the Nile, or to theaters downtown or in Doqqi to see Egyptian and international (subtitled) movies.

Regardless of the later destinations, the evenings would usually start with the young people, mostly in their late teens and twenties, taking a large corner table in Los Amigos, the Mexican-themed bar in the Semiramis with an Irish DJ. They would meet there around 10 or 11 P.M., and stay until midnight or even later, if the dancing was lively, before heading somewhere else. Sometimes Zayd's mother, a very pretty woman with blonde hair who liked to wear miniskirts, would go to the same bar, sitting with another female Saudi friend at a different table than that of her children. It was rumored that their mother was a naturalized Saudi of Lebanese origin, though Zayd and Bandar denied that she wasn't pure Saudi, and the rumor may have just been a commentary on her beauty, since Lebanese women are thought by many Saudis to be among the most beautiful in the Arab world. Her sons would always stop and pay their mother greetings every time they went in and out of the bar.

(One of my Egyptian friends, Hassan, was aghast at the notion that Zayd and Bandar's mother would go to the same bar as her children, wearing miniskirts, no less; he argued that she showed disrespect to her grown sons by dressing so immodestly in public and going to a place where alcohol was served, even if she didn't drink alcohol herself, but he approved of the respectful way her sons treated her. Layla, Hassan's girlfriend, disagreed; she argued that their mother could do as she liked and it was neither the business of her sons nor of Hassan to say anything negative about her behavior. Hassan agreed that it was far better for her to do such things in front of her sons, rather than behind their backs, because at least it meant that she had nothing to hide. Both of these Egyptians thought it very surprising behavior for Saudis, but my Saudi and Emirati friends shrugged it off as not very unusual at all.)

One night each week, there was a "Russian Show" at the Semiramis bar, where a group of six young women from former Soviet countries performed a choreographed dance routine with several costume changes. The tight spaces of the long, narrow bar and the summer crowds meant that the dancers couldn't move quickly enough from the bathroom where they changed their costumes to the slightly raised dance floor at the far end of the bar (next to the table where Zayd and his friends usually sat), so the solution the bar manager had found was to have the women dance on top of the two widest, longest tables in the center of the bar. Before their performance, the bar manager would warn patrons to clear space in the middle of these tables, and the dancers' manager would assist the dancers in climbing up to the top of the table, which was no small feat, especially since they wore high heels. On the nights of the Russian Show, the Saudi group managed to be seated at one of the tables where the women would dance, rather than their usual corner table. One routine had the dancers costumed in G-string leotards worn over fishnet stockings and high-kicking over the heads of the people sitting at the table. I was frankly astonished at the view I had as I looked straight up at fishnet-clad dancing buttocks and thighs, but the Saudis maintained a mien of sophisticated disinterest, sometimes watching the dancers perform, and other times looking away to talk and flirt with each other.

One evening when the group had met at the Semiramis, the handsome Ahmed and his girlfriend, Rania, didn't join the rest of the group until quite late. When they finally appeared together at 1 A.M., they both had self-conscious grins on their face. I wondered if it was because they had just spent several hours together alone in a hotel room, with the rest of their friends downstairs at the bar, but then a cheer went up at the table when they announced that they had just gotten engaged. Early in the morning, after I had gotten home, I called my (then) husband back in the United States to tell him the news. "Really?" he said, in a skeptical voice. "I wonder if it will last. Ahmed is such a ladies' man; he's always dating different women." He told me about all the beautiful Saudi women Ahmed had dated and then broken up with in Jeddah, and wondered what had made Ahmed decide to commit now, especially to Rania, who, in his opinion, was beautiful but fatally boring, with a depressive personality.

Before we got off the phone, my husband told me a funny story about how he and Ahmed used to hang out together in a certain mall in Jeddah. Like other Saudi young men their age, they went to watch the women and flirt, but Ahmed took pleasure in teasing the women to amuse his male friends. During prayer call, all the shops closed, and while other men headed to the mall's mosque, Ahmed and Mohamed loitered in a hallway, trying to stay out of sight of any *mutawwaʿa* who might come to harass them for not praying.[12] In the hallway was the entrance to the women's bathroom. Ahmed and Mohamed watched the door to the bathroom, and when one pretty, young woman came out, dressed in a prettily trimmed ʿabāya (cloak) and matching *tarha* (headscarf), they pointedly stared at her. The woman held her ʿabāya tightly closed at the shoulder with one hand and haughtily looked away, ignoring them. As she passed them, Ahmed said, in a low, friendly voice, "*Shakheiti, ya halwa?*"— "Did you just pee, my pretty?" It was very *Jiddāwī* slang, Mohamed explained to me, laughing. At least it had startled the woman enough to look at them. She had expected them to compliment her, not crudely allude to what she had been doing in the bathroom.

So now, sitting at the coffee shop with Zayd, I asked about his friends and family, and, remembering my husband's skepticism about Ahmed's ability to commit, inquired whether Ahmed and Rania were still engaged. They were, he told me, though he didn't think a date had been set for the wedding. I offered my wishes for their happiness together. Then Zayd asked me how my research was going. I told him that I was spending my days out at the pyramids, looking into the Western fascination with pharaonic Egypt, and that I had also gotten to know a group of Belarusian dancers who had escaped from the abusive clutches of the same man who managed the "Russian" dancers we had seen perform at the Semiramis that summer; he had taken their passports and kept them locked in their apartment during the day, sometimes not even bothering to bring them food; finally they managed to get away from him and found another manager who was kind and put them up in an apartment with his sweet elderly mother who cooked for them, but they were still struggling to get their passports back from the first man, to whom they were indebted for the cost of their airfare from Belarus to Egypt.

As for my research on Arab tourism, I told Zayd that most of my Egyptian friends seemed sure that all Gulf Arabs came to Cairo to visit prostitutes, and that it seemed to me that this wasn't what most were up to at all.

"Oh, no," said Zayd, setting his glass of orange juice on the counter. "Most Saudis don't come to Cairo for prostitutes."

I nodded.

He continued, "The prostitutes in Morocco are far nicer than the Egyptian ones."

I blinked.

▲ ▲ ▲ ▲ ▲ ▲ ▲ ▲ ▲ ▲ ▲ ▲ ▲ ▲ ▲ ▲ ▲ ▲ ▲

CHAPTER 6

PALIMPSEST, EXCAVATION, GRAFFITI,
SIMULACRA: AN ETHNOGRAPHY OF
THE IDEA OF EGYPT

In 1865, Lady Lucie Duff-Gordon, one of the early British tourists in Egypt, commented, "This country is a palimpsest in which the Bible is written over Herodotus, and the Koran over that."[1] In Egypt, people have spent millennia writing over the monuments of the past, using them as temples, churches, mosques, homes, and museums, interpreting them according to their own imaginations, and appropriating them for their own political agendas. In 1400 BCE, King Thutmosis IV undertook the first known restoration of the Sphinx, putting a plaque between the paws to mark his efforts; the Romans dug it out of the sand again in preparation for Nero's visit to Egypt in the first century CE, and French explorers of the 1840s again cleared the sand away from its body.[2] In each case, reverence for the ancient sculpture was fueled by a desire to appropriate the power of a long-lost civilization and harness it to a contemporary political order. Pharaonic Egypt became a Greek, then a Roman, colony; Roman travelers to the outskirts of the empire removed obelisks and sent them back to Rome, setting a precedent for European colonizers, travelers, and antiquities looters nearly two millennia later. Coptic Christianity also left its mark, making chapels out of ancient temples and defacing the heretical inscriptions—but also preserving some of them with the mud they used to plaster over them, which protected paintings from sun and wind erosion until the mud was cleared away by nineteenth- and twentieth-century Europeans.

Since ancient times, Egypt has fueled exotic, and often competing, imaginations of the past. The writing on the various layers of history has often been sufficiently faded to accommodate more inscription—for people to project their imaginations about the past and write their own accounts of history—but this is never without some reference to the traces of what came before, however

Figure 6.1. A postcard mailed in 1908 shows a view of Cairo from a minaret. The author of the postcard describes an itinerary that includes a stop in Alexandria and three weeks in Palestine. Collection of L. L. Wynn.

fanciful the interpretations of those traces might be. Medieval Arabs imagined the ancient Egyptians as a race of giants, and wrote magical treasure-hunting guides that were later translated and sold to nineteenth-century tourists by an Egyptologist. The powdered corpses of ancient Egyptians were eaten and applied topically by Europeans for medicinal purposes, while Arabs still circulate rumors about a mythical embalming fluid said to hold the secret to longevity. And, returning to Herodotus (as, it seems, one always does), we find an ancient Greek fascination with an even more ancient Egypt—combined with amusement as he relates dubious facts, such as that the pyramids were built using funds earned from the prostitution of King Khufu's daughter, and that the outsides of the pyramids were inscribed with a tally of the number of onions fed to the workers who built them. (The morals of this story are threefold: foreigners have long imagined Egypt as a wily seductress; guides tell you what they think you want to hear; and travelers love to relate a fantastic story.)

But Herodotus's sly insinuation that the greatness of the pharaohs was built on the prostitution of their women reminds us that the play of historical imagination is not only a fanciful exercise in myth-making. As scholars such as Edward Said, Rana Kabbani, and Malek Alloula have argued, writing a description of the Other is always a political exercise.[3] The comparison of Arab and Western tourism in Egypt highlights the historical processes which have produced apparently natural icons of national identity. The authors of a recent book on tourism argue that certain cities and countries (like Jerusalem, Rome, and Egypt) are invested with sufficient "historical and cultural significance" that they do not have to engage in the same sort of frenzied competition to create an authentic identity to draw in tourist dollars (Fainstein and Judd 1999:11) as other places do. These locales, they say, possess something called "place luck," which is not far from one Egyptian tourism official's argument that the pharaonic monuments were "intrinsic" tourist attractions. But of course (as Fainstein and Judd recognize), it is not luck at all that invests these places with historical and cultural significance. "Place luck" is the outcome of a long historical process that is always political, in which certain geographical points or archaeological ruins are designated civilizational centers to which modern societies must make their pilgrimage, and those civilizational narratives and pilgrimages are then harnessed to contemporary political projects (Abu El-Haj 2001). That it can later appear as "luck" demonstrates just how hegemonic these discourses become, such that the concept of inevitability or luck can mask the political circumstances that created these objects as icons of national identity.

Yet they are not wholly hegemonic, as the discussion of the contemporary politics of Egyptology has shown. And the fact that the pharaonic past is far from an intrinsic tourist draw for Arab tourists in Egypt is a reminder of the historical particularities that constructed ancient Egypt as a national narrative for certain audiences, but not for others.

This book has shown how tourist agendas and narratives reflect and indeed constitute some of the many different arenas where the political work of describing Egypt—as a country, a people, a culture, and a history—is fought out. In the contemporary politics of Egyptology, for example, we are reminded that the writing of ancient history is an intrinsically political act. In the case of President Anwar Sadat, who famously called himself "the last of the pharaohs," the symbols of ancient Egypt were appropriated in an attempt to harness the greatness of the past to a contemporary political leader, lending not only legitimacy but also an aura of greatness to his reign. But the example of Sadat reminds us that such symbols of the past are multivalent, for his assassins, too, portrayed Sadat as Pharaoh, with all the negative connotations of despotic idolatry that that evoked.

European colonizers were certainly not the first to introduce the pharaonic past to Egyptians. Pharaoh is a constant presence in the Qur'an, where he appears in the stories of Moses and the sexual temptation of Joseph. In the Qur'an, pharaonic times are associated with corruption and portrayed as a great civilization that was destroyed by God for its sins. Pharaoh was not the invention of colonialism, but it was European colonialism and, subsequently, early Egyptian nationalists who gave the pharaonic past some of its more posi-tive renderings, enabling modern Egyptians to speak with pride of their phar-aonic heritage.[4] By the 1950s, Umm Kalthoum, the great Egyptian classical singer, could sing a poem by Hafez Ibrahim which extols the glory and majesty of the pyramids: "And the builders of the pyramids . . . have impressed upon me that indeed, my glory is in the beginnings."[5]

In the battle over Egypt's history, artifacts of antiquity become multivalent symbols that are laden with endless layers of meaning and wielded like holy talismans in the struggle for authority to write and rewrite the past. But the impact of these processes is not an abstract exercise in writing history books; it has more immediate effects on the lives of contemporary Egyptians who live near key tourist sites or over archaeological remains. This point was driven home to me when I interviewed both Egyptologists and inhabitants of the vil-lage of Nazlet el-Semman. The village of Nazlet el-Semman is situated next to the Giza pyramids and the Sphinx and, according to Egyptologists, is built on top of major Old Kingdom archaeological sites, including the Valley Temple of Khufu. Egyptologists have long wanted to excavate this site, and several gener-ations of directors of the Giza Plateau have lobbied the government to have the villagers relocated to different land. They accuse villagers not only of blocking the progress of archaeological knowledge, but of digging beneath their homes to find artifacts to sell on the black market. (Indeed, the number of holes that have recently been dug into the sand near the pyramids under cover of night— making horseback riding in the desert treacherous—shows that some do try, though whether they find portable items to sell is debated.) As one Egyptian Egyptologist told me in an interview,

> There is site pollution here [on the Giza Plateau], and the pyramids are not in the desert anymore, they are in downtown. And we should move the village. I always said that the village should be moved, that the government should build a village for them, and move them to that village. The cam-els and horses are also everywhere. . . . they shit all over the pyramids and they contribute to site pollution. But . . . these people, it's impossible to move them, because they are influential and they are rich! They are *really* rich! Many of them make lots of money from the camels and horses, they used to smuggle antiquities, they do everything.[6]

He claimed that the villagers' wealth translated into substantial political lever-age and so the archaeologists couldn't get enough support from politicians to force a move.

Villagers, in turn, complained to me that Egyptologists, in some esoteric pursuit of knowledge, were trying to uproot them from their traditional land.

Figure 6.2. Camels wait for tourists at the pyramids in the 1930s. Photographer unknown; collection of L. L. Wynn.

They claimed roots in that area that dated back hundreds and sometimes thousands of years. Dr. Mamdouh el-Khattab, an elderly man from a prominent village family, said,

> The village of Nazlet el-Semman [existed] long, long, long ago. . . . The guards of the pyramids, those guides who were working with tourists who came to visit the pyramids, and tourism did not start in the 20th century or the 19th century, but it started long, long, long ago. Let us say, maybe it started during the Old Kingdom itself, or the Middle Kingdom, or the New Kingdom. And maybe we know about the Dream Stele which is in between the two front legs of the Sphinx, the Pharaoh Thutmosis the Fourth was coming in the area and he slept in the shade of the Sphinx . . . so there was a kind of tourism—those people who were guiding the people, telling them stories, right or wrong, but they were the people who were telling the stories about the pyramids.

Not only the village, but also its link to tourism, was as ancient as the monuments themselves, Dr. el-Khattab implied.

What was fascinating, though, was the way these two groups—archaeologists and villagers—used a photograph to argue their case about who had rights to the land. When I interviewed Dr. Zahi Hawass about the issue of excavations and villagers, he pulled out a photograph of the Giza Plateau and pyramids that dated back to the 1940s. "As you can see," he told me, "back then the area was almost empty. The whole area in front of the pyramids was flooded with water, and there were very few houses. And even [if] you see the whole right side, when you go to town, of the Pyramids Road, no houses existed then. And you can see the pyramids from downtown Cairo. Now, the village has expanded to be like 200,000 people—actually almost 200,000 families."

Then one day I interviewed a man whose family had lived in the village of Nazlet el-Semman for, he said, generations. He had spent his youth working as an engineer and living abroad, but eventually he decided to retire, move back to the village, and open a tourist gift shop. As we discussed the village and the conflict between villagers and Egyptologists, he pulled out a postcard with an old picture of the village. "You see?" he said. "They [the Egyptologists] say that we have built our village over an archaeological site. But look at this old photo:

Figure 6.3. A 1930s photograph shows the Sphinx overlooking the village of Nazlet el-Semman. Photographer unknown; collection of L. L. Wynn.

Figure 6.4. A Lehnert and Landrock postcard (date unknown) showing the pyramids and villagers from Nazlet el-Semman during the time of the Nile floods, before the building of the Aswan High Dam. A similar image was shown to me by both villagers and Egyptologists to buttress their conflicting positions on excavating under the current village of Nazlet el-Semman. Collection of L. L. Wynn.

where the village is today, there was nothing but a lake before. Did the ancient Egyptians build their cities in the water? Of course not! Our village is built on empty land; the antiquities area is elsewhere."

It was the same photo that Dr. Hawass had shown me. Similar photos appeared again and again as I talked to both villagers and Egyptologists. Yet another villager produced one to make the same argument as the engineer:

> And if we return back before the Aswan Dam, the High Dam, the annual flood covered the whole area, including the house that we are sitting in now. This area was completely covered with water. My great-grandfathers were living on the high ground just beside the Giza Plateau, what we call in Arabic al-wāya al-ʿālī, which literally means the high ground, because the water would reach a limit and then the people can live above it, and when the flood goes, the people come down from their houses and start cultivating in the area and so on. . . . All these thousands of years and this area was covered with flood[waters]. And even if we look at the contour

of the plateau, we can know where are the areas that were flooded by the Nile. . . . So this area was covered by water, and I don't think the ancient Egyptians came and built in the water.[7]

The issue is of immediate importance to villagers of Nazlet el-Semman, who feel that the Egyptological reverence for the past comes at the expense of respecting the contemporary inhabitants' rights to the land. Regarding the Valley Temple that Egyptologists claim lies beneath Nazlet el-Semman, Dr. Mamdouh el-Khattab argued,

[Even if archaeologists were to find some remains of the Valley Temple,] would it be enough to eliminate the whole village of five thousand houses? About twenty or more thousand people living in this area, eliminated for the sake of the Valley Temple or Mortuary Temple? If that is the case here in Nazlet el-Semman, because it is close to the pyramids, what will happen in Luxor, where the city is between Luxor Temple and Karnak Temple?— so we have to eliminate the entire city of Luxor?! What is the case in Islamic Cairo, in which you will find shops and houses inside the monuments themselves? So we have to eliminate all of Cairo! Believe me, I'm not exaggerating: even under the house of the President [Mubarak], there will be antiquities, because Heliopolis was an ancient site. And we know that if you make a cross section of the land of Egypt, you will find the Predynastic area, then you will find the Old Kingdom, the Middle Kingdom, the New Kingdom, the Greek-Roman period, until you will reach Coptic and Islamic times. These are layers of history over each other. So what will be the archaeologists' answer for this? Eliminate all of Egypt and we will go to Libya and live there and leave it all to the archaeologists?

Again, we return to the palimpsest, to layers and versions of history being written over each other, over the same land, the same monuments, and the same picture. But also we are reminded that excavation, a technique for reading that history, is no abstract intellectual exercise, but a politicized act that has implications not only for scholars but for contemporary Egyptians who live on or near potential excavations. In a sense, excavation parallels the idea of palimpsest. On the surface, the two appear to represent opposite trajectories, with one layering over and the other uncovering traces of the past. But a closer look at the politics of Egyptology shows how the uncovering of monuments is undertaken in the service of a simultaneous layering of historical meaning and interpretation onto the Egyptian past.[8]

It was a European fascination with pharaonic Egypt that has propelled one elaboration of Egyptian identity as an "antique" land. The Enlightenment fervor of the Western world to describe and rule the Orient was the original impetus for what has become, today, multiple industries: tourism, archaeology and anthropology, museums, tour guides and guide books, antiquities reproductions, and a black-market trade in artifacts.[9] The current politics of Egyptology reverberate with the historical process by which a European treasure hunt and large-scale policy of looting was gradually converted to a science of archaeology under Egyptian government supervision.

Arab tourism in Egypt centers on a completely different imagination of Egypt as a people, history, nation, and culture. Just as an Egyptian pharaonic identity was constructed through a history of Egyptology and contact with the West, so too is Egyptian cultural identity partially constituted in the productions of popular culture that are broadcast all over the Arab world, from classical singers such as Umm Kalthoum to pop culture icons such as Amrou Diyab. Arab tourists come to Cairo in the summer to experience the cultural world of their favorite television soap operas, movies, theater productions, and songs. They hope to see a play starring one of their favorite actors, go to a nightclub to see a pop star sing, or, as one Egyptian hotel worker speculated (in Chapter 4), just to meet a friendly Egyptian girl like the ones they see on Egyptian television. In a regional context, Egyptians take pride in a national identity which is constituted as much by a pharaonic past as by the fact that Egypt is the cultural hegemon in the Arab world, where it dominates the Arabic-speaking regional media, and Egyptian is the most widely understood Arabic dialect.

And yet here too we find fissures in the apparent unity of culture and language that facilitate Arab tourism in Egypt. Gulf Arabs, fed a visual diet of relatively racy Egyptian films, may inappropriately assume that the average Egyptian woman they encounter working in the restaurants, hotels, and casinos they frequent is a sexual libertine, while Egyptians I interviewed frequently confessed to being baffled by the dress styles, food and eating preferences, and other markers of Gulf culture. Linguistic differences between Gulf and Egyptian dialects reflect different histories of transnational engagements, and cultural differences in terms of polite address can lead to misunderstandings (see Chapter 4). The regional context of migrant labor and the inequitable distribution of oil wealth throughout the Arab world contribute to Egyptian antipathy toward Arab tourists, and specific events in Egypt and abroad, from the exploits of Prince Tork to the maltreatment of Egyptians working in the Gulf, fan the flames of resentment. On the other hand, popular Egyptian stereotypes that insist (with a mixture of indignation, resentment, and perhaps a twinge of pride) that Gulf Arab tourists come to Egypt to sexually exploit Egyptian women are belied by the vacation activities of young, urbane Gulf tourists who prefer to see their time in Cairo as an opportunity to meet, date, and court their own compatriots, and regard Egyptians with wariness as economic exploiters, trying to take advantage of imagined Gulf wealth (Chapter 5).

STATE NARRATIVES, NARRATIVES OF STATE

These sketches I have drawn of particular forms of Arab and Western tourism do not exhaust the touristic imaginations of Egypt. Far from it. Other forms of tourism that I have neglected in this account of transnational encounters range widely, from sports tourism and religious pilgrimage to desert safaris and hunting trips to the "sun-sea-and-sand" tourism of both Westerners and Arabs (but particularly Europeans) who fly straight to Sinai beaches or to the Red Sea resort of Hurghada for holidays, bypassing Cairo and the monuments altogether.[10] And while I have suggested that Arab tourists engage with a more contemporary image of Egypt than Westerners, with their interest in the pharaonic past, there are certainly Western tourists who are interested in contemporary Egyptian culture; yet even here the vision of contemporary Egyptian culture differs: Western tourists are more likely to visit the whirling dervish show near al-Azhar and the Khan el-Khalili or attend a folkloric dance show than they are to see a play or a musical concert or Egyptian movie, the kinds of performances of Egyptian culture popular among Arab tourists. But while there are certainly other forms of tourism among both Arabs and Westerners, which reveal competing imaginations of Egypt, the types of tourism I have portrayed in this book do represent the most typical touristic destinations and activities for Arabs and Western tourists in Egypt.

The two broad types of tourism being compared in this book—Western and Arab—are not symmetric. I have mapped out images of Western and Arab tourism over the history of European colonialism and the regional political economy to find ways in which imaginations of the other (both touristic imaginations of Egypt as well as Egyptian imaginations of tourists) resonate in these broader political and economic contexts. And these contexts are not equivalent. Egypt has a closer relationship to the Arab world than it does with Western countries. Egyptians have more direct contact with Saudis and other Gulf Arabs than they do with Europeans or Americans because of the degree of regional labor migration engendered by the oil boom; shared language and popular culture give Arab tourists a completely different basis for fantasizing about Egypt and ideas of what to do in Egypt that are not shared by Western tourists. Meanwhile, Western countries (predominantly the United States and Europe) may be more culturally distant, but they make their economic and political presence immediately felt; the occasional outrage in the Egyptian press and public gossip mills over the treatment of Egyptian laborers in the Gulf or the exploits of Prince Tork cannot compare with the anger many Egyptians felt toward Western countries, and in particular the United States, for their economic hegemony, their military incursions in Afghanistan and Iraq, and their support of Israel in its continued occupation of Palestinian and Lebanese and Syrian lands and killing of Palestinian and Lebanese people.

Just as the broader historical, political, and economic contexts of Egypt's relationship with Western and Arab countries cannot simply be seen as minor variations on fundamental equivalents, but rather reflect larger global structures of inequality, so too are the forms of tourism that they have engendered substantially different. So while the Arab belief in a powerful pharaonic elixir called "red mercury" and similar mystical Arab imaginations of ancient Egypt which other authors have traced back to medieval times are proof that it is not only Westerners who creatively construct a monumental pharaonic history, and while some Arab tourists may consult Egyptian *shuyūkh* (popular healers) for magical remedies, which may or may not authorize themselves with reference to a mysterious pharaonic past, these are not simply the Arab equivalent of the Western New Age imagination of ancient Egypt which enthralls Western audiences and drives one particular brand of Western monuments tourism. That is not to say that the majority of Western tourism is New Age tourism. Yet the predominant brand of Western tourism is concerned with ancient monuments, and this vision of Egypt shares with New Age tourism a vision of Egypt as the inheritor of a monumental, and somewhat mysterious, pharaonic past. The popularity of books devoted to the "mysteries of the pyramids" (a common title and subtitle) illustrates that mystical constructions of Egypt's past compete with more orthodox Egyptological narratives for a Western audience in a way that just has no equivalent for Arabs, whose holiday itineraries by and large do not include visits to pharaonic monuments.

Likewise, there is simply no equivalent in Western tourism to the phenomenon of Arabs who come to Egypt on an annual basis to meet up with friends and family, as I have described for the Saudi tourists who regularly spend a month or more on summer holidays in Cairo. And Western tourists do not have the same interest in contemporary Egyptian popular culture because they do not share a language with Egyptians, as do Arab tourists, so they are not going to come to Egypt to see Rashed al-Majed give a private concert in a Cairo hotel, or pay hundreds of pounds to see Ehab Tawfiq and Dina perform at the Semiramis nightclub.

But what the two forms of tourism that I have described do share is economic privilege. The average tourist in Egypt, whether Arab, Western, or Asian, is considerably wealthier than most Egyptians, and tourism is a top earner of

Figure 6.5. Billboards on a Cairo street advertise two Egyptian movies, a New Year's Eve concert by Egyptian pop singer Amrou Diyab in a Cairo luxury hotel, and an album by the Lebanese singer Najwa Karam. Photograph by Mahmoud Abbas Elbadawi.

foreign currency for the Egyptian state. This economic power translates into forms of political and cultural power (Mitchell 1995). This includes the protection of Western and Arab tourists by the tourist police and the way Egyptian authorities turn a blind eye to activities which would probably be prosecuted if engaged in by Egyptians, such as the sexual dalliances of both Western and Arab tourists and the abuses of Egyptians by Prince Tork's bodyguards. The fact that Zayd, my Saudi acquaintance described in the previous chapter, could casually compare the respective merits of Egyptian and Moroccan prostitutes reflects a transnational economy in which the poorer countries supply sexual services to the powerful and wealthy men of neighboring countries, and even those who claim no personal knowledge of prostitution can speak casually of a market in female Arab bodies. This economic power also can be seen in the funding of plays, folkloric dances, and other cultural productions geared toward both Arab and Western tourists, and in the building of museums and the excavation of ancient Egyptian archaeological sites which are primarily visited by Western tourists.

Such elaborations of Egyptian cultural identity for foreign consumption do not exist in a touristic bubble. They also trickle down to have a much wider impact, as they become part of the vocabulary for debating Egyptian national and cultural identity. And it is in this sense that we can speak of tourism's impact on Egyptians who have no immediate personal or economic link to the tourism industry. So the productions of Egyptian popular culture, from plays and belly dance shows that are consumed by shared audiences of both Egyptians and Arab tourists in the summer, to movies and songs that are exported to Arab consumers in the Gulf and elsewhere, may be shaped by their non-Egyptian audiences. And while many Egyptians have never lived and worked in the Gulf, media reports of the negative experiences of those who have, as well as the publicity surrounding Prince Tork's exploits and the summer marriages between wealthy Arab men and poor, young Egyptian villagers, all influence the Egyptian imagination of Arab tourists on holiday in Egypt, even among Egyptians who have little or no contact with Arab tourists.

As for Western tourism in Egypt, its impact on a face-to-face level is light, since most Western tourists have little contact with locals, outside of the relatively small number of Egyptians who work in the tourism industry as guides or hotel receptionists and wait staff. But the Western tourist imagination of Egypt as an ancient and pharaonic land has a much broader impact in the long term, inasmuch as the Egyptian government mandates lessons on the pharaonic past in government schools and uses pharaonic history in discourses on national history and unity, and tries to evict villagers in Giza (Rose 2003) and Luxor (Mitchell 2002) in order to clear the way for development projects, archaeological excavations, and tourist imaginations of what an Egyptian village should look like. Whether Egyptians individually or as a group identify with this pharaonic past or reject it in favor of other markers of identity, they cannot escape its powerful presence as one competing version of Egyptian identity when pharaonic symbols adorn numerous quotidian examples of material culture, from the national currency to stamps to the logo of the state newspaper.

The shared economic power of Arab and Western tourists is the most obvious link between otherwise very different forms of tourism. Perhaps less obvious, however, is the fact that the types of Arab and Western tourism I have described in this book share a common reference point in imagining a powerful Egyptian state. This is apparent in the "Entering the Seventh Millennium" slogan used by the publicity campaign for the Y2K celebrations at the Giza pyramids (what could be more powerful than a timeless nation that persists through six millennia while other empires and civilizations rise and fall?), or in the 1930s appropriation by Egyptian nationalist politicians of pharaonic nationalism following the discovery of Tutankhamun's tomb. Thus we can see instances of when pharaonic identity has been articulated both mimetically in response to Western imaginations of Egypt, and oppositionally, to establish credentials of historical and civilizational greatness against the civilizing dogma of British and French colonialism. On the other hand, Egyptians set aside their pharaonic past in favor of a shared Arab or Islamic identity vis-à-vis the United States and Israel in support of the Palestinian *intifāda* and when opposing Western military actions in Muslim countries like Afghanistan and Iraq. Here, the reference to a national or state image is one in which Egypt is a political giant in the contemporary Arab world, not the inheritor of a pharaonic civilizational past.[11]

Images of state and state-building are apparent, too, in the images that Egyptians hold of Arab tourists. The popular Egyptian images of Arab tourists that portray them as nouveaux riches Bedouins, fondling their toes and eating with their hands and sharing their luxury sedans with barnyard animals, are also constructions of civilizational identity: they reflect a construction of Egypt as a great and powerful centralized state, both historically and in contemporary times, and juxtapose this image of the Egyptian state with an implicit portrayal of fractured Arab tribalism, the absence of both state and civilization. Likewise, I often heard Saudi tourists express disdain for Egyptian obsequiousness and distaste for the Egyptian use of Turkish-derived honorifics such as *pasha* and *bey* and *efendim,* as well as French words and phrases in common use, such as *merci.* And a few Saudis went so far as to claim that such linguistic traits reflected Egypt's history of subjugation to colonial powers, which they contrasted with a portrayal of Saudi culture and history as fiercely defiant vis-à-vis the West and marked by a tribal egalitarianism that they contrasted with a more rigid and hierarchical Egyptian class structure. Again, such constructions of cultural difference between Egyptians and Saudis make implicit or explicit links with forms of statehood and national history.

The state comes into this story in another way. The comparison of Arab and Western travel in Egypt illustrates how national identities, histories, and culture are elaborated through borderland encounters such as tourism. And while individual Egyptians participate in the tourism industry, it is important to recognize how the institutions of the state structure, reproduce, and perpetuate Western and Arab imaginations of Egypt, in the ways that the Egyptian state markets Egypt as a tourist destination, licenses tour guides, trains and employs Egyptologists, writes history books, restores monuments and creates new ones, and funds and regulates cultural performances—from the opera *Aïda,* performed every year at an outdoor performance in front of the pyramids and Sphinx, to the whirling dervishes who perform for tourist audiences twice a week in Islamic Cairo, to summer theater productions that are geared toward Gulf Arab spectators, to Oriental dancers who perform for both Gulf and Western tourist audiences.

And yet Egypt and Egyptian identity are far from determined by a monolithic state acting from above to construct Egyptian culture. These state-approved discourses on history, culture, and identity are not passively absorbed, either by Egyptians or by travelers to Egypt. They are actively consumed in ways that at times acquiesce to dominant narratives but at others challenge them. So, for example, Dr. Zahi Hawass often complained that the majority of Egyptians visiting the pyramids did not sufficiently respect the Giza pyramids but rather vulgarized them by using the lower stones as settings for family picnics during national holidays. In a similar vein, while a very few Egyptian films and television shows have taken the pharaonic past as their subject matter, the pharaonic monuments are more commonly featured in Egyptian popular culture as a backdrop for romantic and even illicit encounters. In Egyptian films, characters visit the pyramids not to appreciate ancient majesty but to kiss in a picturesque spot where they are unlikely to be spied on by their neighbors and relatives. Instead of seeing this popular reading of the pyramids as a mark of ignorance or lack of culture, it is perhaps more useful to see these as acts of antidiscipline (de Certeau 1984:xv) that quietly resist constructions of the monumental gravity of the site. Such "tactics of consumption," as de Certeau calls them, are, in their own way, political acts, because they doggedly resist the imposition of centralized and spectacular elite discourses of Egyptian history and identity.[12]

Seen against the backdrop of European colonialism and its use of Egyptology to serve its own narratives of civilizational history, the Egyptian state's palimpsest-like rewriting of ancient pharaonic history to tell a story of unified and timeless Egyptian nationalism looks like a de Certeauian tactic of resistance. Yet when the practices of contemporary Egyptology are viewed in the context of conflicts with Egyptian citizens whose houses and farmland are located on top of ancient ruins, the prism shifts; suddenly, pharaonic nationalism reads more like the strategic (to stick with de Certeau's vocabulary) imposition of a powerful elite narrative.[13]

Perhaps a more useful metaphor than the palimpsest is that of graffiti. Egyptologists today encounter layers upon layers of graffiti on the monuments—in hieroglyphics, Coptic, Greek, Latin, Arabic, French, English, and German.[14] Graffiti is an individual act (or tactic), not one which is undertaken by a state or a religious movement or even an academic discipline. It is an act which on one level swallows the dominant reading and labeling of a site, accepting elite markers of civilizational distinction, while at the same time it defies the demand for reverence that such dominant narratives make.[15] In trying to overwrite these dominant narratives of civilization and history, graffiti simultaneously requires their underwriting for some of its weight. It is at once oppositional, reinforcing, and mimetic.[16] In this sense, it neatly expresses the complex map of power relations that characterize tourism as a prime site where transnational encounters shape national identities.

ORIENTAL DANCE

Up to this point, I have relied on a heuristic distinction between tourist itiner-aries that neatly divides off a purportedly "Arab" and "Western" imagination of Egypt. But here I want to take one last detour by considering a final touristic arena which confounds such neat categories. Belly dance is an example of a touristic site where Western and Arab imaginations of Egypt are complexly intertwined. Within Egypt, the stereotype of Arab tourists holds that "Arabs" (i.e., Gulf Arabs) are the greatest fans of "Oriental dance," as it is called in Ara-bic (Western audiences know it as "belly dancing"). But Western tourists also figure prominently in the audiences of Oriental dancers who perform on Nile dinner cruises and in the restaurants, discos, and nightclubs of Cairo hotels. And the Western imagination of Egyptian belly dancing played an important role in the transformation of this "traditional" art form.

By the late 1800s, French and English imperialism in Egypt had paved the way for an industry of academics and scholars describing the Middle East, which in turn fired up the interest of Western society in the Orient. Interna-tional expositions and world fairs in American and European cities brought exotic cultures and people to enthralled Western audiences.[17] Travelers like Flaubert published accounts of dancers encountered during their Middle East travels, and world fairs subsequently enacted these exotic fantasies of Middle Eastern culture for Western audiences, with performances of belly dance. As Mitchell (1988) recounts, the 1889 Paris Great Exhibition had a reproduction of a Cairo street in which the exterior of a mosque led to a bustling Egyptian-style coffee shop interior in which dancers performed with music. (Egyptian visitors to the fair were appalled.) So popular were these dancers that they were brought to the 1893 Chicago International Exposition, where they performed for six months. A Syrian dancer who went by the name "Little Egypt" was re-portedly one of the biggest attractions at the fair, where she both titillated and shocked American audiences with dance moves that a puritanical American audience found sexually suggestive and "lewd" (see Buonaventura 1983).

So go most histories of Oriental dance. Yet Donna Carlton (1994) examines the myth of Little Egypt, revealing that it is not at all clear who was the original dancer who performed under that name, nor what her nationality was; turn-of-the-century photographs of "Little Egypt" feature several different women, both Western and Middle Eastern. Even more provocative is Carlton's claim that, despite the number of historical sources, both academic and popular, that report that Little Egypt's debut occurred at the Chicago World's Fair, no contemporary account included any reference to Little Egypt, casting doubt on her presence there, and even whether an original historical Little Egypt

THE ORIENTAL DANCE

© Edward Gross Co., N. Y.   Painted by Alice Luelia Fidler

Figure 6.6. A 1919 postcard features a painting by Alice Luelia
Fidler showing an "Oriental dance" costume that does not
expose the belly. Collection of L. L. Wynn.

ever existed (Carlton 1994:x). If such is the case, then Little Egypt is a simu-
lacrum (Baudrillard 1988), an icon that encapsulates a particular imagination
of women, dance, the Middle East, and World Fairs, without even an original
from which it derives.

Danse du ventre became a faddish hit in the United States, and the myth
of Little Egypt was appropriated by various American dancers who, under
the same name, danced in burlesque shows. The "hootchy-kootchy," as it was
called, was simultaneously a transgressive send-up of bourgeois ideals of femi-

nine modesty and a parody of erotica, and it became standard fare of cabaret shows, music halls, and amusement parks (Badger 1979). Belly dancing made its way into some of the earliest films ever made, and "Danse du Ventre" (1896) was censored for its "indecent movements" (Badger 1979:105); a 1951 film had Rhonda Flemming playing the titular role of the historical Little Egypt.

The Hollywoodization of Oriental dance was responsible for an important change in the dance form back in Egypt: the transformation of the belly dancing costume. The basic outfit worn by the dancers in the international fairs, a vest over a long skirt, was insufficiently exotic, so cabaret shows added beads, spangles, sequins, and veils to fulfill a Western fantasy of Oriental splendor and decadence. There is some debate over how and when the two-piece costume of the beaded bra and the long skirt with slits up the side was introduced to Egypt. Wendy Buonaventura (1989) holds that it was developed in Western cabarets and then brought to Egypt by American film, which had a great influence on Egyptian film, and then filtered down to popular use, while Sarah Graham-Brown (1988:180) believes that it came from an Indian dance costume which was brought to Egypt by the British and later made its way to the West. Either way, what both versions have in common is an argument that the two-piece bra and skirt set as a costume for dancers in Egypt evolved through transnational cultural exchanges sometime between the turn of the century and the early 1930s. Van Nieuwkerk (1995:198) points out that the two-piece costume appeared in early American films well before the 1920s, while it did not appear in Egyptian pictures until the late 1920s. Hollywood's portrayal of Oriental dance in early American films certainly must have had an impact on early Egyptian filmmakers, who were themselves innovators in the art form, and, as van Nieuwkerk points out, the film portrayal of the nightclub later had a greater impact on popular dance circuits in Egypt than the actual nightclubs themselves, since relatively few Egyptians frequented nightclubs, but many were exposed to the media's interpretation of them.

In contemporary Egypt, "belly dancing" continues to be linked to tourism in important ways. First, many dancers perform in front of tourist audiences in the hotels and Nile cruise ships. But second, many of the Oriental dancers performing in Cairo today first came to Egypt as tourists themselves.

A story I heard repeatedly during the course of my research starts with a young woman who is visiting Cairo on vacation or for work; during her stay, she is taken out by friends to see a belly dancer. She is entranced, and when she goes back to Europe or Australia or the United States, she finds someone who teaches Oriental dance and starts taking classes. There is an extended network of teachers, students, and fans of "Oriental dance" (many find the term *belly dancing* offensive) in these countries, and they are linked not only by word of

Figure 6.7. Diana, a Frenchwoman who previously performed as a belly dancer all over the Middle East and Africa before settling in Cairo, where she works as a dance teacher and choreographer. Photograph by L. L. Wynn.
Figure 6.8. Semasem, a Swedish dancer who performed in Cairo for more than ten years. Photograph by L. L. Wynn.

mouth but also by costume shops, dance and exercise studios, the restaurants and clubs which cater to Arab expatriates, dance magazines, and the Internet. (Caroline, an Australian dancer, told me that, while working for Egyptian choreographer Raqia Hassan in 2000 to promote her annual International Oriental Dance Festival, she found a total of 450 Oriental dance schools with an Internet presence, all over the world.)

These women usually start out by taking lessons in their country, then find work dancing in some local venue, and they may return to Cairo several times to take short, intensive classes with teachers and choreographers such as Raqia Hassan, Ibrahim Akef, or Aida Nour, who are Egyptian, or Diana, a French dancer and choreographer based in Cairo. Finally, a few of them move to Egypt, hoping to fulfill their dream of succeeding as a dancer in the center of Oriental dance. For a foreign Oriental dancer, working in Cairo is the pinnacle of her career, and putting this on her résumé guarantees her success as a dancer, teacher, or choreographer back home.

Foreign dancers in Egypt have been on the scene for years, and they wax and wane in popularity both at weddings and also in the nightclubs and discotheques of five-star hotels. During my research, I encountered dancers from Argentina (Asmahan), Australia (Caroline), England (Yasmina), France (Diana), Iran (Liza), Japan (Kazumi), Russia (Katia, Nour, Shams, and Amar), and Sweden (Semasem). I heard of other dancers from the United States, Germany, Spain, Brazil, and virtually every country of the former Soviet Union. Most of them come to Egypt with a dance style that is rather different from that of Egyptian dancers. They are taught in their countries by teachers who often rely heavily on videos that are thirty to fifty years old; the rest is a Hollywoodized, Orientalist imagination of dance which circulates widely in the West, but which many say has little connection with the way dance is actually performed in Egypt. Most foreign dancers start taking classes and choreography with teachers when they come here, which modifies their style and "Egyptianizes" it.

In recent years, foreign dancers have had a major impact on the dance market in Egypt. Most of the dancers I interviewed, both Egyptian and foreign, claimed that foreign dancers have driven down the prices that all dancers can command at hotels. For foreigners, dancing in Cairo is a highly coveted achievement to put on their résumé, and some are willing to sacrifice money to get a job dancing there. There are even stories about dancers who actually *pay* to be able to dance in prestigious venues. It's difficult to ascertain to what extent this is true. Almost any dancer has to give kickbacks to the stage manager in the various places she performs if she wants to keep her place on the program, but some, it is rumored, pay much more than the going rate to be able to dance.

But even if they're not dancing for free or paying people to let them dance, there's another way that the presence of foreign dancers can affect the market. Most come to Cairo without a good knowledge of the business and what the going rates are for dancers. They are easy prey for unknown artists' agents who want to get an edge in the business. Unscrupulous agents will try to keep control over a new dancer by advising her not to talk to any other dancers because, they say, "The others are jealous of you." If she doesn't talk to any other dancers, she doesn't know what prices she should be commanding. Then the agent goes to different venues and offers her for two-thirds or half the going rate. Even if she's not a very good dancer, some stage managers will accept this, at least for a short period of time, because, since clubs have fairly standard prices for all dancers, they know that if they pay one dancer less, they can pocket the

Figure 6.9. Liza, an Iranian-British belly dancer, performing on the *Nile Maxime* cruise ship in Cairo. Photograph by Louise Wynn.

difference. This kind of competition drives down rates for all the other dancers, both Egyptian and foreign, who want to perform in Cairo.

Of course every place has competition and these kinds of movements of supply and demand, but Cairo is unique because of the excess supply of dancers who want to "make it" there, while at the same time, local interest in dance shows is decreasing, with the younger generation of elites preferring to spend nights in discos and bars. According to foreign dancers who have danced in several different countries, the going rate for dancers in Cairo is about half of what it is in Lebanon or Dubai.

But there is another even more important way that the excess supply of foreign dancers is influencing the dance scene in Cairo. It operates at the intersection of the economy and the social valuation of dancers in Egyptian society.
In Egypt, dancers do not only perform at nightclubs, discos, and cabarets—
they are also considered an essential presence at celebrations such as saints'
day celebrations and weddings. Yet there is a social stigma attached to dancers
themselves (see van Nieuwkerk 1995). Many middle-class Egyptians consider
dancers loose women who sell their bodies, and the term *dancer—ra'āsa*—can
be applied as a pejorative epithet and can be almost synonymous with *whore*.
(One famous Egyptian dancer, Fifi Abdou, recounted in a television interview
that her daughter was taunted at university by other students who referred to
her as "You whose mother is a dancer." My Egyptian friends often advised me
to stop hanging out with "those dancers" with whom I socialized during the
course of my research, for the sake of my own reputation and morals.)

The Islamic revival in Egypt, another form of transnational exchange, has
contributed to the stigmatization of an art form that displays and sensualizes
the female body. Van Nieuwkerk (1995) shows how professional Egyptian dancers (it is a trade that many are born into) differentiate dancing at fairs and weddings from dancing in nightclubs. While many consider the former respectable
work, nightclub dancing is not, and many dismiss nightclub dancers as little
better than prostitutes. Yet dancing in prestigious hotels and nightclubs brings
a dancer fame. As long as there is a substantial income to make it worthwhile
for an Egyptian dancer to perform, there will always be those who are willing to
sacrifice social prestige for a lucrative nightclub career. But if there isn't much
money involved, many would prefer to retain their social respectability rather
than work as a nightclub dancer for paltry sums. Foreigners do not have the
same difficult choice to make. Foreign dancers are much less affected by the
social valuation of dancers in Egyptian society, since they are often in Egypt
for only a few years, and for many, dancing is not just a way to make money—it
converts into other kinds of social currency (experience, exposure to different
dance styles, "authenticity," and the prestige of having danced in Cairo), which
can be cashed in on later when they return to their own countries.

With foreigners driving down the price that a dancer in Cairo can command, and with the popularity of dancers and belly dance shows on the wane
as other forms of decadent entertainment, display, and excess are on the rise
(such as the discotheque, which is attracting the young moneyed elite whose
parents might have spent an evening out at a nightclub watching a dancer perform), there is less incentive for Egyptians to subject themselves to the social
stigma of being a dancer in an atmosphere of increasing social conservatism.
This complicated transnational inflection on the moral economy of dance in
Egyptian society is certainly one factor behind the lack of rising Egyptian stars

in the dance scene in Egypt today. While the top three dancers in Egypt (Fifi Abdou, Lucy, and Dina) are Egyptian, there is not a single Egyptian dancer who is perceived to be on her way toward achieving this kind of stardom, and at the time I did my research, at most of the five-star hotels in Cairo where dancers perform (either in the hotel nightclub or on the Nile dinner cruise boats operated by the hotels), at least half (and often more than half) of the dancers on the roster were foreigners.

In August 2003, someone in the Egyptian government decided to intervene. Ahmed El Amawi, Minister of Manpower and Immigration, announced his intention to ban all non-Egyptians from working as belly dancers starting in January 2004.[18] Yasser Allam, a wealthy Egyptian businessman who is the husband of the popular Russian dancer Nour (her stage name), filed suit against the new law. The Australian dancer Caroline Evanoff also sued against enforcement of the law. There were several arguments brought to bear against it. First, many hotel and nightclub managers in Red Sea resorts such as Hurghada would face a sudden shortage of dancers, since they mostly hire Russians to perform in their belly dance shows. There simply aren't enough Egyptians living in these towns who are prepared (trained, costumed, and willing) to work as dancers. Second, Caroline pointed out that most of the money made by foreign dancers ultimately goes back into the Egyptian economy in the form of rent, belly dance costumes, wages paid to their bands, and lessons from the Egyptian dance instructors and choreographers who are popular with foreign dancers and dance students, not to mention the significant portion of their salary which is taxed by the Egyptian government, so wages paid to foreign dancers were hardly a threat to the local economy. But perhaps most interesting was Caroline's objection to the law's presumption that Oriental dance "is a purely Egyptian art form that shouldn't be subject to foreign intrusion."[19] Nour and Caroline argued that the dance form was not purely Egyptian, and as evidence they pointed to not only the historical presence of foreign dancers performing in Egypt but also the long history of transnational artistic exchanges that have shaped the contemporary form of Oriental dance as practiced in Egypt today. They were successful: in early September 2004, the Egyptian government overturned the law banning foreigners from working as belly dancers.

The excess supply of foreign dancers in Egypt is a result of both the popularity of Egyptian dance in Western countries and Japan and of the increasing transnational movements of people in Egypt in the post-*infitāh* (economic "open door" policy) era. All the dancers, teachers, choreographers, and musicians I interviewed, both Egyptian and foreign, agreed that foreign dancers have played a significant role in the economy and development of Oriental dance in

Egypt today.[20] But the influence of transnational movements of people on the development of Oriental dance is not a novel, postmodern phenomenon—it dates back to the nineteenth century (and perhaps well before that, though the historical record is murky); as noted, even the "traditional" Egyptian dance costume was an innovation adapted from an early twentieth-century Holly-wood imagination of Oriental dance. The Hollywoodization of Oriental dance in Egypt illustrates how, in a history of transnational encounters, the imagina-tion of an exotic (and erotic) other intersects with cross-cultural exchanges to create new definitions of "traditional" cultural forms. The court decision per-mitting non-Egyptians to work as belly dancers in Egypt is an unusual public recognition of the fact that this Egyptian dance has been created and defined through a history of such transnational exchanges.

CONCLUSIONS: AN ETHNOGRAPHY OF THE IDEA OF EGYPT

This book tells a story about how Egypt and Egyptian identity have been con-structed through transnational (or borderland) encounters, from European co-lonialism to regional economic migration arising out of the oil economy to the economic forces of contemporary tourism, both Western and Arab.[21] But, of course, the story isn't just about Egyptians; it is also about Americans, Euro-peans, and (non-Egyptian) Arabs. As scholars such as Edward Said and Homi Bhabha have pointed out, if we cannot assume a pre-existent Egyptian identity, neither can we assume a pre-existent European or Gulf Arab identity acting on Egyptians. The stories I have told in this account have also hinted at some of the ways in which people became Westerners or Gulf Arabs through inter-actions with Egyptians and the mutual construction of identities.

This book is also a story about national narratives, as it traces the power of the state to write narratives of history and identity. These national narratives emerge out of dialogue with and through oppositional politics vis-à-vis power-ful outside forces, ranging from European colonialism and Middle Eastern re-gional politics with competing discourses of Islamic and Arab civilization, to the more dispersed but still powerful narrative authority of contemporary non-state actors, from European and American authors writing alternative histories of ancient Egypt to wealthy Gulf tourists who consume a pop-culture version of Egypt.

Yet we also see how popular consumption of those narratives is by no means determined either by the state or by powerful international economic forces of tourism. Small tactics of the less powerful resist dominant discourses of nation and identity. This is true on a local scale, from Egyptian villagers who contest the significance of archaeological investigations around the pyramids, to Cairenes who use the pyramids as their picnic grounds or the setting for romantic interludes rather than contemplating them with reverent awe, to Egyptian shopkeepers who refuse service to Arab tourists as a protest against the treatment of Egyptian migrant laborers in Saudi Arabia. It also applies to the international consumption of national constructions of Egyptian identity, from Western tourists who create alternative histories of pharaonic Egypt that contradict the orthodox Egyptological narrative endorsed by the Egyptian government, to Gulf tourists who ignore the pyramids and reject Egyptian claims to civilizational greatness, to Australian and Russian belly dancers who challenge an attempt by Egyptian lawmakers to define Oriental dance as an intrinsically Egyptian art form.

Travel and cross-cultural encounters are not merely factors contributing to the production of subjectivities in the nation-building project, they are *key* factors. The tourist economy in Egypt illuminates the creative projects of cultural and identity production that occur through processes at once mimetic and oppositional in encounters with national others. The classic examples of postcolonial theory where this concept of culture was developed often focused on the encounters between colonizer and colonized and the productive ambiguity that resulted (compare Bhabha 1990, 1994). But if this ethnography starts with that grand narrative, the narrative of Egyptian history as produced through colonial encounters with the West and engagement with the academic disciplines (such as Egyptology) that emerged from them, it subsequently diverges to examine a rather different sort of postcolonial encounter. In this cross-cultural, transnational encounter, the West has become a marginal character, and the postcolonial encounter is reversed: instead of former colonizers becoming tourists, we contemplate a scenario in which Arabs from the Arabian Peninsula have become tourists in lands of former colonial authority, be they Egypt (formerly a powerful center of Ottoman rule) or Europe. Finally, in my brief digression to explore the contemporary state of Oriental dance in Egypt, we see, to paraphrase from Homi Bhabha (1994:2), the complex negotiation and authorization of new cultural hybridities, which nevertheless masquerade awkwardly as "tradition."

Both Western and Arab travels in Egypt are rooted in millennia of travel, trade, pilgrimage, conquest, colonialism, and tourism. This history of transnational encounters has in turn had a lasting impact on Egyptian national identity. There are important theoretical lessons to be drawn from this which have shaped the writing and the very form of this ethnography. One is the location of identity and even "culture." The study of Arab and Western tourism, dance, and Egyptology in Egypt reveals how national identities are created through encounters with cultural others. It also shows how identities are fluid, situ-

ational, and relative.²² Egypt means many different things in different contexts. It exists in the interstices, and it cannot be pinned down, because it is
constantly shifting and transforming. The shape given it in this ethnography,
where it looks sometimes like a pyramid surrounded by miles of sand and
sometimes like neon lights reflected on the surface of the Nile at night, is
merely one very partial description which is bound to be contested by other
shapes, gleaming with other facets of historical encounters.

The other important issue raised by the study of tourism and, in particular,
the history of Oriental dance in Egypt, is that of cultural "authenticity" and
the discipline of anthropology itself: what should anthropologists study, and
what should they include in their description of a culture, people, or nation? A
recent anthropological study of Oriental dance in Egypt (van Nieuwkerk's 1995
authoritative ethnography of singers and dancers in Egypt) almost completely
ignores the phenomenon of Western belly dancers who perform there. The
ethnographic tradition of focusing on authentic, "traditional," local, and geo-
graphically cohesive groups has effectively made an entire group of people—
the transnational grouping of American, European, and Japanese belly dancers who live and work in Cairo, in luxury apartments scattered all throughout
town, rather than in one distinct district, like the Egyptian singers and dancers
who live on Muhammed Ali Street—invisible in the anthropological literature.
Yet the history of dance in Egypt, as well as the tremendous impact of foreign
dancers on the market today, is an exemplary reminder that no cultural form
exists in isolation, and none can be understood outside of the historical context
of its performance and transnational circulation.

This ethnography, then, has taken as its challenge not to dig for the real, the
traditional, the genuine, or the authentic *Egypt* in the soil of the motherland
and the traditions of its people. Instead, this vision of Egypt is constituted in
the cyberspace circulation of theories about extraterrestrial pyramid builders,
in the flow of Saudi oil through the regional economy, and in the beaded bras
of Russian and Australian dancers on Nile cruise ships. It traces the historically
contingent, the mutually constituted, the creatively narrated and continually
contested *idea of Egypt* in the excavations and graffiti of history, in a matrix of
movement and travel, conquest and revolution.

NOTES

INTRODUCTION

1. Cited in Greener 1966:10. Herodotus is also told by his priest-guides that the money spent on radishes, onions, and garlic for the workers is inscribed in hieroglyphs on the Pyramid. Greener notes, "One wonders if the translator of the radishes and onions was smiling inwardly at his credulous tourist" (ibid.).

2. See Francis Steegmuller, translator and editor, *Gustave Flaubert: Flaubert in Egypt* (1996). Flaubert traveled up the Nile in 1849. For further readings of Flaubert's Oriental fantasies that situate them within the context of European empire, see Said 1978, Tucker 1985, Kabbani 1986, Buonaventura 1989, and Karayanni 2005.

3. See Lockman 2004 for a review of the history of Orientalism, Said's critique, and its impact and subsequent critics.

4. Percy Bysshe Shelley wrote his poem "Ozymandias" in 1817–1818 about ruins found in sand, and it begins, "I met a traveler from an antique land . . ."

5. Sadly, both Ahmed Zaki and Alaa Waly el-Din, two of the biggest Egyptian movie stars during my fieldwork in Egypt (and my personal favorites), died after this chapter was written.

6. See al-Rasheed 2002 for a history of the *mutawwa'īn* in Saudi Arabia, and Wynn 2007 for a brief discussion.

7. Indeed, while many social scientists and popular writers tout the importance of uncovering the black box of Saudi culture and society, a project equally important to that would be to describe and analyze expatriate culture in Saudi Arabia and the way it both objectifies and consumes images of dress forms of the Saudi other (as in the little dolls that many expatriates, including my own family, have of Saudi men and women dressed in traditional clothing).

8. Works that deal with generational cultural differences in Saudi Arabia include Altorki 1986, al-Rasheed 2002, Arebi 1994, Doumato 2000, and Yamani 2000.

9. Some of the finest social science studies of Saudi Arabia published in English are written by a triumvirate of Saudi women anthropologists: Soraya Altorki, Madawi al-Rasheed, and May Yamani.

10. While many have followed MacCannell in characterizing mass tourism as a paradigmatic phenomenon of modernity, others (e.g., Urry 1990, Eco 1986, Jameson 1991) explore it as a feature of postmodernity. For example, Urry (1990) argues that tourism has to be seen in terms of changes in consumption and capitalism, and the quest for authenticity was a historical moment specific to the period of modernity and high capitalism. Current and future patterns of capitalism and consumption, he says, could produce different touristic goals which revel in simulacra and do not demand authenticity—a kind of post-tourism which reflects the state of contemporary patterns of consumption. Cohen (1979) likewise argues that, rather than pursuing a single paradigm of the tourist quest, we should look at different types of tourism with different tourist goals, not all of which can be subsumed under a universal category of either modernity or postmodernity.

11. E.g., MacCannell 1976 and 1992, Valene Smith 1989, and Urry 1990, but see Vitalis 1995, Ossman 1995, Mitchell 1995, and Cole and Altorki 1998 for exceptions within the regional literature, and Chambers 1999 and Graburn 2004, both of whom discuss Japanese tourism.

12. Figures are for 1998 and come from the Egyptian Government Yearbook entry on tourism (Egypt State Information Service 1999). In 1998, visitors to Egypt from Europe represented 56 percent of the total number of visitors, Middle East and North African visitors represented 31 percent of the total, and Americans (from all of North and South America) comprised just 6 percent of the tourists in Egypt.

13. The number of nights tourists stay in Egypt varies widely by nationality every year. According to the Egypt State Information Service (1999), in 1991 and 1994, the total number of nights stayed in Egypt by Arabs exceeded the number of nights that Europeans stayed in Egypt, despite the fact that many more Europeans visited Egypt than Arabs. In 1993 there was near parity in the number of nights stayed, and in 1994, 1995, and 1996, Europeans stayed significantly more nights than Arabs. Several factors contribute to these fluctuations. One is the increasing popularity of post–civil war Lebanon as a tourist destination for Arabs (but as of this writing in August 2006, the Israeli terrorizing of Lebanon is dashing Lebanese hopes of a flourishing tourist economy); another is terrorist acts in Egypt that frighten away European tourists some years, leading to a relative increase in the percentage of Arab tourists in Egypt.

14. When the second edition of Valene Smith's landmark volume on the anthropology of tourism was published in 1989, Greenwood wrote an epilogue in which he critiqued his own 1977 argument, pointing out that anthropological concern with tourism arises from a romanticized view of "the pristine relatively static, traditional communities plunged into the modern capitalist arena" (1989:181–182), and acknowledged that tourism could lead to creative cultural responses rather than destruction of meaning. See also Jonathan Friedman's (1990) exploration of the way people actively use tourism in their cultural projects; a similar perspective is evident in Graburn's (1984) article on

tourist arts and the politics of ethnic identity. See the Introduction to Bruner (2004) for a useful review of the literature on tourism and authenticity.

15. This argument is made by Kathleen Adams (1996) in "Ethnic Tourism and the Renegotiation of Tradition in Tana Toraja." And as Dennison Nash (1977) notes, one cannot account for the character of a tourist site without examining the imposition of "metropolitan dreams" and different "host" responses. See also Ruth Phillips's (1994) analysis of why Native American tourist art was kept out of museums.

16. Examples include anthropologists studying: exiled or refugee communities (Malkki 1995), communities that produce or absorb immigrants and migrant laborers (Ghosh 1986), pilgrimage (V. Turner 1974), cultures which are defined by travel, movement, spatial displacements, and discontinuities (Tsing 1993), and movements of commodities, ideas, information, money, and people (e.g., Appadurai 1990), as well as ethnographic studies of international politics from non-anthropologists, such as Enloe (1989).

17. Again my historical sense of the field failed me: while I was delighted with Clifford's 1997 essays on travel, I was then ignorant of the fact that he had published on the topic of travel and theory in 1989, which happens to be the year I took my very first anthropology course as a senior in high school.

18. The term critiques a putative anthropological tradition of trying to find discrete, self-contained gardens of culture to study and describe.

19. See Crick (1985) and Bruner (2004) for a critique; Mary Louise Pratt (1986) suggests that the dullness of much ethnographic writing is due to its attempts to distance itself from its less scientific cousins, particularly the travel narrative.

20. Edward Bruner (2004) also deals provocatively with the problematic boundaries between ethnography and tourism, ethnographers and tourists, and writing ethnography and writing tourism.

21. See Castañeda (1997) for an ethnography of archaeological tourism in Mexico, and Abu El-Haj (2001) for a detailed examination of the intimate connection between Israeli nationalism and archaeology. See also Taussig 1992:37–52.

22. E.g., Clifford (1997), Anderson (1991), Ghosh (1992). Néstor García Canclini (e.g., 1993, 1995) has examined the nature of hybridity as well as the conflicts between those who want to preserve "tradition"—from elites vested in current power structures to anthropologists for whom "traditional culture" is the currency of their trade—and those who pursue a transforming project of "modernity."

23. Cf. Appadurai (1986), Anzaldua (1987), Gupta and Ferguson (1997), and Rosaldo (1989).

24. V. Adams (1996), Taussig (1992). See also Appiah (1992).

25. These incentives are not necessarily financial.

26. See, for example, Stocking 1991b, Asad 1991, and other contributors to Stocking 1991a.

27. A substantial literature explores the negotiation of disciplinary and other identities during fieldwork for native ethnographers; see Altorki 1986 and Stewart 1989 for two provocative explorations.

CHAPTER 1

1. See Graburn 2002 for a thorough discussion of the methodological problems inherent in tourism research.

2. For an in-depth discussion of fieldwork methods in the Middle East, see Clark 2006, Schwedler 2006, Carapico 2006, and Tessler and Jamal 2006.

3. Sharon Traweek (1988) reports that her publications and grant proposals have often been peer-reviewed by the high energy physicists that she studies.

4. I generally use the term *alternative theorists* rather than *New Agers* to describe people who have positions on the history of the Egyptian monuments that do not agree with the orthodox archaeological theories. This is discussed in Chapter 3.

CHAPTER 2

1. This was technically incorrect since Dr. Hawass was at that time Director General of Giza Antiquities and Undersecretary of State of Culture for Antiquities. Dr. Hawass now heads the Supreme Council of Antiquities.

2. The major names usually include Ahmed Pasha Kamal, working at the beginning of the twentieth century; Selim Hassan, whose publications of his excavations in Giza and Saqqara during the 1920s and 1930s are still considered the basic texts for these sites; and Ahmed Fakhry, whose work during the 1940s and 1950s focused on the Egyptian oases, including Siwa, Farafra, Bahariya, and Fayoum, as well as Dahshour, closer to Cairo. Donald Malcolm Reid's *Whose Pharaohs?* (2002) covers the research of these and other important Egyptian Egyptologists who have been neglected in most histories of Egyptology.

3. My brief summary of the history of European treasure hunting and the early days of Egyptology is drawn from several excellent secondary sources, in particular Greener (1966), Fagan (1975), Hoving (1978), France (1991), and Reid (2002). I refer readers interested in the history of Egyptology to these sources for more complete, exhaustive, and authoritative accounts than I can provide here.

4. For a history of Napoleon's Expedition and the Institute, see Tignor (1993); Greener (1966), Fagan (1975), and France (1991) also have brief accounts. The work of the commission was published in several volumes with large color plates of the artists' illustrations, which caused great excitement in France; a pocket version of the *Description de l'Egypte* is published by Benedikt Taschen (1994).

5. A complete review of the history of Egypt mania is beyond the scope of this work. Some excellent sources are James Stevens Curl's *Egyptomania* (1994) and the essays by Jean-Marcel Humbert and others in the catalogue accompanying the *Egyptomania* exhibit at the Louvre, the National Gallery of Canada, and the Kunsthistorisches Museum in Vienna (1994). Humbert points out that Egyptomania is a recurring theme in Western art and certainly predates Napoleon's arrival: "The phenomenon of Egyptomania has often been reduced to that period of the early nineteenth century referred to as the 'Return to Egypt' or viewed as the expression of specific and fleeting moments (opening of the Suez Canal, discovery of Tutankhamun's tomb). In fact, it is ageless, without genre,

and all-pervasive: during Roman times, from the Renaissance to the post-modern era" (25). The term *Egyptomania* itself has been in use since the nineteenth century (Curran 1996).

6. Such was Frenchman Lelorrain's ruse to prevent the boarding of his ship by European agents of Henry Salt, the British consul, who, armed with a decree from the Pasha's grand vizier, were trying to block him from removing the Zodiac of Dendera. Lelorrain was no diplomat, and he was trying to remove the Zodiac even after the 1835 decree preventing the exportation of antiquities; yet his trick worked, Salt's agents went away frustrated, and the Zodiac was eventually removed to France, where it ended up in the Louvre. See Fagan (1975) for an account.

7. Hawass (2002b:17). See also Hoving (1978) for a discussion of the history of tomb robbing.

8. See D'Auria, Lacovara, and Roehrig (1988), Ikram and Dodson (1998), and Pringle (2001) for more on mummies and mummy research.

9. European interest in this peculiarly Egyptian monumental form long predates the modern period. The first Egyptian obelisk to be removed from the country as the trophy of a European colonial power was the small obelisk of Thutmosis IV, which was taken during the reign of the Emperor Augustus (30 BCE–41 CE). It originally stood in Karnak, and now stands in front of the Lateran in Rome. Romans were fond of Egyptian obelisks and reproduced the form in their own architecture. See Curl (1994) for more on obelisks in European monuments, parks, cemeteries, and garden topiary schemes.

10. Sources that discuss the history of pharaonic nationalism include Colli (2000), Dykstra (1994), Reid (2002), Selim (2001), Walker (1994), and Wood (1998).

11. See Hoving (1978) for a fascinating account of the discovery of Tutankhamun's tomb by Howard Carter, as well as for several previously unrevealed facts about Carter's involvement in the illegal antiquities trade.

12. Hassan (1998:206), however, notes that Zaghloul's mausoleum is practically the only example of pharaonic architecture in downtown Cairo, though several statues by Egyptian artists bear a pharaonic theme.

13. Ludwig Borchardt was excavating an artist's workshop in Tel el-Amarna. The head of Nefertiti, along with a number of other plaster items from the artist's workshop, was left behind when Tel el-Amarna was abruptly abandoned after the death of Akhenaton.

14. The Egyptology Congress is held once every four years; this was only the second time that the Congress was held in Egypt.

15. The expression *zayy al-atrash fil-zaffa* can be roughly translated as the English "like a fish out of water"—the Egyptian *zaffa,* or wedding procession, is very loud, so a deaf man would feel completely excluded and unable to understand what is going on.

16. At the (previous) Seventh International Congress of Egyptologists in Cambridge, papers were published in the following languages: English, 178; French, 30; German, 18; and Italian, 2 (Arabic, 0). When some 248 of the 400 papers delivered at the Eighth International Congress of Egyptologists were published in 2003, the tally was: English, 201; French, 35; German, 11.

17. All quotes from Hassaan (2000) are my translation from Arabic.

18. The breakdown of nationalities of the paper presenters is more diverse than the language breakdown suggests. Of the 248 published papers from the Eighth International Congress of Egyptologists, which took place in Cairo, institutions from the following countries were represented: Egypt, 50; United States, 28; France, 25; Germany, 25; Italy, 20; UK, 17; Poland, 12; Russia, 12; Spain, 10; Argentina, 7; Netherlands, 6; Czech Republic, 4; Portugal, 4; Switzerland, 4; Hungary, 3; Japan, 3; Austria, 2; Canada, 2; Greece, 2; Belgium, 1; Denmark, 1; Sweden, 1; Taiwan, 1; Uruguay, 1. Numbers will not sum to 248 because some papers were published by authors representing more than one national institution, two papers were published by scholars identifying with international institutions (UNESCO, ECHO), and a few papers were published by independent scholars who did not identify with any institution. Many scholars who originally hail from one country were publishing from an institution in another country. The domination of papers by Egyptian scholars at the meeting of course reflects the fact that these scholars did not have to travel internationally to reach the conference (Hawass [2003] says that some 500 Egyptian Egyptologists attended), but it is also testament to the increasing entry of Egyptians into the field, which in turn reflects the opportunities that Egyptian government policies have made for Egyptians to study and work in Egyptology.

19. See Noh (2003) for a recent analysis of the linguistic affinities between modern Arabic and ancient Egyptian.

20. The EAO is the predecessor of the Supreme Council of Antiquities (SCA), the Egyptian government body supervising all excavations and museums in Egypt.

21. The Seventh International Congress of Egyptology in Cambridge hardly did any better than its predecessor, with four out of 228 of the papers published afterward addressing site preservation, but by the time of the Eighth Congress, 25 of the 248 published papers addressed conservation and/or site management.

22. Foreign institutions involved in recent restoration and preservation of ancient antiquities in Egypt include the American Research Center in Egypt (the Sphinx project), the Paul Getty Institute (Nefertari's tomb), Chicago House (in the Valley of the Kings), the Polish Institute of Conservation (Hatshepsut's temple), the German Archaeological Institute (the Northern Pyramid of Sneferu in Dahshour and the reconstructed funerary temple of Sneferu), and the French Institute of Egyptology (in Karnak and South Saqqara, the Pyramid Complex of Pepi I). Of course, the single biggest restorer and preserver of historical sites in Egypt is the Egyptian Department of Restoration and Conservation, under the Supreme Council of Antiquities.

23. Like Hawass, the Egyptologists who contributed to the volume *The Archaeology of the Nile Delta: Problems and Priorities* (van den Brink, ed., 1988) bemoan the loss of archaeological sites in the Delta, but rather than naming water as the chief threat, as Hawass does, they identify the encroaching population of modern Egyptians as the culprits (the threat of water comes from Egyptians attempting to irrigate land for cultivation). Contributor El-Wakil describes, among the "problems met with during excavations" at a Delta archaeology site, how "land reclamation encouraged the local population to attack the site and prepare it for plantation, causing great damage to the archaeological re-

mains" (1988:265). Note the use of the term *attack* to describe local farmers' attempts to use the ground for agriculture. See Mitchell (2002:179–205) and Meskell (2001, 2005) for a discussion of disputes over Egypt's "heritage" and violent attempts by the state to dispossess Egyptian villagers of their land to develop sites for archaeology and tourism, and Rose (2003) for more on issues of political geography on the Giza Plateau.

24. Reid confronts this issue by focusing in his work on Egyptian archaeologists who have researched not only the pharaonic past but also Coptic and Ottoman remains.

25. The curious metaphor of "rape" has frequently been used by revisionist historians to describe the colonial period of treasure looting. Fagan (1975), the Romers (1993), and France (1991) all title their books, "The Rape of . . ." ("the Nile," "Tutankhamun," and "Egypt," respectively). It is curious that, instead of using the term *looting*, which might more appropriately describe the process by which vast quantities of antiquities were removed from Egypt to fill museums and private collections in Europe and elsewhere, these authors all resort instead to a gendered image of violence that expresses the power differential between Europeans and Egyptians by portraying Egypt as a violated woman.

26. It is thus not just a little ironic that Egyptian authors of a pharaonic nationalist bent have long reified the Egyptian peasant as a symbol of the timeless pharaonic identity of Egypt (Selim 2001).

27. But see Dural 2006, which was published as this book was going to press, for an important exception in Turkey.

28. The term *turgomān*, sometimes pronounced *turkomān*, is also (like *khartī*) used to denote a local who lacks formal training and is not employed as an official tour guide, but who befriends travelers and shows them around. The word *turgomān* (also sometimes rendered "Dragoman") derives from the root *targama*, to translate, because they are often skilled linguists, speaking several foreign languages.

29. This percentage ranges from 5 to 65 percent, depending on the type of purchase (with gold and silver bringing the smallest percentage and paintings on papyrus bringing the greatest) and on the relationship between the guide and the shop where the purchase is made. See Wynn (2003:Chapter 3) for a lengthy discussion.

30. Mohammed Bakr (1988:50) discusses the black market for antiquities in a Nile Delta town: "In the past the area was frequented by an antiquities dealer, encouraging the local population and tempting them with money to find him antiquity-objects. The search for antiquities was concentrated—secretly—mainly on the farmlands adjoining the village. It is told by native residents of the area that whenever a pottery object was offered to the dealer, he broke it into pieces, saying it was worthless, but he generously paid for marble, alabaster, and schist vessels, jewelry, and slate palettes. This practice went on until the E.A.O. appointed two guards for the area."

31. A Ptolemaic prophecy called the *Oracle of the Potter* expresses the hope that the colonialist Greeks will be wiped out and their city deserted, that the foreigners will disappear, and that the statues they had taken from Egypt will be returned: "And the belt-wearers [the Greeks] will destroy themselves, for they are followers of Typhon . . . and it will be deserted, the city of foreigners that will be built among us. These things will

come to pass when all evils have come to an end, when the foreigners who are in Egypt disappear as leaves from a tree in autumn. . . . And the Egyptian statues which were carried thither will be restored to Egypt" (Fowden 1993:21).

32. See, for example, Politeyan (1915), Hogarth (1899), Egypt Exploration Society (1894), Brugsch (1880), Robinson (1841).

33. These are numerous, but see in particular books by Graham Phillips (e.g., 1998, 2002, 2003) and Ahmed Osman (1990, 2002, 2004).

34. Hassan (1998:211); see also Selim (2001).

35. There is more to explore here than I have space for, since Akhenaton's queen was Nefertiti, whose bust is discussed in this chapter, and his successor was Tutankhamun, both of whom are popular figures of Egypt's pharaonic past.

36. My brief review here does not do justice to the nuances of pharaonic nationalism in Egyptian politics and the arts, its many expressions, and the key actors articulating these and opposing formulations of Egyptian identity. There are a number of excellent sources to turn to. Some of the articulations of modern Egyptian nationalism that take up the issue of the pharaonic past (not including those by Egyptologists elsewhere cited in this and the next chapter) include: Fuʿād (1978 [1968]), al-Hakīm (1994), Heikal (1965 [1933]), Hussein (1954), and Mūsā (1961). This is an extremely abbreviated list of a wide literature. Secondary sources in English include: Cook (1983), E. Colli (2000), Douglas and Malti-Douglas (1997), Dykstra (1994), Gershoni (1982), Gershoni and Jankowski (1986 and 1995), Haarmann (1996), Hassan (1998), Jansen (1985), Kepel (2003), Reid (2002), Selim (2001), Walker (1994), and Wood (1998).

37. The Metropolitan Museum was eyeing the discovery as an opportunity to add to its Egyptian collection. Carter and Carnarvon sold the London *Times* the right to first report any news from the tomb, infuriating Egyptian and other international journalists and newspapers. See Hoving (1978) for a detailed account.

CHAPTER 3

1. Interview with the owner of a shop in the pyramids area that catered to a tourist clientele. He was talking about *khurateyya*, or tourist hustlers, and he said that they try to pick up tourists in hotels after making snap judgments about how much money they have based on what they are wearing. He said they especially look for people wearing rumpled white linen clothing since that is usually the sign of a "worshipper," i.e., the New Age groups or the people who meditate in the pyramids, because these are considered easiest to part from their money.

2. Martin Bernal's *Black Athena* (1987) is the seminal work on Afrocentric theories of civilizational origin. For a study on the relationship between race and early theories of ancient Egypt, see Trafton (2004). A book on the Joseph Smith papyri (see n. 8 below) that is itself a religious tract is Larson (1985). Elizabeth Mazucci has written an extremely interesting (and hitherto unpublished) essay on the Nuwaubian cult.

3. *The Collected Dialogues of Plato*, Edith Hamilton and Huntington Cairns Edition, 1961, 1159.

4. Jowett 1953, "Introduction" to Vol. 2 of "The Collected Dialogues of Plato," 2.

5. Ibid., "Introduction" to Vol. 3, 703.

6. Garth Fowden (1993) is my primary source for information about the Hermetic texts, their Egyptian foundation, and the relationship between Hermes and Thoth. I also draw on the work of Frances Yates, whose books *Giordano Bruno and the Hermetic Tradition* and *The Rosicrucian Enlightenment* shed light on how these texts were read and appropriated by late Renaissance and early Enlightenment Europe. But see Haarmann (1996) and Cook (1983) for discussions of the Hermetic tradition in medieval Egypt, where it dates to the early eleventh century CE.

7. AMORC website, www.rosicrucian.org, accessed 19 June 2006.

8. In general, both share a nondenominational esoteric approach to religion and an emphasis on brotherhood, ethical teachings, and philanthropic works. However, Freemasons do not share the Rosicrucian interest in scientific research, alchemy, and magic. See Waite 1887:402. A number of other groups were influenced by these movements and by a prevailing European and American fascination with ancient Egypt. For example, Joseph Smith, the founder of the Church of Jesus Christ of Latter-Day Saints (the Mormons), purchased a mummy and several papyri that he incorporated into church scripture.

9. While Ashmole's initiation is usually cited as the first recorded Masonic initiation, Yates points out that there was one earlier than that. The first known record of Masonic initiation is that of Robert Moray—who was very interested in alchemy and chemistry, another affinity between early Freemasons and the Rosicrucian tradition (Yates 1986:210).

10. Lewis, the founder of the American AMORC, was a major collector of Egyptian, Assyrian, and Babylonian artifacts, and his collection formed the basis for the Rosicrucian Egyptian Museum in San Jose, California, which claims to contain "the largest collection of Egyptian artifacts on exhibit in the western United States," including human and animal mummies, jewelry, canopic jars, ushabtis, pottery, bronze tools, and textiles (AMORC website, www.rosicrucian.org, accessed 19 June 2006). A similar adoption of Egyptian symbolism by Freemasons has been amply documented in their architecture, symbols, terms of address, and titles (see Bauval 1999a).

11. When I say "linked the ideas" I do not mean that Cayce made an intentional linkage, or that he had any background in Hermetica or Rosicrucianism. I do not know what Cayce's precise intellectual influences were. (His son, Hugh Lynn Cayce [1968], says that his father had never read Plato's writings on Atlantis or any other book on Atlantis.) I mean only that Cayce is the first source I can identify in which the idea of Atlantis was united with the idea of records of a lost civilization being buried in the sands of Giza.

12. His statements, which Cayce said he did not remember making after the trances were over, were recorded by a secretary whom Cayce believed to be the reincarnation of a daughter from a previous life.

13. Overall, Cayce did some 14,000 "readings" for more than 8,000 different people. Approximately 2,500 of those readings (for 1,600 different people) deal with

the person's past lives and their influence on the subject's present life. About 700 of those people had incarnations in Atlantis (Cayce 1968).

14. Bauval and Hancock (1997) state that these dates come from a Cayce reading given 1 July 1932 (reading no. 5748-6).

15. Cayce, Schwartzer, and Richards 1988:132. They are not specific but many assume that this American student was Mark Lehner.

16. See Bauval and Hancock (1997), Chapter 5, for details about ARE/ECF involvement in various Giza archaeology projects and their relationship to Egyptologist Mark Lehner.

17. I visited the well shaft twice, once in early 2001, and once about six months later. During the first visit, I observed the apparent tunnel leading off from the corner of the well shaft. The second time I visited, the tunnel had been filled in by archaeologists, partly to preserve the structural integrity of the tomb, but also, perhaps, in an attempt to quash speculation about secret underground passageways.

18. Their theory is much more complicated than I have rendered it here, so I refer readers to Bauval and Gilbert (1994:97–196) for a full explanation. Bauval and Hancock (1997:24–86) also summarize the theory. A fascinating connection between Western and Arab mystical approaches to ancient Egypt appears here, too: medieval Egyptian authors also used a kind of precessional astronomy to date the ancient Egyptian ruins to twenty thousand years (Haarmann 1996:616).

19. West calls Schwaller de Lubicz a "renegade Egyptologist," but a British Egyptologist I queried writes him off as a New Ager—albeit one who, she admitted, had produced some very good descriptions of the Egyptian temples he had studied.

20. The 1993 videotape *Mystery of the Sphinx* lists as its "scientific team": John Anthony West, author, Egyptologist; Dr. Robert M. Schoch, geologist, geophysicist; Dr. Thomas Dobecki, seismologist, geophysicist; Professor John Kutzback, paleoclimatologist; and Detective Sergeant Frank Domingo (NYPD), forensics expert.

21. Other refutations of the West-Schoch hypothesis include Gauri, Sinai, and Bandyopadhyay (1995) and Hawass and Lehner (1994a and 1994b); Schoch responded to critics in several letters to *KMT*.

22. Unless identified as coming from a published source, all quotes from West and Schoch come from my transcript of our 2 July 2000 tape-recorded interview.

23. Two other geologists (David Coxill and Colin Reader) later did their own independent investigations into Schoch's argument and agreed with Schoch's line of reasoning, although Reader makes an attempt to reconcile Schoch's theory with that of the Egyptology community, which Schoch disapproves of (Reader 2000, Coxill 1998). While Reader had done "really great work, in my assessment" of the paleohydrogeology of the Sphinx enclosure and surrounding area, Schoch noted that "he's very explicit about that he's looking for reconciliation, between the geological and Egyptological views. Which to me is not the way you do science: you look at the data and you come to your conclusions, and then you evaluate alternative dating, you don't try to . . . find the happy medium to make everyone feel good" (Schoch 2000). See Knorr Cetina (1995:152) for a discussion of how scientific work tends to negotiate consensus in formulating theories and analyzing murky data.

24. The comment comes from a letter written by Dr. Mark Lehner to Robert Bauval and Graham Hancock in 1995, which Bauval and Hancock published in full as an appendix in their *Keeper of Genesis* (1997).

25. This important insight comes from my colleague Ken Croes.

26. Bauval, in each of his books, devotes a considerable amount of space to both Hawass and Lehner. Lehner gets nearly an entire chapter in *Keeper of Genesis*, called "The Case of the Psychic, the Scholar and the Sphinx," where the scholar in question is Lehner, and another chapter is devoted to him in Hancock and Bauval's *Message of the Sphinx* (1996). Bauval and Hancock cleverly blur categories of New Ager and Egyptologist by, for example, quoting from articles and a book Lehner wrote while still a Cayce believer and attributing that material to "Dr. Mark Lehner"—although the material was written long before Lehner ever obtained his doctorate in Egyptology.

27. Stille (1997) provides an account of Lehner's conversion to Egyptology.

28. Bourdieu (1993) discusses the implicit but powerful rules of academic disciplines for how to play the disciplinary game, including rules for how to subvert or contest a theory within that discipline.

29. http://www.think-aboutit.com/Mars/a_master_occultist.htm, accessed February 2000.

30. http://www.enterprisemission.com, accessed February 2000.

31. "Unfortunately, the general lay public is easy prey and the Pyramidiots have always found a ready audience. Their interpretations are interesting, exciting, and romantic, if scientifically unsound" (Hawass 2000d:21).

32. A whole host of factors plague the Sphinx, and conspiracy theories are hardly required to explain why it is falling apart. Sewage water from the neighboring village of Nazlet el-Semman seeps up into the stone and impregnates the sandstone with salts, which then crystallize and cause the stone to crack from the pressure. The wind then blows away large chips of the monument as they flake off. See Stille (1997) for an account of Sphinx preservation efforts and the clash between New Age groups and Egyptologists Hawass and Lehner.

33. After I finished my fieldwork and returned to the United States, Hawass was promoted to Secretary General of the sca; he continues to direct Giza excavations.

34. "And doesn't a caricature capture the essence, making the copy magically powerful over the original?" Taussig 1997:5.

35. Bauval and Hancock (1997:131). My summary of the Gantenbrink/Upuaut incident in all of its complicated twists is too brief. For a complete description of the events and characters involved, see Bauval's *Secret Chamber* (1999a), which devotes about one hundred pages to the matter.

36. The three Giza pyramids are on a rotating schedule whereby each year, one pyramid is closed to the public so that it can be cleaned and ventilated, while the other two are open to a limited number of tourists each day.

37. Although many articles run with the headlines "stealing our civilization" and so on, one recent article in the Arabic press (Khadīr 1999) grudgingly admits that even the craziest theories about Egypt bring in tourist dollars.

38. *Egyptian Gazette*, 16 May 1997, author Mohsen Arishie quotes Farouk Hosni to this effect.

39. Ibid.

40. Hawass, quoted in *Akhbār al-Yaūm*, 8 January 1994.

41. "To find out for myself about the tunnels under the Sphinx I sneaked into the ancient well shaft to become, I believe, one of the few people alive to have been so close to the Hall of Records . . ." (Bauval 1999b:64). It requires no real daring to see the "Tomb of Osiris"—at the time I was in Egypt, Dr. Hawass permitted anybody who asked him to descend into the well, accompanied by an antiquities inspector. And a padlocked gate covers the entrance to the well, so there is no "sneaking" in without a key.

42. The limestone casing was almost entirely stripped off by the Ottoman period and was used for building Cairo, but some remains on the top of Khafre's pyramid.

43. As for the more outlandish theories, they may find an audience because they are symbolically true. People entertain David Icke's theory about the pyramids being controlled by inbreeding, shape-shifting, lizard-people because many politicians *are* somewhat reptilian, they *are* inbreeding to maintain their class status, and they *are* out to rule the world.

44. See Gieryn (1983, 1995) for a useful approach to "boundary-work" whereby science draws boundaries between itself and "non-science."

45. I have not the space for a thorough review of the science studies literature and what it has to say about science's pretensions to neutrality and objectivity, but a few good sources to start with include: Gieryn (1983 and 1995), Knorr Cetina (1995), Latour (1993), Shapin (1995), Watson-Verran and Turnbull (1995), and Jasanoff's edited volume (2004).

46. Feyerabend (1975) writes, "The consistency condition which demands that new hypotheses agree with accepted theories is unreasonable because it preserves the older theory, and not the better theory."

47. As Fujimura (1998:347) points out, the real conflict is "not about science versus antiscience, not about objectivity versus subjectivity, but about authority in science: What kind of science should be practiced, and who gets to define it?" See also Gieryn (1983).

48. In their response, the journal's editors stated that they had in fact asked Sokal to pare out his ridiculous jargon, but he refused.

49. But see Trigger (1979) for a discussion of the problematic relationship between Egyptology and anthropology.

50. See, for example, Larson (1985), in which Egyptological evidence is marshaled for the author to not only refute Smith but to propose "The Alternative: Biblical Christianity," the title of his concluding chapter.

51. Interview with Dr. Nazmy Amin Farag, Undersecretary of State for Planning, Egyptian Tourism Development Authority (TDA), 18 September 2000. The interview was largely conducted in Arabic, but Dr. Farag used the term *absolute merit* in English.

52. According to *Al-Hayat* newspaper of 5 October 1998 (issue no. 12998, special insert on Gulf Tourism in Egypt), Gulf tourism to archaeological sites in Egypt is on

the rise: Arabs visiting the Giza pyramids and the Sphinx numbered 150,000 in 1998, up from only 50,000 the year before. However, when compared to the overall number of yearly visitors to the Giza pyramids and Sphinx, these numbers are small change. In 1995 and 1996 (the latest figures I have), if we look at the breakdown of the languages of the Sound and Light Show at the Giza Pyramids, we find 4,379 attended the Arabic program, which is the lowest number for all the languages (by contrast, 83,209 people attended the English-language show)—and that figure includes, of course, not just Arab tourists, but Egyptians as well (Egyptian Statistical Yearbook, 1996).

CHAPTER 4

1. The question of what people mean when they say either *sharmūta* (in Arabic) or *prostitute* (in English—generally to avoid saying it in Arabic) is a matter which requires further discussion. Briefly: Egyptians, even when speaking Arabic, would often say *prostitute* (even if they knew only a few words of English) because saying *sharmūta* sounds so bad in Arabic. But *sharmūta* might be better translated as "whore," since it makes a moral judgment but doesn't necessarily imply that a woman performs sex acts for money. However, when people were speaking about belly dancers and other women who frequented the same nightclubs as Arab tourists, *prostitute* usually *did* imply a belief that the woman so labeled received some sort of remuneration for sexual services performed.

2. Vatikiotis 1992:13. My too-brief recap of Middle East history cobbles together the work of various historians, but in particular I have relied on Vatikiotis (1992, fourth edition), Goldschmidt (2002, seventh edition), Korany and Dessouki (1991), al-Sayyid Marsot (1996, 1985), Waterbury (1983), and al-Rasheed (2002).

3. Vatikiotis 1992:14.

4. However, it should be noted that there had been significant numbers of influential European merchants and state representatives in Egypt—particularly Alexandria—before Napoleon's 1798 conquest.

5. Western historians usually refer to him as ibn Saud. Here I will refer to him as al-Saud or King Abd al-Aziz to distinguish him from his forebear, Muhammad ibn Saud.

6. This covering is made of black silk (though historically the colors have changed) which is thickly and lavishly embroidered with Qur'anic verses in rich gold thread. It currently uses hundreds of kilos of silk fabric and many pounds of gold embroidery thread, and costs millions of dollars to make. Each year, after the new covering is installed, the old *kiswah* is cut up and the pieces presented to Muslim and other world leaders and institutions.

7. This was the case prior to the exploitation of Saudi Arabia's natural oil resources; now, the oil-rich country substantially subsidizes the pilgrimage.

8. I refer readers to the excellent novel (1996 [1994]) by Saudi author and diplomat Ghazi Algosaibi, *An Apartment Called Freedom,* that portrays the headiness of the days of Arab nationalism when Cairo was the center of the Arab world.

9. Despite its base in the Arabian Gulf, al-Jazeera is widely considered a transnational journalistic enterprise and has many Egyptians working for it, so it is not viewed—by Egyptians, at least—as a Gulf Arab journalistic coup. (Perhaps, however, Gulf Arabs see it differently—I did not ask my Gulf informants about this.)

10. When I speak of "Gulf Arab" tourism throughout this chapter I am referring to tourists coming from the Arabian peninsula, namely Saudi Arabia, Oman, Kuwait, Bahrain, Qatar, and the United Arab Emirates. I briefly discuss Yemeni tourism below, but it is properly a misnomer to refer to this as Gulf tourism since Yemen has no territory bordering the Arabian (Persian) Gulf or the Gulf of Oma4n. The modifiers I use in English, "Gulf Arab," are direct translations from the Arabic terms used by Egyptians to refer to these tourists: in popular use (and especially when said in a derogatory tone), al-'Arab generally refers to non-Egyptian Arabs, from the Gulf, the Levant, and Iraq, as well as Libyans and Egyptian Bedouins. (More positive Egyptian use of the term 'Arab includes urban Egyptians and other North Africans in its meaning; the different ways in which Egyptians use the term 'Arab are discussed elsewhere in this chapter.) The qualifier *Gulf* further narrows the scope of discussion: Egyptians refer to Gulf Arab tourists as *khalīgiyīn* from the Arabic word *khalīj* meaning "gulf," and although Saudi Arabia's territory spreads all the way from the Arabian (Persian) Gulf to the Red Sea, Egyptians include Saudis in the category of *khalīgiyīn*.

11. To be sure, Westerners are the majority of international tourists; according to Williams and Shaw (1992), Europeans comprise over 60 percent of the world's tourists.

12. Nada (1991:1) argues that international rural labor migration was the single greatest factor generating social change in Egypt during the 1970s and 1980s.

13. See Weyland for a discussion of the strategies used by host governments to prevent migrant laborers from becoming settled communities, "the most unwanted side effect of migration" (Weyland 1993:41).

14. The qualifier *so-called* alludes to a debate over terminology that is really a larger debate over religious authority. Outsiders often refer to the Saudi way of practicing Islam as "Wahhabism" after Mohamed Abd al-Wahhab, a seventeenth-century thinker and religious reformer who advocated a return to the fundamentals of Islam and a purging of popular religious practices, such as saint worship, which he said were corruptions of the original revealed religion. The principles of Abd al-Wahhab's religious reform were incorporated as fundamental organizing principles in the revolutionary alliance between Abd al-Aziz al-Saud and the *ikhwān*, Bedouin warriors, that led to al-Saud's "unification" (read "conquest") of the territories which now comprise modern Saudi Arabia. I found many Saudis to be offended by the term *Wahhabism*, which, they said, implied that it was merely one sect among other possible versions of Islam. It was no sect, they argued, but the one true and correct way of practicing religion. But during my fieldwork in Egypt, I found these aspirations to (or just plain assumptions of) religious hegemony challenged by people who maintained that Wahhabism *was*, in fact, just one approach to religion, and not necessarily the most correct one, either. See Lacey (1983) for a discussion of how the term is regarded in Saudi Arabia.

15. For oil economies and labor migration, see Fargues (1980), Ibrahim (1982a and

1982b), Kerr and Yassin (1982), Sirageldin et al. (1984), Beblawi and Luciani (1987), Mursī (1989), Crystal (1990), and Gause (1994).

16. While this was the system practiced by Saudi Arabian Airlines in the early 1990s when I was living in Saudi Arabia, I do not have any concrete information about how pay scales are currently established by that company.

17. See Vitalis (2006) for a discussion of the racial segregation policies implemented by Aramco during its early years in Saudi Arabia, to appreciate these more recent policies within the context of a history of racial hierarchies in Saudi Arabia.

18. One person working in the management of the Ramses Hilton told me that shoot-outs had occurred twice between Tork's bodyguards and Egyptians; in one case, an Egyptian minister was at a function at the hotel so there was heavy security, and the bodyguards of Prince Tork were trying to come through a metal detector with their guns. The minister's security detail would not allow them to enter armed, and the dispute erupted into a fight in which guns were fired. The hotel employee claimed that the incident was kept quiet for political reasons.

19. He was convicted of being a *qawwād*, a pimp or procurer.

20. I am less certain what to make of the toe-fondling stereotype. I myself never saw a Gulf Arab man rubbing his toes. In fact, Saudis have serious qualms about touching the feet in public; even more so than in Egypt, the foot in Saudi Arabia is unclean, and it is an insult to put your foot in close proximity to any person, or even to sit with the sole of the foot facing another person. So I find it hard to imagine there being enough Gulf Arabs rubbing their toes in the public places of Cairo to fuel an entire national stereotype—and yet this is an image of the Gulf Arab that I encountered over and over again among Egyptians. But the sexual symbolism of toe rubbing suggests the Egyptian attribution of an excessive and inappropriately contained libido in their stereotype of Gulf Arabs, as well as the disrespect implied by the gesture.

21. A Saudi friend offered this example of how a Saudi would use *hadritak/hadritik* sarcastically: "A mother might say to her daughter, who hasn't cleaned her room in ages, 'Would you [*hadritik*] kindly clean your room?'"

22. For example, many Levantine and North African singers perform and record songs in the Egyptian dialect to ensure market success. I do not know of any Egyptian singer who sings in the Lebanese, Syrian, Moroccan, or Algerian dialect. Egypt spreads its pop culture throughout the Arab world but is scarcely aware of the popular culture of other countries, with a few notable exceptions of some Moroccan, Algerian, and Lebanese singers who have attained popularity in Egypt.

23. The exceptions to this generalization are the intellectual elite and those who have migrated to the Gulf to work, which, as I have argued, plays its own critical role in creating feelings of difference. (This seems to be changing in recent years, though, with the spread of satellite broadcasting and the recovery of the post–civil war Lebanese economy which has brought Lebanese television shows to Egypt.)

24. It is striking that this terminology is so much an aspect of everyday life in Egypt, and appears an important linguistic marker for identity, yet I find very little mention of it in the scholarly literature, even among political scientists and historians writing

on pan-Arabism. An exception is Fekri Hassan (an Egyptian), who theorizes that one reason why pan-Arabism has failed as an enduring motif of Egyptian national identity is that "Egyptians use the word 'Arab' to refer to Bedouin nomads or the inhabitants of the Arabian Peninsula" (Hassan 1998:209). Ethnographers who have written about Bedouin populations have noted that Bedouins use 'Arab to refer to themselves as distinct from "Egyptians." See for example Abu-Lughod (1993:223, 227). Thus, even among tourism workers in Sinai, where Gulf tourists are less commonly found than they are in Cairo, an Egyptian who speaks of "Arabs" is probably referring to local Bedouins rather than Gulf Arabs, who would instead be referred to as khalīgiyīn.

25. It is often compared to Lebanese Phoenicianism, Israel's identification with the ancient Hebrews, and Ataturk's appropriation of the Hittites (see Reid 1985:239).

26. Significantly, Saad Zaghloul was buried in a massive neo-pharaonic tomb of Aswan granite.

27. For a discussion of Nasser's conversion to Arab nationalism, see Gordon (1971: 126–129) and Copeland (1969:56–57, 162–163, and 168–189). For discussions of the evolution of the ideology of pharaonic nationalism, see Salāma Mūsā (1961:50–51), Wendell (1972, esp. 236–239 and 265–273), Reid (1985:233–246), and Gershoni (1982:59–94). See also Cook (1983), Douglas and Malti-Douglas (1997), Dykstra (1994), Gershoni (1982), Gershoni and Jankowski (1986), Haarmann (1996), Hassan (1998), Jansen (1985), Kepel (2003), Mitchell (2002), Reid (2002), Selim (2001), Walker (1994), and Wood (1998).

28. According to Israeli, "Pharaonism has been in vogue in the Arab world in general and in Egypt in particular since the rise of modern nationalism. The preceding regime, under Nasser's aegis, emphasized pan-Arabism more than ever before; under Sadat's rule allusions to the Pharaonic age appear even more prominently" (Israeli 1985:110).

29. "Our people have a heritage of seven or eight thousand years. It has confronted many invaders, but never lost its personality" (25 May 1971). "Egypt has given man the greatest civilization he ever knew. . . . The Egyptians were the first to invent a writing system and a method of differentiation of labor. They set up the first civilized society" (27 January 1975). "This 7000-year-old people gave humanity its first culture. The first government and the first state ever were established on the banks of the Nile" (26 July 1976). These excerpts from Sadat's speeches are found in Israeli (1981:36–37, 111).

30. It is interesting that, as a Coptic Christian, Emad still saw the relationship between Egypt and Saudi Arabia as closer than that between Egypt and the United States because of, among other things, shared religion (Islam). (He chose Saudi Arabia and the United States to compare because both were wealthy countries with close ties to Egypt, and earlier in the discussion he had been discussing foreign aid to Egypt that came from both Western and Arab countries.) The Arabic phrase that he used that I have translated as "utilitarian relationship" was 'ilāqat maslaha. The difference he described between the Egyptian-Arab relationship versus the Egyptian-Western relationship was 'ilāqat shaqīqa versus 'ilāqat sadīqa, a fraternal bond versus a friendship.

CHAPTER 5

1. See also Behbehanian (2000) for a brief discussion of Western and Arab sex tourism in Egypt.

2. There was a lot of socially approved dating *after* marriage, however. If a young man and woman wanted to get to know each other, they would often get engaged, which involved signing a marriage contract (*kātib al-kitāb*), after which the couple was technically married. The marriage would not be consummated until after a formal wedding celebration took place, months or years later, but the fact that they were formally married protected the woman against any loss of virtue and allowed her to be alone with the man without a chaperone. They could then date. If, on the other hand, the two found that they didn't get along, they could "divorce" and go their separate ways without any blemish on the woman's reputation, so long as she was still a virgin (Wynn 1996). See also Altorki (1986) and Yamani (2000) for more on the lives (including dating and marriage) of Saudi women.

3. Notably, my Egyptian research advisor, Dr. Ali Omar Abdellah, Dean of the Tourism and Hoteliery School of Helwan University, was encouraging and facilitated many interviews with Gulf visitors to Egypt. All the Gulf Arab men I spoke to during the course of my research were polite and respectful.

4. Some details of Meriam's story have been changed to protect her privacy. All names used in this chapter are pseudonyms.

5. A manager of the Semiramis Intercontinental Hotel told me that the changed summer seating arrangement was a deliberate strategy of the hotel to appeal to Gulf tourists.

6. That probably does not hold as true for men who go on vacation only with male friends. However, I often saw and spoke to people who spent their vacation time in mixed groups of men and women. Usually the group was a mix of friends and relatives who either traveled together or coordinated their vacation times to overlap.

7. My knowledge of male-female socializing in Saudi Arabia is limited to Jeddah. I assume that the same kind of socializing (and other similar tactics of youth for subverting authority) exist to varying degrees in other cities of Saudi Arabia and other countries in the Arab Gulf, but to what extent, I cannot say.

8. As Stokowski (1992) argues, we have to examine how social networks affect everything from tourist destinations to the type of tourism a group engages in (e.g., "cultural" versus sun-sand-sea tourism).

9. Some Egyptians call all of them tourists, but more often the word *tourist* is used to speak of Westerners and Asians, while *Arab* denotes visitors from the Gulf and the rest of the Arab world. The term that gets translated "foreigner"—*agānib*—is used only to refer to non-Arabs, usually Westerners and Asians, and is not used to speak of Arabs or Africans.

10. For an interesting comparison, see Nicole Constable's (2003) ethnography of "mail order" marriages between white men and Asian women, in which she points out that there are two competing popular images of the women involved: one portrays them

as poor, helpless, and being taken advantage of by the wealthier white Westerners who trade their sexuality, while another portrays the women as savvy economic mercenaries who take advantage of lovelorn men.

11. This statement applies less to Gulf men than to Gulf women in Egypt. Karim el-Gawhary (1995) has written that there is an extensive network of real estate agents who double as pimps, supplying "maids" who also work as prostitutes to single Gulf Arab men renting furnished flats in Cairo. More research needs to be done on this phenomenon and on the holiday activities of Arab men more generally. See also Behbehanian (2000) for a brief discussion of Western and Arab sex tourism in Egypt.

12. The *mutawwaʿīn* are (in popular slang) representatives of the Committee for the Promotion of Virtue and Prevention of Vice, the quasi-independent entity that enforces morals in the Kingdom of Saudi Arabia. See al-Rasheed (2002) and Doumato (2000) for perspectives on the history of this organization and its complicated relationship with the Saudi state.

CHAPTER 6

1. Cited in Fagan 1975:14.

2. See Porterfield (1998) for a discussion of the French imperial investment in the Sphinx. I thank Kirsten Scheid for drawing this work to my attention.

3. And as Sherry Ortner has pointed out, the "borderland politics" of tourism encompasses discourses of national identity that are inevitably "gendered and eroticized" (1997:182). Flaubert's Egyptian tour down the Nile was an early account of European sex tourism, in which descriptions of his visits to the pharaonic monuments are interlaced with accounts of his liaisons with Egyptian prostitutes. In contemporary times, Western sex tourism has diverted to different global locations, and sex tourism in Egypt is—at least in the popular Egyptian imagination—minimal for Western males; however, European women are thought to come on vacation in the Sinai for sexual liaisons with locals. In contrast, contemporary Egyptian critiques accuse Arab male tourists of using their wealth to spread moral corruption via the sexual exploitation of Egyptian women. For a brief discussion of how Egyptian tourism is gendered and eroticized, see Wynn (2006).

4. Professor Abdellah Hammoudi has related to me that when he was in Egypt and visited the mosque of Ibn Touloun, what primarily struck him was the scale of the mosque, which is unparalleled elsewhere in North Africa. He felt that its vast, gigantic proportions were built to resonate with pharaonic proportions, as if the Egyptian builders sought to build an Islamic structure that could contest the legacy of the pharaonic past, both in its monumental architecture and in its claim to a unique historical position.

5. The song is "Waqafa al-khalq (Misru tatahaddathu ʿan nafsiha)" by composer Riad al-Sunbat. I am indebted to Abdellah Hammoudi for drawing it to my attention as a key example of how Egyptians revere their pharaonic past. There are nationalistic resonances in such a song being sung by Umm Kalthoum because she was a favorite of

Gamal Abd el-Nasser, and her voice and her songs provided continuity of Egyptian identity and popular culture in the transition from the monarchy to the post-1952 revolution era.

6. Another Egyptologist shared the first's disdain for the villagers, and she also claimed that there was incredible wealth in the village ("Have you ever tried counting how many Mercedes are parked in front of houses in Nazlet el-Semman?"), but she doubted that they made their money out of antiquities smuggling. "They make all the money they need from being astute businessmen and from fleecing tourists for all they can get. They don't need to smuggle antiquities. Nowadays there's really nothing left on the Giza Plateau that's worth smuggling or that would fetch any sort of decent price on the international market. All the statues and so forth have been found, and all that is left of interest now would be rubble foundations of buildings, bits of potsherds and strange-looking mud and so forth that archaeologists would love to analyze for clues but which would be of absolutely no interest to the black market."

7. Egyptologists, of course, point out that the course of the river has changed many times over the millennia, and its course in the middle of the twentieth century was no indicator of where water stood thousands or even hundreds of years ago.

8. I am indebted to Sarah Pinto for this astute observation about the links between excavation and palimpsest.

9. Just how closely linked description and domination were in the European occupation of Egypt is described in Mitchell (1995).

10. See Cole and Altorki (1998:162–167) for an overview of the history of Arab and Western tourism in Egypt and the standard tourist activities and destinations for each. Cole and Altorki's book is a fascinating study of the impact of touristic development on local communities on Egypt's northwest coast.

11. On nationalism, tourism, and the state, see: Abu El-Haj 2001, Bernhardsson 2006, Baranowski 2004, Dawson 2004, Edensor 2003, Hitchcock 1995, Hutt 1996, Koshar 1998, Neatby 2003, Shaffer 2001, and Zuelow 2004, 2005a, 2005b, 2007, and forthcoming.

12. See E. Colli's (2000) dissertation for more on how Egyptians resist narratives of pharaonic greatness.

13. See Castañeda (1996) for a far more in-depth application of de Certeau's concepts of map, strategy, and tactic to the practices of monumental tourism.

14. For an Egyptological reading of graffiti on the monuments, see Vachala and Ondráš (2000), for example.

15. MacCannell (1976) and Culler (1981) are the definitive sources for thinking about how sites are labeled and given markers for touristic consumption. See also Bruner (2004) on the processes of site sacralization.

16. I am most gratefully indebted to Kirsten Scheid for her provocative insights on the meaning of graffiti in this monumental context. For an extended anthropological reading of graffiti, see Merle (1998).

17. See Rydell (1984) for a description of the world fairs as well as an analysis of the international political order that they visually enacted.

18. The Arabic-language daily that published the news, *Al-Gomhouriyya*, claimed that some five thousand foreign belly dancers worked in Cairo alone, but this is a ridiculously inflated figure. At that time there were probably no more than a hundred, and not all of them could find work at the same time.

19. Khaled Moussa al-Omrani, "Foreign Dancers Reply to Decree." *Business Monthly*, November 2003, American Chamber of Commerce in Egypt.

20. I should note that when Egyptians speak about "foreign dancers" they are often including Armenian Christians who are Egyptian citizens, have been born and raised in Egypt, and speak flawless, unaccented Egyptian Arabic.

21. I mostly use the term *transnational encounters* for the exchanges described in this book, but others have productively applied the concept of "borderlands" or "borderzones" to touristic encounters. See both Ortner (1997:181–182) and Bruner (2004:17–19) for lucid reviews of this interdisciplinary literature.

22. I am indebted to Mitch Rose for his insights in discussions we had about this subject in Cairo.

BIBLIOGRAPHY

Abdel Meguid, Ibrahim. 1997. *The Other Place*. Translated by Farouk Abdel Wahab. Cairo: American University in Cairo Press.

Abu El-Haj, Nadia. 2001. *Facts on the Ground: Archaeological Practice and Territorial Self-Fashioning in Israeli Society*. Chicago: University of Chicago Press.

Abu-Lughod, Lila. 1989. "Zones of Theory in the Anthropology of the Arab World." *Annual Review of Anthropology* 18:267–306.

———. 1991. "Writing against Culture." In *Recapturing Anthropology*, edited by Richard Fox, 137–162. Santa Fe, New Mexico: School of American Research Press.

———. 1993. *Writing Women's Worlds: Bedouin Stories*. Berkeley: University of California Press.

———. 2004. *Dramas of Nationhood: The Politics of Television in Egypt*. Chicago: University of Chicago Press.

Abu Nader, Muris. 1997. "Al-Haraka al-qaumiyya: Asbab al-ta'athur wa subul al-nahud." *Al-Hayaa*, 24 March.

Adams, Kathleen M. 1997. "Ethnic Tourism and the Renegotiation of Tradition in Tana Toraja (Sulawesi, Indonesia)." *Ethnology* 36:4.

Adams, Vincanne. 1996. *Tigers of the Snow and Other Virtual Sherpas: An Ethnography of Himalayan Encounters*. Princeton: Princeton University Press.

Adler, Judith. 1989. "Origins of Sightseeing." *Annals of Tourism Research* 16:7–29.

Al-Akhbār. 1999. "Ihtifālan bi qudūm al-alfiyya al-thālitha . . . haram dhahabiyya fauq qimmat Khūfū." *Al-Akhbār*, 19 February.

Algosaibi, Ghazi A. 1996 [1994]. *An Apartment Called Freedom*. Translated from the Arabic by Leslie McLoughlin. London: Kegan Paul International.

al-'Ālim, Mahmūd Amīn. 1986. *Wa'y wa-al-wa'y al-zā'if fi al-fikr al-'Arabī al-mu'āsir*. Cairo: Dar al-Thāqafa al-Jadīda.

Altorki, Soraya. 1986. *Women in Saudi Arabia: Ideology and Behavior among the Elite*. New York: Columbia University Press.

American Anthropology Association. 1971, revised through 1986. "Statement on Ethics: Principles of Professional Responsibility." Available online at http://www.aaanet .org/stmts/ethstmnt.htm, accessed 14 June 2006.

Amin, Galal. 2000. *Whatever Happened to the Egyptians? Changes in Egyptian Society from 1950 to the Present.* Cairo: American University in Cairo Press.

ʿAmrān, ʿEsām. 2000. "Wazīr al-thaqāfa . . . ʾākher man yaʿlam." *Al-Gomhoriyya,* 29 June.

Anderson, Benedict. 1991. *Imagined Communities: Reflections on the Origin and Spread of Nationalism.* New York: Verso.

Anzaldua, Gloria. 1987. *Borderlands/La Frontera: The New Mestiza.* San Francisco: Spinsters/Aunt Lute.

Appadurai, Arjun, ed. 1986. *The Social Life of Things: Commodities in Cultural Perspective.* Cambridge, New York: Cambridge University Press.

Appadurai, Arjun. 1990. "Disjuncture and Difference in the Global Cultural Economy." *Public Culture* 2(2):1–24.

Appiah, Kwame Anthony. 1992. *In My Father's House: Africa in the Philosophy of Culture.* New York, Oxford: Oxford University Press.

Al-ʿAqad, Sāleh. 1987. "Hawiyyat al-shakhsīyya al-misrīyya min khilāl al-tarīkh." *Al-Ahrām,* 21 August.

Arebi, Saddeka. 1994. *Women and Words in Saudi Arabia: The Politics of Literary Discourse.* New York: Columbia University Press.

El-Aref, Nevine. 2002a. "Home at Long Last." *Al-Ahrām Weekly,* 31 January–6 February, 23.

———. 2002b. "The Night of Counting the Years." *Al-Ahrām Weekly,* 31 January–6 February, 22.

Armbrust, Walter. 1996. *Mass Culture and Modernism in Egypt.* New York, Cambridge: Cambridge University Press.

Asad, Talal. 1991. "Afterword: From the History of Colonial Anthropology to the Anthropology of Western Hegemony." In *Colonial Situations: Essays on the Contextualization of Ethnographic Knowledge.* History of Anthropology, vol. 7, edited by George W. Stocking, Jr., 314–324. Madison: University of Wisconsin Press.

Badger, Reid. 1979. *The Great American Fair: The World's Columbian Exposition and American Culture.* Chicago: N. Hall.

Badone, Ellen, and Sharon R. Roseman, eds. 2004. *Intersecting Journeys: The Anthropology of Pilgrimage and Tourism.* Urbana and Chicago: University of Illinois Press.

Bakr, Mohammed I. 1988. "The New Excavations at Ezbet El-Tell, Kufur Nigm; The First Season 1984." In *The Archaeology of the Nile Delta: Problems and Priorities,* edited by E. C. M. van den Brink, 49–62. Amsterdam: Netherlands Foundation for Archaeological Research in Egypt.

Baranowski, Shelley. 2004. *Strength through Joy: Consumerism and Mass Tourism in the Third Reich.* Cambridge: Cambridge University Press.

Baudrillard, Jean. 1988. "Simulacra and Simulations." In Jean Baudrillard, *Selected Writings,* edited by Mark Poster, 166–184. Stanford: Stanford University Press.

Bauval, Robert. 1999a. *Secret Chamber: The Quest for the Hall of Records*. London: Century.

———. 1999b. "Is the Great Pyramid about to Reveal Its Deepest Secret?" *Guardian*, 11 July, 64.

Bauval, Robert, and Adrian Gilbert. 1994. *The Orion Mystery: Unlocking the Secrets of the Pyramids*. London: Heinemann.

Bauval, Robert, and Graham Hancock. 1997. *Keeper of Genesis: A Quest for the Hidden Legacy of Mankind*. London: Arrow Books.

Beblawi, Hazem, and Giacomo Luciani, eds. 1987. *The Rentier State*. London: Croom Helm.

Behbehanian, Laleh. 2000. "Policing the Illicit Peripheries of Egypt's Tourism Industry." *Middle East Report* 216.

Beinin, Joel. 1998. *Workers on the Nile: Nationalism, Communism, Islam and the Egyptian Working Class, 1882–1954*. Princeton: Princeton University Press.

Bennett, Tony. 1988. "The Exhibitionary Complex." *New Formations* 4:73–102.

Berg, Robert. 2002. "Searching for Zerzura." *Saudi Aramco World* 53(6).

Bernal, Martin. 1987. *Black Athena: The Afroasiatic Roots of Classic Civilization*. London: Free Association Books.

Bernhardsson, Magnus. 2006. *Reclaiming a Plundered Past: Archaeology and Nation Building in Modern Iraq*. Austin: University of Texas Press.

Bhabha, Homi. 1990. *Nation and Narration*. London, New York: Routledge.

———. 1994. *The Location of Culture*. London, New York: Routledge.

Blavatsky, Helena Petrovna. 1925. *The Secret Doctrine: The Synthesis of Science, Religion and Philosophy*. Covina, CA: Theosophical University Press.

Boon, James. 1992. "Cosmopolitan Moments: Echoey Confessions of an Ethnographer-Tourist." In *Crossing Cultures: Essays in the Displacement of Western Civilization*, edited by Daniel Segal, 226–253. Tucson: University of Arizona Press.

Bourdieu, Pierre. 1993. *Sociology in Question*. Translated from the French by Richard Nice. London: Sage.

Brier, Bob. 1999. "Napoleon in Egypt." *Archaeology Magazine* 52(3):44–53.

Brugsch, Heinrich Karl. 1880. *The True Story of the Exodus of Israel, Together with a Brief Review of the History of Monumental Egypt. Comp. from the Work of Dr. Henry Brugsch-Bey; Edited with an Introduction and Notes by Francis H. Underwood*. Boston: Lee.

Bruner, Edward M. 2004. *Culture on Tour: Ethnographies of Travel*. Chicago: University of Chicago Press.

Buonaventura, Wendy. 1983. *Belly Dancing: The Serpent and the Sphinx*. London: Virago Press.

———. 1989. *Serpent of the Nile: Women and Dance in the Arab World*. New York: Interlink Books.

Butler, Judith. 1989. *Gender Trouble: Feminism and the Subversion of Identity*. New York: Routledge.

———. 1993. *Bodies That Matter: On the Discursive Limits of "Sex."* New York: Routledge.

Carapico, Sheila. 2006. "No Easy Answers: The Ethics of Field Research in the Arab World." *Political Science and Politics* 39:429–431.

Carlton, Donna. 1994. *Looking for Little Egypt*. Bloomington, IN: I.D.D. Press.

Castañeda, Quetzil. 1996. *In the Museum of Maya Culture: Touring Chichen Itza*. Minneapolis: University of Minnesota Press.

Cayce, Edgar Evans (Hugh Lynn Cayce, ed.). 1968. *Edgar Cayce on Atlantis*. New York: Hawthorn Books.

Cayce, Edgar Evans, Gail Cayce Schwartzer, and Douglas G. Richards. 1988. *Mysteries of Atlantis Revisited: Edgar Cayce's Wisdom for the New Age*. San Francisco: Harper and Row.

de Certeau, Michel. 1984. *The Practice of Everyday Life*. Translated by Steven Rendall. Berkeley: University of California Press.

Cervé, Wishar Spenle. 1963 (1931). *Lemuria: The Lost Continent of the Pacific*. San Jose, CA: Supreme Grand Lodge of AMORC.

Chambers, Erve. 1999. *Native Tours: The Anthropology of Travel and Tourism*. Waveland Press.

Clark, Janine A. 2006. "Field Research Methods in the Middle East." *Political Science and Politics* 39:417–423.

Clifford, James. 1989. "Notes on Theory and Travel." *Inscriptions* 5:177–188.

———. 1997. *Routes: Travel and Translation in the Late Twentieth Century*. Cambridge: Harvard University Press.

Cohen, Erik. 1979. "A Phenomenology of Tourist Experiences." *Sociology* 13:179–201.

———. 1984. "The Sociology of Tourism: Approaches, Issues, and Findings." *Annual Revue of Sociology* 10:373–392.

Cole, Donald P., and Soraya Altorki. 1998. *Bedouin, Settlers, and Holiday-Makers: Egypt's Changing Northwest Coast*. Cairo: American University in Cairo Press.

Colli, Elliott. 2000. "Hooked on Pharaonics: Literature and Appropriation of Ancient Egypt." Ph.D. dissertation, Department of Comparative Literature, University of California at Berkeley.

———. 2002. "*Whose Pharaohs?* by Donald Malcolm Reid" (book review). *MIT Electronic Journal of Middle East Studies*, vol. 2. Electronic document, http://web.mit.edu/CIS/www/mitejmes/issues/200210/colla.htm, accessed 8 June 2006.

Constable, Nicole. 2003. *Romance on a Global Stage: Pen Pals, Virtual Ethnography, and "Mail Order" Marriages*. Berkeley: University of California Press.

Conway, Moncure Daniels, ed. 1896. *The Writings of Thomas Paine*. New York: G. P. Putnam's Sons.

Cook, Michael. 1983. "Pharaonic History in Medieval Egypt." *Studia Islamica* 57:67–103.

Copeland, Miles. 1969. *The Game of Nations: The Amorality of Power Politics*. New York: Simon and Shuster.

Coxill, David. 1998. "The Riddle of the Sphinx." *Inscription: Journal of Ancient Egypt* 2:13–19.

Crick, Malcolm. 1985. "'Tracing' the Anthropological Self: Quizzical Reflections on Field Work, Tourism, and the Ludic." *Social Analysis* 17:71–92.

Crone, Patricia, and Michael Cook. 1977. *Hagarism: The Making of the Islamic World*. Cambridge: Cambridge University Press.

Crystal, Jill. 1990. *Oil and Politics in the Gulf: Rulers and Merchants in Kuwait and Qatar*. London: Cambridge University Press.

Culler, Jonathan. 1981. "Semiotics of Tourism." *American Journal of Semiotics* 1(1–2): 127–140.

Curl, James Stevens. 1994. *Egyptomania: The Egyptian Revival: A Recurring Theme in the History of Taste*. Manchester, England: Manchester University Press.

Curran, Brian A. 1996. "Egyptomania: Egypt in Western Art, 1730–1930" (book review). *Art Bulletin*, December.

Danforth, Loring. 1989. *Firewalking and Religious Healing: The Anastenaria of Greece and the American Firewalking Movement*. Princeton: Princeton University Press.

D'Auria, Sue, Peter Lacovara, and Catharine Roehrig, eds. 1988. *Mummies and Magic: The Funerary Arts of Ancient Egypt*. Boston: Museum of Fine Arts.

Dawson, Michael. 2004. *Selling British Columbia: Tourism and Consumer Culture, 1890–1970*. Vancouver: University of British Columbia Press.

Description de l'Egypte. 1994. Germany: Benedikt Taschen.

Díaz-Andreu, Margarita, and Timothy Champion, eds. 1996. *Nationalism and Archaeology in Europe*. London: University College London Press.

Donnelly, Ignatius. 1882. *Atlantis: The Antediluvian World*. New York: Harper.

Douglas, Allen, and Fedwa Malti-Douglas. 1997. "Film and Pharaonism: Shādī 'Abd al-Salām's *Eloquent Peasant*." In *Tradition and Modernity in Arabic Literature*, edited by Issa J. Boullata and Terri DeYoung. Fayetteville: University of Arkansas Press.

Doumato, Eleanor Abdellah. 2000. *Getting God's Ear: Women, Islam, and Healing in Saudi Arabia and the Gulf*. New York: Columbia University Press.

Dural, Sadrettin. 2006. *Protecting Çatalhöyük: Memoir of an Archaeological Site Guard*. With contributions by Ian Hodder; Foreword by Ian Hodder; translated by Duygu Camurcuoglu Cleere. Walnut Creek, CA: Left Coast Press.

Dykstra, Darrell. 1994. "Pyramids, Prophets, and Progress: Ancient Egypt in the Writings of Ali Mubarak." *Journal of the American Oriental Society* 114(1):54–65.

Eco, Umberto. 1986. *Travels in Hyperreality: Essays*. New York: Harcourt Brace and Co.

Edensor, Tim. 2003. *National Identity, Popular Culture and Everyday Life*. Oxford: Berg.

Edwards, Amelia. 1983 [1878]. *A Thousand Miles Up the Nile*. Boston: Houghton Mifflin.

Egypt Exploration Society. 1894. *An Atlas of Ancient Egypt: With Complete Index, Geographical and Historical Notes, Biblical References, etc.* London: K. Paul, Trench, Trübner.

Egypt State Information Service. 1999. *Egypt Yearbook: Tourism*. Cairo: State Information Service Publications.

Egyptian Museum Berlin (museum catalogue, n.d.). Berlin: Ägyptisches Museum.

Ellis, Richard. 1998. *Imagining Atlantis*. New York: Alfred Knopf.

Eltahawy, Mona. 1999. "Egyptians Disown Celluloid 'Prince.'" *Guardian*, 17 April, 17.

Enloe, Cynthia. 1989. *Bananas, Beaches and Bases: Making Feminist Sense of International Politics*. Berkeley: University of California Press.

Fagan, Brian M. 1975. *The Rape of the Nile: Tomb Robbers, Tourists, and Archaeologists in Egypt*. New York: Charles Scribner's Sons.

Fainstein, Susan S., and Dennis R. Judd. 1999. "Global Forces, Local Strategies, and Urban Tourism." In *The Tourist City*, edited by Dennis R. Judd and Susan S. Fainstein, 1–7. New Haven: Yale University Press.

Fargues, Philippe. 1980. *Réserves de Main-d'Oeuvre et Rente Pétrolière: Étude Démographique des Migrations de Travail vers les Pays Arabes du Golfe*. Beirut: Centre d'études et de recherches sur le Moyen-Orient contemporain.

Faucher, Jean Andrew. 1986. *Les Francs Maçons et le Pouvoir*. Paris: Ed. Perrin.

Feldman-Savelsberg, Pamela, Flavien T. Ndonko, and Bergis Schmidt-Ehry. 2000. "Sterilizing Vaccines or the Politics of the Womb: Retrospective Study of a Rumor in Cameroon." *Medical Anthropology Quarterly* 14(2):159–179.

Feyerabend, Paul. 1975. *Against Method: Outline of an Anarchistic Theory of Knowledge*. London: NLB.

Forster, John. 1964. "The Sociological Consequences of Tourism." *International Journal of Comparative Sociology* 5(2):217–227.

Fowden, Garth. 1993. *The Egyptian Hermes*. Princeton: Princeton University Press.

Fox, Richard, ed. 1991. *Recapturing Anthropology*. Santa Fe, NM: School of American Research Press.

France, Peter. 1991. *The Rape of Egypt: How the Europeans Stripped Egypt of Its Heritage*. London: Barrie and Jenkins.

Friedman, Jonathan. 1990. "Being in the World: Globalization and Localization." In *Global Culture: Nationalism, Globalization and Modernity*, edited by M. Featherstone, 311–328. London: Sage Publications.

Fu'ād, Ni'māt Ahmad. 1978 [1968]. *Shakhsīyat Misr*. Cairo: al-Hay'ah al-Misrīyah al-'Āmmah lil-Kitāb.

Fujimura, Joan. 1998. "Authorizing Knowledge in Science and Anthropology." *American Anthropologist* 100(2):347–360.

García Canclini, Néstor. 1993. *Transforming Modernity: Popular Culture in Mexico*. Translated by Lidia Lozano. Austin: University of Texas Press.

———. 1995. *Hybrid Cultures: Strategies for Entering and Leaving Modernity*. Translated by Christopher Chippari and Sylvia López. Minneapolis: University of Minnesota Press.

Gauri, K. Lal, John J. Sinai, and Jayanta K. Bandyopadhyay. 1995. "Geologic Weathering and Its Implications on the Age of the Sphinx." *Geoarchaeology* 10(2):119–133.

Gause, F. Gregory, III. 1994. *Oil Monarchies: Domestic and Security Challenges in the Arab Gulf States*. New York: Council on Foreign Relations.

el-Gawhary, Karim. 1995. "Sex Tourism in Cairo." *Middle East Report* 195:26.

Geertz, Clifford. 1973. "Thick Description: Toward an Interpretive Theory of Culture." In *The Interpretation of Cultures*, 3–30. New York: Basic Books.

———. 2002. "Le Proche-Orient en Extrême-Orient: sur l'Islam en Indonésie." In Lucette Valensi, ed., *À L'oeuvre: Une histoire anthropologique de l'Islam méditerranéen*, 197–214. Paris: Editions Bouchene.

Gershoni, Israel. 1982. "The Emergence of Pan-Nationalism in Egypt: Pan-Islamism and Pan-Arabism in the 1930s." *Asian and African Studies* 16:59–94.

Gershoni, Israel, and James Jankowski. 1986. *Egypt, Islam, and the Arabs: The Search for Egyptian Nationhood, 1900–1930*. New York: Oxford University Press.

———. 1995. *Redefining the Egyptian Nation, 1930–1945*. Cambridge: Cambridge University Press.

Gharib, Samir. 1997. "Finding a New Home for Egypt's Ancient Treasures." UNESCO *Courier* 50(12):45–46.

Ghīsh, Ibtihāl. 1999. "Al-hurayim al-dhahabī mā zāl taht al-dirāsa." *'Uktūbir*, December.

Ghosh, Amitav. 1986. "The Imam and the Indian." *Granta* 20:135–146.

———. 1992. *In an Antique Land*. London: Granta Books.

Gieryn, Thomas. 1983. "Boundary-Work and the Demarcation of Science from Non-Science: Strains and Interests in Professional Ideologies of Scientists." *American Sociological Review* 48:781–795.

———. 1995. "Boundaries of Science." In *Handbook of Science and Technology Studies*, edited by Jasanoff et al., 393–443. London: Sage.

Gillespie, Kate, and Liesl Riddle. 2003. "Case-Based Business Education in the Arab Middle East and North Africa." Paper presented at the Business Education Systems in Emerging Market Economies: Trends and Prospects Conference, Atlanta, Georgia, 7 November. Electronic document available at http://www.ciber.gatech.edu/workingpaper/2003/04-013.pdf, accessed 15 June 2006.

Goffman, Erving. 1959. *The Presentation of Self in Everyday Life*. Garden City, NY: Doubleday.

Goldschmidt, Arthur, Jr. 2002. *A Concise History of the Middle East*, 7th ed. Boulder: Westview Press.

Gordon, David C. 1971. *Self-Determination and History in the Third World*. Princeton: Princeton University Press.

Graburn, Nelson. 1989 (1977). "Tourism: The Sacred Journey." In *Hosts and Guests*, edited by Valene Smith. Philadelphia: University of Pennsylvania Press.

———. 1984. "The Evolution of Tourist Arts." *Annals of Tourism Research* 11:393–419.

———. 2002. "The Ethnographic Tourist." In *The Tourist as a Metaphor of the Social World*, edited by Graham M. S. Dann. Wallingford, UK: CABI Publishing.

———. 2004. "The Kyoto Tax Strike: Buddhism, Shinto, and Tourism in Japan." In *Intersecting Journeys: The Anthropology of Pilgrimage and Tourism*, edited by Ellen Badone and Sharon R. Roseman, 125–139. Urbana and Chicago: University of Illinois Press.

Graham-Brown, Sarah. 1988. *Images of Women*. London: William Heinemann.

Green, Peter. 1979. "Tut-Tut-Tut." *New York Review of Books* 26(15).

Greener, Leslie. 1966. *The Discovery of Egypt*. London: Cassell.

Greenwood, Davydd. 1989. "Culture by the Pound: An Anthropological Perspective on Tourism as Cultural Commoditization." In *Hosts and Guests*, edited by Valene Smith. Philadelphia: University of Pennsylvania Press.

Griffiths, J. Gwyn. 1991. *Atlantis and Egypt*. Cardiff: University of Wales Press.

Gupta, Akhil, and James Ferguson, eds. 1997. *Anthropological Locations: Boundaries and Grounds of a Field Science*. Berkeley: University of California Press.

Ha, Marie-Paule. 1997. "Relations of Cultures: A Review of Ali Behdad's *Belated Travelers*, Xiaomei Chen's *Occidentalism*, and Chris Tiffin and Alan Lawson's *De-Scribing Empire, Post-Colonialism and Textuality*." *Research in African Literatures* 28(4):154–164.

Haarmann, Ulrich. 1980. "Regional Sentiment in Medieval Islamic Egypt." *Bulletin of the School of Oriental and African Studies* 43:62–64.

————. 1996. "Medieval Muslim Perceptions of Pharaonic Egypt." In *Ancient Egyptian Literature: History and Forms*, edited by A. Loprieno, 605–627. Leiden, New York: Brill.

Habachi, Labib. 1988. *The Obelisks of Egypt*. Cairo: American University in Cairo Press.

al-Hakīm, S. 1994. *Misr al-Farʿō-ʿArabīa*. Cairo: Marz al-Hadāra al-ʿArabīa lil-ʿIlm wal-Nashr.

Hamilakis, Yanni. 1996. "Through the Looking Glass: Nationalism, Archaeology and the Politics of Identity." *Antiquity* 70:975–978.

Hamilton, Edith, and Huntington Cairns, eds. 1961. *The Collected Dialogues of Plato, including the Letters*. Translated by Lane Cooper and others. New York: Pantheon Books.

Hammoudi, Abdellah. 2002. "L'intuition du Maghreb: un rêve paradoxal." *À L'oeuvre: Une histoire anthropologique de l'Islam méditerranéen*, edited by Lucette Valensi, 163–174. Paris: Editions Bouchene.

Hancock, Graham. 1995. *Fingerprints of the Gods*. London: Heinemann.

————. 1998. *Heaven's Mirror: Quest for the Lost Civilization*. New York: Crown Publishers.

Hancock, Graham, and Robert Bauval. 1996. *Message of the Sphinx: A Quest for the Hidden Legacy of Mankind*. New York: Three Rivers Press.

Haraway, Donna. 1994 (1983). "Teddy Bear Patriarchy: Taxidermy in the Garden of Eden, New York City, 1908–1936." Reprinted in *Culture/Power/History: A Reader in Contemporary Social Theory*, edited by Dirks, Eley, and Ortner, 49–95. Princeton: Princeton University Press.

Harrell, James A. 1994. "The Sphinx Controversy: Another Look at the Geological Evidence." *KMT: A Modern Journal of Ancient Egypt* 5(2):70–74.

Hassaan, Yousry. 2000. "Failure knows its friends at the Egyptology Congress: those responsible for Egyptian antiquities speak every language . . . except for Arabic." *al-Masaa*, 11 March.

Hassan, Fekri A. 1998. "Memorabilia: Archaeological Materiality and National Identity in Egypt." In *Archaeology under Fire: Nationalism, Politics and Heritage in the Eastern Mediterranean and Middle East*, edited by L. Meskell, 201–216. London: Routledge.

Hawass, Zahi. 1996. "The Workmen's Community at Giza." In *House and Palace in Ancient Egypt*, edited by Manfred Bietak, 53–67. Wien: Verlag der Osterreichischen Akademie der Wissenshaft.

————. 1997. "Tombs of the Pyramid Builders." *Archaeology Magazine* 50(1):39–44.

————. 2000a. *Valley of the Golden Mummies*. New York: Harry Abrams.

———. 2000b. *Silent Images: Women in Pharaonic Egypt*. New York: Harry Abrams.

———. 2000c. "Innahum yuzayyifūn al-tārīkh." *Al-Ahrām*, 20 May.

———. 2000d. "The Five Secret Chambers." *Al-Ahrām Weekly*, 1–7 November, 21.

———. 2001a. "Al-zī'baq al-ahmar." *Al-Ahrām*, 13 January.

———. 2001b. "The Sphinx Cried Twice." *Al-Ahram Weekly*, 24–30 May.

———. 2002a. *al-Sayyida fi Misr al-Qadima*, 2nd edition. Cairo: Egyptian Ministry of Culture.

———. 2002b. "More Dances with Tomb Robbers." *Al-Ahrām Weekly*, 3–9 January, 17.

———. 2003. "Site Management and Conservation." In *Egyptology at the Dawn of the Twenty-First Century: Proceedings of the Eighth International Congress of Egyptologists*, edited by Z. Hawass, vol. 3, 48–61. Cairo, New York: American University in Cairo Press.

Hawass, Zahi, and Mark Lehner. 1994a. "The Sphinx: Who Built It and Why?" *Archaeology* 47(5):30–41.

———. 1994b. "Remnants of a Lost Civilization?" *Archaeology* 47(5):44–47.

———. 1997. "Builders of the Pyramids." *Archaeology Magazine* 50(1):30–37.

Hawass, Zahi, and Miroslav Verner. 1996. "Newly Discovered Blocks from the Causeway of Sahure." *MDAIK* 52:177–186.

Hazbun, Waleed. 2006. "The East as an Exhibit: Thomas Cook & Son and the Origins of the International Tourism Industry in Egypt." In *The Business of Tourism: Place, Faith, and History*, edited by Philip Scranton and Janet F. Davidson. Philadelphia: University of Pennsylvania Press.

Heikal, Mohamed. 1965 [1933]. *Thawrat al-Adab*. Cairo: Maktabat al-Nahda al-Misrīya.

———. 1983. *Autumn of Fury: The Assassination of Sadat*. New York: Random House.

Hess, David J. 1993. *Science in the New Age: The Paranormal, Its Defenders and Debunkers, and American Culture*. Madison: University of Wisconsin Press.

Hitchcock, Michael. 1995. "Inter-ethnic Relations and Tourism in Bima-Sumbawa." *Sojourn* 10(2):233–258.

Hodder, Ian. 2003. "Archaeological Reflexivity and the 'Local' Voice." *Anthropological Quarterly* 76:55–69.

Hogarth, David George. 1899. *Authority and Archaeology, Sacred and Profane: Essays on the Relation of Monuments to Biblical and Classical Literature, with an Introductory Chapter on the Nature of Archaeology by the Editor*. London: Scribner.

Hope, Murray. 1990. *Ancient Egypt: The Sirius Connection*. Dorset: Element Books.

———. 1991. *Atlantis: Myth or Reality?* London: Penguin Books.

Horn, Miriam. 1992. "The Vanishing Past." *U.S. News & World Report* 113(11):80–86.

Hoving, Thomas. 1978. *Tutankhamun, the Untold Story*. New York: Simon and Schuster.

Humbert, Jean-Marcel. 1994. "Egyptomania: A Current Concept from the Renaissance to Postmodernism." In *Egyptomania: Egypt in Western Art 1730–1930* (catalogue accompanying the exhibit at the Louvre, the National Gallery of Canada, and the Kunsthistorisches Museum in Vienna). Ottawa: National Gallery of Canada.

Hussein, Taha. 1954. *The Future of Culture in Egypt*. Translated from the Arabic by Sidney Glazer. Washington: American Council of Learned Societies.

Hutt, Michael. 1996. "Looking for Shangri-La: From Hilton to Lamichane." In *The*

Tourist Image: Myths and Myth Making in Tourism, edited by T. Selwyn, 49–60. Chichester: John Wiley and Sons.

Ibrahim, Saad Eddin. 1982a. "Oil, Migration and the New Arab Social Order." In *Rich and Poor States in the Middle East: Egypt and the New Arab Order,* edited by Malcolm Kerr and El Sayed Yassin. Cairo: American University of Cairo Press.

———. 1982b. *The New Arab Social Order: A Study of the Social Impact of Oil Wealth.* Boulder: Westview.

Ikram, Salima, and Aidan Dodson. 1998. *The Mummy in Ancient Egypt: Equipping the Dead for Eternity.* Cairo: American University in Cairo Press.

Israeli, Raphael. 1981. *I, Egypt: Aspects of President Anwar Al-Sadat's Political Thought.* Jerusalem: Magnes Press, Hebrew University.

———. 1985. *Man of Defiance: A Political Biography of Anwar Sadat.* Totowa, NJ: Barnes and Noble Books.

Iversen, Erik. 1993 (1961). *The Myth of Egypt and Its Hieroglyphs in European Tradition.* Princeton: Princeton University Press.

Jameson, Fredric. 1991. "Introduction." *Postmodernism, or, The Cultural Logic of Late Capitalism.* Durham: Duke University Press.

Jansen, J. J. G. 1985. "The Creed of Sadat's Assassins: The Contents of 'The Forgotten Duty' Analysed." *Die Welt des Islams* XXV (Leiden: Brill), 1–30.

Jasanoff, Sheila, ed. 2004. *States of Knowledge: The Co-Production of Science and Social Order.* New York: Routledge.

Jobbins, Jenny. 2002. "Law from an Antique Land." *Al-Ahrām Weekly,* 31 January–6 February, 22.

Jowett, Benjamin. 1953. *The Collected Dialogues of Plato. Vol. 2: Republic, Gorgias, Parmenides. Vol. 3: Cratylus, Phaedrus, Theaetetus, Sophist, Statesman, Philebus, Timaeus, Critias.* Translated into English with analyses and introductions by B. Jowett. Fourth Edition. Oxford: Clarendon Press.

Judd, Dennis R., and Susan S. Fainstein, eds. 1999. *The Tourist City.* New Haven: Yale University Press.

Kabbani, Rana. 1986. *Europe's Myths of the Orient: Devise and Rule.* London: Pandora Press.

Karayanni, Stavrous Stavrou. 2005. "Dismissal Veiling Desire: Kuchuk Hanem and Imperial Masculinity." In *Belly Dance: Orientalism, Transnationalism, and Harem Fantasy,* edited by Anthony Shay and Barbara Sellers-Young, 114–143. Costa Mesa, CA: Mazda Publishers.

Kepel, Gilles. 2003. *Muslim Extremism in Egypt: The Prophet and Pharaoh.* Berkeley: University of California Press.

Kerr, Malcolm, and El-Sayed Yassin, eds. 1982. *Rich and Poor States in the Middle East: Egypt and the New Arab Order.* Boulder: Westview.

Khadīr, Haīdar. 1999. "Takhrīb al-āthār . . . am daʿāya lahā?" *Al-Ahrām,* 12 September.

Knorr Cetina, Karen. 1995. "Laboratory Studies: The Cultural Approach to the Study of Science." In *Handbook of Science and Technology Studies,* edited by S. Jasanoff et al., 140–166. London: Sage.

Kohl, Philip L., and Clare Fawcett, eds. 1995. *Nationalism, Politics, and the Practice of Archaeology*. Cambridge: Cambridge University Press.

Korany, Bahgat, and Ali E. Hillal Dessouki, eds. 1991 [1984]. *The Foreign Policies of Arab States: The Challenge of Change* (second edition). Boulder: Westview Press.

Koshar, Rudy. 1998. "What Ought to Be Seen: Tourists, Guidebooks and National Identities in Modern Germany and Europe." *Journal of Contemporary History* 33(3):323–340.

Kuhn, Thomas. 1962. *The Structure of Scientific Revolutions*. Chicago: University of Chicago Press.

Kuklick, Henrika. 1991. "Contested Monuments: The Politics of Archaeology in Southern Africa." In *Colonial Situations: Essays on the Contextualization of Ethnographic Knowledge. History of Anthropology*, vol. 7, edited by George W. Stocking, Jr., 135–169. Madison: University of Wisconsin Press.

Lacey, Robert. 1983. *The Kingdom: Arabia and the House of Saud*. New York: Avon Books.

Larson, Charles M. 1985. *By His Own Hand upon Papyrus: A New Look at the Joseph Smith Papyri*. Grand Rapids, MI: Institute for Religious Research.

Latour, Bruno. 1993. *We Have Never Been Modern*. Translated from the French by Catharine Porter. New York: Harvester Wheatsheaf.

LaTowsky, Robert J. 1984. "Egyptian Labor Abroad: Mass Participation and Modest Returns." *MERIP Reports* No. 123, 11–18.

Lavie, Smadar, and Ted Swedenburg, eds. 1996. *Displacement, Diaspora, and Geographies of Identity*. Durham: Duke University Press.

Lawton, Ian, and Chris Ogilvie-Herald. 1999. *Giza: The Truth*. London: Virgin Publishing.

Lehner, Mark. 1994. "Notes and Photographs on the West-Schoch Sphinx Hypothesis." *KMT: A Modern Journal of Ancient Egypt* 5(3):40–48.

Lévi-Strauss, Claude. 1981 [1955]. *Tristes Tropiques*. Translated by John and Doreen Weightman. New York: Atheneum.

———. 1993. *Scientific Practice and Ordinary Action: Ethnomethodology and Social Studies of Science*. Cambridge, New York: Cambridge University Press.

Limón, José E. 1991. "Representation, Ethnicity, and the Precursory Ethnography: Notes of a Native Anthropologist." In *Recapturing Anthropology*, edited by Richard Fox, 115–136. Santa Fe, NM: School of American Research Press.

Lockman, Zachary. 2004. *Contending Visions of the Middle East: The History and Politics of Orientalism*. Cambridge: Cambridge University Press.

Lynch, Michael. 1985. *Art and Artifact in Laboratory Science: A Study of Shop Work and Shop Talk in a Research Laboratory*. London, Boston: Routledge and Kegan Paul.

———. 1993. *Scientific Practice and Ordinary Action: Ethnomethodology and Social Studies of Science*. Cambridge/New York: Cambridge University Press.

MacCannell, Dean. 1976. *The Tourist: A New Theory of the Leisure Class*. New York: Schocken Books.

———. 1992. *Empty Meeting Grounds: The Tourist Papers*. New York: Routledge.

Malkki, Liisa. 1995. *Purity and Exile: Violence, Memory and National Cosmology among Hutu Refugees in Tanzania*. Chicago/London: University of Chicago Press.

Martin, Emily. 1987. *The Woman in the Body: A Cultural Analysis of Reproduction*. Boston: Beacon Press.

Mauss, Marcel. 1990. *The Gift: The Form and Reason for Exchange in Archaic Societies*. Translated by W. D. Halls. New York: W. W. Norton.

Mayes, Stanley. 1959. *The Great Belzoni*. London: Putnam.

Melton, J. Gordon. 1988. "A History of the New Age Movement." In *Not Necessarily the New Age*, edited by Robert Basic. Buffalo: Prometheus Books.

Merle, Florence. 1998. *The International Graffiti Movement: Mixed Metaphors and Aesthetic Disruption*. Ph.D. dissertation, Department of Anthropology, Princeton University.

Meskell, Lynn. 2001. "The Practice and Politics of Archaeology in Egypt." In *Ethics and Anthropology*, edited by Anne-Marie Cantwell, Eva Friedlander, and Madeleine Tramm. New York: New York Academy of Sciences.

———. 2005. "Sites of Violence: Terrorism, Tourism, and Heritage in the Archaeological Present." In *Embedding Ethics*, edited by Lynn Meskell and Peter Pels. New York: Berg.

Mitchell, Timothy. 1988. *Colonizing Egypt*. Berkeley/Los Angeles: University of California Press.

———. 1995. "Worlds Apart: An Egyptian Village and the International Tourism Industry." *Middle East Report* 196(25/5):8–11, 23.

———. 2002. *Rule of Experts: Egypt, Techno-Politics, Modernity*. Berkeley, Los Angeles: University of California Press.

Mullen, Patrick B. 1972. "Modern Legend and Rumor Theory." *Journal of the Folklore Institute* 9(1):95–109.

Munif, Abdelrahman. 1987 [1984]. *Cities of Salt*. Translated by Peter Theroux. New York: Random House.

———. 1991. *The Trench*. Translated by Peter Theroux. New York: Pantheon.

———. 1993 [1989]. *Variations on Night and Day*. Translated by Peter Theroux. New York: Pantheon.

Mursī, Muhammed 'Abd el-'Alīm. 1989. *al-Tarbīya wa Mushkilāt al-Mujtama' fī Duwal al-Khalīj al-'Arabīya: Mushkilat al-'Amāla al-Ajnabīya: Mu'ālaja Islāmīyah*. al-Riyād: Dār 'Ālam al-Kutub.

Mūsā, Mūshīra. 1999. "Dr. Zahi Hawass: al-hurayim fikra misriyya 100%." *Al-Akhbār*, 11 February.

Mūsā, Salāma. 1961. *The Education of Salāma Mūsā*. Leiden: E. J. Brill.

Nada, Atef Hanna. 1991. *The Impact of Temporary International Migration on Rural Egypt*. Cairo: American University in Cairo Press.

Nader, Laura. 1996. *Naked Science: Anthropological Inquiry into Boundaries, Power, and Knowledge*. New York: Routledge.

Nash, Dennison. 1977. "Tourism as a Form of Imperialism." In *Hosts and Guests*, edited by Valene Smith. Philadelphia: University of Pennsylvania Press.

———. 1981. "Tourism as an Anthropological Subject." *Current Anthropology* 22(5)461–481.

National Geographic News. 2002. "Update: Third 'Door' Found in Great Pyramid." *National Geographic News,* September 2002, electronic document available online at: http://news.nationalgeographic.com/news/2002/09/0923_020923_egypt.html, accessed 20 June 2006.

Neatby, Nicole. 2003. "Meeting of Minds: North American Travel Writers and Government Tourist Publicity in Quebec, 1920–1955." *Histoire Sociale/Social History* 36(72):465–495.

Noakes, Aubrey. 1962. *Cleopatra's Needles.* London: H. F. & G. Witherby.

Noh, Heba Moustafa. 2003. "Distinction (=Arabic *Tamyiz*) and Its Manifestation in Egyptian." In *Egyptology at the Dawn of the Twenty-First Century: Proceedings of the Eighth International Congress of Egyptologists,* edited by Z. Hawass, vol. 3, 315–321. Cairo, New York: American University in Cairo Press.

Ortner, Sherry. 1997. "Borderland Politics and Erotics." In *Making Gender: The Politics and Erotics of Culture,* 181–212. Boston: Beacon Press.

Osman, Ahmed. 1990. *Moses: Pharaoh of Egypt: The Mystery of Akhenaten Resolved.* London: Grafton.

———. 2002. *Moses and Akhenaten: The Secret History of Egypt at the Time of the Exodus.* London: Bear and Company.

———. 2004. *Jesus in the House of the Pharaohs: The Essene Revelations on the Historical Jesus.* London: Bear and Company.

Ossman, Susan. 1995. "Boom Box in Ouarzazate: The Search for the Similarly Strange." *Middle East Report* 196(25/5):12–15.

Owen, R. 1985. *Migrant Labour in the Gulf.* London: Minority Rights Group.

Paine, Thomas. 1818. "Origin of Free-Masonry." In *The Writings of Thomas Paine,* edited by Moncure Daniels Conway, 1896. New York: G. P. Putnam's Sons.

Phillips, Graham. 1998. *Act of God: Tutankhamun, Moses and the Myth of Atlantis.* London: Sidgwick and Jackson.

———. 2002. *The Moses Legacy: In Search of the Origins of God.* London: Sidgwick and Jackson.

———. 2003. *Atlantis and the Ten Plagues of Egypt: The Secret History Hidden in the Valley of the Kings.* London: Bear and Company.

Phillips, Ruth B. 1994. "Why Not Tourist Art? Significant Silences in Native American Museum Representations." In *After Colonialism: Imperial Histories and Post-Colonial Displacements,* edited by Gyan Prakash. Princeton: Princeton University Press, 98–125.

Picknett, Lynn, and Clive Prince. 1999. *The Stargate Conspiracy: The Truth about Extraterrestrial Life and the Mysteries of Ancient Egypt.* London: Little, Brown.

Politeyan, J. 1915. *Biblical Discoveries in Egypt, Palestine and Mesopotamia.* London: E. Stock.

Pollock, Susan, and Reinhard Bernbeck. 2004. *Archaeologies of the Middle East.* Oxford: Blackwell Publishing.

Porterfield, Todd. 1998. *The Allure of Empire: Art in the Service of French Imperialism, 1798–1836.* Princeton: Princeton University Press.

Pratt, Mary Louise. 1986. "Fieldwork in Common Places." In *Writing Culture: The Poet-*

ics and Politics of Ethnography, edited by James Clifford and George Marcus, 27–50. Berkeley: University of California Press.

Prentice, Chris. 1994. "Some Problems of Response to Empire in Settler Post-Colonial Societies." In De-Scribing Empire: Post-Colonialism and Textuality, edited by Chris Tiffin and Alan Lawson, 45–58. London: Routledge.

Pringle, Heather. 2001. The Mummy Congress: Science, Obsession, and the Everlasting Dead. New York: Theia.

Raafat, Samir. 1999. "Freemasonry in Egypt: Is It Still Around?" Insight Magazine, 1 March. Available online at http://www.egy.com/community/99-03-01.shtml, accessed 20 June 2006.

Rabinow, Paul. 1986. "Representations Are Social Facts: Modernity and Post-Modernity in Anthropology." In Writing Culture: The Poetics and Politics of Ethnography, edited by James Clifford and George E. Marcus, 234–261. Berkeley: University of California Press.

al-Rasheed, Madawi. 2002. A History of Saudi Arabia. Cambridge: Cambridge University Press.

al-Rasheed, Madawi, ed. 2005. Transnational Connections and the Arab Gulf. New York: Routledge.

Reader, Colin D. 2000. "A Geomorphological Study of the Giza Necropolis, with Implications for the Development of the Site." Archaeometry 43(1):149–159.

Reid, Donald M. 1985. "Indigenous Egyptology: The Decolonization of a Profession." Journal of the American Oriental Society 105(2):233–246.

———. 2002. Whose Pharaohs? Archaeology, Museums, and Egyptian National Identity from Napoleon to World War I. Berkeley: University of California Press.

Reybaud, J. 1828. Histoire de l'expedition française en Egypte. London.

Roberts, David. 2000. The Holy Land: Egypt and Nubia. From Drawings Made on the Spot by David Roberts R.A. With Historical Descriptions by the Reverend George Croly, LLD. Cairo: American University in Cairo Press.

Robinson, Edward. 1841. Biblical Researches in Palestine, Mount Sinai and Arabia Petraea: A Journal of Travels in the Year 1838. Undertaken in Reference to Biblical Geography. London: J. Murray.

Romano, David. 2006. "Conducting Research in the Middle East's Conflict Zones." Political Science and Politics 39:439–441.

Romer, John, and Elizabeth Romer. 1993. The Rape of Tutankhamun. London: Michael O'Mara Books Ltd.

Rosaldo, Renato. 1989. Culture and Truth: The Remaking of Social Analysis. Boston: Beacon Press.

Rose, Mitch, n.d. The Problem of Power and the Politics of Landscape: Stopping the Greater Cairo Ring Road. Unpublished manuscript.

———. 2003. "Monumental Vistas: Narratives of Heritage and the Landscape of the Giza Plateau." Ph.D. dissertation, Department of Geography, University of Cambridge.

Rydell, Robert W. 1984. All the World's a Fair: Visions of Empire at American International Expositions, 1876–1916. Chicago: University of Chicago Press.

Sabagh, G. 1982. "Migration and Social Mobility in Egypt." In *Rich and Poor States in the Middle East: Egypt and the New Arab Order,* edited by Malcolm Kerr and El Sayid Yassin. Cairo: American University in Cairo Press.

Sadek, Hind. 1990. "Treasures of Ancient Egypt." *National Parks* 64(5/6):16–17.

Said, Edward. 1978. *Orientalism.* New York: Pantheon Books.

Samper, David. 2002. "Cannibalizing Kids: Rumor and Resistance in Latin America." *Journal of Folklore Research* 39(1):1–32.

Sapir, Edward. 1985 [1924]. "On Culture, Genuine and Spurious." In *On Culture, Language and Personality,* edited by David G. Mandelbaum, 308–331. Berkeley: University of California Press.

al-Sayyid Marsot, Afaf Lutfi. 1996 [1984]. *Egypt in the Reign of Muhammad Ali.* Cambridge: Cambridge University Press.

———. 1985. *A Short History of Modern Egypt.* Cambridge: Cambridge University Press.

Scheper-Hughes, Nancy. 1996. "Theft of Life: The Globalization of Organ Stealing Rumors." *Anthropology Today* 12(3):3–11.

Schoch, Robert. 1992a. "Redating the Great Sphinx of Giza." *KMT: A Modern Journal of Ancient Egypt* 3(2):52–59, 66–70.

———. 1992b. "A Modern Riddle of the Sphinx." *Omni* 14(10):46–48, 68–69.

———. 1993. "Reconsidering the Sphinx." *Omni* 15(6):31.

———. 1999. *Voices of the Rocks: A Scientist Looks at Catastrophes and Ancient Civilizations.* New York: Harmony.

———. 2000. Personal Interview. 2 July.

Schoch, Robert, and Robert Aquinas McNally. 2003. *Voyages of the Pyramid Builders: The True Origins of the Pyramids from Lost Egypt to Ancient America.* New York: Jeremy P. Tarcher.

Scholch, Alexander. 1981. *Egypt for the Egyptians! The Socio-political Crisis in Egypt.* London: Ithaca Press.

Schwaller de Lubicz, Rene. 1998 (1957). *The Temple of Man.* Translated from the French by Deborah and Robert Lawlor. Rochester, VT: Inner Traditions International.

Schwedler, Jillian. 2006. "The Third Gender: Western Female Researchers in the Middle East." *Political Science and Politics* 39:425–428.

Selim, Samah. 2001. "The New Pharaonism: Nationalist Thought and the Egyptian Village Novel, 1967–1977." *Arab Studies Journal* 8(2):10–24.

Shaffer, Marguerite S. 2001. *See America First: Tourism and National Identity, 1880–1940.* Washington and London: Smithsonian Institution Press.

Shapin, Steven. 1995. "Here and Everywhere: The Sociology of Scientific Knowledge." *Annual Review of Sociology* 21:289–321.

Shay, Anthony, and Barbara Sellers-Young, eds. 2005. *Belly Dance: Orientalism, Transnationalism, and Harem Fantasy.* Costa Mesa, CA: Mazda Publishers.

Shelley, Percy Bysshe. 1998 (1818). "Ozymandias." In *The Norton Anthology of British Literature,* 8th ed., edited by M. H. Abrams, et al. New York: Norton.

Silberman, Neil Asher. 1989. *Between Past and Present: Archaeology, Ideology, and Nationalism in the Modern Middle East.* New York: Henry Holt.

———. 1991. "Desolation and Restoration: The Impact of a Biblical Concept on Near Eastern Archaeology." *Biblical Archaeologist* 54:76–86.

———. 1995. "Promised Lands and Chosen Peoples: The Politics and Poetics of Archaeological Narratives." In *Nationalism, Politics, and Archaeology,* edited by P. L. Kohl and C. Fawcett, 249–262. Cambridge: Cambridge University Press.

———. 2000. "Sultans, Merchants, and Minorities: The Challenge of Historical Archaeology in the Modern Middle East." In U. Baram and L. Carroll, eds., *A Historical Archaeology of the Ottoman Empire: Breaking New Ground.* New York: Kluwer Academic/Plenum Publishers, 243–251.

Silverman, Helaine. 2004. "Subverting the Venue: A Critical Exhibition of Pre-Columbian Objects at Krannert Art Museum." *American Anthropologist* 106(4):732–738.

Sirageldin, Ismail, Naiem Sherbiny, and M. Ismail Serageldin. 1984. *Saudis in Transition: The Challenges of a Changing Labor Market.* New York: Oxford University Press for the World Bank.

Smith, Valene. 1989. "Introduction" to the 2nd edition of *Hosts and Guests: The Anthropology of Tourism.* Philadelphia: University of Pennsylvania Press.

———. 1992. "*Hosts and Guests* Revisited." *American Behavioral Scientist* 36(2):187–199.

Sokal, Alan. 1996a. "Transgressing the Boundaries: Toward a Transformative Hermeneutics of Quantum Gravity." *Social Text,* 46–47.

———. 1996b. "The Problem with Cultural Studies." *Lingua Franca* 6(4):62–64.

Stadelmann, Rainer. 2003. "The Great Sphinx of Giza." In *Egyptology at the Dawn of the Twenty-First Century: Proceedings of the Eighth International Congress of Egyptologists,* edited by Z. Hawass, vol. 1, 464–469. Cairo, New York: American University in Cairo Press.

Steegmuller, Francis, trans. and ed. 1996. *Gustave Flaubert: Flaubert in Egypt.* New York, NY: Penguin Books.

Stewart, John O. 1989. *Drinkers, Drummers, and Decent Folk: Ethnographic Narratives of Village Trinidad.* Albany: State University of New York Press.

Stille, Alexander. 1997. "Perils of the Sphinx." *New Yorker,* 10 February, 54–66.

———. 2003. *The Future of the Past.* New York: Picador.

Stocking, George W., Jr., ed. 1991a. *Colonial Situations: Essays on the Contextualization of Ethnographic Knowledge. History of Anthropology,* vol. 7. Madison: University of Wisconsin Press.

———. 1991b. "Maclay, Kubary, Malinowski: Archetypes from the Dreamtime of Anthropology." In *Colonial Situations: Essays on the Contextualization of Ethnographic Knowledge. History of Anthropology,* edited by George W. Stocking, Jr., vol. 7, 9–74. Madison: University of Wisconsin Press.

Stokowski, Patricia. 1992. "Social Networks and Tourist Behavior." *American Behavioral Scientist* 36(2):212–221.

Taussig, Michael. 1992. "Violence and Resistance in the Americas: The Legacy of Conquest." In *The Nervous System,* 37–52. London: Routledge Press.

———. 1997. *The Magic of the State.* New York, London: Routledge.

————. 2004. *My Cocaine Museum*. Chicago, London: University of Chicago Press.

Tessler, Mark, and Amaney Jamal. 2006. "Political Attitude Research in the Arab World: Emerging Opportunities." *Political Science and Politics* 39:433–437.

Tignor, Robert. 1993. "Introduction" to *Al-Jabart's Chronicles of Napoleon in Egypt*. Princeton, New York: Markus Wiever Publishing.

Tomas, Andrew. 1972. *From Atlantis to Discovery*. London: Robert Hale.

Tonkin, Boyd. 1996. "Riddles of the Sphinx." *New Statesman and Society* 9(402):39–40.

Trafton, Scott. 2004. *Egypt Land: Race and Nineteenth-Century American Egyptomania*. Durham: Duke University Press.

Traweek, Sharon. 1988. *Beamtimes and Lifetimes: The World of High Energy Physicists*. Cambridge, MA: Harvard University Press.

Trigger, Bruce G. 1979. "Egypt and the Comparative Study of Early Civilizations." In *Egyptology and the Social Sciences*, edited by Kent Weeks, 23–56. Cairo: American University in Cairo Press.

Tsing, Anna. 1993. *In the Realm of the Diamond Queen: Marginality in an Out-of-the-Way Place*. Princeton: Princeton University Press.

————. 2005. *Friction*. Princeton: Princeton University Press.

Tucker, Judith E. 1985. *Women in Nineteenth-Century Egypt*. Cambridge: Cambridge University Press.

Turner, Patricia A. 1993. *I Heard It through the Grapevine: Rumor in African-American Culture*. Berkeley: University of California Press.

Turner, Terence. 1991. "Representing, Resisting, Rethinking: Historical Transformations of Kayapo Culture and Anthropological Consciousness." In *Situations: Essays on the Contextualization of Ethnographic Knowledge. History of Anthropology*, edited by George W. Stocking, Jr., vol. 7, 285–313. Madison: University of Wisconsin Press.

Turner, Victor. 1974. "Pilgrimage as Social Process." In *Dramas, Fields, and Metaphors: Symbolic Action in Human Society*, 166–230. Ithaca: Cornell University Press.

United Nations Educational, Scientific and Cultural Organization. 1970. "Convention on the Means of Prohibiting and Preventing the Illicit Import, Export and Transfer of Ownership of Cultural Property," adopted by the General Conference at its sixteenth session, Paris, 14 November.

United States Information Agency. "Curbing Illicit Trade in Cultural Property: U.S. Assistance under the Convention on Cultural Property Implementation Act." Washington, D.C.: USIA.

Urry, John. 1990. *The Tourist Gaze: Leisure and Travel in Contemporary Societies*. London: Sage Publications.

————. 1992. "The Tourist Gaze 'Revisited.'" *American Behavioral Scientist* 36(2):172–186.

Vachala, Břetislav, and František Ondráš. 2000. "An Arabic Inscription on the Pyramid of Neferefra." *Abusir and Saqqara in the Year 2000*. Prague: Academy of Sciences of the Czech Republic Oriental Institute.

van den Brink, E. C. M., ed. 1988. *The Archaeology of the Nile Delta: Problems and Priorities*. Amsterdam: Netherlands Foundation for Archaeological Research in Egypt.

van Nieuwkerk, Karin. 1995. *A Trade Like Any Other: Female Singers and Dancers in Egypt.* Austin: University of Texas Press.

Vatikiotis, P. J. 1992. *The History of Modern Egypt: From Muhammad Ali to Mubarak,* 4th ed. Baltimore: Johns Hopkins University Press.

Vitalis, Robert. 1995. "The Middle East on the Edge of the Pleasure Periphery." *Middle East Report* 96(25/5):2–7.

———. 2006. *America's Kingdom: Mythmaking on the Saudi Oil Frontier.* Stanford: Stanford University Press.

Waite, Arthur Edward. 1887. *The Real History of the Rosicrucians Founded on Their Own Manifestoes, and on Facts and Documents Collected from the Writings of Initiated Brethren.* London: G. Redway.

El-Wakil, Abdel Latif. 1988. "A Brief Report on the Problems Met with During Excavations at Silvago, Delingat, Behera Governate" [sic]. In *The Archaeology of the Nile Delta: Problems and Priorities,* edited by E. C. M. van den Brink, 265. Amsterdam: Netherlands Foundation for Archaeological Research in Egypt.

Walker, Dennis. 1994. "The Collapse of Neo-Pharaonic Nationalism in Egyptian High Culture after 1930." *Islam and the Modern Age* 25(4):234–252.

Walz, Terence. 1996. "The American Experience in Egypt." *Archaeology* 49(1):70–75.

Waterbury, John. 1983. *The Egypt of Nasser and Sadat: The Political Economy of Two Regimes.* Princeton: Princeton University Press.

Watson-Verran, Helen, and David Turnbull. 1995. "Science and Other Indigenous Knowledge Systems." In *Handbook of Science and Technology Studies,* edited by Sheila Jasanoff et al., 115–139. London: Sage.

Weeks, Kent, ed. 1979. *Egyptology and the Social Sciences.* Cairo: American University in Cairo Press.

Wendell, Charles. 1972. *The Evolution of the Egyptian National Image: From Its Origins to Ahmad Lutfi al-Sayyid.* Berkeley: University of California Press.

West, John Anthony. 1985. *The Traveler's Key to Ancient Egypt: A Guide to the Sacred Places of Ancient Egypt.* New York: Alfred A. Knopf.

———. 2000. Personal Interview. 2 July.

West, John Anthony (Producer), and Charlton Heston (Narrator). 1993. *The Mystery of the Sphinx* [videotape]. Livonia, MI: Sphinx Project.

Weyland, Petra. 1993. *Inside the Third World Village.* London: Routledge.

Williams, Allan M., and Gareth Shaw. 1992. "Tourism Research: A Perspective." *American Behavioral Scientist* 36(2):133–143.

Wilson, Colin. 1996. *From Atlantis to the Sphinx.* London: Virgin Books.

Wilson, John A. 1964. *Signs and Wonders upon Pharaoh: A History of American Egyptology.* Chicago: University of Chicago Press.

Wissa, Karim. 1989. "Freemasonry in Egypt 1798–1921: A Study in Cultural and Political Encounters." *Bulletin (British Society for Middle Eastern Studies)* 16(2):143–161.

Wood, Michael. 1998. "The Use of the Pharaonic Past in Modern Egyptian Nationalism." *Journal of the American Research Center in Egypt* 35:179–196.

Wynn, Lisa. 1996. "Marriage Contracts and Women's Rights in Saudi Arabia." In *Shift-*

ing Boundaries in Marriage and Divorce in Muslim Communities, 106–121. Special Dossier, Women and Law Program, Montpelier, France: Women Living under Muslim Laws.

———. 1997. "The Romance of Tahliyya Street: Youth Culture, Commodities and the Use of Public Space in Jiddah." *Middle East Report* 204:30–31.

———. 1998–2002. Unpublished fieldnotes. Cairo and Giza, Egypt.

———. 2003. *From the Pyramids to the Nightclubs of Pyramids Road: An Ethnography of the Idea of Egypt.* Ph.D. dissertation, Department of Anthropology, Princeton University.

———. 2006. "Women, Gender, and Tourism: Egypt." In *The Encyclopedia of Women and Islamic Cultures, Vol. IV: Economics, Education, Mobility, and Space,* edited by Suad Joseph. Leiden: Brill.

———. Forthcoming (2008). "Women in Saudi Arabia: Orientalism, Occidentalism, and the Political Discourse of Islam and Tradition." In *Women's Movements and Gender Debates in the Middle East and North Africa,* edited by Homa Hoodfar. Contemporary Issues in the Middle East Series. Syracuse, NY: Syracuse University Press.

Yamani, May. 2000. *Changed Identities: The Challenge of the New Generation in Saudi Arabia.* London: Royal Institute of International Affairs.

Yared, Nazik Saba. 1996. *Arab Travellers and Western Civilization.* Translated from the Arabic by Sumayya Damluji Shahbander, revised and edited by Tony P. Naufal and Jana Gough. London: Saqi Books.

Yates, Frances. 1964. *Giordano Bruno and the Hermetic Tradition.* London: Routledge and Keegan Paul.

———. 1986 (1972). *The Rosicrucian Enlightenment.* London, NY: Ark Paperbacks.

Zuelow, Eric. 2004. "Enshrining Ireland's Nationalist History inside Prison Walls: The Restoration of Kilmainham Jail." *Eire-Ireland* 39 (Fall/Winter 2004): 180–201.

———. 2005a. "The Tourism Nexus: The Meanings of Tourism and Identity since the Irish Civil War." In *Ireland's Heritages: Critical Perspectives on Memory and Identity,* edited by Mark McCarthy, 189–213. Hampshire: Ashgate.

———. 2005b. "The Tourism Nexus: Tourism and National Identity since the Irish Civil War." Ph.D. dissertation, Department of History, University of Wisconsin at Madison.

———. 2007. "National Identity and Tourism in 20th Century Ireland: The Role of Collective Re-Imagining." In *Globalization and Nationalism: The Persistence of Nations,* edited by Andreas Sturm, Mitchell Young, and Eric Zuelow. Routledge Studies in Nationalism and Ethnicity. New York, London: Routledge.

———. Forthcoming. *Making Ireland Irish: Tourism and National Identity since the Irish Civil War.* Syracuse: Syracuse University Press.

INDEX

Yates, Frances, 94–95, 235n6, 235n9
Yemen, 135, 137, 149, 240n10
York, Malachi, 100

Zaghloul, Saad, 60, 165–168, 231n12,
242n26

Zakaria, Sally Ahmed, 48
Zaki, Ahmed, 7, 227n5
Ziwar, Ahmed, 60
Zodiac of Dendera, 54, 231n6
Zuelow, Eric, 245n11